# CONTENTS

W9-CAH-658

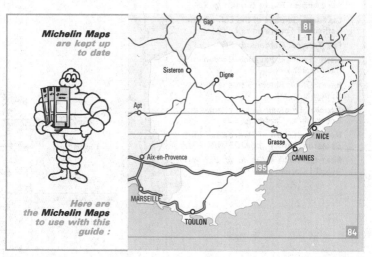

*Michelin Maps
are kept up
to date*

*Here are
the **Michelin Maps**
to use with this
guide :*

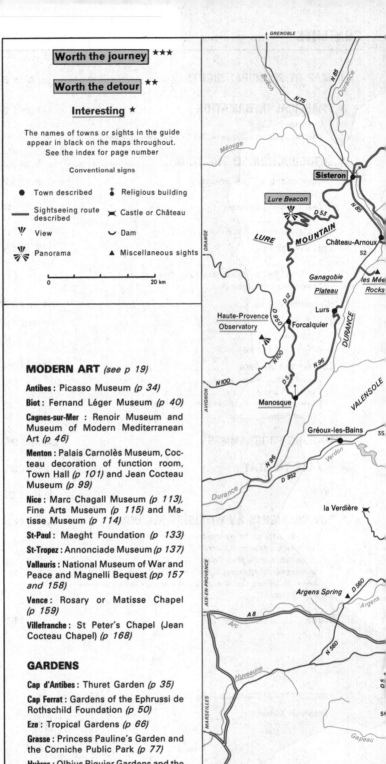

**Worth the journey** ★★★

**Worth the detour** ★★

**Interesting** ★

The names of towns or sights in the guide
appear in black on the maps throughout.
See the index for page number

Conventional signs

● Town described     ☨ Religious building

— Sightseeing route    ⚔ Castle or Château
described

💹 View            ⌣ Dam

🎆 Panorama      ▲ Miscellaneous sights

0                20 km

## MODERN ART *(see p 19)*

**Antibes :** Picasso Museum *(p 34)*

**Biot :** Fernand Léger Museum *(p 40)*

**Cagnes-sur-Mer :** Renoir Museum and
Museum of Modern Mediterranean
Art *(p 46)*

**Menton :** Palais Carnolès Museum, Coc-
teau decoration of function room,
Town Hall *(p 101)* and Jean Cocteau
Museum *(p 99)*

**Nice :** Marc Chagall Museum *(p 113)*,
Fine Arts Museum *(p 115)* and Matisse Museum *(p 114)*

**St-Paul :** Maeght Foundation *(p 133)*

**St-Tropez :** Annonciade Museum *(p 137)*

**Vallauris :** National Museum of War and
Peace and Magnelli Bequest *(pp 157
and 158)*

**Vence :** Rosary or Matisse Chapel
*(p 159)*

**Villefranche :** St Peter's Chapel (Jean
Cocteau Chapel) *(p 168)*

## GARDENS

**Cap d'Antibes :** Thuret Garden *(p 35)*

**Cap Ferrat :** Gardens of the Ephrussi de
Rothschild Foundation *(p 50)*

**Eze :** Tropical Gardens *(p 66)*

**Grasse :** Princess Pauline's Garden and
the Corniche Public Park *(p 77)*

**Hyères :** Olbius Riquier Gardens and the
St-Bernard Park *(p 83)*

**Menton :** Tropical Garden and the
Colombières Garden *(p 101)*

**Monaco :** Tropical Gardens and
St-Martin Garden *(pp 103 and 104)*

**Nice :** Gardens in Cimiez *(p 82)* and
Albert I Garden *(p 109)*.

# PRACTICAL INFORMATION

The French Government Tourist Office at 178 Piccadilly, London WIV OAL, ℡ (01) 499.76.22 and 610 Fifth Avenue, New York 1020, ℡ (212) 757 – 1125 will provide information and literature.

**Travel.** – There are scheduled flights direct to Marseilles or via Paris by national airlines; commercial and package tour flights, with rail or coach connections; cross-Channel ferry or hovercraft services from England continuing by train or car. Enquire at any good travel agent.

The high tourist season in France is July and August, so remember to make reservations for travel and accommodation well in advance if you are visiting then or at Christmas, Easter or Whitsun.

**Essential documents.** – A valid national **passport** (or British Visitor's Passport) is required.

For the car, a valid **driving licence, international driving permit, car registration book** and a nationality plate of the approved size are required. Insurance cover is compulsory and although the Green Card (an International Insurance Certificate) is no longer a legal requirement for France it is the most effective proof of insurance cover and is internationally recognized by police and other authorities.

Caravan owners will require a **caravan log-book** and an **inventory** for customs clearance; also Green Card endorsement for caravan and trailer. A carnet is required for the temporary import of certain vehicles: pleasure craft over 5.5 m long and motor boats.

Certain motoring organisations run accident insurance and breakdown service schemes for their members. Enquire before leaving. A **red warning triangle** or breakdown lights are obligatory in case of a breakdown.

In France it is compulsory for the front passengers to wear **seat belts** if the car is equipped with them. Children under ten should always be on the back seat.

Regulations in France on speeding and drinking and driving are strictly interpreted – usually by an on the spot fine and/or confiscation of the vehicle.

**Speed limit regulations.** – Liable to modification: motorways – 130 kph – 80 mph ; national trunk roads – 110 kph – 68 mph ; other roads – 90 kph – 56 mph ; in town – 60 kph – 37 mph.

**Medical Treatment.** – Form E111, obtainable from the Department of Health and Social Security in the UK, confirms entitlement to medical benefits and can be used to obtain urgent medical treatment in EEC countries and a refund of part of the cost on application to the French Social Security Offices *(Caisse Primaire de Sécurité Sociale)*. It is still advisable however to take out comprehensive insurance cover.

**N.B.** Body temperature: 37°C – 98.4°F.

**Currency.** – Exchange regulations are liable to alteration. Banks or international travel agencies will know how much foreign currency can be purchased, how much currency can be exported and can advise on travellers' cheques.

A passport must be presented for the purchase of currency or cheques and for the cashing of cheques. Commission charges vary; hotels charge more highly than banks and very highly indeed when obliging non-residents at weekends or on bank holidays.

**Consulates:** British – 13006 Marseille, 24 Avenue du Prado ( ℡ 53 43 32).
American – 13006 Marseille, 9, rue Armeny (℡ 33 78 33).
06000 Nice, 3, rue du Docteur Barety ( ℡ 88 89 55).

**Local Tourist Information Centres** *(Syndicats d'Initiative)* are to be found in most large towns and many tourist resorts. They can supply large scale town plans, timetables and information on local entertainment facilities, sports and sightseeing.

**Accommodation.** – The **Michelin Guide France** *(revised annually)* gives a selection of hotels at various prices in all areas. It also lists local restaurants together with prices.

For camping or caravanning consult the **Michelin Guide Camping Caravaning France**, revised annually.

**Electric Current.** – Mostly 220-230 volts ; in some places however it is still 110 volts. European circular two pin plugs are the rule – remember to take an adaptor.

**Poste Restante.** – Name, Poste restante, Poste centrale, Department's postal number followed by the town's name, France. The **Michelin Guide France** gives local postal code numbers.

Postage via air mail to: UK letter: 2.10 F    postcard: 1.60 F
US letter: 5.20 F    postcard: 3.25 F

**Public Holidays in France.** – National museums and art galleries are closed on Tuesdays. The following are days when museums and other monuments may be closed or may vary their hours of admission:

| | | |
|---|---|---|
| New Year's Day | Whit Sunday and Monday | All Saints' Day, **1 November** |
| Easter Sunday and Monday | France's National Day, **14 July** | Armistice Day, **11 November** |
| May Day (**1 May**) | The Assumption, **15 August** | Christmas Day |
| Ascension Day | | |

# THE FRENCH RIVIERA

The Côte d'Azur one of the most inviting names in the world! Properly speaking, the name of Riviera applies to the French Coast between Nice and Menton and to the Italian Coast between Ventimiglia and Genoa. English visitors, at first for the sake of health but later more and more in search of pleasure, were attracted to the Riviera (especially Nice) in the 18C. The Côte d'Azur (Les Lecques to Menton) has become widely known as the French Riviera to millions.

**The Seasons.** – Due essentially to its climate the Riviera is now popular at all times of the year.

**Winter.** – The proverbial mildness of the French Riviera is due to a number of factors : a low latitude, the presence of the sea which moderates temperature variations, a wholly southern aspect, and the screen of hills and mountains which protects it from cold winds. The average temperature for January in Nice is 8°C. (46°F.–7°C. higher than in London)

The unfavourable wind is that from the southeast which brings rain. Fog and sea-mists are rare except on the coast in the height of summer ; snow is practically unknown.

The thermometer may rise to 22°C. (72°F); but at sunset and during the night the temperature drops suddenly and considerably. There is little rainfall : it is the dew that keeps the vegetation fresh. Evergreens and flowers, which bloom for months on end, provide colour.

The hinterland is cold and often snow covered : Castellane reckons on 100 days of frost each year. But the air is limpid and the sun brilliant. It is the ideal climate for the winter sports which have been highly developed in this area *(pp 30-31)*.

**Spring.** – Short but violent showers are characteristic of the Riviera springtime. This is when the flowers are at their best and a joy to look at. The only blot is the Mistral which blows most frequently at this season, especially west of Toulon.

The Romans made a dreaded god of this fearsome wind. It comes from the northwest in cold gusts; after several days this powerful blast of clean air is said to have purified everything and the swept sky to be bluer than ever.

**Summer.** – The coast offers an unchanging blue and average temperature of 22°C. (72°F.) throughout July and August. However, the heat is bearable because it is tempered by the fresh breeze that blows during the daytime. This is not the season of flowers : the vegetation, overwhelmed by drought, seems to sleep. When the hot breath of the Sirocco comes out of the south everyone grumbles.

The hinterland offers a wide variety of places to stay at varying altitudes *(pp 30 and 31)* up to 2000 m – 6560 ft ; the higher one climbs the more vital the air.

**Autumn.** – Autumn is the season for violent storms after which the sun reappears, brilliant and warm. In the whole year, there is an average of only 86 days of rain in Nice (150 in London), but the quantity of water which falls is higher (34 in in Nice against 23 1/2 in in London). There is no lack of ideal days during the Mediterranean autumn; and, after the summer rest, the flowers burst out again everywhere.

## VOCABULARY

| | | | |
|---|---|---|---|
| **Barrage** | dam | **Marais** | saltmarsh |
| **Carrefour** | crossroads | **Marché couvert, halles** | covered market |
| **Château-fort** | fortified castle | | |
| **Col** | pass | **Moulin** | mill |
| **Coteau** | hillside, slope | **Palais** | palace |
| **Cour** | courtyard, court, square | **Parterre, pelouse** | flowerbed, lawn |
| **Couvent** | convent, monastery | **Pavillon** | pavilion, wing (of a building) |
| **Donjon** | keep | | |
| **École** | school | **Pont** | bridge |
| **Escalier** | stairs, staircase, stairway | **Pont-levis** | drawbridge |
| | | **Porte de ville** | town gate |
| **Étage** | storey, tier | **Prieuré** | priory |
| **Étang** | pool, pond | **Quartier** | town quarter |
| **Évêché** | bishopric | **Rempart** | rampart |
| **Falaise** | cliff | **Romain** | Roman |
| **Fontaine** | fountain, spring | **Roman** | Romanesque (architecturally in Europe ; Norman in England) |
| **Forêt domaniale** | state forest | | |
| **Forteresse** | fortress | | |
| **Fossé** | moat, ditch | **Route** | road, route |
| **Fresque** | fresco | **Rue** | street |
| **Grand'Place** | main square | **Site** | site, setting |
| **Gratuit** | free | **Sortie** | way out, exit |
| **Hôtel particulier** | private house | **Syndicat d'Initiative** | local tourist office |
| **Ile** | island | **Tapisserie** | tapestry |
| **Jardin** | garden | **Tour** | tower |
| **Logis** | dwelling, house | **Val, vallée** | valley |
| **Mairie** | town hall | **Vigne, vignoble** | vine, vineyard |
| **Manoir** | manor house | **Ville** | town |

**Clue** – a fault in the rock, giving rise to a steep sided rift, often tree-covered, with a stream running along its course.

**Corniche** – a road often constructed at the top or bottom of a cliff overlooking the sea or even halfway up the face which is hewn away to take the road emplacement.

**Calanque** – a creek or inlet formed by the "drowning" by the sea of the end of a river valley.

# INTRODUCTION TO THE TOUR

## APPEARANCE OF THE COUNTRY

This guide describes the Riviera from Les Lecques to Menton and the mountainous hinterland which forms Haute-Provence and Nice Pre-Alps in the far east. The adjacent regions are described in the Michelin Green Guides *Provence* – available in English – and *Alpes* – available only in French.

**A Poet's Phrase.** – Côte d'Azur – the Azure Coast – is a poet's phrase which was felt to be so apt for the beauty of the Provençal coast and the Mediterranean sunshine that it has stuck long after the late 19C poet, Stephen Liégeard, has faded into obscurity, together with his poem which was honoured by the French Academy of the time.

What promises of blue sea and sky, of shining beaches and brilliant sunshine. The region's natural beauty has been extolled in a thousand ways in almost every language – "spell", "enchantment", "magic" are words which frequently recur.

To the splendour of this magnificent coastline is added the charm of the eastern part of inland Provence, so typically Mediterranean, as well as the grandeur of the Verdon Grand Canyon and the rifts *(clues)* of Haute-Provence. Although not so well known, it justly claims its own enthusiasts.

These two regions complement each other and it is nature's miracle to bring together such a variety of scenery. The regions constitute a holiday area unique in France and perhaps in the whole world.

## CONTRASTS

This is a country of contrasts :

**... in coastline.** – The Riviera extends from Les Lecques to Menton and is extremely varied *(p 11)*. The little sheltered inlets between the porphyry promontories of the Esterel differ markedly from the great sweeping bays with flat shores which gently breach the coast; while elsewhere on the coast mountains drop into the sea, sheer as a wall as at Cap Sicié.

**... in relief.** – A countryside just as varied lies inland. The fertile plains and foothills of Provence are typically Mediterranean in their vegetation, but among them are barren, rugged heights like those to the north of Toulon.

Then follow the mountain masses of the Maures and the Esterel which rise to no more than 800 m – 2 600 ft: the first is crisscrossed by many valleys and ravines and covered with fine forests of cork oak and chestnut; separated from the former by the Argens valley, the second massif with its harsh relief and vivid colouring is dominated by the outlines of Mount Vinaigre, the Ours and the great Cap Roux Peaks. All three summits offer spectacular panoramas, although that of the Ours Peak is all embracing including the coast and stretching as far as the Alps and then round inland over the Esterel Massif to Mount Vinaigre.

The country behind Cannes and Nice is one of undulating hills stretching to the Pre-Alps of Grasse, where the gorges and rifts of the plateaux and mountain chains are among the attractions of Haute-Provence.

Further to the west the Verdon Grand Canyon provides the grandiose spectacle of a great winding gorge with its sheer rock sides in a wild setting.

Lastly, behind the Riviera the Pre-Alps of Nice rise to more than 2 000 m – 6 560 ft. While further to the north and north-east tower the true Alpine heights on the border with Italy.

**... in climate.** – There is a winter warmth on the Nice coast (the average temperatures for January in Nice are max 13°C – 55°F ; min 4°C – 39°F) and, two hours away by car, the icy air of the ski slopes; the summer heat of the coast and the exhilarating coolness of the mountain resorts; the cold mistral wind and the burning sirocco; long days of drought, dried up rivers and, suddenly, tremendous downpours and overflowing torrents.

**... in vegetation.** – The forest of Turini, with its centuries old beeches and firs, is like that of a northern land; the woods of the Maures and the Esterel are typically southern with their cork oaks and pines, periodically ravaged by forest fires. The wild scrub and underbrush of the *maquis* is far from the orderly rows of the orange and lemon orchards; the lavender and thyme growing wild from the vast cultivated fields of flowers; the palm trees, agaves and cacti of the coast from the firs and larches of the highlands.

**... in activity.** – The coast attracts all the activity of the area: the busiest roads, the most important towns and the varied and best equipped resorts are concentrated there. One comes across sleepy little towns like Lorgues or Riez and old villages, perched like eagles' nests high up in the hillside but now almost deserted *(p 21)*.

Tourrette-sur-Loup

**... in economy.** – Nice is the coast's tourist capital; Monte-Carlo, a great gambling city. The tourist passes from the busy flower trade and the production of perfume to the new computer research centre within the space of a few miles.

**Land of the Sun.** – Everywhere the tourist will find the Land of the Sun in which the Provençal poet Mistral gloried. The sun shines continually (2 725 hours annually in Nice compared with 1 465 hours in London). Outlines are sharpened and natural features stand out architecturally in the clear air. The shining blue of the sea and sky blends with the green of the forests, the silver-grey of the olive trees, the red porphyry rock and the white limestone.

# LAND FORMATION

**Primary Era.** – Beginning about 600 million years ago. The western basin of the Mediterranean did not exist originally, there being in its place the vast continent of Tyrrhenia. This continent, formed of crystalline rock, was contemporary with the Massif Central and the Armorican Massif (Brittany). A sea covered what is now Provence.

**Secondary Era.** – Beginning about 200 million years ago. Tyrrhenia was progressively levelled by streams and as the alternation of rain, sun and frost eroded the land, the soil was slowly carried off by the rivers and deposited on the bottom of the sea. With the passing of time, these deposits were transformed into horizontal layers of rock (strata), composed of limestone, clay, schist, sandstone or sand.

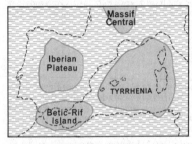

Primary Era : Tyrrhenia

Quaternary Era : The Mediterranean

**Tertiary Era.** – Beginning about 60 million years ago. The slow but powerful pressure, which had already formed the Pyrenees, now came to bear on these rock layers, forcing them upwards to considerable heights. The strata bent, forming undulations or folds in an east-west direction.

These are now the Provençal hills to the north of Marseilles, Toulon and Draguignan. Later, the Alpine thrust, moving in a north-south direction, collided with the already formed heights resulting in an inter-crossing of the east-west and north-south mountain formations of the Pre-Alps of Nice and Digne.

**Quaternary Era.** – Beginning about 2 million years ago. Tyrrhenia had by now disappeared beneath the sea, leaving behind only the mountainous formations of the Maures, the Esterel and Cap Sicié.

The Mediterranean as we know it today covers the vanished continent, although some traces of Tyrrhenia still exist, namely Corsica, Sardinia and parts of Sicily in the east and the Balearic Islands in the west.

# LANDSCAPE

Provence, therefore, was formed from two mountain systems: one very old – the Maures and the Esterel – the other much younger – the Provençal ranges of Pyrenean and the Pre-Alps of Alpine origin.

**The Maures.** – This crystalline mountain mass spreads from the River Gapeau in the west to the Argens Valley in the east, from a long depression in the north, on the far side of which are the limestone Pre-Alps, to the sea in the south.

Long low parallel ranges, covered with fine forests of pine, cork oak and chestnut, make up the Maures Massif whose highest point is La Sauvette (779 m – 2 556 ft – *excursion to the Maures p 94*).

**The Esterel.** – The Esterel, separated from the Maures by the lower Valley of the Argens, has also been eroded by time and is therefore also of low altitude, its highest peak being Mount Vinaigre at 618 m – 2 027 ft. The deep ravines cut into its sides and its jagged crests dispel any impression of mere hills *(excursion to the Esterel p 61)*.

The Esterel, like the Maures, was once entirely covered with forests of pine and cork oak, but these have been ravaged periodically by forest fires *(p 14)*.

Quantities of shrubs and bushes grow beneath the trees: tree heathers, arbutus, lentisks and lavender, while *maquis* or scrub covers open land. In spring the red and white flowers of the cistus, yellow mimosa and broom and white heather and myrtle form a brilliant floral patchwork.

**The Provençal Ranges.** – These short limestone chains, arid and rugged rise to heights of 400 to 1 150 m – 1 200 to 3 500 ft. Of Pyrenean origin with a highly complex structure, these chains do not have the continuity of those of Alpine origin such as the Southern Pre-Alps.

The most southerly mountain chains are the Gros Cerveau (429 m – 1 407 ft) cut by the Ollioules Gorges and Mount Faron (542 m – 1 778 ft) which dominates the town of Toulon. Others include the Coudon and further north Ste-Victoire and La Loube Mountain.

Between the ranges are fertile valleys where the traditional crops of cereals, vines and olives are cultivated.

**Maritime Alps and Mercantour.** – Away to the north-east the horizon is dominated by a vast mountainous mass (altitude: 1 500 to 2 900 m – 4 922 to 9 515 ft) which is dissected by the upper valleys of the Verdon, Var, Tinée, Vésubie and Roya. On the Italian border these mountains abut the great crystalline massif, Le Mercantour, the summits of which exceed 3 000 m – 9 843 ft.

**Pre-Alps.** – This region has a large part of the Southern Pre-Alps. To the west of the Durance they include the unbroken spine of crests of the **Lure Mountain** *(p 91)* and the **Lubéron**.

The strike of the **Digne Pre-Alps** is more complicated, while in the **Castellane Pre-Alps** it runs in a north-west to south-east direction. The mountain chains have been cut transversally by torrents to form wild and narrow rifts. The towns of Sisteron, Digne and Castellane occupy sites commanding these narrow passages. The limestone Pre-Alps are the poorest, the least-populated and the most desolate of the French Alps. The slopes, beneath white denuded rock summits, support a meagre and sparse vegetation.

Between the rivers Verdon and Var, the **Grasse Pre-Alps** are a series of parallel east-west chains, with altitudes varying between 1 100 and 1 600 m (3 609 and 5 249 ft). The area is described under the heading Haute-Provence Rifts *(p 79)*.

Finally the **Nice Pre-Alps** rise from the coast in tiers to a height of 1 000 m – 3 281 ft, affording a wide variety of scenery inland from Nice and Menton. Of Alpine origin these ranges run north-south before changing direction abruptly to end parallel with the coast.

**Provençal tableland.** – From Canjuers Plateau to the Vence Pass the Pre-Alps are rimmed with a tableland of undulating limestone plateaux. Not unlike the *causses*, all water infiltrates, penetrating by rifts to feed resurgent streams like the Siagne. Here also the rivers have formed extraordinary gorges: Verdon, Artuby *(both p 161)* and Loup *(p 90)* Canyons. Below lies a **depression** or "lowland" where the towns of Vence, Grasse and Draguignan are situated. Arms of the depression extend down the Argens river to Fréjus, west towards Brignoles while the main axis is south-west to Toulon to the northern slopes of the Maures and Le Luc Basin.

## THE COAST

From Les Lecques to Menton the inland area of deep valleys and different types of mountain range and plateaux has resulted in combinations of cliffs and rocks and sea – a grouping characteristic of this coast.

**The Toulon Coast.** – Highly indented, this section of the coast provides well sheltered harbours: Bandol and Sanary Bays and the outstanding Toulon roadstead. The stretches of almost vertical cliffs are interrupted by some fine beaches.

**The Maures Coast.** – Between Hyères and St-Raphaël the Maures Massif meets the sea and the coastal scenery offers charming sites and enchanting views.

The Giens Peninsula, formerly an island is now joined to the mainland by two sandy isthmuses. Nearby are the Islands of Hyères, densely covered with vegetation, and the Fréjus Plain, once a wide bay but now filled by alluvial deposits brought down by the Argens. Characteristic also of this particular section of the coast are great promontories such as Cap Bénat and the St-Tropez Peninsula and narrow tongues of land such as Caps Nègre and Sardinaux dividing from each other wide bays like the Bormes roadstead and the Gulf of St-Tropez.

**The Esterel Coast.** – The blood-red porphyry rocks of the Esterel Massif steep and rugged, make a striking contrast with the blue of the sea. Along this stretch of coast the mountains thrust great promontories into the sea, with between inlets *(calanques)* and small bays. Offshore, the surface of the sea is scattered with thousands of rocks and small, green moss covered islets while beneath, submerged reefs can be seen through clear water.

The Golden Corniche *(p 61)* is reputed internationally for its breathtaking scenery, superb viewpoints and various resorts.

**Antibes Coast.** – The vista changes once again between Cannes and Nice. The shore is no longer eaten away by the sea ; it is flat and opens into wide bays. It is a calm, soft coast on which the Cap d'Antibes Peninsula is the sole promontory.

**Riviera Proper.** – From Nice to Menton the Alps plunge abruptly into the sea. Here the coastline forms a natural terrace, facing the Mediterranean but at the same time isolating it from its hinterland. Cap Ferrat and Cap Martin are the two main promontories along this coastal stretch. The term Riviera, which has already passed into the language of geography, is applied to this part of the coast. A triple roadway has been cut over the steep slopes, lined with villas and terraced gardens.

## THE MEDITERRANEAN

The Mediterranean is Europe's bluest sea. The shade – cobalt blue to artists – comes from the clarity of the water. Visitors soon realise that the colour often changes depending on the clearness of the sky, the light, the seabed and the depth of water so that at times the "blue Mediterranean" is opal or a warm grey.

**The water.** – The temperature of the water, governed on the surface by the sun's heat, is constant from 200 m to 4 000 m – 650 ft to 13 000 ft – down (13 °C – 55.4 °F), whereas in the Atlantic it drops from 14 °C. to 2 °C. (57.2 °F. to 35 °F.). This is an important factor in the climate, for the sea cools the air in summer and warms it in winter. Rapid evaporation makes the water noticeably more salty than that of the Atlantic.

The great Atlantic swells are unknown here since these need immense space in which to form. Instead the waves are small, short and choppy, easily becoming rough. Storms come and go quickly.

**The tides.** – Tides are almost non-existent, averaging about ten inches. Sometimes when the wind is very strong the tide may reach as much as three feet. These figures are markedly different from the tides of the Atlantic or from the tides of 13 to 15 m – 40 to 50 ft round Mont-St-Michel. This relative tidal stability has resulted in the Mediterranean being chosen as the base level for all French coastal altitudes.

In contrast to the coast of Languedoc, the Provençal coastline drops sharply into water that becomes relatively deep a short distance from the shore. Between Nice and Cap Ferrat soundings indicate a depth of 500 m – 1 600 ft – about half a mile out.

**The fish.** – The Mediterranean is less rich in fish than the other seas off the coast of France. However, rockfish are plentiful: these include the *rascasse* (hog-fish) – the basis of *bouillabaisse* – red mullet, conger and marine eels, as well as many varieties of crab, crayfish and lobster.

Shoals of sardines, anchovies, tunny and mackerel swim offshore pursued by dolphins, porpoises and various kinds of shark some of which reach a length of 5 m – over 16 ft.

## RIVERS

Mediterranean rivers are really torrents and their volume, which varies considerably, is governed by melting snow, rainfall and evaporation.

The lack of rain and the intense evaporation of the summer months dry up the rivers to mere trickles of water along their stony beds. In spring and autumn the rains fall suddenly and violently and even the smallest streams are immediately filled with rushing water; little brooks, trickling through the undergrowth, become torrents in a short time, their raging waters having the speed of a galloping horse.

The flow of the Argens varies from 3 m³ to 600 m³ – 660 to 132 000 gallons a second and that of the Var from 17 m³ to 5 000 m³ – 3 790 to over a million gallons. At its peak the Var is more than half a mile wide and the stain of its muddy waters can be seen in the sea as far away as the other side of Nice at Villefranche. The Durance and the Verdon are exactly the same.

In the limestone hills the rains seep into the ground through numerous fissures to reappear often at considerable distance as large springs gushing out from the sides of valleys. Some of the springs rise in riverbeds, when they are known as *foux* or gushers, often causing the river to flood, as happens with the Argens.

Most of the rivers with torrential rates of flow transport material, but the Argens is the only one to have built up an alluvial plain comparable to those of the Languedoc coast. All the torrential rivers have created beautiful valleys with deep gorges (the Verdon Grand Canyon and the Loup Gorges) or rifts *(clues* – the Aiglun Rift), making them among the tourist attractions of inland Provence.

*The companion guides in English in this series on France are*

*Brittany, Châteaux of the Loire,*

*Dordogne, Normandy,*

*Paris, Provence*

*Other **Michelin Green Guides** available in English*

*Austria, Canada, Germany, Italy*

*New England, Portugal, Spain, Switzerland*

*London, New York City*

# THE VEGETATION

Plants and trees do not grow in the same way on the Riviera as they do further north. New shoots appear, as they do elsewhere, in the spring but a second growth begins in the autumn and continues throughout most of the winter. The dormant period is during the summer when the heat and dryness of the climate only permit plants to grow which are especially adapted to resist drought. These have long tap roots, glossy leaves which reduce transpiration, bulbs which act as reservoirs of moisture and perfumes which they release to form a kind of protective vapour.

## TREES

**The Olive.** – The Greeks, brought olive trees to Provence 2 500 years ago where they grow equally well in limestone or sandy soils. The olive has been called the immortal tree for, grafted or wild, it will always grow from the same spot in the ground. Those grown from cuttings die relatively young, at about hundred years of age.

Along the coast, the trees reach gigantic dimensions, attaining 20 m – 65 ft in height, their domes of silver foliage 20 m – 65 ft in circumference and trunks 4 m – 13 ft round the base.

The olive tree, which has more than sixty varieties, is found up to an altitude of 600 m – 2 000 ft and marks the limit of the Mediterranean climate. It grows mainly on valley floors and on the hillsides. The trees begin to bear fruit between their sixth and twelfth year and are in full yield at twenty or twenty-five. They are harvested every two years.

Olive groves are numerous in the areas around Draguignan, Sospel and Breil in the Roya valley.

Olive tree

**Oak Trees.** – The oaks native to the Mediterranean region are evergreen.

### Holm oak

This grows in chalky soil at altitudes below 800 m – 2 500 ft.
As scrub-oak it is a characteristic feature of the *garrigue*.
In its fully developed state it is a tree with a short thick-set trunk covered in grey–black bark and with a dense, rounded crown.

### Cork oak

This tree is distinguished by its large dark coloured acorns and its rough bark.
Every 8 to 12 years the thick cork bark is stripped off exposing a reddish brown trunk.

**Pine Trees.** – The three types of pine to be found in the Mediterranean region have unmistakable silhouettes.

#### Sea pine

The sea pine, which grows only in lime free soil, has dark, blue tinged green needles and deep red bark.

#### Umbrella pine

The umbrella pine is typically Mediterranean and owes its name to its easily recognisable outline.
It is often found alone.

#### Aleppo pine

This Mediterranean species which grows well in chalky soil along the coast, has a twisted, grey trunk and lighter, less dense, foliage.

**Other Trees.** – In towns and villages the smooth barked **plane trees** shade courtyards, streets and squares, and also line the roadsides where at times the **lotus tree** (micocoulier) is also to be found. Dark **cypresses** are a common feature of the countryside whereas the **almond tree** lends a certain charm to the landscape. Robust **chestnuts** flourish on the Maures Massif, certain mountain species of **firs** and **larches** in the Alps and pines, as fine as any found in northern climes, in the Turini Forest *(p 153)*.

#### Almond tree

This small fruit tree is grown for its nut. Wide spread in Provence it blossoms early giving a pink flower.

#### Cypress

This evergreen conifer planted in serried ranks acts as a wind break.

#### Lotus tree

This typically Mediterranean tree still shades squares and avenues. The easily worked wood is used for fork making.

**Exotic Trees.** – Magnificent **eucalyptus** trees can now also be seen lining avenues and standing singly or in groups in parks and gardens. These trees which originally came from Australia, flourish and grow to a great height in the south of France.

The greatest concentration of **palm trees** is to be found in the Hyères district. The two types most common to the Riviera are the date palm with its smooth, tall trunk sweeping upwards and the Canary palm which is much shorter and has a rough scaly trunk.

**Orange** and **lemon** groves flourish on the coastal stretches between Cannes and Antibes and Monaco and Menton.

## BUSHES AND SHRUBS

The **kermes oak** is a bushy evergreen shrub which rarely grows more than three feet in height. Its name comes from the kermes, an insect halfway between a cochineal fly and a flea which lives throughout its existence attached to the oaks' stems.

Other plants emphasising the Mediterranean character of the country are the lentisk or mastic tree and the pistachio.

| **Lentisk** | **Pistachio** |
|---|---|
| This is an evergreen shrub with paired leaves on either side of the main stem but without a terminal leaf. | This tree sometimes grows to a height of 13 or 16 ft. It is deciduous and has leaves growing in groups of five to eleven, one forming the terminal. |

This is an evergreen shrub with paired leaves on either side of the main stem but without a terminal leaf.
The fruit is in the form of a small globular berry which turns from red to black on maturity.

This tree sometimes grows to a height of 13 or 16 ft. It is deciduous and has leaves growing in groups of five to eleven, one forming the terminal. The fruit is a very small berry, red at first, ripening to brown.

**The Garrigue.** – Some of the limestone areas are so stony that even thorns (thistles, the kermes oak and gorse) and aromatic plants (thyme, lavender and rosemary) can only survive here and there, leaving bare large stretches of rock: these areas are the *garrigue*. This country can be found by following the D 2, the Vence Pass road or the D 955 from Draguignan to Pont-de-Soleils in the direction of Montferrat and Comps.

**The Maquis.** – The *maquis* or scrub is to be found on sandy soil and, in contrast to the *garrigue*, is characterised by a thick carpet of greenery completely covering the country. In May and June when the rock plants are in flower it is a wonderful sight, especially in the coverts of the Esterel.

## SUCCULENTS

Some succulents are definitely African in character: Barbary figs, agaves, cacti and aloes grow in open ground. Ficoids with large pink and white flowers cling to old walls. The tropical gardens of Monaco *(p 103)*, the garden of the Villa Thuret on the Cap d'Antibes *(p 35)* and the botanical gardens at Menton *(p 101)* all have specimens of tropical plants.

**Cactus**

A succulent spiny growth of unusual shape.
The main stem is round and grooved.
The leaves take the form of spines.
Some types of cactus have amazingly brilliant flowers in vivid colours.

**Aloe**

The leaves are thick and fleshy.
The flowers are greenish-yellow or deep red or often enough a mixture of all these colours.
A bitter juice is extracted from the leaves for medicinal use.

**Barbary fig**

An odd-shaped plant, originating from Central America, it has broad thick leaves, bristling with spines, and flourishes in the most arid soil in the hottest climate.
The Moroccans call it the Christian fig; it is also known as the "prickly pear".

**Agave**

The leaves, long, broad, thick and sea-green in colour, are bordered with brown thorns and terminate in a sharp black spike.
Thousands of yellow flowers adorn the upright flower stems which gleam like candelabra.

## FOREST FIRES

From time immemorial the plague of the Provençal forests, especially in the Maures and the Esterel, has been the forest fire. This causes more damage than the deforestation by man, now carried out with far more prudence than formerly, and are more harmful than the destruction caused by the herds of goats which live on the tender young shoots. During the summer the dried-up plants of the underbrush, pine needles, resins exuded by leaves and twigs are highly combustible and sometimes catch fire spontaneously. Once a fire has started, it spreads to the pines and if the wind is strong disaster may follow.

Enormous walls of flame, sometimes 10 km – 6 miles in length and 30 m – 100 ft high, spread at speeds of 5 to 6 km – 2 to 3 miles an hour. When the fire has passed, nothing remains standing except the blackened skeletons of the trees while a thick layer of white ash covers the ground.

Forest guards, soldiers and local residents unite to fight the outbreaks by clearing parts of the forest of all brushwood and shrubs, and by starting counter fires to clear areas where the forest fire will burn out for lack of fuel. Often the fire wins, stopping only at the coast unless the wind drops or alters direction.

Protective measures against forest fires are improving and include the organization of a systematic watch, with the help of local aviation and also the use of planes to douse the flames with sea water. When a fire is tackled at its start, it is generally possible to master it. In addition, efforts are being made to clear the undergrowth periodically, to create fire-breaks, and to substitute for the pines less inflammable tress such as the cork oak and chestnut.

# FLOWERS, FRUIT AND VEGETABLES

**Cut Flowers.** – Alphonse Karr *(p 127)*, a political refugee living in Nice before the annexation, is generally credited with having founded the trade in flowers. Karr, with the help of an associate, began large scale cultivation and had the idea of sending bunches of fresh violets and small packets of mixed seeds to Paris. From this modest start has developed the trade in cut flowers and mimosa, in which 4 000 firms are engaged between Toulon and Menton.

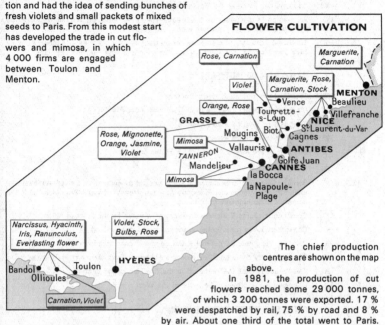

## FLOWER CULTIVATION

The chief production centres are shown on the map above.

In 1981, the production of cut flowers reached some 29 000 tonnes, of which 3 200 tonnes were exported. 17 % were despatched by rail, 75 % by road and 8 % by air. About one third of the total went to Paris.

**Flowers and Scented Plants of the Grasse Region.** – The two main flower crops of this area are roses and jasmine. The May tea-rose is the same as that grown in the east, but the Mediterranean variety has a fine scent.

Jasmine is of the large flowered variety which has been grafted on to officinal jasmine. This is a particularly costly and delicate plant which flowers from the end of July to the first winter frosts.

The orange blossom used for perfume is obtained from the bitter fruit tree, known as the *bigaradier* or Seville orange. Orange-flower water is made from direct distillation.

The cherry laurel, eucalyptus and cypress are distilled both for essence and for toilet water. Mimosa is used for the production of essence by extraction. Sweet basil, clary (sage), tarragon, melissa or balm mint, verbena, mignonette, peppermint and geranium all yield products used in perfumery, confectionery and pharmacy, etc. Scented plants include wild lavender, aspic, thyme, rosemary, sage, etc.

Le Bar-sur-Loup, Golfe-Juan and Vallauris as well as Seillans (Var Department), are major centres for the production of aromatic raw materials although it is Grasse which is number one in this domain.

Known the world over as the home of the French perfume industry in reality the essences obtained locally are treated with a fixative and sent to Paris where the great perfume houses blend them according to secret formulas to produce the fascinating creations for which France is famous. *(For further details on the perfume industry see under Grasse.)* This luxury industry, which caters mostly for the export market, is supplemented by the synthetic perfume industry.

The French perfume industry's exports exceed 800 million francs ($ 73 000 000), the most important customers being the United States, Japan, West Germany and the United Kingdom.

**The Lavenders of Haute-Provence.** – For many the smell of lavender recalls the hills of Haute-Provence. At the beginning of the century the gathering of these flowers, which grow wild on the mountains was only a minor harvest.

As the cultivation of cereals declined at the beginning of the 20C, the systematic growing of lavender was introduced on the plateaux and the higher slopes above 700 m – 2 240 ft.

Ideally adapted to both the climate and soils, the plant has given a new lease of life to many estates; land that had been fallow for nearly twenty years is now covered with the green plants whose mauve flowers scent the July air.

Later, *lavandin* (a hybrid obtained by crossing true lavender and great lavender), which has a more abundant yield than true lavender but produces an essence of inferior quality, was introduced on the lower slopes and in the valleys between 400 and 700 m – 1 280 and 2 240 ft.

Field after field of sturdy *lavandin* bushes can be seen on the Valensole plateau along the road from Digne to Gréoux-les-Bains (Puimoisson, Riez, St-Martin-de-Brômes). The annual output of lavender essence for southeast France is about 80 tonnes for lavender and 800 – 900 tonnes for *lavandin*, of which the Grasse manufacturers are large buyers. The main outlet is export to the United States.

**Early vegetables.** – After North Africa, Spain and Italy the region of Toulon and Hyères provides the earliest vegetables and fruit. The Var is noted for the cherries of Solliès-Pont and the peaches of the Fréjus area. In 1981 the Var Department alone, despatched 2 059 tonnes of fruit and vegetables of which 189 tonnes left from the railway station of Hyères.

15

# HISTORICAL FACTS

| | |
|---|---|
| **BC** | **ORIGINS** |
| 1000 | The Ligurians occupy the Mediterranean seaboard. |
| 600 | Foundation of Marseilles by the Greeks. They bring olive, fig, nut, cherry trees, the cultivated vine; they substitute money for barter. |
| 5-4C | The Greek colonists in Marseilles set up trading posts : Hyères, St-Tropez, Antibes, Nice and Monaco. The Celts invade Provence mingling with the Ligurians. |

## GALLO-ROMAN PROVENCE

| | |
|---|---|
| 122 | The Celts are defeated by the Romans. |
| 102 | Marius defeats the Teutons from Germania, near Aix. |
| 58-51 | Conquest of Gaul by Julius Caesar. |
| 49 | Julius Caesar founds Fréjus (p 69). |
| 6 | Building of the Alpine Trophy at La Turbie (p 152). |
| **AD** | |
| 1, 2 and 3C | Roman civilisation in evidence in some coastal towns (Fréjus, Cimiez, Antibes) and inland (Digne, Manosque, Riez) ; the Aurelian Way (Ventimiglia-Brignoles-Aix) is the country's main highway (p 65). |
| 313 | Constantine grants Christians freedom of worship by the Edict of Milan. |
| 4, 5C | Christianity takes roots in the seaboard towns, then inland. |
| 5, 6C | Vandals, Visigoths, Burgundians, Ostrogoths, Franks invade Provence in turn. |
| 496 | Clovis, King of the Franks, defeats the Alamanni, from Germany at Tolbiac. |
| 8C | The Saracens sack the seaboard in the first half of the century. |
| 800 | Charlemagne is crowned Emperor of the West. |

## PROVENCE UP TO THE "REUNION"

| | |
|---|---|
| 843 | Treaty of Verdun regularises the division of Charlemagne's Empire between the three sons of Louis the Debonair. Provence is restored to Lothaire (one of Charlemagne's grandsons) at the same time as Burgundy and Lorraine. |
| 855 | Provence is made a kingdom by Lothaire for his son, Charles. |
| 884 | The Saracens capture the Maures and for a century terrorise the land (p 73). |
| 962 | Restoration of the Western Empire as the Holy Roman Empire, in favour of Otto I. |
| 10, 11C | Provence, after passing from hand to hand, is finally made part of the Holy Roman Empire. Despite this, the Counts of Provence enjoy effective independence. The towns are freed and proclaim their autonomy. |
| 12C | The County of Provence passes to the Counts of Toulouse, then to the Counts of Barcelona. The Counts maintain an elaborate court at Aix. |
| 1226 | Accession of Saint Louis. |
| 1246 | Charles of Anjou, brother of Saint Louis, marries the daughter of the Count of Barcelona and becomes Count of Provence. |
| 1254 | Landing of Saint Louis at Hyères on return from 7th Crusade. |
| 1270 | Death of Saint-Louis. End of 8th and last Crusade. |
| 1308 | Overlordship of Monaco is bought from the Genoese by a member of the Grimaldi family (p 102). |
| 1337 | Start of the Hundred Years War, ending in 1453. |
| 1343-1382 | Queen Jeanne becomes Countess of Provence. Plague decimates the population. |
| 1338 | Nice hands itself over to the Count of Savoy (p 108). |
| 1419 | Nice is officially ceded to the Duke of Savoy. |
| 1434 | René of Anjou becomes Count of Provence. The reign of "good King René" opens an era of prosperity for Provence. |
| 1461 | Accession of Louis XI. |
| 1481 | Charles of Maine, nephew of René of Anjou, bequeaths Provence (except Nice, which belongs to Savoy) to Louis XI. |
| 1486 | Reunion of Provence with France is ratified by the "Estates" of Provence (assembly of representatives of the three orders). Henceforth, Provence is attached to the Kingdom "as one principal to another". |

## PROVENCE AFTER THE "REUNION"

| | |
|---|---|
| 1501 | Establishment of Parliament at Aix (Parliament of Provence), sovereign court of justice, which later claims certain political prerogatives. |
| 1515 | Accession of François I. |
| 1524 | Provence is invaded by the Imperialists, commanded by the High Constable of Bourbon. |
| 1536 | Invasion of Provence by the Emperor Charles V. |
| 1539 | Edict of Villers-Cotterêts decrees French as the language for all administrative laws in Provence. |
| 1543 | Nice besieged by French and Turkish troops. Catherine Ségurane (p 108) instrumental in causing the Turks to withdraw. |
| 1589 | Accession of Henri IV. |

| | |
|---|---|
| 1562-1598 | Wars of Religion end with promulgation of the Edict of Nantes. |
| 1610 | Assassination of Henri IV. He is succeeded by Louis XIII. |
| 1622 | Louis XIII visits Provence. |
| 1643 | Accession of Louis XIV. |
| 1691 | Nice taken by the French. |
| 1696 | France returns Nice to Savoy. |
| 1707 | Invasion of Provence by Prince Eugene of Savoy. |
| 1718 | County of Nice becomes part of the newly created Kingdom of Sardinia. |
| 1720 | The great plague decimates Provence. |
| 1746 | Austro-Sardinian offensive is broken at Antibes. Austrian War of Succession. |
| 1787 | Reunion of the "Estates" of Provence. |
| 1789 | The French Revolution. |

### REVOLUTION-EMPIRE

| | |
|---|---|
| 1790 | Provence is divided into three departments : Bouches-du-Rhône, Var, Basses-Alpes. |
| 1793 | Execution of Louis XVI, 21 January.<br>Siege of Toulon, in which Bonaparte distinguishes himself *(p 145)*.<br>Nice is reunited to France. |
| 1799 | On 9 October, Bonaparte lands at St-Raphaël on his return from Egypt *(p 134)*. |
| 1804 | Coronation of Napoleon. |
| 1814 | Abdication of Napoleon, at Fontainebleau, 6 April. |
| 1814 | Embarkation of Napoleon at St-Raphaël, 28 April, for the Island of Elba *(p 134)*. The County of Nice is restored to the King of Sardinia. |
| 1815 | Landing of Napoleon at Golfe-Juan, 1 March *(p 50)*.<br>Battle of Waterloo, 18 June. |

### 19th CENTURY

| | |
|---|---|
| 1830 | Accession of Louis-Philippe. |
| 1832 | The Duchess de Berry lands at Marseilles, hoping to raise Provence in favour of a legitimist restoration. |
| 1852 | Accession of Napoleon III. |
| 1860 | County of Nice restored to France *(p 108)*. |
| 1864 | Nice linked to the railway network. |
| 1878 | Opening of the Monte-Carlo Casino. Development of the winter tourist season on the Riviera. |
| late 19C | St-Tropez School of Painting *(p 136)*. |

### 20th CENTURY

| | |
|---|---|
| 1940 | The Italians occupy Menton. |
| 1942 | The Germans invade the Free Zone. The scuttling of the French Fleet in Toulon harbour *(p 146)*. |
| 1944 | Liberation of Provence. |
| Since 1946 | Development of summer tourist trade on the Riviera. Harnessing of the rivers Durance and Verdon. |
| 1980 | The A8 or Provençale Motorway, links up, the Rhône and Italian networks. |

## MILITARY OPERATIONS, AUGUST 1944

At a critical moment in the Battle of Normandy, the Allies landed the American 7th Army on the coast of Provence under General Patch. American and French divisions were to hasten the German defeat and assure possession of the port of Marseilles. In the early hours of 15 August, 1944, Anglo-American airborne troops were dropped around Le Muy, French commandos landed on the left wing at Cap Nègre, and on the right wing at Esquillon Point, American Special Forces attacked the Islands of Hyères. Thus protected, the main American forces landed at 8am on the beaches of the Maures and the Esterel. Despite a rapid advance these two sectors were still separated at the end of the day owing to German resistance at St-Raphaël and Fréjus, which only fell next day.

On the 16th, the troops of General de Lattre de Tassigny began disembarking around St-Tropez and, having relieved the Americans at the outlet of the Maures, attacked the defences of Toulon on the 19th. General de Montsabert outflanked the town to the north, and Magnan and Brosset attacked from the east, taking Solliès and Hyères. Toulon, attacked on the 21st, fell on the 26th. From the 20th, the troops of Mantsabert moved on to Marseilles; the resistance points of Aubagne and Cadolive were taken on the 21st and 22nd and the town surrounded. The Old Port was reached on the 23rd, but the German garrison did not surrender until the 28th.

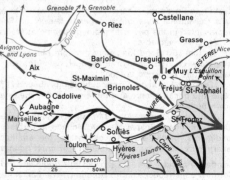

During this time, the Americans passed Castellane, reaching Grenoble on the 22nd and attempted to cut the Valley of the Rhône, the German line of retreat pressed by units from Brignoles and Barjols, via Aix and Avignon.

To the east, the Americans advanced towards Nice and the Alpes-Maritimes on the 21st. Nice fell on the 30th. In less than fifteen days, Provence had been liberated. The Allies pursued the Germans to the gates of Alsace and joined up with the troops coming from Normandy.

# THE ARTS

Compared with Provence, rich in monuments of all sorts, the Riviera and Haute-Provence have less to offer. Here however the sightseer will discover side by side, art in its earliest and most modern forms, from the many Roman ruins to the most striking contemporary buildings.

Right up until the 19C the art of the region remained highly conservative. When the Romanesque and Gothic styles were flourishing elsewhere in France, the area remained untouched by these movements for even longer than neighbouring Provence.

## ARCHITECTURE

**Gallo-Roman Antiquities.** – Provence and particularly the Riviera have been vital areas since Roman times. But later generations, interested in the future rather than the past, took materials used by the Romans to construct their own new buildings and so have left only fragments of the prosperous civilisations of former times.

The Roman world, however, can still be seen: at Cimiez *(p 113)* are arenas, at Riez *(p 121)* stand four fine granite columns which formed part of a temple built at the end of the first century AD. Fréjus *(p 69)* in addition to arenas, can still show traces of the harbour installations. La Turbie, a ruin *(p 152)*, which has been restored in part, is of especial interest: the Alpine Trophy, a grandiose construction elevated to the glory of Caesar, is one of the few such Roman trophies still in existence.

Buildings from the Merovingian and Carolingian periods include: the baptistries of Riez *(p 121)* and Fréjus *(p 70)*, octagonal or square buildings flanked by apsidal chapels ; the Chapel of Notre-Dame-de-Pépiole *(p 139)* and the Chapel of the Trinity on Saint-Honorat Island *(p 89)*.

**Romanesque Period.** – In the 12C an architectural renaissance in Provence produced a harvest of churches. The Romanesque style here is more inventive than creative so that it is not capital buildings such as exist in Burgundy that will be found, but small churches, remarkable for the bonding of their evenly cut stones with fine mortar work.

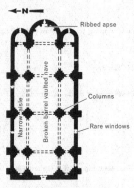

Plan of a Provençal Romanesque Church

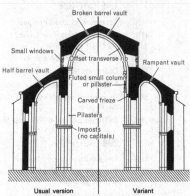

Vertical section of a Provençal Romanesque Church

The churches are plain outside, their façades being often poor in style; the only break in the flatness of the sides comes from powerful buttresses. The square belfries are sometimes decorated with applied blind arcades, known as "Lombard bands" and evidence of northern Italian influence.

On entering, the visitor is struck by the simplicity and austerity of the interior which often consists of a single nave and a shallow transept. If aisles form part of the plan, the apse ends in a semicircle flanked by two apsidal chapels.

The interesting Abbey of Thoronet *(p 143)* contains a church of the Cistercian Order with the wide transept and bare appearance characteristic of the churches built by the Benedictines. In contrast, however, the roof of broken barrel vaulting and the semicircular apse show the influence of the local craftsmen.

**Gothic to Baroque.** – There are few Gothic buildings now in the region. Provençal Gothic is a transitional style which depends heavily on Romanesque traditions. The style is represented in the powerful groined vaulting at Fréjus and Grasse. The Fréjus Cloisters *(p 71)* are remarkable.

In the 15C Good King René brought numerous Italian craftsmen to Provence. But strangely enough, though Provençal painting was influenced by the Renaissance, architecture remained untouched.

On the other hand, Classical buildings abound (17 and 18C). Design lost its original style and became more and more severe and majestic. In the towns the wealthier built town houses.

The development of the Baroque style is to be seen in ecclesiastical buildings in the County of Nice at Sospel, Menton, Monaco, la Turbie and Nice. Façades are adorned with pediments, niches and statues; inside, the architectural lines are often hidden by altarpieces, panelling and baldaquins of great richness.

**Modern Period.** – The 19C showed little originality and Baroque continued to be favoured for new constructions and restorations. The Romanesque-Byzantine style was employed at Our Lady of Victory, St-Raphaël, the Neo-Gothic on the west front of the church at Cimiez and Neo-Romanesque for Monaco's Cathedral.

Examples of 20C works include the Church of St-Joan of Arc, Nice, the country church of St-Martin-de-Peille and the Matisse Chapel at Vence *(p 159)*. The Marc Chagall Museum, Nice and the striking property development, the Baie des Anges Marina *(p 46)* are other fine examples of modern architecture.

# SCULPTURE

**Pierre Puget (1620-1694).** – Man of Marseilles, painter and architect, Pierre Puget was one of the greatest French sculptors of the 17C. He began his chisel work on boat ornaments and was later to devise huge carved poops on men-of-war. He developed his talent at the side of Pietro da Cortona, whose pupil he became during one of his journeys to Italy. Following the fall of his patron Fouquet, he chose to live far from the court at Versailles, but nevertheless received favours from Colbert who appointed him to supervise the decoration of the port of Toulon.

Jealousy and intrigue caused his disgrace and he therefore devoted himself solely to the embellishment of Marseilles and Toulon. The atlantes that once supported the balcony of the Toulon Town Hall and that fortunately were spared when the old harbour was destroyed in 1943 are, with the statue of Milo (on exhibition in the Louvre in Paris), his best known works. Though he may have sacrificed elegance of appearance for strength, he knew how to portray in his work, which was sometimes of grandiose proportions, power, movement and pity.

# PAINTING

**15-16C.** – From the middle of the 15C to the middle of the 16C a school of painting, at first purely Gothic then influenced by the Italian Renaissance, flourished in the County of Nice. The names of **Bréa** and **Durandi**, for many years unknown, are now famous. It is said of Louis Bréa that he was a "Provençal Fra Angelico" – praise justified by the sincerity and sobriety of his brush and his gift for stressing the humanity of his subjects. However, his simplicity is a far cry from the mysticism of Fra Angelico, and his colours and dull tones have not the quality of the genius of the great Italian. These Provençal artists worked mainly for the penitent brotherhoods, which explains why their paintings are scattered in many churches and pilgrim chapels. They can be seen in Nice, Cimiez (Antoine, his brother and nephew François), Lucéram, Gréolières, Biot, Antibes, Fréjus, Grasse and Lieuche.

During the same period, the humblest churches of the County of Nice were decorated with the most striking mural paintings. These are to be seen at St-Étienne-de-Tinée, Venanson, Lucéram, Auron, Saorge and Our Lady of the Fontaines *(p 129)* where **Giovanni Canavesio** created a work of exceptional quality. St Sebastian is often portrayed since, if invoked, he was said to ward off the plague (the scourge of the countryside) as easily as he tore the arrows from his body.

Although anonymous many of these artists were highly talented such as the unknown master who worked at Villars.

*(After photo : Archives photographiques)*

Louis Bréa – St. Martin
(detail from Pietà, Cimiez)

**The Classical Period.** – The 17 and 18C were marked by the fine pictures of the Parrocels, the Vanloos, Joseph Vernet and Hubert Robert. It is **Fragonard**, however, who is the pride of Provence. Rakish scenes were his favourites; he painted them with great enthusiasm and exquisitely. He often took as background to his gay party paintings the landscapes flooded with light which he knew so well and the gardens full of flowers to be seen all round his native town of Grasse.

**Modern painting.** – The Riviera became the chosen land for painters at the end of the 19C. Numerous artists, representing the main trends in modern painting have been fascinated by the clear light of the Mediterranean South.

**Impressionism.** – The Impressionists sought to portray the subtle effects of light on the Mediterranean landscapes. Berthe Morisot lived at Nice, Monet at Antibes and **Renoir** at Cagnes *(p 46)* where he spent his last years, painting flowers and fruits, landscapes and people of the South. Impressionism gave birth to a new school, **Pointillism**, a method of painting created by Seurat, which consisted of dividing shades into tiny dots of pure colour. **Signac**, the follower of Seurat established himself in St-Tropez in 1892, to which he attracted some of his friends, among whom were Manguin, Bonnard and Matisse.

**Fauvism.** – Reacting against Impressionism, **Matisse** and **Dufy** living in Nice aimed to set painting loose as an act of pure instinct – brillant colours with simplified forms and perspectives, no longer the fleeting sensations before nature's great spectacles but the sentiments and thoughts of the artist.

**Contemporary Movements.** – **Picasso**, founder with Braque of Cubism – an art concerned above all with form – was in his turn seduced by the Riviera, and lived at Vallauris in 1946, then at Cannes and finally at Mougins. Braque spent his last years painting in Le Cannet while **Fernand Léger**, another Cubist painter, lived at Biot. **Dunoyer de Segonzac** was untiring in his portrayal of St-Tropez. **Chagall**, Surrealist painter, found the light and flowers of Vence a marvellous stimulus to his multicoloured dreams.

Other artists, such as **Kandinsky** at La Napoule, **Cocteau** at Menton, **Van Dongen** at Cannes, **Magnelli** at Grasse and **Nicolas de Staël** at Antibes although not resting too long in the region, nevertheless marked their stay in an unforgettable manner.

# LIFE ON THE RIVIERA

Ways of life contrast sharply on the Riviera: the coast, with its towns, resorts and innumerable villas, seems to live only for the tourist; the interior, on the other hand, more inward looking, preserves its Provençal character.

## HAUTE-PROVENCE

Haute-Provence has few large towns unlike the coast, but many small market towns, whose flat roofed houses covered with red tiles of stone shingles, press their high narrow façades along the equally narrow, winding and sometimes uneven streets. Urban development is sited according to the topography, in the basins (Forcalquier, Brignoles and Draguignan) or on the plateaux (Riez); but most of the time the localities are to be found at strategic points in the valley, like Sisteron, Digne, Draguignan and Castellane.

## ON THE COAST

On the contrary, the coast since earliest times has attracted man and strongholds have been built on isolated hills; the curious village of Èze *(p 65)* is the best example.

Since the great development of tourist traffic, life on the Riviera, nearly all the year round, is dominated by the beach and holiday atmosphere. The great influx of visitors has gradually hidden local life.

**Holiday Resorts.** – The visitor who is seeking fashionable and elegant surroundings can choose between the animation of Cannes and Monte-Carlo or the quieter and more discreet existence of Hyères, Beaulieu, Cap Ferrat or Cap Martin. Those who are looking for the liveliness of a large town with all its amusements will undoubtedly turn to Nice. Lively St-Tropez will attract a large number of summer visitors; the seeker of solitude will find isolated inlets and localities and hotels of all kinds. The less wealthy tourist has a choice of hotels to suit his pocket in most of the great resorts.

There are also charming country houses, built in Provençal rustic style, with pink or ochre coloured walls, overhanging red tiled roofs and arbours covered with wisteria and climbing plants. There are, too, beautiful gardens where great earthenware jars, which once held olive oil or wine, are now purely decorative. Parks offer fine views from their terraces and everyone can enjoy the light and colour in an atmosphere of charm and relaxation.

Thus there is a veritable colonisation by tourists which becomes increasingly hectic, posing real accommodation problems to the towns of the Riviera. Numerous constructions are invading the coast, land is becoming scarce, and one can see here and there towns built over water, such as the lake town of Port-Grimaud *(p 97)*, the Marinas of Cogolin and the sea city of Port-la-Galère.

Inevitably, the success of these seaside resorts has not been achieved without some loss of natural beauty. Building developments have arisen on all sides; great blocks of flats have sprung up in the towns; far too many private properties are situated along the coast itself, barring access to the sea. Poky little houses as well as pretentiously battlemented and turreted villas make the occasional eyesore.

**Ports, harbours and catches.** – The naval port of Toulon is a place apart on the recreational coast. Cannes, Monaco and Menton are in character with pleasure boat harbours which have always been characterised by their beautiful yachts with shining brasswork and gleaming paint lying at anchor in the bay or moored to the quays.

Fishing on the Riviera is confined to the coast and, as the catch is insufficient for the area, has to be supplemented by shipments from the Atlantic. There are no trawlers or large fishing combines, but small boats manned by individual sailors. The *tartane,* the classic craft of the Mediterranean with a triangular sail – said to be of Roman origin – has completely disappeared.

There are no large fishing ports, but numerous little harbours along the coast – Bandol, St-Tropez, St-Raphaël, Villefranche – are adapting to the demands of tourists and equipping themselves with moorings for pleasure boats. They offer a colourful spectacle. After they have been fishing the men mend their nets, thrusting their big toes into the meshes to keep them taut.

For some years past in the region, efforts have been made to modernise the fishing industry and increase the number of boats in use. This has been

Villefranche – The fishing port

made practical through the use of very large running nets known as *lamparos* and *seinches* and the transfer of the N. African fleets to the French coast and the construction of fish canneries which can absorb the hauls quickly. Owner fishermen have replaced the traditional one or two ton pointed ship *(pointu)* by a 5-6 tonner.

An unusual sight in the harbour at Nice is a fleet of about 50 tunny fishing-boats, which come from all along the Mediterranean coast.

**The Markets.** – Most of the coastal towns – Nice, Cannes and Toulon especially – have their own flower and fishmarkets where, to the colouful banks of flowers and stalls of gleaming fish, are added the noisy bustle and the warmth of the local accents of buyers and sellers thus providing a truly meridional scene.

# INLAND

The interior reveals the last vestiges of what was once a rough and precarious way of life. Valley sides and hill slopes were terraced with stone walls retaining small strips of soil. On these narrow plots cereals were planted or two or three rows of vines and a few olive and almond trees grew. These meagre assets were often completed by small flocks of sheep and goats, roaming on the *garrigues*.

It is hardly surprising that there has been a gradual drift from these difficult plateaux and mountainous areas. The contrast with the fertile valleys and irrigated plains of the lowlands and the coast, where cereals, early vegetables and flowers were harvested and vines and fruit trees flourished, was too evident. This evolution is a feature of the countryside as shown by the lonely villages clinging to solitary ridges (*details below*) and small farms lying abandoned among their terraced walls. They bear no resemblance to the market towns of the plains, spread along the main roads, or to the *mas* in the midst of large cultivated areas.

Since the 16C, local townsmen have been in the habit of spending their Sundays and, if possible, the hot days of the year in a country cottage or *bastide*, or sometimes a simple herdsman's hut.

The centre of the village is the little square or *cours*, shaded by plane trees round a small fountain. This is where the cafés are to be found, always full in this region where people love social life, conversation and politics and where much of the day is spent away from the houses which are kept shuttered to keep out the heat and the flies.

# THE HILL VILLAGES

Many old villages may be seen perched like eagles' nests on a hilltop or set on the flank of a hill, some are practically deserted while others have been restored. For centuries the peasants built their villages in this way, at a distance from their lands and water supplies, and surrounded them with ramparts.

This was a wise precaution in the days of the great Germanic invasions, the Moslem pirates, and the attacks by the mercenaries of the Middle Ages and the Renaissance. The coming of security, better communications and the development in agricultural techniques in the 19C ended this isolation. The villages now flourish in the plains and the peasant is able to live on his land and build his house there.

Gourdon, Èze, Utelle, Peille and many other villages (*see map above*) still bear witness to the ancient Provençal way of life.

These villages are picturesque to visit. Built with stones from the hillsides, they seem to blend with the countryside. The winding streets and alleyways, steeply sloped and only to be traversed on foot, are paved with flagstones or cobbles, intersected by tortuous stairways and crossed overhead by vaults and arches. Sometimes arcades follow one another at ground level, affording the passerby shelter from the sun and rain.

The houses, roofed with curved tiles, have high narrow fronts, worn by the centuries. They buttress each other and surround the church or château which dominates the village. Old nail studded doors, wrought iron hinges and bronze knockers, still adorn the more substantial dwellings. Sometimes the little townships are still enclosed by ramparts and one enters by a fortified gate.

## PROVENÇAL COOKERY

The main features of Provençal cooking are garlic and frying in oil. Garlic has its own poets who have described it as the "Provençal truffle", the "divine condiment" and the "friend of man". Oil – preferably olive oil – takes the place of butter in all its northern uses. "A fish lives in water and dies in oil," says a local proverb.

**Bouillabaisse.** – Honour to whom honour is due, and we here salute the most celebrated of Provençal dishes. The classic bouillabaisse must consist of the "three fishes": *rascasse* (hog-fish), red gurnet and conger eel. Several other kinds of fish and some crustaceans are usually added: crabs, spider crabs, etc. Crayfish is also included as a luxury. The seasoning is just as important as the fish: salt, pepper, onion, tomato, saffron, garlic, thyme, bay leaves, sage, fennel and orange peel. Sometimes a glass of white wine or brandy gives the final flavour to the broth which is poured on to thick slices of bread.

A first class bouillabaisse, with the indispensable presence of *rascasse*, is distinguished by the freshness of the fish, the purity of the olive oil and the excellence of the saffron.

**Aïoli.** – *Aïoli* is another Provençal speciality and is a mayonnaise made with olive oil, strongly flavoured with crushed garlic. Comparing the northern variety of mayonnaise with *aïoli* Mistral dismissed it as insipid "jam". *Aïoli* is served with *hors-d'œuvre* and with *bourride* (a soup of frog-fish, bass and whiting, etc.) which some people prefer to bouillabaisse.

**Fish and Shellfish.** – One of the Mediterranean's tastiest fish is the red mullet, which the famous chef, Brillat-Savarin, called the "woodcock of the sea" probably because gourmets cook it without first scaling or cleaning it. The *loup* (local name for bass), grilled with fennel or vine shoots, is also a delicious dish. *Brandade* of cod is a *purée* of pounded cod mixed with olive oil, milk, some cloves of garlic and slices of truffle.

**Specialities of Nice.** – These are numerous and we will mention here only the best known: *Pissaladiera,* an onion flan flavoured with a *purée* of anchovies and black olives; *Socca,* a pastry made from chick-pea flour; *Ratatouia,* a kind of vegetable stew consisting of tomatoes, egg-plant, green pepper and baby vegetable marrows cooked in oil; *Pan Bagnat,* a sandwich of raw onions and tomatoes, black olives and anchovies, sprinkled with oil and vinegar; *Pistou,* a vegetable soup flavoured with a *pommade* or paste of fat, garlic, basil, olive oil and parmesan blended with a pestle and mortar; *Tourte de Bléa,* a tart garnished with chopped cardoon leaves, pine nuts and currants ; *Stocaficada,* cod stewed with aromatic herbs, anchovies and black olives ; *Ravioli,* little envelopes of noodle paste, stuffed with seasoned chopped meat and cardoons, a celery-like vegetable.

**Wines.** – Vines have been grown in Provence since the days of the ancients, but now wine-growing is becoming ever more important.

The **rosé wines**, iridescent in hue and made from grapes grown on vines brought to Provence by Good King René of Anjou, are gaining great favour; pleasant and fruity to the palate, they go well with any dish. The **white wines** are generally dry in character but have a good bouquet and go excellenty with shellfish and Mediterranean fish. Finally there is a wide variety of full flavoured **red wines**: full-bodied or subtle and delicate depending on whether they come from Bandol, the southern slopes of the Maures or, on the other hand, from the Argens Valley or St-Tropez. The most popular wines are those from Ollioules, Bandol, Pierrefeu, Cuers, Taradeau, La Croix-Valmer, and those from the Nice area – Bellet, La Gaude, St-Jeannet and Menton.

## THE GAME OF BOULES

This, the most popular game of the region, is played with ironclad balls. Matches are between teams of three players *(triplettes)* or four *(quadrettes)*, usually watched by a crowd of excited spectators. The *pointeurs* (attackers) must throw their balls as close as possible to a small ball (*cochonnet*), acting as a jack, which is set at the limit of the pitch. The *tireurs* (defenders) must knock away the balls of their opponents by striking them with their own and the best players can do this so that their ball takes the exact place of the one knocked away. Over short distances in which it is forbidden to move the feet the play is *à la pétanque*. Over long distances of 10 m – 30 ft or more the players throw their balls after making three hopping steps from the throwing mark and the game is known as *à la longue*.

## HANDICRAFTS

In numerous inland villages, restored with taste, are craftsmen dedicated to the production of objects by traditional methods.

**Moustiers-Ste-Marie.** – *Description p 106*. Examples of the famous Moustiers ware can be seen at the workshop, Atelier de Ségries 4 km – 2 ½ miles to the north-west of Moustiers.

**Biot.** – *Description p 40*. Biot owes its growing reputation to its glass craftsmanship. The glass workers can be seen working – using the secrets of their ancestors. The production of the large earthenware jars dating from the Phoenicians (who exported them from the port of Antibes) is perpetuated. Another craft perfected in the town is jewellery: gold and silver are worked and decorated with precious and semi-precious stones.

**Vallauris.** – *Description p 157*. This town's pottery has world wide fame. In spite of the large scale production, many potters continue producing in the traditional manner – baking by wood. Besides pottery there are other interesting crafts to be noted: handmade marionettes, olive wood furniture, sculptured objets and weaving.

**Tourrette-sur-Loup.** – *Description p 90*. It represents the most striking example of an old mediaeval village which has been reborn thanks to crafts. The weavers installed in the narrow winding alleyways, offer a whole range of varied and beautiful materials (shops and workshops are open to the public). Potters, painters, olive wood carvers have also chosen as their home this picturesque village.

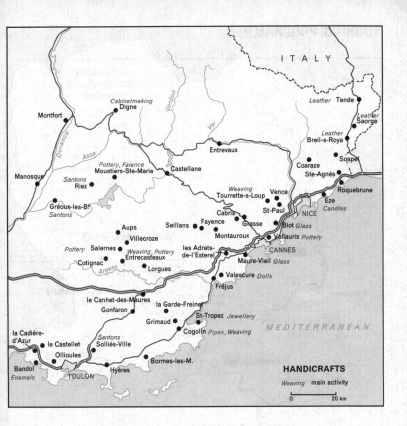

## PRINCIPAL FESTIVALS

| DATE AND PLACE | PAGE | NATURE OF FESTIVAL |
|---|---|---|
| **Cannes** ................... February | 47 | Mimosa Festival |
| May | 47 | International Film Festival |
| **Cap d'Antibes (La Garoupe)** .......... First or second Sunday in July | 35 | Sailors Festival: Procession of Our Lady of Safe Homecoming |
| **Digne** ....... First Sunday in August | 56 | Flower decked lavender *Corso* |
| **Forcalquier**. .................. August | 67 | Haute-Provence Music Festival |
| **Grasse** ...... First Sunday in August | 74 | Jasmine Festival |
| **Hyères**   Late August-early September | 82 | Experimental cinema |
| **Juan-les-Pins, Antibes** ............. July | 87 | World Jazz Festival |
| **Lucéram** .............. 24 December | 91 | The Shepherd's Christmas Offering |
| **Menton** ........ The week of Shrove Tuesday | 99 | Lemon Festival, *Corso* of the Golden Fruits |
| August | 99 | Chamber Music Festival |
| **Monaco (La Condamine)**. 27 January | 105 | Feast of St Dévote |
| May | 103 | Grand Prix |
| **Nice** ...... Weeks preceding Shrove Tuesday | 108 | Carnival ★★★ |
| April | 109 | International Book Fair |
| (at Cimiez) .................. May | 113 | May Festival |
| (at Cimiez) ................. July | 115 | Jazz Festival |
| **Peille** ... First Sunday in September | 119 | Folk Festival |
| **Roquebrune-Cap-Martin**. .... Evening of Good Friday | 125 | Procession of the Entombment of Christ |
| 5 August | 125 | Procession of the Passion |
| **St-Tropez** ....... 16, 17 and 18 May | 136 | *Bravade* |
| 15 June | 136 | The "Spanish" *Bravade* |
| **Seyne** .. Second Saturday in August | 57 | Horse and mule fair |
| **Sisteron** ... Mid July to early August | 141 | Music, dance and drama Festival |
| **Toulon (Châteauvallon)** ......... July | 146 | International Dance Festival |
| **Vence** .. Easter Sunday and Monday | 159 | Episcopal Mass: Provençal dancing, Flower Battle |

*The events listed above are a selection only. For further details and to avoid
disappointment check with the local tourist information centres.*
*The addresses, telephone numbers and any special closing times or dates of
the information centres are given in the current* **Michelin Guide France.**

# TOURING PROGRAMMES

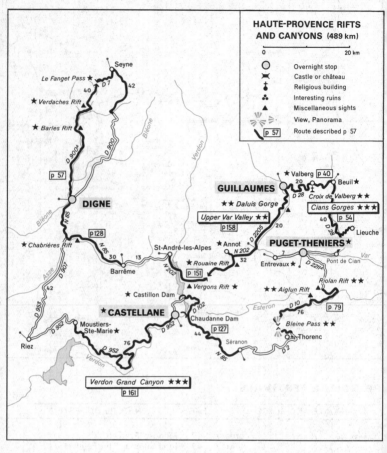

**HAUTE-PROVENCE RIFTS AND CANYONS** (489 km)

0                    20 km

○ Overnight stop
⚓ Castle or château
♁ Religious building
♣ Interesting ruins
▲ Miscellaneous sights
✿ View, Panorama
p 57 Route described p 57

Seyne

Le Fanget Pass ★
40    42
D 7
★★ Verdaches Rift
★ Barles Rift ▲
D 900A    D 900
Biléone

p 57
DIGNE
N 85    p 128

★ Chabrières Rift ▲
N 85    30    13
Barrème
N 202
D 907
Asse
42
D 951
Riez
Moustiers-Ste-Marie ★
Verdon
D 952    76
D 952    44
p 127
Chaudanne Dam
D 102
★ CASTELLANE
★ Castillon Dam
▲ Vergons Rift ★
★ Rouaine Rift ▲
p 151
St-André-les-Alpes
N 202    32
Annot ★
N 202    D 908
Séranon
N 85
D 2
Thorenc
★★ Bleine Pass ★★
p 79
D 10    76
★★ Aiglun Rift
Esteron
Riolan Rift ★★
Entrevaux ▲
7    D 211A
Pont de Cian
Var
PUGET-THENIERS ★
Lieuche
40    D 28
★★★ Cians Gorges
Croix de Valberg ★★
D 28
Beuil ★
Valberg p 40
20
GUILLAUMES
★★ Daluis Gorge
Upper Var Valley ★★
p 158
D 2205    20

Verdon Grand Canyon ★★★
p 161

# MAURES MASSIF-HAUT-VAR (546 km)

0                    30 km

Bel-Homme Pass ★
Seillans ★
D 19    21    Fayence ★
Bargemon
D 562
6    D 19
p 58
★ Châteaudouble Gorges ★
25
D 557
65
D 51
Tourtour
Villecroze
Cotignac
p 35
Entrecasteaux
D 13
Carcès
Thoronet Abbey ★
Brignoles
D 79    21
Cabasse
p 42
D 5
♣♣ Celle Abbey
la Loube Mountain ★
Signes
64    D 2
D 5
le Castellet ★
BANDOL ★
★ Sanary-38 s-Mer
p 149
18
★ Our Lady of the May Tree ★★
✿ Mount Faron ★★★
TOULON ★★
19    D 276    Hyères ★
38
N 98
★ Bormes-les-Mimosas
★ Babaou Pass
Pierre d'Avenon ♣
Collobrières
6
La Verne Charterhouse
p 94
★★★ Maures Massif
14
D 98
Grimaud
★ Port-Grimaud
St-Tropez ★★
60
D 98
Gassin
36
Canadel Pass ★★
N 559
Paillas Windmills ★★
12
Ramatuelle ★
34
★ Ste-Maxime
p 97
N 98
Roquebrune-s-Argens
Argens
62
p 59
D 25
Roquebrune Mountain ★
FRÉJUS
DRAGUIGNAN
★ Ste-Roseline (Former Abbey)
LE LAVANDOU ★

24

## ESTEREL-PRE-ALPS OF GRASSE (247 km)

0         20 km

47   N 85

p 77

Mons ★

la Faye Pass ★★

Gourdon ★

Courmes Waterfall ★

▲ Tourrette-s-Loup

Vence ★

St-Paul ★★

Loup Valley ★★
p 90

Magagnosc

D 2210

41

9

D 36

Var

★ St-Cézaire Caves

D 613

D 37

59

Siagne

GRASSE ★★

★ CAGNES-S-MER

Biot ★

N 7

28

Antibes ★

p 50

St-Cassien Lake

CANNES ★★★

★ Golfe-Juan

Juan-les-Pins ★★

Cap d'Antibes ★★

D 37

Tanneron Massif ★
p 143

N 98

la Napoule-Plage ★

Théoule-s-Mer ★

Mount Vinaigre ★★★

11   4

N 98

Esterel Massif ★★★
p 62

le Trayas ★

Argens

★ FRÉJUS

St-Raphaël ★

Agay ★

44

N 98

---

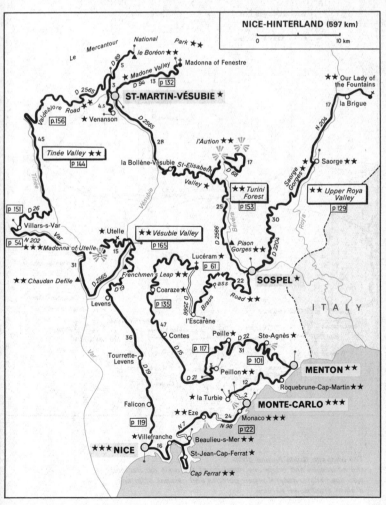

## NICE-HINTERLAND (597 km)

0         10 km

Le Mercantour National Park ★★

▲ le Boréon ★★

D 89

5

Madone Valley ★

† Madonna of Fenestre

D 2565

3

D 94   13   p 132

★★ Our Lady of the Fountains

ST-MARTIN-VÉSUBIE ★

4.5

17

la Brigue ★

Valdeblore Road

p.156

★ Venanson

D 2565

N 204

45

Tinée Valley ★★
p 144

2R

l'Aution ★★

la Bollène-Vésubie

St-Elisabeth

17

Saorge ★★

Tinée

Vésubie

Valley

D 68

Saorge Gorges

★★ Upper Roya Valley
p 129

p 151

D 26

★★ Turini Forest
p 153

25

Roya

Villars-s-Var

Var

30

D 2204

Bévéra

D 2566

p 54   N 202

★★ Madonna of Utelle

★ Utelle

★★ Vésubie Valley
p 165

▲ Piaon Gorges

31

15

Frenchmen's Leap ★★

Lucéram ★

p 61

SOSPEL ★

★★ Chaudan Defile ▲

D 2565

D 19

Coaraze ★

p 135

22

Braus

Pass Road ★★

ITALY

Levens

D 2566

l'Escarène

47

36

Contes ○

D 15

Peille ★

D 22

Ste-Agnès ★

p 117

31

p 101

MENTON ★★

Tourrette-Levens

D 19

D 21

3

Peillon ★★

12

Roquebrune-Cap-Martin ★★

Falicon ○

★ la Turbie

2

MONTE-CARLO ★★★

p 119

★★ Eze

N 7

24

Monaco ★★★

N 98

★ Villefranche

16

Beaulieu-s-Mer ★★

★★★ NICE

St-Jean-Cap-Ferrat ★

Cap Ferrat ★★

# PLACES TO STAY

The map below and the tables on the following pages give information concerning the accommodation and leisure facilities offered by a selection of towns in the region covered by this guide.

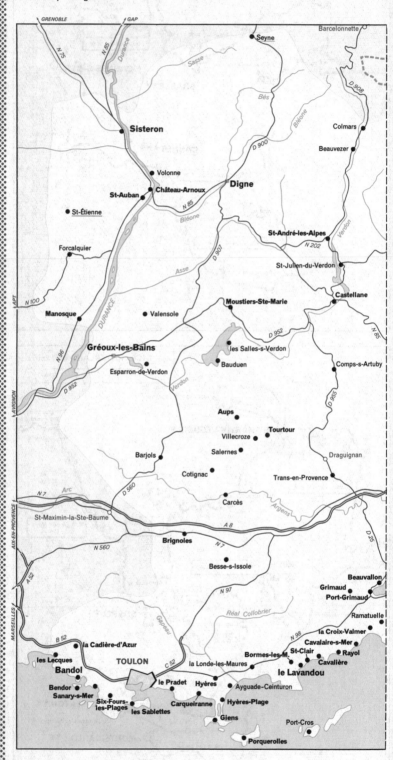

*The **Michelin Guide France** gives :*
*the addresses and telephone numbers of the main car dealers,*
*tyre specialists, general repair garages and garages offering*
*a night breakdown service.*

## Suggestion for an outing...

Take one of the two single track railway lines which wend inland from **Nice**. The first follows the Var valley to **Digne** while the second goes over the Tende Pass to **Cuneo**.

Both lines are real feats of civil engineering with their twisting and at times audacious alignments. The train journey reveals some dramatic countryside and affords some unusual views of the inland highland area.

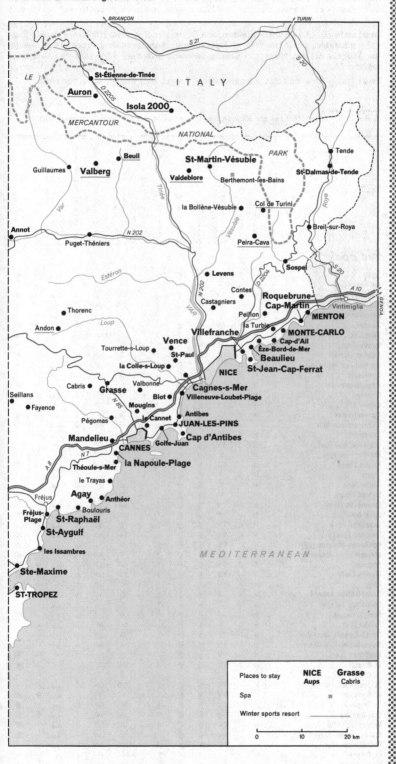

The ***Michelin Camping Caravaning Guide*** to ***France*** provides a selection of camping sites throughout the country and enumerates their characteristics, and facilities (installations and amusements)

**Hotels (H).** – A selection of the town's hotels is given in the current Michelin Red Guide **France**. This annual guide gives a choice of pleasant or secluded hotels with a list of their facilities as well as the periods when seasonal hotels are open *(1)*.

**Camping (C).** – This covers sites included in the current Michelin **Camping Caravaning France**. The sites selected are classified and the individual headings cover such topics as : shops, bars, laundries, games rooms, miniature golf, swimming pools and children's amusements *(1)*.

**Tourist centre (T).** – Local Tourist Information Centres or *Syndicats d'Initiative* supply town plans, timetables and information on local entertainment facilities, sports and sightseeing. The Michelin Guides **France** and **Camping Caravaning** give their addresses and telephone numbers *(1)*.

**Cinema ( ▦ ).** – This indicates a cinema which has at least one showing per week.

*(1) For further information see the Michelin Red Guide France and Camping Caravaning France*

### THE COAST

| | Hotels = H | Camping site = C | Tourist centre = T | Room reservation service = V | Doctor | Chemist | Pleasant site | Particularly attractive town | Beach (S = Sand, G = Pebbles) | Park or public gardens | Pleasure boat harbour | Fishing port | Casino | Cinema |
|---|---|---|---|---|---|---|---|---|---|---|---|---|---|---|
| Agay | H | C | T | | ✓ | ✓ | ◁ | – | S | – | – | 🎣 | – | ▦ |
| Anthéor | H | – | | | | | ◁ | – | S | – | – | – | – | – |
| Antibes | H | C | T | V | ✓ | ✓ | ◁ | ◇ | SG | ❀ | ⚓ | 🎣 | ♠ | ▦ |
| Antibes (Cap d') | H | – | T | V | | – | ◁ | ◇ | SG | ❀ | – | – | – | – |
| Ayguade-Ceinturon | H | C | | V | ✓ | – | | – | S | – | ⚓ | 🎣 | – | – |
| Bandol | H | – | T | V | ✓ | ✓ | ◁ | – | SG | ❀ | ⚓ | 🎣 | ♠ | ▦ |
| Beaulieu | H | – | T | V | ✓ | ✓ | ◁ | – | G | ❀ | – | – | ♠ | ▦ |
| Beauvallon | H | – | | V | | – | | – | S | – | – | – | – | – |
| Bendor Island | H | – | T | | | | ◁ | – | S | – | – | – | – | – |
| Bormes-les-Mimosas | H | C | T | V | ✓ | ✓ | ◁ | ◇ | S | ❀ | ⚓ | 🎣 | – | – |
| Boulouris | H | C | | V | ✓ | ✓ | | – | S | ❀ | – | – | – | – |
| Cagnes-sur-Mer | H | C | T | V | ✓ | ✓ | | ◇ | S | ❀ | – | – | – | ▦ |
| Cannes | H | C | T | V | ✓ | ✓ | ◁ | ◇ | S | ❀ | ⚓ | 🎣 | ♠ | ▦ |
| Cap-d'Ail | H | – | T | V | ✓ | ✓ | ◁ | – | S | ❀ | – | – | – | ▦ |
| Carqueiranne | H | C | T | V | ✓ | ✓ | | – | S | – | ⚓ | 🎣 | – | – |
| Cavalaire-sur-Mer | H | C | T | V | ✓ | ✓ | | – | S | ❀ | ⚓ | 🎣 | – | – |
| Cavalière | H | C | | V | ✓ | – | ◁ | – | S | – | – | – | – | – |
| Croix-Valmer (La) | H | C | T | V | ✓ | ✓ | ◁ | – | S | – | – | – | – | – |
| Èze-Bord-de-mer | H | – | | V | | ✓ | ◁ | – | G | – | – | – | – | – |
| Fréjus-Plage | H | – | T | V | ✓ | ✓ | | – | S | ❀ | – | – | – | ▦ |
| Giens | H | C | | V | ✓ | ✓ | ◁ | – | SG | – | ⚓ | 🎣 | – | – |
| Golfe-Juan | H | – | T | | ✓ | ✓ | | – | S | ❀ | ⚓ | 🎣 | – | – |
| Hyères-Plage | H | – | | V | ✓ | ✓ | | – | S | – | ⚓ | – | – | – |
| Issambres (Les) | H | – | T | V | ✓ | ✓ | ◁ | – | SG | ❀ | ⚓ | 🎣 | – | ▦ |
| Juan-les-Pins | H | – | T | V | ✓ | ✓ | ◁ | – | SG | ❀ | ⚓ | 🎣 | ♠ | ▦ |
| Lavandou (Le) | H | C | T | V | ✓ | ✓ | ◁ | – | S | ❀ | ⚓ | 🎣 | – | ▦ |
| Lecques (Les) | H | C | T | V | ✓ | ✓ | | – | SG | ❀ | – | – | – | ▦ |
| Londe-les-Maures (La) | H | C | T | V | ✓ | ✓ | | – | S | – | ⚓ | 🎣 | – | ▦ |
| Mandelieu-la-Napoule | H | C | T | V | ✓ | ✓ | ◁ | – | S | ❀ | ⚓ | 🎣 | – | ▦ |
| Menton | H | C | T | V | ✓ | ✓ | ◁ | ◇ | SG | ❀ | ⚓ | 🎣 | ♠ | ▦ |
| Monte-Carlo | H | – | T | V | ✓ | ✓ | ◁ | ◇ | SG | ❀ | ⚓ | 🎣 | ♠ | ▦ |
| Nice | H | – | T | V | ✓ | ✓ | ◁ | ◇ | G | ❀ | ⚓ | 🎣 | ♠ | ▦ |
| Porquerolles Island | H | – | | V | ✓ | ✓ | ◁ | – | S | – | ⚓ | – | – | – |
| Port-Cros Island | H | – | | | | | ◁ | – | S | – | – | – | – | – |
| Port-Grimaud | H | C | | | ✓ | ✓ | ◁ | ◇ | S | – | ⚓ | – | – | – |
| Pradet (Le) | H | C | T | | ✓ | ✓ | | – | SG | ❀ | ⚓ | – | – | ▦ |
| Rayol-Canadel-sur-Mer | H | – | T | V | ✓ | ✓ | ◁ | – | S | ❀ | – | – | – | ▦ |
| Roquebrune-Cap-Martin | H | – | T | V | ✓ | ✓ | ◁ | – | G | ❀ | – | – | – | ▦ |
| Sablettes (Les) | H | – | T | V | ✓ | ✓ | | – | S | – | ⚓ | – | – | ▦ |
| St-Aygulf | H | C | T | V | ✓ | ✓ | | – | SG | ❀ | – | – | – | ▦ |
| St-Clair | H | C | | | | | ◁ | – | S | – | – | – | – | – |
| St-Jean-Cap-Ferrat | H | – | T | V | ✓ | ✓ | ◁ | – | SG | ❀ | ⚓ | – | – | – |
| St-Raphaël | H | C | T | V | ✓ | ✓ | ◁ | – | S | ❀ | ⚓ | – | ♠ | ▦ |
| St-Tropez | H | – | T | V | ✓ | ✓ | ◁ | ◇ | S | ❀ | ⚓ | 🎣 | – | ▦ |
| Ste-Maxime | H | – | T | V | ✓ | ✓ | ◁ | – | S | ❀ | ⚓ | 🎣 | ♠ | ▦ |
| Sanary-sur-Mer | H | – | T | V | ✓ | ✓ | ◁ | – | SG | ❀ | ⚓ | 🎣 | – | ▦ |
| Six-Fours-les-Plages | H | C | T | V | ✓ | ✓ | | – | S | ❀ | ⚓ | 🎣 | – | ▦ |
| Théoule-sur-Mer | H | – | T | V | ✓ | ✓ | ◁ | – | S | ❀ | ⚓ | 🎣 | – | ▦ |
| Le Trayas | H | – | | | | | ◁ | – | S | – | – | – | – | – |
| Villefranche | H | – | T | V | ✓ | ✓ | ◁ | ◇ | G | ❀ | ⚓ | 🎣 | – | – |
| Villeneuve-Loubet-Plage | H | C | T | V | ✓ | ✓ | | – | G | ❀ | ⚓ | 🎣 | – | – |

*The **Michelin Red Guides, Green Guides** and **Maps** are cross referenced. Use them together.*

**Swimming pool or bathing place.** – The symbol ⌐ denotes a heated swimming pool ; (⌐), an unheated pool and ≋ supervised bathing in fresh water. The **Michelin** yellow map series, at a scale of 1:200 000 *(see the layout diagram on p 3 for coverage of the region)* indicates swimming pools, beaches and bathing places on rivers, lakes, or other stretches of water.

**Sailing ( ₰ ).** – This symbol indicates official sailing schools.

**Skin diving.** – Only resorts with clubs affiliated to a federation are included in this column.

**Tennis.** – Courts are indicated only if they are available for hire by visiting tourists.

**Mountaineering.** – For safety it is strongly recommended to use the services of officially approved guides. Details from the Tourist Information Centre. The **Michelin** 1:200 000 maps situate mountain refuge huts.

**Angling.** – The symbol ⌐ indicates the existence of an angling club in the town.

**Cross-country skiing.** – This is differentiated from downhill skiing in the table.

**Gliding.** – The two main centres are Fayence *(p 66)* and Château-Arnoux–St-Auban *(p 30)*.

### THE COAST

| Swimming pool | Sailing school ₰ | Boats/pedal boats L | Water skiing | Motor boats M | Skin diving | Footpaths (signposted) | Tennis | Horse riding | Bicycles for hire B | Golf (holes) | Page / Michelin map | Place |
|---|---|---|---|---|---|---|---|---|---|---|---|---|
| – | ● | L | ● | – | ● | ● | ● | ● | – | – | 62 | Agay |
| – | ● | L | ● | M | – | ● | ● | ● | – | – | 63 | Anthéor |
| ● | ● | L | ● | M | ● | ● | ● | ● | B | 18 | 33 | Antibes |
| ● | ● | L | ● | M | ● | ● | ● | ● | B | – | 34 | Antibes (Cap d') |
| – | – | L | ● | – | – | – | ● | – | B | 18 | 84 | Ayguade-Ceinturon |
| – | ● | L | ● | – | ● | ● | ● | ● | B | – | 36 | Bandol |
| ● | ● | – | ● | M | ● | – | ● | ● | – | – | 39 | Beaulieu |
| – | – | L | ● | M | – | ● | ● | ● | – | 9 | 98 | Beauvallon |
| ● | ● | L | – | – | ● | ● | ● | – | – | – | 37 | Bendor Island |
| – | ● | L | ● | M | ● | ● | ● | ● | B | 18 | 41 | Bormes-les-Mimosas |
| – | – | L | ● | M | – | ● | – | – | – | – | 62 | Boulouris |
| ● | ● | L | ● | M | ● | ● | ● | ● | B | 18 | 44 | Cagnes-sur-Mer |
| ● | ● | L | ● | M | ● | ● | ● | ● | B | 18 | 47 | Cannes |
| – | ● | – | ● | M | – | – | – | – | – | – | 124 | Cap d'Ail |
| ● | ● | L | – | M | – | – | – | – | B | – | 84-⑮ | Carqueirane |
| – | ● | L | ● | M | ● | ● | ● | ● | B | – | 95 | Cavalaire-sur-Mer |
| – | ● | L | ● | M | – | – | ● | – | – | – | 95 | Cavalière |
| ● | – | L | ● | M | – | ● | – | ● | – | – | 95 | Croix-Valmer (La) |
| – | ● | – | – | M | – | – | – | – | – | – | 124 | Eze-bord-de-Mer |
| – | ● | L | ● | M | ● | ● | ● | ● | B | 18 | 72 | Fréjus-Plage |
| – | – | – | – | ● | ● | – | – | ● | – | – | 84 | Giens |
| ● | ● | L | ● | M | ● | – | ● | – | – | – | 50 | Golfe-Juan |
| – | – | – | ● | M | ● | – | – | ● | – | – | 84 | Hyères-Plage |
| – | ● | L | ● | M | ● | ● | ● | ● | B | – | 98 | Issambres (Les) |
| ● | ● | L | ● | M | ● | ● | ● | ● | B | 18 | 87 | Juan-les-Pins |
| – | ● | L | ● | M | ● | ● | ● | ● | B | – | 87 | Lavandou (Le) |
| – | ● | L | – | – | ● | – | ● | – | – | – | 87 | Lecques (Les) |
| – | ● | L | – | – | ● | ● | ● | ● | – | 18 | 84-⑯ | Londe-Les-Maures (La) |
| ● | ● | L | ● | M | ● | ● | ● | ● | – | 18 | 143-64 | Mandelieu-La-Napoule |
| ● | ● | L | ● | M | ● | ● | ● | ● | B | – | 99 | Menton |
| ● | ● | L | ● | M | ● | ● | ● | ● | B | 18 | 105 | Monte-Carlo |
| ● | ● | L | ● | M | ● | ● | ● | ● | B | – | 108 | Nice |
| – | – | – | – | – | ● | ● | – | ● | B | – | 85 | Porquerolles Island |
| – | – | – | – | – | ● | ● | – | – | – | – | 86 | Port-Cros Island |
| – | – | – | – | – | – | – | – | – | – | – | 97 | Port-Grimaud |
| – | ● | L | – | – | ● | ● | ● | ● | B | – | 84-⑮ | Pradet (Le) |
| – | – | L | – | M | – | – | – | – | B | – | 95 | Rayol-Canadel-sur-Mer |
| ● | ● | L | ● | M | – | ● | ● | ● | – | 18 | 125 | Roquebrune-Cap-Martin |
| – | ● | L | – | M | – | – | – | – | – | – | 150 | Sablettes (Les) |
| – | – | L | ● | M | – | ● | ● | – | – | – | 98 | St-Aygulf |
| – | ● | L | ● | M | – | – | – | – | – | – | 95 | St-Clair |
| ● | ● | L | ● | M | ● | ● | ● | – | B | – | 51 | St-Jean-Cap-Ferrat |
| ● | ● | L | ● | M | ● | ● | ● | ● | B | 18 | 134 | St-Raphaël |
| ● | ● | L | – | M | ● | ● | ● | ● | B | 9 | 136 | St-Tropez |
| – | ● | L | – | M | ● | ● | ● | – | B | – | 138 | Ste-Maxime |
| – | ● | L | – | – | ● | ● | ● | – | B | – | 138 | Sanary-sur-Mer |
| ● | ● | L | ● | M | ● | ● | ● | ● | – | – | 142 | Six-Fours-les-Plages |
| – | ● | L | ● | M | ● | – | ● | – | – | 18 | 64 | Théoule-sur-Mer |
| – | – | L | – | – | ● | – | – | – | – | – | 63 | Le Trayas |
| – | ● | L | – | – | ● | ● | – | ● | – | – | 167 | Villefranche |
| – | ● | L | ● | M | – | ● | ● | ● | – | 18 | 46 | Villeneuve-Loubet-Plage |

*Travel with the* **Michelin 1:200 000 Map** *Series,*
*they are revised regularly.*

| | Altitude in metres | Hotels = H | Camping site = C | Tourist centre = T / Room reservation service = V | Doctor = ⚕ | Chemist = ℞ | Pleasant site = ◁ | Particularly attractive town = ◇ | River, lake or stretch of water = ● | Park, or public gardens = ❀ | Casino = ♠ | Cinema = ▦ |
|---|---|---|---|---|---|---|---|---|---|---|---|---|
| **INLAND** | | | | | | | | | | | | |
| Andon | 1182 | H | – | V | – | – | ◁ | – | – | ❀ | – | – |
| Annot | 700 | H | – | TV | – | – | ◁ | ◇ | – | ❀ | – | ▦ |
| Aups | 505 | H | C | V | ⚕ | ℞ | ◁ | ◇ | – | ❀ | – | – |
| Auron | 1608 | H | C | TV | ⚕ | ℞ | ◁ | – | – | ❀ | – | ▦ |
| Barjols | 288 | H | – | TV | ⚕ | ℞ | ◁ | – | ● | – | – | – |
| Bauduen | 483 | H | – | T | – | – | ◁ | – | ● | – | – | – |
| Beauvezer | 1150 | H | – | T | – | – | ◁ | – | ● | ❀ | – | – |
| Besse-sur-Issole | 258 | – | C | TV | ⚕ | ℞ | ◁ | – | ● | – | – | – |
| Beuil | 1450 | H | – | TV | ⚕ | ℞ | ◁ | – | – | ❀ | – | – |
| Biot | 80 | H | C | TV | ⚕ | ℞ | ◁ | ◇ | – | – | – | – |
| Bollène-Vésubie (La) | 690 | H | – | TV | ⚕ | ℞ | ◁ | ◇ | – | ❀ | – | – |
| Breil-sur-Roya | 286 | H | – | TV | ⚕ | ℞ | ◁ | ◇ | ● | ❀ | – | – |
| Brignoles | 215 | H | C | T | ⚕ | ℞ | – | ◇ | ● | – | – | ▦ |
| Cabris | 545 | H | – | V | ⚕ | ℞ | ◁ | – | – | – | – | – |
| Cadière-d'Azur (La) | 144 | H | C | TV | ⚕ | ℞ | ◁ | – | – | – | – | – |
| Cannet (Le) | 110 | H | – | TV | ⚕ | ℞ | ◁ | – | – | ❀ | – | – |
| Carcès | 138 | H | – | TV | ⚕ | ℞ | – | – | ● | – | – | – |
| Castagniers | 340 | H | – | – | – | – | – | – | – | – | – | – |
| Castellane | 724 | H | C | TV | ⚕ | ℞ | ◁ | ◇ | ● | ❀ | – | ▦ |
| Château-Arnoux-St-Auban | 440 | H | C | T | ⚕ | ℞ | ◁ | – | ● | ❀ | – | – |
| Colle-sur-Loup (La) | 96 | H | C | TV | ⚕ | ℞ | ◁ | – | ● | – | – | – |
| Colmars | 1235 | H | C | TV | ⚕ | ℞ | ◁ | – | ● | ❀ | – | – |
| Comps-sur-Artuby | 898 | H | – | TV | ⚕ | – | ◁ | – | – | – | – | – |
| Contes | 260 | H | – | – | ⚕ | ℞ | – | ◇ | ● | – | – | ▦ |
| Cotignac | 260 | H | – | TV | ⚕ | ℞ | ◁ | ◇ | ● | – | – | – |
| Digne | 608 | H | C | TV | ⚕ | ℞ | ◁ | – | ● | ❀ | – | ▦ |
| Esparron-de-Verdon | 386 | – | C | – | – | – | ◁ | – | ● | – | – | – |
| Fayence | 325 | H | – | TV | ⚕ | ℞ | ◁ | ◇ | – | – | – | ▦ |
| Forcalquier | 550 | H | – | TV | ⚕ | ℞ | ◁ | – | ● | ❀ | – | ▦ |
| Grasse | 333 | H | C | TV | ⚕ | ℞ | ◁ | ◇ | – | ❀ | ♠ | ▦ |
| Gréoux-les-Bains | 360 | H | C | TV | ⚕ | ℞ | ◁ | – | ● | ❀ | – | – |
| Grimaud | 100 | H | – | T | ⚕ | ℞ | ◁ | – | – | – | – | – |
| Guillaumes | 819 | H | – | T | ⚕ | ℞ | ◁ | – | ● | ❀ | – | – |
| Hyères | 40 | H | C | TV | ⚕ | ℞ | – | ◇ | ● | ❀ | ♠ | ▦ |
| Isola 2000 | 2000 | H | – | V | ⚕ | ℞ | ◁ | – | ● | – | – | ▦ |
| Levens | 570 | H | – | TV | ⚕ | ℞ | ◁ | – | – | ❀ | – | – |
| Manosque | 387 | H | C | TV | ⚕ | ℞ | – | ◇ | ● | – | – | ▦ |
| Mougins | 260 | H | – | T | ⚕ | ℞ | ◁ | ◇ | – | – | – | – |
| Moustiers-Ste-Marie | 631 | H | C | T | ⚕ | ℞ | ◁ | ◇ | ● | – | – | – |
| Pégomas | 22 | H | C | T | ⚕ | ℞ | ◁ | – | ● | – | – | – |
| Peillon | 376 | H | – | T | ⚕ | – | ◁ | ◇ | – | – | – | – |
| Peïra-Cava | 1450 | H | – | TV | ⚕ | ℞ | ◁ | – | – | ❀ | – | – |
| Puget-Théniers | 410 | H | – | TV | ⚕ | ℞ | ◁ | ◇ | ● | – | – | ▦ |
| Ramatuelle | 135 | H | C | – | ⚕ | ℞ | ◁ | – | – | ❀ | – | – |
| St-André-les-Alpes | 894 | H | C | TV | ⚕ | ℞ | ◁ | – | ● | ❀ | – | – |
| St-Dalmas-de-Tende | 696 | H | – | TV | ⚕ | ℞ | ◁ | – | ● | ❀ | – | – |
| St-Étienne | 697 | H | – | TV | ⚕ | ℞ | ◁ | – | ● | ❀ | – | ▦ |
| St-Étienne-de-Tinée | 1144 | H | – | V | ⚕ | ℞ | ◁ | ◇ | – | ❀ | – | ▦ |
| St-Julien-du-Verdon | 914 | H | – | TV | – | – | ◁ | – | ● | – | – | – |
| St-Martin-Vésubie | 960 | H | C | TV | ⚕ | ℞ | ◁ | ◇ | – | ❀ | – | – |
| St-Paul | 150 | H | – | TV | ⚕ | ℞ | ◁ | ◇ | – | ❀ | – | – |
| Salernes | 222 | H | C | – | ⚕ | ℞ | – | – | ● | – | – | ▦ |
| Salles-sur-Verdon (Les) | 503 | H | C | V | ⚕ | – | ◁ | – | ● | – | – | – |
| Seillans | 366 | H | – | TV | ⚕ | ℞ | ◁ | ◇ | – | – | – | – |
| Seyne | 1200 | H | C | TV | ⚕ | ℞ | ◁ | – | ● | ❀ | – | – |
| Sisteron | 482 | H | C | T | ⚕ | ℞ | ◁ | ◇ | ● | – | – | ▦ |
| Sospel | 349 | H | – | T | ⚕ | ℞ | ◁ | ◇ | ● | – | – | – |
| Tende | 816 | H | – | T | ⚕ | ℞ | ◁ | – | ● | – | – | ▦ |
| Thorenc | 1250 | H | – | T | ⚕ | – | ◁ | – | – | ❀ | – | – |
| Tourrette-sur-Loup | 400 | H | C | TV | ⚕ | ℞ | – | ◇ | ● | – | – | – |
| Tourtour | 633 | H | – | – | ⚕ | – | ◁ | ◇ | – | ❀ | – | – |
| Trans-en-Provence | 146 | H | – | TV | ⚕ | ℞ | – | – | ● | – | – | – |
| La Turbie | 480 | H | – | T | ⚕ | ℞ | ◁ | ◇ | – | – | – | – |
| Turini Pass | 1607 | H | – | – | – | – | ◁ | – | – | – | – | – |
| Valberg | 1669 | H | – | TV | ⚕ | ℞ | ◁ | – | – | ❀ | – | – |
| Valbonne | 202 | H | C | TV | ⚕ | ℞ | – | – | ● | ❀ | – | – |
| Valdeblore | 1000 | H | – | TV | ⚕ | ℞ | ◁ | – | – | ❀ | – | – |
| Valensole | 569 | H | C | TV | ⚕ | ℞ | – | – | ● | – | – | ▦ |
| Vence | 325 | H | C | TV | ⚕ | ℞ | ◁ | ◇ | – | ❀ | – | ▦ |
| Villecroze | 350 | H | – | T | ⚕ | ℞ | ◁ | – | ● | – | – | – |
| Volonne | 500 | H | C | T | – | ℞ | – | – | ● | ❀ | – | – |

(A) Skiing at the Turini Pass   (C) Skiing at Auron (7 km – 4 miles to the south)
(B) Skiing at Refuge de Lure

Legend of columns:
- SP = Swimming pool
- BP = Bathing place
- SS = Sailing school
- BH = Boats or pedal boats for hire = L
- MB = Motor boats = M
- FP = Footpaths (signposted)
- TN = Tennis
- HR = Horse riding
- MT = Mountaineering
- AC = Angling club
- GC = Golf course and no of holes
- SK = Skilifts, cable car
- TO = Skilifts, tows for skiers only
- CC = Cross country skiing
- PG = Page in guide or Michelin map and fold numbers

### INLAND

| SP | BP | SS | BH | MB | FP | TN | HR | MT | AC | GC | SK | TO | CC | PG | Place |
|----|----|----|----|----|----|----|----|----|----|----|----|----|----|----|-------|
| ✓ | – | – | – | – | – | – | – | – | – | – | ✓ | 7 | ✓ | 195-23 | Andon |
| ✓ | – | – | – | – | ✓ | ✓ | – | – | ✓ | – | – | – | – | 55 | Annot |
| ✓ | – | – | – | – | ✓ | ✓ | ✓ | – | ✓ | – | – | – | – | 35 | Aups |
| – | – | – | – | – | ✓ | ✓ | – | – | – | – | 3 | 22 | – | 36 | Auron |
| ✓ | – | – | – | – | ✓ | ✓ | – | – | ✓ | – | – | – | – | 38 | Barjols |
| – | ✓ | L | – | – | – | – | – | – | ✓ | – | – | – | – | 84-17 | Bauduen |
| ✓ | – | – | – | – | ✓ | ✓ | – | – | ✓ | – | – | – | – | 165 | Beauvezer |
| ✓ | – | – | – | – | ✓ | ✓ | – | – | ✓ | – | – | – | – | 84-16 | Besse-sur-Issole |
| ✓ | – | – | – | – | ✓ | ✓ | – | – | ✓ | – | – | 6 | ✓ | 40 | Beuil |
| ✓ | – | – | – | – | ✓ | ✓ | – | – | ✓ | 18 | – | – | – | 40 | Biot |
| ✓ | – | – | – | – | ✓ | ✓ | – | – | ✓ | – | – | (A) | – | 155 | Bollène-Vésubie (La) |
| ✓ | – | – | – | – | ✓ | ✓ | – | – | ✓ | – | – | – | – | 42 | Breil-sur-Roya |
| ✓ | – | – | – | – | ✓ | ✓ | – | – | ✓ | – | – | – | – | 42 | Brignoles |
| ✓ | – | – | – | – | ✓ | ✓ | – | – | – | – | – | – | – | 77 | Cabris |
| ✓ | – | – | – | – | ✓ | ✓ | – | – | ✓ | 18 | – | – | – | 37 | Cadière-d'Azur (La) |
| ✓ | – | – | – | – | ✓ | ✓ | – | – | ✓ | – | – | – | – | 50 | Cannet (Le) |
| ✓ | – | – | – | – | ✓ | ✓ | – | – | ✓ | – | – | – | – | 42 | Carcès |
| ✓ | – | – | – | – | ✓ | ✓ | – | – | ✓ | – | – | – | – | 195-26 | Castagniers |
| ✓ | – | – | – | – | ✓ | ✓ | ✓ | – | ✓ | – | – | – | – | 52 | Castellane |
| ✓ | – | – | – | – | ✓ | ✓ | ✓ | – | ✓ | – | – | – | – | 59 | Château-Arnoux-St-Auban |
| ✓ | – | – | – | – | ✓ | ✓ | – | – | ✓ | – | – | – | – | 91 | Colle-sur-Loup (La) |
| ✓ | – | – | – | – | – | ✓ | – | – | – | – | – | – | ✓ | 55 | Colmars |
| – | – | – | – | – | – | ✓ | – | – | ✓ | – | – | – | – | 161 | Comps-sur-Artuby |
| ✓ | – | – | – | – | – | ✓ | – | – | – | – | – | – | – | 118 | Contes |
| ✓ | – | – | – | – | ✓ | ✓ | – | – | ✓ | – | – | – | – | 55 | Cotignac |
| ✓ | – | – | – | – | ✓ | ✓ | – | – | ✓ | – | – | – | – | 56 | Digne |
| – | ✓ | L | – | – | – | – | – | – | ✓ | – | – | – | – | 157 | Esparron-de-Verdon |
| – | ✓ | L | – | – | ✓ | ✓ | – | – | ✓ | – | – | – | – | 66 | Fayence |
| ✓ | – | – | – | – | ✓ | ✓ | – | – | ✓ | – | – | – | – | 67 | Forcalquier |
| ✓ | – | – | – | – | ✓ | ✓ | – | – | ✓ | 18 | – | – | – | 74 | Grasse |
| – | ✓ | L | – | – | ✓ | ✓ | ✓ | – | ✓ | – | – | – | – | 157 | Gréoux-les-Bains |
| ✓ | – | – | – | – | ✓ | ✓ | – | – | ✓ | – | – | – | – | 96 | Grimaud |
| ✓ | – | – | – | – | ✓ | ✓ | – | – | ✓ | – | – | – | – | 159 | Guillaumes |
| ✓ | – | – | – | – | – | ✓ | ✓ | ✓ | ✓ | 18 | – | – | – | 82 | Hyères |
| – | – | – | – | – | ✓ | ✓ | – | – | – | – | 1 | 21 | ✓ | 145 | Isola 2000 |
| ✓ | – | – | – | – | ✓ | ✓ | – | – | ✓ | – | – | – | – | 165 | Levens |
| ✓ | – | – | – | – | ✓ | ✓ | – | – | ✓ | – | – | – | – | 93 | Manosque |
| ✓ | – | – | – | – | – | ✓ | – | – | ✓ | 18 | – | – | – | 106 | Mougins |
| ✓ | ✓ | L | – | – | – | – | – | – | – | – | – | – | – | 106 | Moustiers-Ste-Marie |
| – | – | – | – | – | – | ✓ | – | – | ✓ | – | – | – | – | 195-24 34 | Pégomas |
| – | – | – | – | – | – | – | – | – | ✓ | – | – | – | – | 120 | Peillon |
| – | – | – | – | – | – | ✓ | – | – | – | – | – | 2 | ✓ | 154 | Peïra-Cava |
| – | – | – | – | – | ✓ | ✓ | – | – | ✓ | – | – | – | – | 120 | Puget-Théniers |
| – | ✓ | – | – | – | ✓ | – | – | – | ✓ | – | – | – | – | 97 | Ramatuelle |
| – | – | – | – | – | ✓ | ✓ | – | – | ✓ | – | – | – | – | 165 | St-André-les-Alpes |
| – | – | – | – | – | ✓ | ✓ | – | – | ✓ | – | – | (B) | – | 129 | St-Dalmas-de-Tende |
| – | – | – | – | – | ✓ | ✓ | – | ✓ | ✓ | – | (C) | (C) | (C) | 92 | St-Étienne |
| – | ✓ | L | M | – | ✓ | – | – | – | ✓ | – | – | – | – | 131 | St-Étienne-de-Tinée |
| – | – | – | – | – | ✓ | – | – | – | ✓ | – | – | – | – | 152 | St-Julien-du-Verdon |
| – | – | – | – | – | ✓ | ✓ | ✓ | ✓ | ✓ | – | – | – | – | 132 | St-Martin-Vésubie |
| – | – | – | – | – | ✓ | ✓ | – | – | ✓ | – | – | – | – | 133 | St-Paul |
| ✓ | – | – | – | – | – | ✓ | ✓ | – | ✓ | – | – | – | – | 36 | Salernes |
| – | – | L | – | – | – | – | – | – | ✓ | – | – | – | – | 84-6 | Salles-sur-Verdon (Les) |
| ✓ | ✓ | L | – | – | ✓ | ✓ | – | – | ✓ | – | – | – | – | 67 | Seillans |
| – | – | – | – | – | ✓ | ✓ | – | – | ✓ | – | – | (D) | (D) | 57 | Seyne |
| ✓ | ✓ | – | – | – | ✓ | ✓ | – | – | ✓ | – | – | – | – | 140 | Sisteron |
| ✓ | – | – | – | – | ✓ | ✓ | – | – | ✓ | – | – | – | – | 142 | Sospel |
| ✓ | – | – | – | – | – | ✓ | – | – | ✓ | 9 | – | – | – | 143 | Tende |
| ✓ | – | – | – | – | ✓ | ✓ | – | – | – | – | – | – | ✓ | 79 | Thorenc |
| ✓ | – | – | – | – | ✓ | ✓ | ✓ | – | ✓ | – | – | – | – | 90 | Tourrette-sur-Loup |
| ✓ | – | – | – | – | ✓ | – | – | – | ✓ | – | – | – | – | 36 | Tourtour |
| ✓ | – | – | – | – | ✓ | ✓ | – | – | ✓ | – | – | – | – | 59 | Trans-en-Provence |
| – | – | – | – | – | ✓ | – | – | – | ✓ | – | – | – | – | 152 | La Turbie |
| – | – | – | – | – | ✓ | – | – | – | ✓ | – | – | 2 | ✓ | 153 | Turini Pass |
| ✓ | – | – | – | – | ✓ | ✓ | ✓ | – | ✓ | – | 2 | 20 | ✓ | 155 | Valberg |
| ✓ | – | – | – | – | ✓ | ✓ | – | – | ✓ | 18 | – | – | – | 155 | Valbonne |
| ✓ | – | – | – | – | ✓ | ✓ | – | ✓ | ✓ | – | – | 10 | – | 156 | Valdeblore |
| ✓ | – | – | – | – | ✓ | ✓ | – | – | ✓ | – | – | – | – | 156 | Valensole |
| ✓ | – | – | – | – | ✓ | ✓ | ✓ | – | ✓ | – | – | – | – | 159 | Vence |
| ✓ | – | – | – | – | – | ✓ | ✓ | – | ✓ | – | – | – | – | 167 | Villecroze |
| – | – | – | – | – | ✓ | – | – | – | ✓ | – | – | – | – | 128 | Volonne |

(D) Skiing at St-Jean Pass (12 km – 8 miles to the north) and at Grand Puy (6 km – 4 miles to the south)

# KEY

★★★ **Worth a journey**
★★ **Worth a detour**
★ **Interesting**

Sightseeing route with departure point and direction indicated
on the road                             in town

The following symbols, when accompanied by a name or a letter in heavy type,
locate the sights described in this guide

*Mainly on local maps*

| | | |
|---|---|---|
| ✕ | ∴ | Castle − Ruins |
| ⚑ | ✝ | Chapel − Cross or calvary |
| ☀ | Ⴃ | Panorama − View |
| ⚓ | ⚙ | Lighthouse − Mill (wind or water) |
| ◡ | ✿ | Dam − Factory or power station |
| ☆ | ∪ | Fort − Quarry |
| ▲ | | Miscellaneous sights |

*Mainly on town plans*

| | | |
|---|---|---|
| ⌂ | ⚐ | Catholic, Protestant Church |
| ◣ | | Building with main entrance |
| ⚯ | | Ramparts − Tower |
| ‖ | | Gateway |
| ◎ | | Fountain |
| ▪ | | Statue or building |
| ▨ | | Gardens, park, woods |
| B | | Letter locating a sight |

## Conventional signs

| | |
|---|---|
| ▬▬▬ | Motorway (unclassified) |
| ▬▬▬ | Dual carriageway |
| ▬▬▬ | Major through road |
| ▬▬▬ | Tree-lined street |
| ▭▭▭ | Stepped street |
| ╫╫ | Pedestrian street |
| ========= | Impassable or under construction |
| - - - - - | Footpath |
| ·▬·▬· | Trolleybus, tram |
| ▬█▬ | Station |
| A ┃ B | Reference grid letters for town plans |
| ③ | Reference number common to town plans and MICHELIN maps |
| 12 | Distance in kilometres |
| 1429 | Pass − Altitude |

| | |
|---|---|
| ▰ | Public building |
| ⊞ | Hospital |
| ⬭ | Covered market |
| ⚔ | Barracks |
| ⸸⸸⸸ | Cemetery |
| ⛷ ⛳ | Racecourse − Golf course |
| ⊿ ⊡ | Outdoor or indoor swimming pool |
| ⛸ ⊤ | Skating rink − Viewing table |
| ⊤ | Telecommunications tower or mast |
| ⬭ ⬚ | Stadium − Water tower |
| ✈ ✈ | Airport − Airfield |
| ⬛ | Coach station |
| ▣ | Main post office (with poste restante) |
| ⓘ | Tourist information centre |
| P | Car park |

In all MICHELIN guides, plans and maps are always oriented with north at the top.
Main shopping streets are printed in a different colour at the beginning of the list of streets.

## Abbreviations

| | |
|---|---|
| A | Motorway (Autoroute) |
| A | Local agricultural office (Chambre d'Agriculture) |
| c | Chamber of Commerce (Chambre de Commerce) |
| D | Secondary road (Route Départementale) |
| G | Police station (Gendarmerie) |
| GR | Long distance footpath (Sentier de Grande Randonnée) |
| H | Town Hall (Hôtel de Ville) |
| J | Law Courts (Palais de Justice) |
| M | Museum |
| N | Trunk road (Route Nationale) |
| P | Préfecture Sous-préfecture |
| POL. | Police |
| R.F. | Forest Road (Route Forestière) |
| T | Theatre |
| U | University |

## Additional signs

Ferry services

| | |
|---|---|
| ⛴ | Passengers and cars |
| ⛵ | Passengers only |

The towns and sights described in this guide are shown in **black** on the maps.

32

# TOWNS, SIGHTS
# AND TOURIST REGIONS

## ANTIBES ★
Michelin map **195** fold 35 – Pop 48 013 – *Facilities p 28*

The much frequented resort town of Antibes lies on the far side of the Baie des Anges facing Nice. It has its own harbour and the Cap d'Antibes *(p 34)*, nearby, is a pleasant place to explore. The Antibes region is one of Europe's great centres for the commercial production of flowers. About 800 firms keep some 300 hectares – 750 acres under glass frames or greenhouses. Roses take first place, followed by carnations, anemones and tulips. Evergreens and spring vegetables are also grown.

### HISTORICAL NOTES

**Greek Antipolis.** – From the 4C BC the Greeks of Massalia set up a chain of trading-posts with the Ligurian tribes along the coast. A new city sprang up opposite Nice; Antipolis, the Greek name for Antibes, may mean the town opposite but the derivation is disputed.

Antipolis was contained between the present Cours Masséna and the sea, the Greeks holding only the area commanded by their ships, their warehouses and their ramparts. Mistrust reigned; the Ligurians never entered the town, which had only one gate – opposite the present town hall; all transactions took place outside the town walls.

The Greeks were succeeded by the Romans and they by Barbarians whose invasions ruined the city's prosperity.

**Antibes, frontier outpost.** – The kings of France realised the important military role that Antibes could play, above all from the end of the 14C when the town stood at the Franco-Savoyard frontier. Each reign brought improvement or enlargement to its fortifications until the work was finally completed by Vauban in the 17C. Only the Fort Carré and the sea-front remain.

**Bonaparte at Antibes.** – In 1794 Bonaparte, charged with defending the coast, installed his family at Antibes. He was a general, but his pay seldom arrived on the appointed day. Times were hard. Mme Lætitia, his mother, did the household laundry herself in a nearby stream. His sisters made furtive expeditions to the artichoke and fig plantations and were chased away by the landowner but the future princesses were fleet of foot and escaped. After the fall of Robespierre, Bonaparte was imprisoned for some time in the Fort Carré.

**Return from Elba (1815).** – Twenty years later, after his exile on Elba, directly he landed on the soil of France at Golfe-Juan *(p 50)*, Napoleon sent General Bertrand and twenty grenadiers to Antibes to reconnoitre. But the garrison, instead of fraternising with them, flung them into prison. Emissaries sent by the Emperor to find out what had happened suffered the same fate. Disappointed, Napoleon turned towards Cannes.

**Championnet and Reille.** – General Championnet, born at Valence, died at Antibes in 1800, struck down by the epidemic of cholera which was decimating his army; this unselfish leader, who had distinguished himself in the German and Italian campaigns, was only thirty-eight. He asked to be buried in the moat of the Fort Carré. His bust stands on the Cours Masséna.

Marshal Reille (1775-1860) was born at Antibes. Aide-de-camp to Masséna, Reille distinguished himself in all Napoleon's campaigns. Later, rallying to the monarchy, he was made a marshal by Louis-Philippe and died a senator during the Second Empire.

### ■ THE OLD TOWN★ *time: 1 3/4 hours*

**Avenue de Verdun.** – From this road, skirting St-Roch Bay, there is a good view of the 16C Fort Carré isolated on its rock with Cagnes and the heights of Nice in the background to the right.

*Enter by the old sea gate (V) and follow Montée des Saleurs as far as Avenue Amiral de Grasse.*

**Avenue Amiral-de-Grasse.** – This road runs along the only remaining part of 17C ramparts facing the sea and gives a fine view★ of the coastline towards Nice with the Alps rising in the background, snow-covered for most of the year.

**Archaeological Museum (M¹).** – *Open 9am to noon and 2 to 6pm (7pm 1 July to 30 September); closed 1 May and in November; 6F.*

The St-André Bastion, part of Vauban's fortifications, houses a collection of some 300 000 archaeological items illustrating 4 000 years of history. Local excavations are continually adding to the exhibits of pottery and coins and Etruscan, Greek and Roman jewellery as well as objects salvaged from shipwrecks from the Middle Ages to 18C.

**Old streets (Vieilles rues).** – Retracing your steps enter Rue de la Touraque. To left and right are picturesque side streets, bright with flowers in season and barely a stone's throw from the sea. Cours Masséna serves as the market place. From there Rue de l'Orme and Rue du Bateau lead to the castle.

**Grimaldi Castle (B).** – *Open 10am to noon and 3 to 6pm (7pm July to September); closed 1 May, Tuesdays and in November; 10F.*

The original castle was built in 12C on a terrace overlooking the sea on the foundations of a Roman camp. It was reconstructed in 16C but the square Romanesque tower, the battlement walk and pairs of windows remain from the original structure.

**Inner courtyard.** – There is a charming pool in the courtyard. In a small rear room hangs the **Deposition from the Cross★** (1539) by Antoine Aundi, also called the Fainting Virgin, which contains the earliest known view of Antibes.

**Archaeological Collection.** – The Picasso Museum *(see below)* contains Roman pottery, friezes, funerary urns and stelae, one bearing the touching inscription: to the spirit of Septentrion, 12 years, who danced at the Antibes theatre for two days and was a success.

**Picasso Museum★.** – *Staircase and first floor.* Soon after his arrival on the Riviera in the autumn of 1946, Pablo Picasso (1881-1973), who had part of the castle at his disposal, started work on some large scale paintings. His output is amazing; the majority of the paintings and some of the lithographs, drawings and ceramics on view in the castle were the result of one season's work.

**Drawings, engravings** and **lithographs** line the staircase well *(Woman with Hairnet, Goat's Head, Three Women and the Torero, the Couple...)*; others hang in the rooms (mythological scenes); many are grouped in the corridors *(Paloma and her Doll; Family of Acrobats, the Picador...).*

His Antibes **paintings** *(first floor)*, are wholly inspired by the marine and mythological life of the Mediterranean, expressing joy and fantasy: *Ulysses and the Sirens, Symphony in Grey, the Goat* and a huge triptych-*Satyr, Faun and Centaur.* Two still-lifes – *Fish* and *Watermelon* – are of exceptional quality. *La Joie de Vivre*, a huge work in fibro-cement, is a smiling pastoral composition of a plant-woman dancing among exuberant goats and satyrs.

The showcases hold an impressive collection of Picasso's **ceramics**. His great powers of imagination and ingenuity are revealed in the variety of decoration and the beauty and originality of form, often quite humorous. In some pieces decoration and form combine to suggest a silhouette: woman, vulture, owl... *(illustration p 157)*.

**Terrace.** – In the terrace garden overlooking the sea are four statues by Germaine Richier.

**Second Floor.** – There is a fine **still-life** by Nicolas de Staël among other contemporary canvasses but the rooms are generally reserved for temporary exhibitions.

*On leaving, turn right down the steps towards the church.*

**Church of the Immaculate Conception (D).** – Of the original Romanesque building, which served as a cathedral in the Middle Ages, only the east end remains. The belfry is a 12C watchtower converted. The nave and west front are in the 17C Classical style. Among the art treasures are: a wooden Crucifix (1447) in the choir; a former pagan stone altar in the south absidal chapel; an **altarpiece** (1515) by Louis Bréa in the south transept – the centre panel has been touched up but the 13 surrounding panels and the predella are treated like miniatures; a 16C **Recumbent Christ** carved in lime wood.

Take Rue de l'Horloge *(right)*, Rue du Revely *(left)* and Rue Aubernon *(right)* to return to the port by a picturesque route.

## EXCURSION

**Marineland.** – *4 km – 2 1/2 miles. Leave Antibes by ① (see plan of Cap d'Antibes p 35) on the N 7. After 4 km – 1/2 miles turn left into the D 4, the road to Biot. The zoo is on the right in the angle between the N 7 and the D 4.*
*Open all year round, performances from 2.30pm to sunset; in July and August last performance at 9.30pm; 30F, children 15F.*

Marineland, the first marine zoo in Europe, has performing **dolphins**, an orc (a killer whale), sea elephants, sea lions, seals, tortoises, penguins and other sea birds.

## ANTIBES, Cap d' ★★

Michelin map **195** fold 35 – *Facilities p 28*

Strictly speaking the name Cap d'Antibes refers only to the most southerly tip of land but it has come to mean the whole peninsula, which is an enchanting garden dotted with sumptuous hotels and villas catering for summer and winter visitors.

■ **SIGHTS** *Round tour of 10 km – 6 miles – about 2 hours*

*Leave Antibes (p 33) by D 2559 going south and follow the route marked on the plan.*

**Bacon Point** (Z). – View★ of Antibes and the Fort Carré, extending across the Baie des Anges in front of Nice and the surrounding countryside to Cap Ferrat and even Cap Martin near the Italian frontier.

**La Garoupe Plateau.** – There is a fine **panorama★★** from the viewing table stretching from the Esterel to the Alps.

**La Garoupe Church** (Sanctuaire de la Garoupe) (Z E). – Two wrought iron grilles stand outside the church.
Inside, two adjoining chapels, communicating by wide arches, form two aisles.

**ANTIBES**

Albert-I^er (Bd)
Nationale (Pl.) \_\_\_\_\_35
République (R. de la)

Bateau (R. du) \_\_\_\_\_4
Clemenceau (R. G.) 13
Horloge (R. de l') \_\_25

Maizière
(Av. du Gén.) \_\_\_\_30
Masséna (Cours) \_\_\_32
Orme (R. de l') \_\_\_\_37
Revely (R. du) \_\_\_\_40
Safranier (Pl. du) \_\_48
Saleurs
(Montée des) \_\_\_\_49
Vandenberg (R.) \_\_\_59

The aisle of Our Lady of La Garde, which is the wider, is ornamented with a fresco by J. Clergues. It also contains an interesting **collection of votive offerings**, placed on either side of the altarpiece of the high altar: on the left is the **Sebastopol ikon**, a magnificent Russo-Byzantine work, believed to be 14C, and on the right the *plachzanitza* of the Woronzoffs, a splendid painted silk, also brought back at the time of the siege of Sebastopol.

In the second aisle, decorated with frescoes by Edouard Collin, are some sixty naval votive offerings and maritime souvenirs as well as a gilded wood statue of **Our Lady of Safe Homecoming** (Notre-Dame-de-Bon-Port), patron saint of sailors.

Each year on the first or second Sunday in July the statue of Our Lady, taken on the previous Thursday to the Cathedral at Antibes, is brought back in procession to La Garoupe by the seamen.

Beside the sanctuary stands the curious Oratory of St-Helen, first patron of Antibes, who has been worshipped here since 5C AD in what was originally a pagan shrine.

**The Lighthouse.** – *Guided tours 9am to noon and 2 to 6pm (4.30 in winter).*

The light, one of the most powerful on the coast, has a beam which carries 60-70 km – 40-50 miles out to sea and 100 km – 33 000 ft up to aircraft. The radio beam has a range of 185 km – 100 nautical miles.

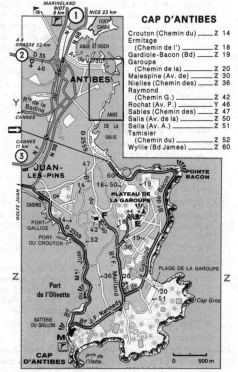

**CAP D'ANTIBES**

| | |
|---|---|
| Crouton (Chemin du) | Z 14 |
| Ermitage (Chemin de l') | Z 18 |
| Gardiole-Bacon (Bd) | Z 19 |
| Garoupe (Chemin de la) | Z 20 |
| Malespine (Av. de) | Z 30 |
| Nielles (Chemin des) | Z 36 |
| Raymond (Chemin G.) | Z 42 |
| Rochat (Av. P.) | Y 46 |
| Sables (Chemin des) | Z 47 |
| Salis (Av. de la) | Z 50 |
| Sella (Av. A.) | Z 51 |
| Tamisier (Chemin du) | Z 52 |
| Wyllie (Bd James) | Z 60 |

**Thuret Garden★** (Z F). – *Open 8am to 12.30pm and 2 to 5.30pm; closed Saturdays, Sundays and holidays.*

The garden bears the name of the scientist who created it in 1856 for the acclimatisation of plants and trees from hot countries. Now, financed by the Ministry of Agriculture, the garden contains a magnificent collection of rare plants and trees which, as a result of early experiments, have become common throughout the region. The Villa Thuret is at the centre of the buildings which house the Antibes Institute of Agronomic Research (I.R.A.A.).

**Naval and Napoleonic Museum** (Z M). – *Open 15 June to 15 September, 10am to noon and 3 to 7pm; 16 September to 14 June, 10am to noon and 2 to 5pm; closed Tuesdays, 1 January, 1 May, 25 December and 30 October to 15 December; 8F.*

The former Le Grillon battery has been transformed into a museum. At the entrance stand two replicas of a magnificent Louis XV bronze cannon. Inside, the construction of ocean-going sailing ships is explained using models in showcases. Also on display are **Napoleon's bust** sculpted by Canova in 1810, model soldiers and officers of the Great Army, Napoleon's autograph and imperial proclamations.

From the roof there is a fine **view★** over the wooded headland to the Lérins Islands (SW) and to the distant Alps (NE).

**Olivette Harbour** (Port de l'Olivette) (Z). – From the harbour there is a view over the Golfe Juan, the heights of Super-Cannes, La Croisette point and the Lérins Islands.

The coast road follows the seashore to Juan-les-Pins *(p 87)*.

## AUPS

Michelin map **84** fold 6 – Pop 1 504 – *Facilities p 30*

From the foot of the Espiguières hills, Aups overlooks the Uchane plain, a fertile area of gently rounded hillocks which is bordered to the northwest by the steep highlands of Haute-Provence. To the south the Maures Massif dominates the horizon. Aups is renowned for its honey.

Ramparts and a ruined castle recall the past. The huge main square planted with magnificent plane trees and the many fountains add to the charm of the picturesque old streets; there is a fine wrought-iron belfry in Rue de l'Horloge.

**St-Pancrace Church.** – *To visit, apply at the presbytery.*

The church is 15C Provençal Gothic with a Renaissance doorway; the simple nave ends in a square apse. Several gilded wood altarpieces adorn the interior, particularly a 16C triptych *(2nd chapel on the right)* of the martyrdom of St Bartholomew.

**Simon Segal Museum.** – *Rue du Maréchal Joffre. Open 1 June to 30 September, 10am to noon and 2 to 7pm; closed the rest of the year; 6F.*

A collection of modern art, 300 pictures, of which 175 are by the Paris School, is on display in the chapel of the former Ursuline Convent.

## *EXCURSIONS*

**The Haut-Var★**. – *Round tour of 53 km – 33 miles. Leave Aups by D 77 going east.*
The road winds along the steep slopes of the Espiguières hills. Soon after La Beaume
château bear left into D 51 towards Tourtour.

> **Tourtour.** – Pop 311. *Facilities p 30.* The hill village is set among green woods and
> flanked by two ruined castles. The two enormous elms in the main square were planted
> in 1638. The houses and 11C church have been restored. From the south-east corner
> of the village a vast **panorama★** opens up of the Argens (S) and Nartuby (NE) valleys
> extending on a fine day to the Maures (S), Ste-Baume (SSW), Ste-Victoire (SW) and
> the Lubéron (WSW) mountains.

*Return to the T junction and turn left (D 51) towards Villecroze.*

A winding wooded road soon passes some caves and strangely shaped rocks. 1 km –
1/2 mile outside Villecroze there is a parking place near a *viewing table* from which the
**view★** extends *(left to right)* from Tourtour, over Villecroze to Salernes and beyond to the
tree-covered peak of Bessillon; in the distance are the Maures and Ste-Baume.

> **Villecroze.** – *Description p 167.*

*Continue on D 51 to Salernes.*

> **Salernes.** – Pop 2 522. *Facilities p 30.* An agricultural and industrial centre, Salernes
> is known for the manufacture of floor tiles and pottery. The church, set among 17C
> houses, boasts a belfry at either end. Fountains abound and trees shade the main
> square.

*D 31 follows the Bresque valley south-east to Entrecasteaux.*

> **Entrecasteaux.** – Pop 472. Built halfway up the hill above the Bresque river, the village
> is proud of its public garden, said to be designed by Le Nôtre. A network of pleasant
> Provençal streets surrounds the fortified church; one of the buttresses juts out over
> the road. The main avenue is lined by age-old plane trees. Olive oil and carpets are
> produced in the village.
> The **castle** is an austere 17C building, long and narrow, where Mme de Sévigné stayed
> when it belonged to the Grignan family. It has been restored and converted into a
> museum displaying furniture and *objets d'art* from a variety of sources and periods,
> particularly porcelain and 17–18C Chinese furniture. *Open 1 October to 31 March,
> 10am to 6pm; 1 April to 30 September, 10am to 8pm; 10F.*

*Leave Entrecasteaux by D 31 going south; turn right into D 50.*

> **Cotignac.** – *Description p 55.*

Leave by D 22 going north, which gives a good view back over the site of Cotignac. Further
on to the right the Sillans waterfall can be spied through the trees.

> **Sillans Waterfall.** – *1/2 hour on foot Rtn. Just before the village take the signposted
> path to the right.* In a sylvan setting the Bresque cascades over a 42 m – 138 ft drop;
> in summer the volume of water is diminished.

> **Sillans-la-Cascade.** – Pop 313. An attractive, once fortified, village on the banks of the
> Bresque, with a few picturesque streets near the Post Office which boasts a pinnacle
> turret.

*Continue on D 22 to return to Aups.*

## AURON ★★

Michelin map **195** fold 4 – *Facilities p 30*

Auron, which occupies a sunny plateau, surrounded by high peaks 1 608 m – 5 276 ft
up, has developed into a pleasant winter and summer holiday resort; it is the main ski
station in the Provençal Alps.
According to legend, when St-Aurigius (whence Auron), who died in 604, was
returning from Rome to Gap, where he was bishop, he was set upon by brigands. In one
bound his horse cleared the 500 m – 1 640 ft which separate Auron from the river Tinée.

**St-Aurigius Chapel.** – *Key from the Tourist Centre (Syndicat d'Initiative).* A square
bell-tower with nailhead ornamentation looks down on the single nave 12C Romanesque
chapel with its parallel apses roofed in painted saw-toothed larch shingles. The interior
is decorated with **wall paintings★** depicting the life of St Aurigius, St Denis, Mary Magdalene
and St Christopher, which date from 1451; one, an Angel of the Annunciation, is 13C.
From the chapel precinct there is a fine **view★** of the ring of mountains encircling Auron.

**Las Donnas★★**. – *Teleferic from Auron, 9am to 4.30pm, except May, June, October and
November; 4 minutes.* From the Las Donnas rock (2 256 m – 7 420 ft) there is an extensive
view of the upper Tinée valley and the Franco-Italian Alps.

## BANDOL ★

Michelin map **84** fold 14 – *Local map p 37* – Pop 6 204 – *Facilities p 28 – See town
plan in the current Michelin Guide France*

Bandol is a pleasant small resort lying beside a pretty bay and sheltered from the
north wind by high wooded slopes. Bandol has three sandy beaches: the Lido facing east,
the well sheltered Renecros facing west and the Casino facing due south.
Beyond the villas scattered in groves of pine and mimosa behind the sea front are
fields of flowers and vineyards which produce the best known Côtes-de-Provence wine.
The **Allée Jean-Moulin★** and the Allée Vivien which line the harbour are bordered with
pines, palms and flowers.
From the **corniche road** which runs round the perimeter of the little peninsula there is
a good view along the coast from Cap de l'Aigle to Cap Sicié.

**Bendor Island★.** – *Facilities p 28. Ferry service every 1/2 hour; 7 minutes; Rtn 10F.*

The boat trip makes a pleasant summer excursion. The island is an attractive tourist centre offering a fine beach harbour, Provençal village with craft shops, zoological gardens, exhibition gallery, theatre (cine-club), conference centre with lectures and concerts and courses on yoga, dancing, drawing, painting and guitar.

**Universal Wines and Spirits Exhibition.** – *Open 10am to 12.30 pm and 2 to 6pm; closed Wednesdays.*

In a large hall decorated with frescoes this curious exhibition covers the production of wine, aperitifs and liqueurs in 45 different countries; 7 000 bottles are on display as well as a collection of glasses and decanters.

## EXCURSION

**Le Castellet★.** – *Round trip of 46 km – 29 miles – about 3 hours. Leave Bandol by N 559 going north-east and turn left into D 559 B towards Le Beausset. Go under the railway bridge, ignore the right hand turning to the motorway and 550 m – 550 yds further on turn right.*

> **Sanary-Bandol Zoological Gardens.** – *Open 8am (10am Sundays and holidays) to noon and 2 to 7pm (6pm out of season); closed Sunday mornings and Tuesdays out of season; 12F, children 6F.*
>
> In the rock garden and greenhouses rare tropical plants – cacti, succulents and flowering trees – grow to enormous sizes. The birds and animals include flamingoes, storks, exotic birds, monkeys (black gibbons), gazelles, deer and antelopes.

*Return to D 559 B; in Le Beausset turn right into N 8 towards Toulon.*

1 km – 1/2 mile beyond Le Beausset turn right into a narrow winding road which climbs through olive groves, orchards and vineyards dotted with broom and cypress trees.

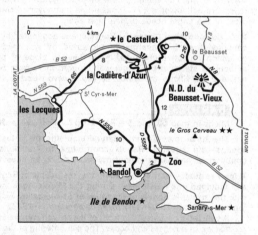

> **N.-D. du Beausset-Vieux Chapel.** – *Leave the car below the chapel. Open all day Saturdays, afternoon only Sunday, holidays and 1 July to 15 September.*
>
> The chapel has been restored by voluntary workers. It is a bare Provençal Romanesque structure with tunnel vaulting in the nave and oven vaulting in the apse. The Virgin and Child in the choir comes from

Pierre Puget's studio. In the lefthand niche a group of 400-year old **santons** illustrate the Flight into Egypt. Some of the votive offerings collected in a side aisle date back to 18C.

From the terrace above the chapel a circular **view★** takes in the neighbouring village of Le Castellet (NW), Ste-Baume (NW), the Gros Cerveau (S) and the coast from Bandol westwards to La Ciotat.

*Return to N 8; in Le Beausset take D 26 on the right to Le Castellet.*

> **Le Castellet★.** – Pop 2 038. Perched on a wooded hill above the vineyards, this remarkable stronghold, formerly owned by the Lords of Les Baux and then by King René, has well preserved ramparts, a carefully restored 12C church, a castle dating back in part to 11C. From beyond the gate in Place de la Mairie there is an attractive **view** inland towards Ste-Baume. Many of the houses date from 17 and 18C and have been used in film sequences. Art and craft workshops – painting, pottery, hollow-ware, weaving and leatherwork – contribute to the local commerce.

*Continue downhill by D 82 and cross over the motorway into D 66.*

> **La Cadière-d'Azur.** – Pop 2 044. *Facilities p 30.* This very old hill town, which numbered some 4 000 citizens at the Revolution, gains its living by producing Bandol wine. Some of its former defences remain. The 13C Pei Gate, near the town hall leads to a maze of picturesque old streets. From the eastern end of the village there is a fine **view★** inland over le Castellet to Ste-Baume.

*Follow D 66 westwards to Les Lecques.*

> **Les Lecques.** – *Description p 87.*

From Les Lecques the road south via La Madrague runs along near the coast before joining N 559 which returns to Bandol.

## BARGEME

Michelin map **84** north of fold 7 – 9 km – 5 miles north-east of Comps-sur-Artuby – Pop 77

This tiny hill village stands at 1 097 m – 3 600 ft on the slopes of Mount Brouis. The church, the ruined wall and two round towers of the castle are visible from afar.

*The village is closed to motor vehicles.* Enter on foot through the watch gate. Narrow streets climb steeply between houses decked with hollyhocks.

**Church.** – *Key at the Town Hall Thursday, Saturday, Sunday, 10 to 11.30am.*
The church is built of large stone blocks in the Romanesque style and contains a precious, carved and painted, wooden **altarpiece★** devoted to St Sebastian. Next to it is an early naive painting which was uncovered behind the altarpiece.

**Castle ruins.** – The overgrown but imposing ruins of the Château des Pontevès are being restored. The **view★** from here extends eastwards to Mount Malay and the Pre-Alps of Grasse and south over the Canjuers Plateau to the distant Maures Massif.

## EXCURSION

**Lachens Beacon★.** – *17 km – 10 miles eastwards. Return to D 21 and turn left.* At Col de Clavel a narrow wooded road branches off to the right. Just beyond Varneige, park the car and climb *(1/2 hour on foot Rtn)* to the Lachens Beacon (1 715 m – 5 627 ft) for an immense **panorama★** over the Pre-Alps and the Mediterranean coast from Toulon to the Italian border.

## BARGEMON

Michelin map 🔲 fold 7 – *Local map p 66* – Pop 820

An old stronghold at the foot of the Provençal plateau, Bargemon still recalls its past in its old streets, its broken ramparts, ruined castle and 12C fortified gateways (in particular the so-called "Roman" gate (Place de la Mairie). Large shady squares and many fountains add to the charm while the presence of mimosa and orange trees indicate a mild climate.

**Church.** – The 15C building near the town gateway was incorporated in the defences. Its square bell-tower is 17C. It has a fine flamboyant **doorway**. Pierre Puget is the putative artist of the angel heads on the high altar.

**N.-D. de Montaigu Chapel.** – The village is dominated by the spire of the chapel which contains three fine altarpieces supported by wreathed columns and an interesting collection of votive offerings. It has been a place of pilgrimage since 17C when a miraculous statue of the Virgin was brought there from Belgium by a monk who was a native of the village *(the statue, carved in olive wood, is shown only on Easter Monday).*

## BARJOLS

Michelin map 🔲 fold 5 – *Pop 2 092* – *Facilities p 30*

The small town lies in a natural amphitheatre in lush green country fed by many springs and streams. Barjols contributes to traditional Provençal life by making tambourines and flutes *(galoubets)* and holding an unusual festival.

**Tripe Festival.** – From time immemorial the people of Barjols have killed an ox each year and indulged in a lavish feast. During the Middle Ages the feast came to be associated with the arrival in Barjols of the relics of St–Marcellus. Nowadays the feast is held every four years about 16 January *(next celebration in 1985).*
A well fed ox is blessed in front of the church and then led round the town in a solemn procession of butchers and cooks. The slaughtering of the ox is greeted with singing and dancing. On the following day the ox is roasted on a spit to be sold off in pieces afterwards while the old "tripe" dance is executed to the accompaniment of flutes and tambourines, fire crackers and musket fire. People come from all over Provence to join in the festivities and perform their own songs and dances.

■ **SIGHTS** *time: 1/2 hour*

**Old town.** – The chief of the 20 **fountains** which ornament the town is near the town hall, a huge mossy basin in the shade of the largest plane tree in Provence, 12.50 m – 41 ft round the bole. A handsome Renaissance doorway graces Pontevès House in the lower town.

**Church.** – The original Romanesque structure was rebuilt in 16C with a fine Gothic nave. The organ loft, choir panelling and carved misericords, are 17C. To the right of the entrance, behind a beautiful 12C font, is the original carved tympanum.

## EXCURSIONS

**Source d'Argens** – *15 km – 10 miles to the south-west. Leave Barjols by D 560.*

**Font-Taillade Valley.** – The road plunges into a green valley of fields and meadows and follows a winding stream. On the slopes vineyards alternate with pines and holm oaks.

*500 m – 550 yds after Brue-Auriac a narrow path to the left leads to a chapel.*

**Notre-Dame Chapel.** – Within a graveyard stands an abandoned Romanesque chapel built from the local red stone. The distinctive features of the pleasant façade are being steadily obscured by the undergrowth.

*Return to D 560 and turn left. Park the car 3 km – 2 miles before the bridge.*

**Argens Spring (Source d'Argens).** – On the right of the road a path leads through the bushes straight to the spring which is one of the sources of the Argens river.

**La Verdière.** – *Round trip 30 km – 20 miles – about 1 3/4 hours. Leave Barjols by the road going north-west towards Varages along the river valley.*

**Varages.** – Pop 722. The pleasant village shaded by plane trees once rivalled Moustiers in the production of chinaware. The Romanesque church *(if closed apply at the presbytery)* with its multicoloured glazed roof, contains a series of china medallions illustrating the life of St Claude.

On leaving Varages, take D 554 northwards, between terraced slopes of vineyards and olive groves interspersed with pines and holm oaks.

**La Verdière.** – Pop 505. The village extends over the hillside beneath the church and **castle.** The latter is of interest although only two rooms and the terrace are open to the public *(guided tour 2 to 5pm; 1/2 hour; 3F).*

The original austere 10C fortress was made more comfortable and elegant in 18C by various additions; among them are the south wing, the grand staircase and some fine and delicate plasterwork.

From the terrace there is a fine view★ to the woods in La Verdière valley. Clearly visible are Ste-Victoire (SW), Ste-Baume (SSW), La Loube (S) and Faron (S) mountains.

*Return to Varages and take D 554 eastwards towards Tavernes. On the right fine views of Ste-Baume.*

**Tavernes.** – Pop 427. Pleasant village set in rich farmland.

*The D 560 returns to Barjols beside the crayfish stream (Ruisseau des Écrevisses).*

## Le BAR-SUR-LOUP

Michelin map ▐195▌ fold 24 – *Local map p 90* – Pop 1 691

Between the Loup river and its tributaries, Le Bar is attractively **sited**★ on a hillside surrounded by terraces of orange trees and beds of jasmine and violets. There is a perfume factory on the edge of the village.

■ **SIGHTS** time: 1/2 hour

**The town.** – The narrow streets of the old town wind round the massive 16C castle with its four corner towers and ruined keep.

**St James' Church** (Église St-Jacques). – Embedded in the stonework at the foot of the tower is a Roman tombstone. The magnificently carved **panels** of the Gothic door are attributed to Jacques Bellot, who was responsible for the choir stalls in Vence *(p 160).*

*Time switch for the paintings.*

A fine **altarpiece** by Louis Bréa consists of 14 scenes painted on a gold background *(high altar).* Under the gallery is the **Dance of Death★,** a curious 15C painting on wood, naive in technique and including a poem in Provençal. The composition illustrates a legend: the Count of Bar gave a ball in Lent and his guests were struck dead in the middle of the revels. The Dance of Death was painted to record the divine displeasure. Death, in the guise of an archer, strikes down the dancers with his arrows and their souls, escaping from their bodies through the mouths as little naked figures, are weighed in the balance by St Michael at the feet of Christ and flung headlong into the gaping maw of a monster representing the entrance to Hell.

**Viewpoint★.** – From the church square there is an oblique view up the Loup Gorge and eastwards over the hills to Vence.

## BEAULIEU ★★

Michelin map ▐195▌ fold 27 – *Local map p 122* – Pop 4 273 – *Facilities p 28*

This fashionable winter resort lies close in to a ring of hills which protect it against north winds and make it one of the warmest spots on the Riviera – an asset especially in winter.

The town is also an oasis of peace and quiet.

For the tourist, the charm of Beaulieu is centred chiefly round **Les Fourmis Bay★** (Baie des Fourmis) and Alsace-Lorraine Boulevard, lined with attractive gardens.

**Villa "Kerylos"★** (M). – *Open July and August, 3 to 7pm; the rest of the year, 2 to 6pm; closed on Mondays and in November; 3/4 hour; 10F.*

This faithful reconstruction of a sumptuous Greek villa of ancient times was conceived and realised by the archaeologist Theodore Reinach, who left it to the French Institute in 1928. On a **site★** reminiscent of the Aegean, the villa stands in a pleasant garden above the sea looking out over Les Fourmis Bay, Cap Ferrat (W), Èze and Cap d'Ail (E).

Precious materials such as Carrara marble, alabaster and rare and exotic woods were used on the interior. The frescoes are reproductions or variations of originals. The furniture, made of wood inlaid with ivory, bronze and leather, is modelled on examples seen on vases and in mosaics. Some of the pieces are originals: mosaics, amphora, vases, lamps, statuettes.

**BEAULIEU-SUR-MER**

| | |
|---|---|
| Marinoni (Bd) | 19 |
| Albert-Ier (Av.) | 2 |
| Blundell Maple (Av.) | 3 |
| Clemenceau (Place et Rue) | 5 |
| Doumer (R. P.) | 6 |
| Gaulle (Pl. Ch. de) | 12 |
| Gauthier (Bd Eug.) | 13 |
| Hellènes (Av. des) | 14 |
| Joffre (Bd Mar.) | 15 |
| Leclerc (Bd Mar.) | 18 |
| May (Av. F.) | 21 |
| Orangers (Montée des) | 22 |
| St-Jean (Pont) | 25 |
| Yougoslavie (R. de) | 27 |

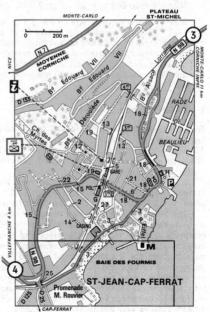

39

# BEAULIEU ★★

## ■ WALKS

**St-Michel Plateau★★.** – *1 3/4 hours on foot Rtn – stiff climb.*

Starting from Boulevard Edward VII. The path leads up to the Riviera escarpment, affording wonderful views on the way.

**Promenade Maurice-Rouvier★.** – *1 hour on foot Rtn.*

This remarkable promenade runs parallel to the shore from Beaulieu to St-Jean-Cap-Ferrat. On one side are fine white villas in beautiful gardens and on the other the sea with distant views of the Riviera and peninsular point of St–Hospice.

## BEUIL ★

Michelin map **195** fold 4 – Pop 343 – *Facilities p 30*

Beuil perches like an eagle's nest on the southern slope of a steep hill in the upper Cians valley. Its attractive **site★** is dominated by Mount Mounier (2 817 m – 9 243 ft) which is snow-covered for several months and provides good skiing. Beuil is also a pleasant and peaceful summer resort.

From the 14 to the 17C Beuil belonged to the powerful **Grimaldi** family, who were continually at war with the Dukes of Savoy. These often had recourse to treachery: the barber of a lord of Beuil was bribed, and when the latter was waiting for his shave, his chin raised for the razor, his throat was cut; on another occasion a valet stabbed his master while helping him put on his doublet.

The Grimaldis sometimes sought help from Spain, sometimes from France, thus it was that in 1617 Hannibal Grimaldi who was the last Count of Beuil sought and obtained the official protection of Louis XIII. But in 1621 a treaty was signed between the King of France and the Duke of Savoy, Charles-Emmanuel. Louis XIII forgot his promise to protect his "dear and well loved Hannibal", and the Count, therefore, took refuge in one of his strongest fortresses, Tourrette-le-Château. The Duke of Savoy did not risk an assault but once again treachery opened the gates for him.

**Church.** – Despite its 15C Romanesque belltower the church is 17C and contains some interesting paintings: *Adoration of the Magi* (Veronese School) *(right)*; altarpiece fragment (St-Lucy) and part of a predella *(Marriage of the Virgin)*; early altarpiece of the Rosary in 16 sections, showing Christ rising from the dead and St-Catherine of Sienna *(high altar).*

**Chapel of White Penitents.** – *To visit apply to the priest only in the morning. Closed Sundays and holidays.*

In Renaissance style, the Chapel was built with the stones from the castle of the Counts of Beuil. Despite its dilapidated state it has some interesting works of art: Renaissance *Pietà* at the high altar, 18C processional cross.

## *EXCURSION*

**Road★ from Beuil to Guillaumes.** – *20 km – 12 miles westwards – about 3/4 hour.* By way of Col de Valberg, D 28 links the Cians Gorges *(p 54)* to the upper reaches of the Var known as the Daluis Gorge *(p 159).*

**Valberg.** – *Description p 155.*

The road descends steadily from Valberg to Guillaumes *(p 159)* through picturesque and varied country. The forests of the northern slope contrast with the cornfields, vineyards and orchards on the southern side.

## BIOT ★

Michelin map **195** fold 25 – Pop 2 745 – *Facilities p 30*

Biot is a picturesque village on rising ground some 4 km – 2 1/2 miles inland. Long known for its pottery, it has recently diversified and is developing into a craft centre *(details p 22)*; its name is now inseparably linked with that of Fernand Léger. Cut flowers – roses, carnations, mimosa and anemones – are grown here for market.

## ■ SIGHTS *time: 2 hours*

**Fernand Léger Museum ★★.** – *South-east of the village, just off D 4 (signpost). Open 1 April to 30 September, 10am to noon and 2 to 6pm; 1 October to 31 March, 10am to noon and 2 to 5pm; closed Tuesdays and 1 May; 8F.*

Designed by A. Svetchine, architect from Nice, the museum contains 348 works by Léger (1881-1955) given to the French nation by Mme Nadia Léger.

The façade is decorated by a monumental **mosaic** in vivid colours designed for the Hanover Stadium to celebrate sport. In contrast the stark and functional interior houses a collection of ceramics, tapestries, stained glass and mosaics on the ground floor and **paintings** and carpets upstairs. The work is displayed in chronological order tracing the artist's development from Cubism, his fascination with the impersonal and rhythmic movement of machinery, his use of contrasting primary colours and simple geometric forms.

*(After photo : National Museum Collection, Paris)*

F. Léger – Child with bird (ceramic)

**Biot Glassworks.** – *Just outside the village on D 4 going south-east. Open 1 June to 30 September, 9am to 8pm (3 to 7pm Sundays); the rest of the year, 8am to noon and 2 to 6pm (except Sunday mornings); closed 1 January, 1 May and 25 December.*

The works were opened in 1957 and produce a great variety of articles. Visitors can watch the different stages of glass blowing – in this case the characteristic Biot bubble glass.

**Old village.** – The evening is the best time to appreciate the authentic charm of the picturesque streets, starting from the Tourist Centre (Syndicat d'Initiative) and following the arrows, through the Grenadiers' Gate (Porte des Migraniers) and the Tines Gate (both 16C) and emerging into the beautiful **Place des Arcades** with its rounded and ogival arches.

**Church.** – The two fine altarpieces are of the Nice school *(details p 19)*: one by Louis Bréa, **the Virgin of the Rosary★**, is divided into eight panels; the other, with four panels, an **Ecce Homo** *(restoration in progress)*, attributed to Canavesio *(time switch)*.

## BORMES-LES-MIMOSAS ★

Michelin map **84** fold 16 – *Local map p 94* – Pop 3 093 – *Facilities p 28*

Bormes-les-Mimosas stands in an agreeable **setting★**, near the sea and on a steep slope at the entrance to the Dom Forest. It is an attractive place to stay abounding in mimosa, camomile and eucalyptus. Bormes has three sandy beaches and eight hundred and fifty pleasure boats can berth at the marina.

■ **SIGHTS** *time: 1 hour*

**Place St-François.** – A statue commemorating Francesco di Paola, who is said to have saved Bormes from the plague in 1481, stands in front of the solid 16C St Francis' Chapel surrounded by dark cypress trees. Among the exotic plants in the neighbouring graveyard is the tomb of the painter, Paul Cazin, who was particularly attached to the place.

The **terrace** in front of the chapel affords a good **view** of Bormes roadstead and Cap Bénat. The round tower to be seen in the distance is the base of an old mill.

**Town Hall** (Hôtel de Ville). – *Closed for restoration.*

A century of regional painting, particularly the works of Cazin (1841-1901), landscape painter and decorator, are on show.

**St-Trophyme Church.** – The robust three-aisled edifice was built in 18C in the Romanesque style. The façade bears a sundial with the Latin inscription: *Ab hora diei ad horam Dei* (from daily time to divine time). The interior is decorated with 14 oil paintings by Alain Nonn, (1980) depicting the Way of the Cross.

**Old streets.** – Below the church the streets of old Bormes are typical of a Provençal village, so steep and slippery that one is known by the expressive name of neck-breaker *(rompi-cuou).*

**Castle.** – The signs *"parcours fleuri"* near the church lead to a flower–lined walk round the castle which has been partially restored to provide a dwelling. Beyond the castle there is a **view** over Bormes, the roadstead and the Hyères Islands.

## BRAUS Pass ★★

Michelin map **195** folds 16 and 17

The Braus Pass road, the D 2204, which links the Paillon and the Bévera valleys *(p 153)* is noted for the succession of startling hairpin bends by which the road rises from l'Escarène (357 m – 1 171 ft) to the pass.

### L'Escarène to Sospel – *22 km – 13 miles – about 3/4 hour*

*Leave Escarène (p 118) by D 2204 going north beside the Braus stream.*

**Toüet-de-l'Escarène.** – Pop 137. Charming village with a Baroque church.

The olive groves give way to a poorer landscape of Spanish broom.

**Braus Rift.** – The rift which opens up beyond Toüet village is short but impressive.

The village of St-Laurent sees the start of a series of sixteen hairpin bends which extend for nearly 3 km – 2 miles. As the road climbs the **view★** widens to include the white cupola of the Nice Observatory (NE) on Mount Gros and Cap d'Antibes and the Esterel Massif which stand out on the coast (SW).

**Braus Pass.** – Alt 1 002 m – 3 287 ft. There is an impressive view of the hairpin bends by which the road reaches the pass.

Beyond the pass the road descends through 18 hairpin bends offering extensive **views★★** of the mountains of the Bévera valley, in particular l'Aution and the Cime du Diable (Devil's Peak) to the north.

The road winds round the south face of Mount Barbonnet with its fort and reaches Sospel *(p 142)* where the Merlanson flows into the Bévera.

MICHELIN GUIDES

*The Red Guides (hotels and restaurants)*

**Benelux – Deutschland – España Portugal – France – Great Britain and Ireland – Italia**

*The Green Guides (picturesque scenery, buildings and scenic routes)*

**Austria – Canada – Germany – Italy – London – New England – New York City – Portugal – Spain – Switzerland and 7 guides on France**

## BREIL-SUR-ROYA

Michelin map **195** fold 18 – *Local map p 130* – Pop 2 232 – *Facilities p 30*

Breil lies astride the Roya river 8 km – 5 miles north of the Italian border below the summit of l'Arpette (1 610 m – 5 282 ft) on the main road from Ventimiglia to Turin via the Tende Pass. Several small industries – leather, olives and dairy farming – sustain the town which is known for fishing and water sports (canoeing competitions).

The old town on the east bank consists of picturesque streets where traces of the ramparts can be seen among the old buildings. St-Catherine's Chapel on the south side of the parish church has a fine Renaissance doorway. **Sancta-Maria-in-Albis** *(closed for restoration)* is a vast 18C church with carved doors (1719) and a Baroque interior in which the **organ loft** (17C) of carved and gilded wood and an early **altarpiece** (1500) on the left in the choir are much admired.

## BRIGNOLES

Michelin map **84** fold 15 – *Local map p 43* – Pop 10 482 – *Facilities p 30*

The narrow twisting streets of old Brignoles terrace the northern side of a low hill crowned by the venerable crenelated castle of the counts of Provence. The new town is developing in the plain. All around spreads a green countryside in the now wide Carami valley.

Brignoles is the most important French centre for the extraction of bauxite – some 2 million tonnes were produced in 1981 – and its marble quarries are famous. Local products include peaches, olives and honey and the exhibition–fair, which is held annually in the first fortnight in April, has made the town the wine capital of the Var and of Provence.

**Brignoles Plums.** – Brignoles plums were famous throughout the kingdom until the 16C. As sugar-plums, they were an important addition to the sweet boxes of the time : the Duke of Guise was nibbling one a few minutes before he was assassinated at Blois.

All the plum trees used to belong to a local lord but during the League troubles in the 16C, the people of Brignoles destroyed 180 000 trees. Since then «Brignoles plums» have actually come from Digne.

### ■ SIGHTS
*time: 1 1/2 hours*

**Old Brignoles.** – South of Place Carami, picturesque old streets – Rue du Grand Escalier, Rue St-Esprit and Rue des Lanciers with a **Romanesque house (E)** – lead to the church and the house of the Counts of Provence.

**St Saviour's** (Église St-Sauveur) **(B).** – The church has a lovely exterior Romanesque doorway.

Inside is an altar dating from the early period of the Christian Church.

The door to the sacristy is 15C. The **Descent from the Cross** is by Barthélemy Parrocel, who died at Brignoles in 1660.

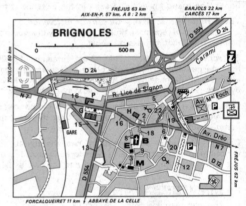

**BRIGNOLES**

FRÉJUS 63 km
AIX-EN-P. 57 km, A 8 : 2 km
BARJOLS 22 km
CARCÈS 17 km
FORCALQUEIRET 11 km ▪ ABBAYE DE LA CELLE

| | | | |
|---|---|---|---|
| Carami (Pl.) | 2 | Mistral (Av. Frédéric) | 13 |
| Comtes de Provence (Pl. des) | 3 | Ottaviani (R. Louis) | 15 |
| Dr-Barbaroux (R. du) | 5 | République (R. de la) | 16 |
| Ferry (R. Jules) | 6 | St-Esprit (R.) | 18 |
| Grand Escalier (R. du) | 8 | St-Louis (Bd) | 19 |
| Lanciers (R. des) | 9 | St-Pierre (Pl.) | 20 |
| Liberté (Cours de la) | 12 | 8 Mai 1945 (R. du) | 22 |

**Museum of the Brignoles Region (M).** – *Open 16 March to 14 September, 9am to noon and 2.30 to 6pm; 16 October to 15 March, 10am to noon and 2.30 to 5pm; closed Mondays, Tuesdays, 1 May and 15 September to 15 October; 5F.*

The building which dates in part from 12C was formerly the house of the Counts of Provence. The chief exhibit is the **Le Gayole tombstone★** dating from 2–3C and illustrating the transition from pagan to Christian iconography. Also on show are a reconstruction of an 18C Provençal interior and the original chapel with its fine 17C woodwork. Parrocel and Montenard are represented in the picture gallery upstairs which also contains an exhibition on local customs and an **automated crib** created in 1952 in the Provençal tradition but using a cement boat by J. Lambor, inventor of reinforced concrete.

### *EXCURSIONS*

**Brignoles Region★.** – *Round tour of 51 km – 32 miles – about 1 1/2 hours.* The undulating countryside of vineyards and pine plantations is stained red by the bauxite mines.

*Leave Brignoles by D 554 going north-east. In Val turn right into D 562.* Vineyards alternate with lavender fields and pine plantations.

**Carcès.** – Pop 1 807. *Facilities p 30.* Tall narrow houses beneath flat roofs cover the hillside below the Gros Bessillon. The town produces oil, honey and lavender and has extensive wine cellars.

*2 km – 1 mile south of Carcès (towards Cabasse)* the tree-lined D 13 comes to a **waterfall** where the river drops 7 m – 22 ft in several stages.

**Carcès Lake.** – The pine-clad shores are a favourite haunt of fishermen. The reservoir of water retained by the beaten earth dam supplies Toulon and other coastal towns. There is a fine **view** from the southern end of the lake.

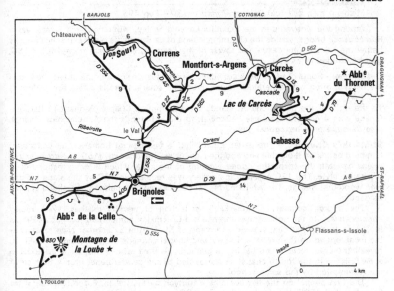

*Continue along D 13.* Red bauxite mines become more frequent. Turn left into D 79 for Thoronet Abbey.

**Thoronet Abbey★.** – *Description p 143 .*

*Return to D 13 and turn left towards Cabasse along the valley of the Issole.*

**Cabasse.** – The green valley site has seen many generations of human habitation as the nearby dolmens and standing stones prove. The charming village grouped round a mossy fountain is on the Provence wine road. The **church of St-Pons** *(key from the Bar-Tabac in the square)* is 16C although the tympanum was carved in 19C and there are Gallo-Roman remains in the side aisle. Most noteworthy is the **high altar★** of carved and gilded wood in Spanish Renaissance style (1543).

Return to Brignoles by D 79 past more red bauxite deposits.

**Sourn Valley.** – *Round trip 39 km – 25 miles – about 1 hour. Leave Brignoles by D 554 going north.* In Val turn right into D 562 and then left into D 22 which crosses the Argens river.

**Montfort-sur-Argens.** – Pop 440. Ramparts and the ruins of a forbidding feudal castle mark this former Templar commandery which now produces excellent grapes and peaches.

*Return to crossroads and turn right into D 45 which follows the Argens upstream.*

**Correns.** – Pop 414. This charming riverside village with its many fountains beneath the towering Gros Bessillon is known for its white wine. The castle keep has some interesting gargoyles.

**Sourn Valley.** – In Provençal "sourn" means sombre. Here the Argens is enclosed between steep cliffs riddled with caves where people sought refuge during the Wars of religion.

*In Châteauvert turn left into D 554 to return to Brignoles.*

**Celle Abbey; La Loube Mountain★.** – *14 km – 10 miles – about 3 hours. Leave Brignoles by D 554 going south. Turn right into D 405.*

**Celle Abbey.** – *Open 20 May to 30 September with the permission of the Hostel Manager.* In 13C the Benedictine convent attracted the daughters of the Provençal nobility but by 16C standards had fallen so low that the nuns were distinguished from other women only by their dress and their lovers. Efforts at reform failed and the convent was closed in 1660 on the orders of Mazarin.

The 17C Prior's house has been converted into a country hotel. The cloister, chapter house and refectory can be visited. The austere Romanesque abbey church, of inhospitable appearance, is now the parish church, containing a striking 15C Crucifixion.

*Continue on D 405 and then turn left into D 5 going south.* The countryside is pitted with red bauxite mines. 1 km – 1/2 mile before La Roquebrussanne, turn left into a narrow road closed to traffic where there is room to park.

**La Loube Mountain★.** – *2 hours on foot Rtn.* Take the narrow road which is bordered by flowers in springtime and passes strangely shaped rocks resembling animals and human beings.

*The last stage of the ascent is a rock climb (not dangerous) near the telecommunications mast.*

From the summit (830 m – 2 723 ft) there is an interesting **panorama★**. In the valleys the farmland is laid out like multicoloured gems in a rock setting and on the hillsides the bauxite mines show like red gashes in the green covering of pine and holm oak. Beyond the Carami valley to the north are the hills of Haute Provence; to the east are the Alps; to the south the mountains round Toulon and to the west the long ridge of Ste-Baume.

*Return to Brignoles by D 5 and N 7.*

## La BRIGUE

Michelin map 195 fold 9 – *Local map p 130* – Pop 493

Among the vineyards in the beautiful Levense valley, tributary of the Roya, near a Romanesque bridge, stands the charming village of La Brigue. Its old green schist houses below the ruins of the castle and tower of the Lascaris, local rulers from 14C to 18C, give some idea of its age.

**Old village.** – Some of the houses are built over arcades; on some of the others the lintels are carved, often with a heraldic device. From the square there is a fine view of Mount Bégo (W).

To the right of the parish church stands the Assumption Chapel (Penitents) : Baroque façade with a graceful Genoese bell-tower; to the left stands the Annunciation Chapel: also Baroque on a hexagonal plan.

**St-Martin's Church★.** – The parish church has a fine square Romanesque bell-tower; Lombard bands on the gable end and the side aisles. The doorway (1501) of green schist opens beneath the sexpartite ribbed vaulting of the nave, which is richly decorated in the Italian style. The 17C organ in the gallery was repaired in 19C by the same Italians who worked at Saorge. The white marble font is covered by a painted and gilded conical baldaquin.

The church contains a remarkable collection of **primitive paintings**. *Walk round anticlockwise.* On the right of the entrance is a Crucifixion comparable with Louis Bréa's in Cimiez. In the first chapel is an altarpiece of Ste-Martha by another Nice artist with the local legend on the predella. The second chapel contains the Sufferings of St-Elmo, revealing a cruel realism unusual in the gentle Louis Bréa, whose **altarpiece of the Adoration of the Child★** is in the fourth chapel, accompanied by the central panel from a triptych of the Assumption by the same school.

The first chapel on the left contains a triptych by the Italian, Fuzeri, **Our Lady of the Snows★**, dated 1507; the Baroque frame is 18C.

*The **Michelin Guide France** lists hotels and restaurants serving good meals at moderate prices. Use the current guide.*

## BROUIS Pass ★

Michelin map 195 fold 18

The Brouis Pass links the Bévera and the Roya Valleys. The upper valley of the latter can be explored in a pleasant drive from Breil-sur-Roya to Tende *(p 129)*.

### Sospel to La Giandola – *21 km – 13 miles – about 3/4 hour*

*Leave Sospel (p 142) by D 2204 going north-east.* Look back at the Barbonnet fortress commanding Sospel. *At the T junction bear left.*

**Pérus Pass.** – Alt 654 m – 2 146 ft. After the T junction *(bear left)* the road looks down on the Bassera ravine *(right)* as it climbs over the Pass.

**Brouis Pass★.** – Alt 879 m – 2 884 ft. A broad view★ opens up over the peaks on the far bank of the Roya.

By a steep and twisting descent the road winds down to the hamlet of La Giandola *(p 129)* in the Roya valley.

It is possible to return to the coast via **Breil-sur-Roya** *(p 42)* and Italy along the picturesque valley of the Roia river which flows into the sea at Ventimiglia.

## CAGNES-SUR-MER ★

Michelin map 195 folds 25 and 26 – Pop 29 538 – *Facilities p 28*

Cagnes-sur-Mer is set in a landscape of hills covered with olive and orange trees and cultivated flowers (carnations, roses, mimosa). The town comprises : Haut-de-Cagnes, dominated by a mediaeval castle , Cagnes-Ville, the modern residential and commercial quarters and Cros-de-Cagnes, an unusual fishing village and beach. The mild climate makes it a favourite winter resort.

The picturesque upper town has become the second home of many painters who come each year in great numbers, attracted by the beautiful setting and the incomparable light.

A large racecourse, serving the whole of the Riviera coast, has a varied programme throughout the season from December to March and in August and September each year.

**The Grimaldis of Cagnes.** – The history of Cagnes is that of its castle. This was originally a fortress built by Raynier Grimaldi, Lord of Monaco and Admiral of France, after he became Lord of Cagnes in 1309. A branch of the Grimaldi family *(details p 102)* remained in possession of Cagnes up to the Revolution.

Raynier's castle was converted in 1620 by Henri Grimaldi into a finely decorated château. Entirely loyal to the King of France, he persuaded his cousin, Honoré II of Monaco, to renounce Spanish protection and to place himself, by the Treaty of Péronne (1641), under French protection. Heaped with honours and riches by Louis XIII and Richelieu, Henri led a life of luxury at Cagnes. This was the zenith of the family's power. When the Revolution broke out, the reigning Grimaldi was driven out by the inhabitants and took refuge in Nice.

**International Art Festival.** – During the three summer months each year an exhibition of contemporary art is put on at Cagnes Castle.

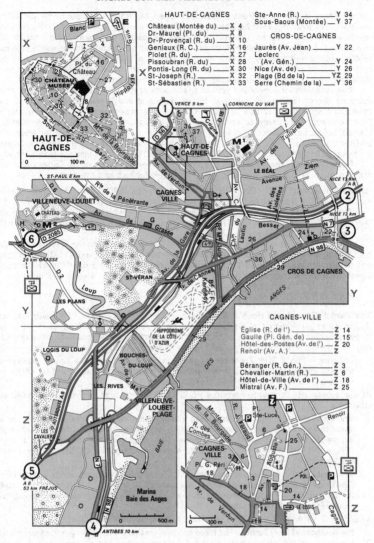

## ■ SIGHTS *time: 2 hours*

**Cagnes Heights★ (Haut-de-Cagnes) (X).** – *It is advisable to walk up to Cagnes Heights by Montée de la Bourgade.*

The **old town★** has retained its ramparts. The steep streets, with steps and vaulted passageways, contain many 15C and 17C houses (in particular Renaissance houses with arcades near the castle). The Nice Gate near the church tower is 13C.

**St-Pierre Church (X B).** – The door opens into the gallery. The early Gothic nave contains the Grimaldi tombs; at the end on the left is a permanent large scale santon crib. The larger nave added in 18C houses an altarpiece of the 18C Spanish School and 18C statue of the Virgin and Child.

**N.-D.-de-Protection Chapel (X E).** – *Open in summer, 2 to 6pm; in winter, 2 to 5pm; closed Tuesdays in summer and Fridays in winter.*

The Italianate porch and bell-tower gave inspiration to Renoir. The apse is decorated with 16C **frescoes**. The altarpiece in the north chapel is 17C.

**The Castle-Museum★ (X).** – *Open 15 April to 30 September, 10 am to noon and 2 to 6pm; 15 November to 15 April, 10am to noon and 2 to 5pn; closed Tuesdays, 1 January, 1 May and 1 October to 15 November; 2 F.*

Enter by a double staircase and a Louis XIII doorway. The small Renaissance **patio★★** which dates from the alterations to the feudal castle carried out by Henri Grimaldi, has an agreeable freshness and elegance in sharp contrast to the castle's sunbaked façades with their few openings. Two storeys of marble columned galleries surmount the courtyard where a note of green is given by the light foliage of a pepper tree.

On the **ground floor** are eight low vaulted mediaeval rooms which open on to the patio galleries; rooms 1 and 2, which boasts a fine Renaissance fireplace, present mediaeval history; rooms 3, 4 and 5 form a **Museum of the Olive Tree** – its history and culture, the use of its wood, pressing and olive oil. Room 6 contains Roman sculpture dating from the 2C discovered in Cagnes.

Receptions were held on the **first floor** where the audience chamber still has its original panelled ceiling. The ceiling of the banqueting hall which represents the **Fall of Phaethon★** was painted between 1621 and 1624 by the Genoese, Carlone, and conveys an

**45**

extraordinary illusion of perspective. Once finished, the artist could not bring himself to leave it : "My beautiful Fall" he sighed, "I shall never see you again." In fact, he died six weeks after he left Cagnes. The ceiling became celebrated and many came from far off to admire it. It suffered considerably under the Sardinian occupation : the favourite pastime of the soldiers being target practice at Louis XIV's son. Between these two great rooms is the oratory with a ceiling decorated with Louis XIII style plasterwork *(gypseries)*. Adjoining rooms are devoted to local history and Mediterranean sea fishing.

The second floor, where the private apartments of the Grimaldis were situated, now contains the collections of paintings of the **Museum of Modern Mediterranean Art**. In it are assembled works by painters of the 20C who were either born on the shores of the Mediterranean, lived there or came repeatedly to work there; Chagall, Brayer, Kisling, Carzou, Seyssaud, Chabaud, Van Velde and others. In the former boudoir of the Marquise of Grimaldi, there are 40 portraits, the **Suzy Solidor bequest★**, given by the famous singer; paintings of herself done by such well known artists as : Dufy, Marie Laurencin, Picabia, etc.

From the top of the **tower** there is a fine **view★** over the roofs of Old Cagnes and the modern town to the sea, from Cap Ferrat to Cap d'Antibes and the Alps.

**Renoir Museum** (Y M¹). – *Open 15 April to 14 October, 2.30 to 6.30pm; 15 November to 14 April, 2 to 5pm; closed Tuesdays, holidays and 15 October to 15 November; 2F.*

The Renoir Memorial Museum is at Les Collettes, the house where the artist passed the last twelve years of his life. The visitor, on entering, is welcomed in the outer hall by a bust of Madame Renoir.

The house has been preserved just as it was. The two studios on the first floor contain his painting materials. Sculptures and sketches in red chalk are displayed upstairs; bronzes and two small canvasses, in particular **Les Collettes Landscape★** on the ground floor. His bronze statue of **Venus★** stands in the garden among fruit trees – olive, orange and lemon.

## EXCURSIONS

**The Peaks (Baous) and the Var Corniche★**. – *Round trip of 32 km – 20 miles – about 1 1/4 hours (excluding the ascent of Baou de St-Jeannet).* Leave Cagnes by Avenue Auguste-Renoir and D 18 going north through elegant residential property, olive groves, market gardens and flower fields, with **views** of Vence, the hills and La Gaude.

La Gaude. – Pop 2 309. From the ridge above the river Cagne, La Gaude surveys a tranquil scene of vineyards which produce an excellent wine. The 14C castle is supposed to have been built by the Templars.

At the crossroads in Peyron continue north on D 18 through orchards and terraced vineyards.

St-Jeannet. – Pop 1 865. The charming village occupies a remarkable **position★** on a scree terrace at the foot of Baou St-Jeannet, among orange groves, flower fields and vineyards producing good quality wine. Behind the church on the left a sign "Panorama" points to a terrace offering a **view★** of the peaks *(baous)*, the coast and the Var valley.

Baou St-Jeannet★★. – *2 hours on foot Rtn. The signposted path starts from Place Ste-Barbe by the Auberge St-Jeannet.* A sheer cliff 400 m – 1 312 ft high dominates the village. From the top *(viewing table)* a huge **panorama★★** extends from the Esterel to the French and Italian Alps.

*Return to D 18 going south. Turn left into D 118 towards Plan-du-Bois.*

IBM Research and Study Centre. – The huge building on the left consisting of two opposing Y-shapes, raised on concrete pillars to accommodate the uneven ground, were designed by Breuer and are a good example of architecture harmonising with its natural surroundings.

Var Corniche Road★. – The road follows the ridge or clings to the hillside on the west bank of the Var with a clear view of the Nice hinterland.

St-Laurent-du-Var. – Pop 15 503. Until the County of Nice passed to France, the Var formed the frontier with the Kingdom of Sardinia. Passengers usually forded the river, often on another man's back. The first permanent bridge was built downstream in 1864.

*Leave by D 118 towards Cagnes and turn right into N 7.*

**Villeneuve-Loubet; Baie des Anges Marina.** – *9 km – 5 miles west. Take Avenue de Grasse, D 2085.*

Villeneuve-Loubet. – Pop 6 119. The village on the banks of the Loup, is dominated by its mediaeval castle *(not open)*. Provençal pelota is still played here without a glove.

Culinary Museum★ (Y M²). – *Open 2 to 6pm; closed Mondays, holidays and in November; 10F.* Established in the house where Auguste Escoffier (1847-1935) was born, the museum contains mementoes of his career, as head chef at the London Carlton and as creator of Peach Melba, and a huge collection of culinary art: show pieces in almond paste and icing sugar. The room arranged as a typical Provençal kitchen leads to an upstairs room containing 15 000 menus, some dating from 1820.

Baie des Anges Marina (Z). – *Take D 2 going south, turn right into N 7 and, after crossing the motorway, turn left to Villeneuve-Loubet–Plage. Facilities p 28.*

The shallow S bends of the four pyramidal blocks of flats are the brainchild of André Minangoy and one of the most amazing property developments on the Riviera. Each floor diminishes in surface area towards the top storey providing terraces at every level. A swimming pool, beach and marina together with cafés, shops and restaurants form an impressive complex.

*The main shopping streets are indicated
at the beginning of the list of streets, which
accompany town plans.*

Against a backdrop of hills Cannes stands on the shores of La Napoule Bay, a superb anchorage dominated by the Esterel Heights. The town owes its popularity to the beauty of its **setting★**, its mild climate and magnificent festivals. From its early fame as the winter salon of the world's aristocracy, it has developed into an important summer resort and conference centre.

## HISTORICAL NOTES

**Cannes, the Coastal Watch Tower.** – By 10C, following earlier Ligurian and Roman settlements, a little cluster of dwellings stood at the foot of the rock, known today as Mount Chevalier. The Place itself was called Canoïs – cane harbour after the reeds *(cannes)* that grew in abundance in the surrounding marshes. The abbots of Lérins became the owners and built a tower and fortifications to protect the fishermen against possible attack from the Saracens.

As soon as the first suspect sails appeared on the horizon, the Lérins watchers gave the alarm. The defences were directed by the monks – first the Templars, then the Knights of Malta. The Fathers of Mercy dealt with the ransoming of prisoners.

**Lord Brougham and the Origin of the Resort (1834).** – Cannes' riches and renown are due to the misfortune of a Lord Chancellor of England, Lord Brougham, who was on his way to Nice in 1834.

Cholera in Provence prevented the wealthy traveller crossing the *cordon sanitaire* to Nice, he, therefore, returned to Cannes. The place then a small fishing village, pleased him so much that he built himself a house there. For the next thirty-four years, right up to the time of his death, Lord Brougham exchanged the winter fogs of London for the Mediterranean sunshine. His example was soon followed by the English aristocracy of the time and the town's population of 4 000 grew rapidly.

Two famous writers dearly loved Cannes: Prosper Mérimée died there in 1870; Guy de Maupassant anchored his yacht in the bay between 1884 and 1888 and wrote his enthusiastic impressions of the town in his story *On the Water*. Frédéric Mistral, the Provençal poet, celebrated Cannes and there is scarcely a famous name in art or literature that has not visited Cannes.

**Cannes Festivals.** – The Cannes festivals are world famous. Among the most popular are the battles of flowers, the international regattas and the mimosa festival (February) which invites contributions from all the plantations in the neighbourhood, particularly Le Tanneron, and uses several tonnes of cut flowers. An International Record and Music Market (MIDEM) takes place in January.

The International Film Festival is the most brilliant artistic gathering on the Riviera; each year in May Cannes becomes the film capital of the world.

## ■ SEA FRONT ★★ *by car: 1/2 hour*

**La Croisette Boulevard★★** (BCZ). – Here the local residents stroll in winter between 10am and 1pm. This elegant promenade, bordered by palm trees and gardens decked with rare flowers, is the setting for the Battle of Flowers. It overlooks fine sandy beaches, both public and private.

Luxury hotels and elegant shops line the front and the side streets as far as Rue d'Antibes. Here among the galleries and antique shops, the cinemas and night clubs, the smart set are to be found. Here also is the Conference Centre already outgrown by many festivals.

Further on beyond the rose gardens is the new Port-Canto, a modern sports and cultural centre.

All along the promenade there are fine views of La Napoule Bay and the Esterel Heights.

Cannes – Boulevard de la Croisette

# CANNES ★★★

**La Croisette Point★** (X). – The spit of land at the east end of the Promenade owes its name to a small cross which used to stand there. It offers splendid views of Cannes, La Napoule Bay and the Esterel, particularly at sunset. In addition to the beautiful gardens, modern tourist developments have provided artificial beaches and the Palm Beach and Moure Rouge marinas.

Beyond Palm Beach (summer casino) round the point, a **view★** of Golfe Juan and Cap d'Antibes opens up. Boulevard Gazagnaire follows the sea front and Avenue Maréchal Juin goes back into town.

## ■ OLD CANNES AND THE HARBOUR *time: 1 1/2 hours*

**Allées de la Liberté** (BZ). – Beneath the plane trees a morning flower market is held overlooking the harbour where pleasure craft and fishing boats are moored.

*From the east end of the Allées turn north, cross over Rue Félix Faure, take Rue Rouguière and turn left into Rue Meynadier.*

**Rue Meynadier** (BZ). – Formerly the High Street linking the new town with Le Suquet, it is lined with a variety of shops and some fine 18C doorways.

*At the end of Rue Meynadier, turn left and right into Rue Georges-Clemenceau and at the far end turn right into Rue du Mont Chevalier going uphill.*

**Le Suquet** (AZ). – The old town, built on the site of the former Canoïs castrum, is known locally as Le Suquet.

Rue Perissol leads to Place de la Castre surrounded by a defensive wall and dominated by the Church of Our Lady of Good Hope, which was built in 16C and 17C in the Provençal Gothic style.

The old bell-tower leads to a long tree-lined terrace offering a fine **view** of the town and harbour and Ste-Marguerite Island. Here stand St-Anne's, a deconsecrated Romanesque chapel, a square tower and the remains of the castle of the Abbots of Lérins, which now houses a museum.

## CANNES - LE CANNET - VALLAURIS

| | | |
|---|---|---|
| André (R. du Cdt) ____ CZ | Dollfus (R. Jean) ____ AZ 22 | Observatoire (Bd de l') ____ X 54 |
| Antibes (R. d') ____ BCZ | Ferrare (Bd de la) ____ BYZ 23 | Oxford (Bd d') ____ V 55 |
| Belges (R. des) ____ BZ 5 | Fiesole (Av.) ____ V 24 | Pastour (R. L.) ____ AZ 56 |
| Chabaud (R.) ____ CZ 15 | Fournas (Av. de) ____ V 26 | Perrier (Bd) ____ V 57 |
| Croisette (Bd de la) ____ BCZ | Gambetta (Bd) ____ V 27 | Perrissol (R. L.) ____ AZ 59 |
| Félix-Faure (R.) ____ ABZ | Gaulle | Pins (Bd des) ____ X 60 |
| Foch (R. du Mar.) ____ BZ 25 | (Pl. du Gén.-de) ____ BZ 28 | République |
| Hôtel-de-Ville (Pl. de l') ____ AZ 33 | Grasse (Av. de) ____ V 29 | (Bd de la) ____ X 62 |
| Joffre (Bd du Mar.) ____ BZ 35 | Haddad-Simon (R. J.) ____ CY 30 | République (R. de la) ____ V 63 |
| Riouffe (R. du Mar.) ____ BZ 64 | Hôpital (Av. de l') ____ V 32 | Roi-Albert-Ier |
| | Isnard (Pl. Paul) ____ V 34 | (Av. du) ____ DZ 65 |
| Alexandre-III (Bd) ____ X 2 | Lacour (Bd. A.) ____ V 36 | Rouguière (R.) ____ BZ 66 |
| Amouretti (R. F.) ____ CZ 3 | Lattre-de-Tassigny | Rouvier (Bd M.) ____ V 67 |
| Beau-Soleil (Bd) ____ V 4 | (Av. J.-de) ____ ABY 37 | St-Charles (⊞) ____ V 69 |
| Bellevue (Pl.) ____ V 6 | Leader (Bd) ____ VX 38 | St-Joseph (⊞) ____ AY 70 |
| Bréguières (Ch. des) ____ V 7 | Lérins (Av. de) ____ X 39 | St-Nicolas (Av.) ____ BY 72 |
| Broussailles (Av. des) ____ V 8 | Macé (R.) ____ BZ 42 | Ste-Philomène (⊞) ____ V 73 |
| Buttura (R.) ____ BZ 10 | Montaigne (R.) ____ BY 43 | Sardou (R. L.) ____ V 74 |
| Carnot (Bd) ____ V 13 | Mont-Chevalier (R. du) ____ AZ 44 | Serbes (R. des) ____ BZ 75 |
| Castre (Pl. de la) ____ AZ 14 | Montfleury (Bd) ____ X 45 | Souvenir (⊞) ____ CY 76 |
| Christ-Roi (⊞) ____ V 16 | Myron-T.-Herrik (Bd) ____ V 46 | Tapis-Vert (Av. du) ____ V 77 |
| Clemenceau (Av. G.) ____ V 17 | N.-D.-de- | Tuby (Bd Victor) ____ AZ 78 |
| Coteaux (Av. des) ____ V 18 | Bon-Voyage (⊞) ____ BZ 49 | Vallauris (Av. de) ____ V 79 |
| Dr-Pierre- | N.-D.-d'Espérance (⊞) ____ AZ 50 | Victor-Hugo (R.) ____ V 80 |
| Gazagnaire (R.) ____ AZ 20 | N.-D.-des-Pins (⊞) ____ DZ 52 | Vidal (R. du Cdt) ____ CZ 82 |

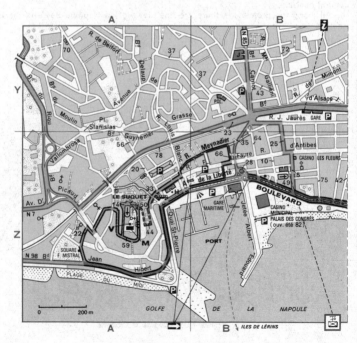

**La Castre Museum**★ (**AZ M**). – *Open 1 April to 30 June, 10am to noon and 2 to 6pm; 1 October to 31 March, 10am to noon and 2 to 5pm; closed Mondays, 1 November to 16 December and holidays; 3F.*

Archaeological and ethnographical collections from all over the world are well presented.

Rooms 1 and 2 display old Persian portraits and Babylonian seals and inscriptions in cuneiform script. Rooms 3 and 4 are devoted to the Far East – Thailand, Laos, China and Japan – note in particular a 17C Chinese statue of a benign Bhuddist god with 40 arms each bearing a symbolic object, fine porcelain and feudal Japanese armour. Rooms 5 and 6 contain exhibits of primitive Polynesian culture and Room 7 Pre-Columbian civilisation in South America – textiles, sculptures and Aztec divinities. Rooms 8 and 9 contain a **Mediterranean archaeological collection** from Egypt, the Lebanon, Cyprus, Greece, Etruria, Rome and Mahgreb.

**Le Suquet or Mount Chevalier Tower** (**AZ V**). – *Apply to the Keeper of the Museum.*

The 12C square tower, 22 m – 72 ft high, is the old watch tower. From the platform there is an extensive **view**★ of La Croisette, La Napoule Bay, the Lérins Islands, the Esterel Heights and the hills to the north of Cannes.

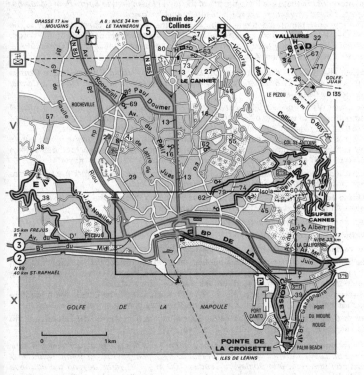

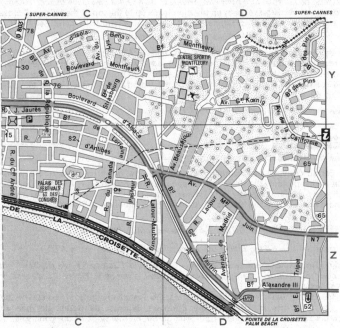

# CANNES ★★★

Follow Rue J.-Hibert and Rue J.-Dollfus to reach F.-Mistral Square where a statue of the "immortal bard of Provence" was erected in 1930 to commemorate the centenary of his birth.

**The Harbour.** – Boulevard J.-Hibert runs parallel with Midi Beach round the point to the harbour with its ranks of fishing boats and luxury yachts. Larger cruise liners and merchant shipping anchor further out. The west side of the harbour is lined with shops and restaurants. In the north east corner is the booking office and embarkation quay for trips to the Lérins Islands *(p 88)*.

## EXCURSIONS

**Lérins Islands★★** (Iles de Lérins). – *Boat trip 1/2 day.*
*Information on the boat service and description of the islands, p 88.*

**Super-Cannes Observatory★★★** (VX). – Alt 325 m – 1 066 ft. *Round tour of 8 km – 5 miles. Leave Cannes by Avenue de Vallauris, D 803, going north towards St-Antoine Pass. Turn off right into Boulevard Beau-Soleil.* A righthand turning leads to the Observatory, where there is a lift to the top of the tower *(open 9am to 8pm – 6pm December to March; closed November except weekends and holidays)*.

The immense panorama is one of the best on the Riviera: the coast from Italy to the Esterel, the hinterland of Cannes and Nice as well as the snow–capped Alps on the border and Corsica on a fine day *(viewing table)*. Return to town by Boulevard de l'Observatoire, Alexandre Lacour, des Pins, Avenue Fiesole and Isola Bella.

**Tour into the Hills★.** – *Round tour of 19 km – 12 miles – about 2 hours. Leave Cannes by Boulevard Carnot (N 85) initially going north; continue in a straight line to Le Cannet which merges with Cannes.*

**Le Cannet** (V). – Pop 33 915. *Facilities p 30.* Sheltered from the wind in a natural amphitheatre of wooded hills, Le Cannet is a popular resort which the painter Bonnard (1867-1947) visited several times before spending his last years there.

After a long righthand bend turn sharp left into Rue de la République which enters **old Le Cannet** with its 18C houses, small shady squares and steep footpaths. **Place Bellevue** (V 6) overlooks the neighbourhood; nearby is 12C Calvis tower.

*Continue along Rue Centrale; turn right into Rue Victor Hugo; at the fork bear right into Chemin des Bréguières which leads into Chemin des Collines.*

**Chemin des Collines★** (V). – This pleasant road winding through the hills above Cannes gives fine views over the town to the islands in the bay.

*At St-Antoine Pass turn left into D 803.*

**Vallauris** (V). – *Description p 157.*

*Leave Vallauris by D 135 which runs down to the coast at Golfe-Juan.*

**Golfe-Juan★.** – *Facilities p 28.* This popular resort at the foot of the Vallauris hills with 1 km – 3/4 mile of fine sandy beach extending in a shallow curve, overlooks a fine anchorage protected by Cap d'Antibes and the Lérins Islands.

**Napoleon** disembarked here in March 1815 after escaping from Elba in the brigantine Inconstant with 1 100 men. A mosaic on the quay commemorates the event.

*Return to Cannes by N 7. The road skirts Super-Cannes. The view of the Esterel and the Lérins Islands is particularly beautiful at sunset.*

**The Croix des Gardes★** (V E). – *Round tour of 8 km – 5 miles (steep climb) plus 1/4 hour on foot Rtn. Leave Cannes by Avenue Dr-Picaud (N 7 going west). At traffic lights near the Solhôtel turn right into Boulevard Leader. 100 m – 100 yards beyond the entrance to the Pavillon de la Croix, turn right into Avenue J. de Noailles and leave the car 100 m – 100 yards further on.* A gravel path on the right leads up to the top of the hill (small cross fixed in the rock) for a **view★** of Cannes, the Lérins Islands and the Esterel Heights.

*Continue along Avenue J.-de-Noailles to return to Cannes.*

**Tour of the Esterel Massif★★★.** – *96 km – 60 miles – 1/2 day. Description pp 61–65.*
We recommend that the round tour is made in the direction in which it is described, from Cannes to St-Raphaël by the inland route *(p 65)* and from St-Raphaël to Cannes by the coast road *(p 62)*. Tours of the interior of the massif can be made using the local map on pp 62–63.

**Tanneron Massif★.** – *Round tour of 56 km – 35 miles – 1 1/2 hours. Description p 142.*

## CAP FERRAT ★★

Michelin map ▉▉▉ fold 27 – *Local map p 122*

Cap Ferrat, originally the southernmost tip, has now given its name to the whole peninsula, which protects the Villefranche Roads and Les Fourmis Bay towards Beaulieu. Elegant houses shelter discreetly in the dense vegetation which tends to hinder a view of the shore except from the streets of St-Jean, the lighthouse or St-Hospice Point.

■ **SIGHTS** *round tour of 10 km – 6 miles – about 2 1/2 hours*

*Starting from St-Jean bridge follow the route shown on the plan on p 51.*

**Ephrussi de Rothschild Foundation★★** (M). – *Guided tour 1 July to 31 August, 3 to 7pm; 1 September to 30 June, 2 to 6pm; closed Mondays, 1 January, 1 May, 25 December and in November; 15F.*

The foundation which was bequeathed to the French Institute on behalf of the Academy of Fine Arts in 1934 by the Baroness Ephrussi de Rothschild, has an incomparable **setting★★** in magnificent gardens on the narrow neck of the peninsula.

## ST-JEAN-CAP-FERRAT

*Walkers,*
*campers,*
*smokers*

**ATTENTION au FEU**

*please*
*take care*

*Fire*
*is the scourge*
*of forests everywhere.*

**Ile de France Museum★★**. – The villa was built in the Italian style soon after 1900 to hold the furniture and works of art that the Baroness collected throughout her life. Her favourite period was 18C.

Marble columns surround a covered patio in which on an 18C Savonnerie carpet on a mosaic floor stand pieces of mediaeval and Renaissance furniture; the walls are hung with 16C and 17C Flemish tapestries.

In the surrounding rooms and galleries are displayed works of art from various periods: 18C furniture – some items belonged to Marie-Antoinette –, Savonnerie carpets, Beauvais and Aubusson tapestries, canvasses by Boucher, Coypel, Fragonard, Lancret, Hubert Robert, terracottas by Clodion and bronzes by Thomire.

An exceptional collection of porcelain from Vincennes, Sèvres and Dresden and the curious "monkey room" add a brilliant note. Two Chinese lacquer panels open into the gallery of Far-Eastern art, arranged in a Gothic decor and including lacquerwork from Coromandel, Chinese vases and carpets and a series of Mandarin costumes in an adjoining room. The Impressionists' Gallery contains landscapes by Monet, Renoir and Sisley.

**Gardens★**. – 7 ha – 17 acres of magnificent gardens surround the villa. The French garden abounds in Mediterranean plants and terminates in a stepped cascade spilling into a rockery by a Temple of Love copied from Versailles. Broad steps lead down among the arums, papyrus, pomegranates and daturas of the Spanish garden, which is followed by the Florentine garden with its graceful marble statue. Fountains, columns, gargoyles and sculptures, both mediaeval and Renaissance, ornament the Stone Garden. A delightful Japanese garden contrasts with the unusual plants in the tropical garden. A huge rose garden leads into the English garden.

**Passable Beach (Plage de Passable)**. – A beach of soft sand facing Villefranche.

**Zoo**. – *Open 15 June to 15 September, 9am to 7pm, the rest of the year, 9.30am to 6pm; 17F, children 10F.*

A dried out lake in grounds which once belonged to Leopold II of Belgium has been converted into a **tropical garden** in which a zoo covering some 3 ha – 7 acres has been established. It contains 350 species of animals and exotic birds, in particular a Condor with a 3 m – 10 ft wing span and fine gibbons. There is also a vivarium maintained at tropical conditions of temperature and humidity and a collection of exotic butterflies.

Several times a day there is a performance given by a troop of chimpanzees.

**Lighthouse (Phare)**. – *Open 1 May to 30 September, 9.30am to noon and 2 to 7pm; the rest of the year, 9.30am to noon and 2 to 4pm.*

Its beam is visible at 46 km – 30 miles. From the top (164 steps) there is a **panorama★★** from Bordighera Point in Italy to the Esterel Heights including the Alps and Pre-Alps. The Sun Beach swimming pool has been hollowed out of the rocks nearby.

**St-Jean-Cap-Ferrat★**. – *Pop 2 268. Facilities p 28.* Formerly a fishing village, St-Jean is now a quiet resort, its old houses looking down on the harbour of pleasure craft.

The stepped street to the south of Boulevard de la Liberation leads to a **viewpoint★** from which Èze, the Tête de Chien, Mount Agel and the Alps on the Italian border can be seen.

**St-Hospice Point**. – A pleasant stroll up between the private houses, past an 18C prison tower, leads to a 19C chapel, which replaces an old oratory dedicated to St-Hospice, a hermit from Nice. From the chapel there is a good **view★** of the coast and inland from Beaulieu to Cap Martin.

## WALKS

From St-Jean, visitors can take pleasant walks, mostly in the shade.

**Maurice Rouvier Walk★.** – *1 hour on foot Rtn.* Starting at the northern end of St-Jean beach, the walk follows the coast towards Beaulieu.

**St-Hospice Point Walk★.** – *1 hour on foot Rtn.* Take Avenue J.-Mermoz to the Paloma Beach restaurant and the steps on the left. The path winds along the shore past Paloma Beach with a view of Èze, Monaco and Cap Martin. Once round St-Hospice Point it skirts Le Colombier Point and Les Fossettes Bay before rejoining Avenue J.-Mermoz.

## CASTELLANE ★

Michelin map **81** fold 18 – *Local map pp 128-129* – Pop 1 261 – *Facilities p 30*

Castellane is a tourist centre, well placed at the point where the Route Napoléon and the Upper Verdon roads cross, north east of the famous canyon. Its **setting★**, one of the most striking in Haute Provence, is dramatised by a gigantic limestone cliff, the Rock (Roc) which dominates it from 184 m – 604 ft.

### CASTELLANE

| | |
|---|---|
| Nationale (R.) | 6 |
| Sauvaire (Pl. Marcel) | 13 |
| | |
| Bains (R. des) | 2 |
| Blondeau (R. du Lt) | 3 |
| Liberté (Pl. de la) | 4 |
| Mitan (R. du) | 5 |
| République (Bd de la) | 7 |
| Roc (Chemin du) | 8 |
| St-Michel (Bd) | 9 |
| St-Victor (R.) | 12 |

*The town plans are orientated with north at the top.*

■ **SIGHTS** time: 2 hours

**N.-D. du Roc Chapel.** – *The key is obtainable from the Presbytery, No 35 opposite the north west side of the Parish Church.*

From the Parish Church take the narrow path northwards *(signpost)* until it meets a broader track; turn right.

A pleasant **walk★** marked by the stations of the Cross leads up to the Chapel. There are constant views of the town. On the north side the machicolated **Pentagonal Tower**, part of the old fortifications, is clearly visible. The ruined walls which appear to the left formed part of the feudal township of Petra Castellana. The Chapel was built in 1703; it is a place of pilgrimage and covered in votive offerings.

From the terrace there is a **view★** of the town, its setting, the semicircle of mountains and the northern end of the Verdon Gorges.

**Old town.** – Local life centres on **Place Marcel Sauvaire (13)** with its cafés, shops and buildings grouped round a fountain and Rue Nationale, where Napoleon stopped on 3 March 1815 at No 34 (**E**), the former sub-prefecture. The old town to the north of the square is dominated by the Pentagonal Tower. Rue Milan leads to the **Lion Fountain (B)** at the heart of the picturesque and winding streets. Rue Victor Hugo leads into Boulevard St-Michel through one of the old town gateways. Known as the Clock Tower, it is a Gothic archway beneath a wrought-iron campanile.

**St-Victor Church (D).** – *Key obtainable from the Tourist Centre (Syndicat d'Initiative).*

The stout intersecting ribs of the nave recall Fréjus Cathedral. The side aisles are 16C and 17C. In the apse is a 17C medallion-shaped wood carving. The tower is in the Lombard style.

## EXCURSIONS

**Verdon Grand Canyon★★★.** – *154 km – 96 miles. Description p 161.*

**The Lakes★★.** – *Round trip of 26 km – 16 miles – about 1 hour. Local map opposite.*
Leave Castellane by N 85, ③ on the map, going north west. Turn right into D 955. As the road rises to the Blache Pass, there is a view back over the Castellane basin dotted with simple farmsteads.

**Blaron Road**. – *7 km – 5 miles detour north west of D 955*. At Blache Pass turn left into D 402, a steep narrow road overlooking Castillon Lake. Between La Baume chapel and Blaron itself, there are fine **views★** of the lake, the little island and the inclined folds of the valley.

*Return to D 955 and turn left.*

**Castillon Dam★**. – Stop at the viewing place created on the west bank to see the dam. *Explanatory panel.*

The narrow horizontal arch dam is only 26 m – 85 ft thick at the base. It is 200 m – 219 yds long at the top and 100 m – 328 ft high.

The road runs along the top of the dam.

**Castillon Lake★**. – *Continue along D 955 for about 1 km – 1/2 mile; turn right into the road to Demandolx*. Cut into the hillside above the Verdon, it has remarkable **views★★** of the dam, the artificial lake (500 ha – about 2 sq miles) and its strangely ridged banks.

*Before reaching Demandolx, turn right into D 102, a narrow winding road.*

**Chaudanne Lake★**. – As the road descends there are **views★★** down to the dam and the dark green waters of the lake. The **dam** is the horizontal arch type (overall height 70 m – 230 ft, length at top 95 m – 312 ft) and is situated at a narrow point on the Verdon downstream from the Castillon dam.

*Return to Castellane by N 85.*

## CASTILLON Pass Road ★

Michelin map **195** folds 18 and 28 – north of Menton

The road over Castillon Pass – also called the Garde Pass – makes its way through a break in the ridge of hills running parallel to the coast and dividing the Menton district from the Sospel basin. From the pass the river Carei flows south to the Mediterranean and the river Merlanson north to join the river Bévera.

### Menton to Sospel – *21 km – 13 miles – about 3/4 hour*

*Leave Menton by Avenue de Sospel, D 2566*. After passing under the motorway, the road climbs, through many turns, up the beautiful **Carei Valley★** beneath the bare ridges of the Franco-Italian border to the east. The lemon groves give way to olives and then pine trees.

Once past the hamlet of Monti, the road skirts Menton Forest, offering fine views of Menton, the sea and the hill village of Castellar.

**Menton Forest**. – A variety of trees contributes to the beauty of the forest which caters for walkers. To the left of the forest refuge a path *(1 hour on foot Rtn)* leads to a **viewing table★** which overlooks the coast.

The road soon passes the graceful curve of the Caramel **viaduct** formely used by the tramway from Menton to Sospel.

**Castillon**. – Pop 55. To the right of the road a new village, a model of rural urbanisation in Provençal style, has been built half way up the hillside. From the top there is a **view** down the Carei valley to the sea.

A long loop round the old road tunnel above the ruined Castillon village brings the road up to the Pass.

**Castillon Pass**. – Alt 707 m – 2 320 ft. The **view** to the north shows the Bévera valley with the Peira-Cava (NNW) and Aution (N) peaks in the background. D 54 takes a picturesque route to St-Jean Pass.

From here begins the long descent of the Merlanson valley. Gradually the forest is replaced by olive groves and terraced vineyards. First the stronghold on Mount Barbonnet comes into view and then the town of Sospel *(p 142)* and the surrounding heights.

## CHAMPS Pass ★

Michelin map **81** folds 8 and 9

The road over the Champs Pass links the Upper Var valley with the Upper Verdon valley and bestows a sense of isolation and absolute solitude.

### St-Martin d'Entraunes to Colmars – *29 km – 18 miles – abour 1 hour*

*Leave St-Martin by D 78 going west.*

After Monnard hamlet the road affords a **view★** of St-Martin d'Entraunes and the narrow passage of the Var below and up to the high peaks separating the Var from the Tinée to the north east.

**Chastelonnette**. – Also called Val Pelens, the hamlet includes the mountain refuge of the Nice Ski Club, facing the Pelens Needles; the highest is 2 523 m – 8 278 ft.

The road climbs through a bleak and stony terrain, inhospitable to trees.

**Champs Pass★**. – The road crosses the departmental border between Alpes-Maritimes and Alpes de Haute-Provence at 2 095 m – 6 874 ft in a bare grey desert landscape. The view is obstructed by the Tête des Muletiers (N) and the Frema Peak (S) (2 747 m – 9 013 ft).

D 78 descends in a succession of double bends to the forest and high pastures. At the first righthand bend there is an oblique **view** up the Lance valley (SE) and the Upper Verdon (SW). Below to the west lies the fortified town of Colmars *(p 55)*.

## CIANS Gorges ★★★

Michelin map 195 folds 4 and 14

The gorges formed by the Cians, a tributary of the Var, are among the finest in the Alps.

The river Cians drops 1 600 m – 5 250 ft in 25 km – 15 1/2 miles carving out deep gorges to reach the Var. The superb walls are of red slate in the upper reaches and limestone lower down.

### La Mescla Bridge to Beuil – 55 km – 34 miles – about 2 1/4 hours

N 202 runs westwards up the narrow rocky Var valley. To the north the ground rises to the Pointe des Quatre Cantons while beyond the ridge to the south lies the rift region of Haute-Provence (p 79).

**Touët-sur-Var★.** – Pop 307. The tall narrow houses flattened against the cliff form a maze of partially roofed streets. The top floor is often open to the midday sun for drying figs. The 17C parish church is built out on arches over a torrent which can be seen through a window let into the floor of the central aisle.

*2 km – 1 mile further on turn right into D 28.*

**Lower Cians Gorge★★.** – Water seeps from the walls bristling with spikes and jagged projections. The roadway snakes along the bottom of the gorge following every curve.

*After leaving the gorge turn right into D 128, a steep narrow road demanding careful driving.*

**Lieuche.** – Pop 17. The tiny mountain village is set in a **landscape★** of black schist.

Its humble church *(key available from Mme Daniel, on the right going down the main street)* contains an **altarpiece★** depicting the Annunciation, one of Louis Bréa's earliest works. It is mounted in a carved and gilded wood surround with statuettes in niches and angels bearing candles (17C). From the church step there is a **view★** of the Dome de Barrot (NW), the line of the Cians Gorge (N and S) and the Var valley (E and W).

*(After photo : Editions Giletta, Nice)*

Louis Bréa, Altarpiece of the Annunciation, Lieuche

*Return to D 28 and continue northwards. 1 km – 1/2 mile later turn left into D 228 which climbs through impressive scenery above the Cians valley.*

**Rigaud.** – Pop 111. Beneath a former Templar fortress, the village stands in a beautiful **setting★**, with an **all-round view** from near Place de la Mairie. The interior of the fortified church *(key available from Mme Pauline Champoussin)* is Baroque and contains several 17C paintings particularly a Descent from the Cross at the high altar and on the left a 1626 canvas of the Virgin.

*Return to D 28 and turn left.*

**Upper Cians Gorge★★★.** – 1.6 km – 1 mile beyond Pra-d'Astier look back down on the torrent and its confluence with Pierlas stream some 100 m – 320 ft downstream. The road climbs steadily, sometimes beside, sometimes above the water which tumbles downstream in great steps.

The sheer walls present a strange jagged profile except where rock falls have worn them smooth. The vivid red rock contrasts with the dark green moss which clings to it. The narrowest places, which are also the most beautiful, are called the little rift *(petite clue)* and the great rift *(grande clue)*. Here the rock walls meet overhead in great arches which are hung with row upon row of icicles in winter.

After 6.5 km – 4 miles the road reaches **Beuil★** *(p 40)* at the north end of the gorge.

## COGOLIN

Michelin map 84 fold 17 – Local map pp 94-95 – Pop 4 606

This village with trading and industrial interests lies along the foot of a slope overlooked by an ancient tower and a ruined mill.

Many of the villagers are employed in the manufacture of carpets, pipes and bottle corks, and in the collection of reeds and canes from the marshes suitable for use in clarinets, fishing rods, furniture, etc. It is also a wine growing centre.

**Cogolin Carpets and Fabrics (Les Tapis et Tissus de Cogolin).** – *Entrance 98 Boulevard Louis-Blanc which is off the Avenue G.-Clemenceau (N 98). Open 8.30am to noon and 2 to 6pm (5.30pm Fridays); closed Saturdays, Sundays and holidays; 1/2 hour.*

On the tour of the workshops you see furnishing fabrics and carpets being woven by hand – the latter are pure wool and knotted.

**Cogolin Marina (Marines de Cogolin).** – *Take N 98 towards the coast and then D 98A.* 4 km – 2 1/2 miles northeast of the village is a fine beach and a marina of 22 ha – 54 acres, part of a residential complex built in a unique architectural style.

Michelin map 🔢 folds 8 and 18

The easy Colle-St-Michel road links the Upper Verdon valley to the Var valley from which Entrevaux and Puget-Théniers and then Nice and the Riviera are accessible.

### Beauvezer to Entrevaux – *41 km – 26 miles – about 1 1/2 hours*

From Beauvezer *(p 165)* to Pont de Villaron, the road follows the green Verdon valley between alternating woods and fields.
From Pont-de-Villaron to St-Michel-Peyresq the road is cut into the rocky slopes or winds round the dried up ravines as it climbs above the Verdon.

**La Colle St-Michel Pass.** – Alt 1 431 m – 4 695 ft. The road is bordered by peaceful pastureland.

Beyond the pass the road descends the **Vaire valley** between wooded slopes and bare lime stone outcrops.

The picturesque villages are also linked by the Digne-Nice railway line which required several impressive feats of civil engineering to carry it up the valley.

**Méailles.** – Pop 102. A curious village following the line of a fold in the limestone high on the east bank of the Vaire.

Beyond Fugeret blocks of sandstone project from the valley's slopes which are clothed in walnut, chestnut and pine trees interspersed with lavender fields.

**Annot★** – Pop 885. *Facilities p 30.* The part-Alpine, part-Provençal town stands on the banks of the Vaire at 600 m – 1 968 ft. It is the oldest settlement in the valley and lay on the Roman road which linked it to Riez.
The local stone, known to geologists as Annot sandstone, has weathered into curiously shaped **rocks** *(Rochers)* forming natural arches, which are the object of several pleasant walks.
A large Provençal style square *(cours)* planted with magnificent plane trees is the focal point of the **old town★**. The Grande Rue which leads from the fortified gate to the church gives a good view of the steep winding streets, covered alleys and ungainly façades of the houses. There are some fine 16C, 17C and 18C carved doorways. The local stone has been used in the buildings and to pave the streets.
The Romanesque **church** is of curious appearance owing to a raised apse which forms a defensive tower. An attractive Renaissance belfry is quartered by the four Evangelists.

D 908 passes the curious Annot sandstone **rocks** *(Rochers)* before rejoining N 202 which follows the deep valley of the Coulomp from Les Scaffarels to its confluence with the Var.

**Entrevaux.** – *Description p 61.*

## COLMARS ★

Michelin map 🔢 south of fold 8 –
Pop 311 – *Facilities p 30*

The charming southern town with its narrow streets and minute squares each with its fountain makes an un-usual holiday resort, set on a wooded hillside at 1 235 m – 4 052 ft, and still surrounded by a 17C wall with flank-ing towers and loopholes. **The two forts** – Savoy to the north and France to the south – date from 14C when Colmars was on the Provençal frontier. Even the town's name has a military origin being derived from the latin "collis Martis" (hill of Mars) after a temple dedicated to the Roman god of war. The church which is built into the town walls shows the transition from Romanesque to Gothic; the side door is signed Mathieu Davers (1530).

**COLMARS**

Basse (R.) _____ 2
Baudouin (Traverse) ___ 3
Église (Pl. de l') _____ 4
Girieud (Pl. J.) _____ 5
Grande Rue _____ 6
St-Pierre (Pl.) _____ 8

## COTIGNAC

Michelin map 🔢 folds 5 and 6 – Pop 1 636 – *Facilities p 30*

Two ruined towers, once part of Castellane castle, dominated the village which seems to flow from a cliff of variegated tufa, which is riddled with caves and tunnels. Several fountains and elm and plane trees add to the charm of the old streets with their 16C and 17C doorways.

From Place de la Mairie the bell-tower leads to the 16C Romanesque church the front of which was rebuilt in 18C.

A path goes up from the church to a two-storey cave which gives a good **view** of the village and its surroundings. At the foot of the rock is an open air theatre where performances are given in summer.

The village is well known for its honey, oil and wine.

**N.-D.-de-Grâce.** – *1 km – 1/2 mile south by D 13 and a side road to the right.*
The chapel, surmounting Verdaille hill, is connected with an appearance of the Virgin in 16C commemorated on a tablet above the altar. In 1660 young Louis XIV came on pilgrimage with his mother Anne of Austria.

Michelin map **BB** fold 17 – Pop 16 576  – *Facilities p 30*

In its mountain **setting**★ on the banks of the Bléone on the Route Napoléon, Digne is an important tourist centre particularly as an overnight stop. Fruit and lavender are the main products of the district; each year there is a flower procession in August and a Lavender Fair in September.

The thermal baths specialise in the treatment of rheumatism.

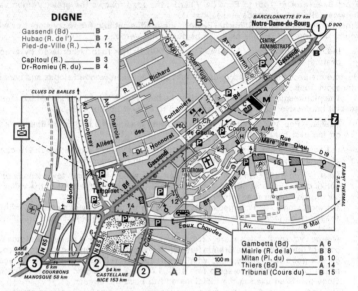

**DIGNE**

| | |
|---|---|
| Gassendi (Bd) | B 7 |
| Hubac (R. de l') | B 7 |
| Pied-de-Ville (R.) | A 12 |
| Capitoul (R.) | B 3 |
| Dr-Romieu (R. du) | B 4 |

| | |
|---|---|
| Gambetta (Bd) | A 6 |
| Mairie (R. de la) | B 8 |
| Mitan (Pl. du) | B 10 |
| Thiers (Bd) | A 14 |
| Tribunal (Cours du) | B 15 |

■ **SIGHTS** *time: 1 3/4 hours*

**Boulevard Gassendi** (AB). – It is pleasant to stroll under the magnificent plane trees of the main street which runs through Place Charles de Gaulle where stands a statue of Gassendi, a local philosopher (1592-1655) who debated with Descartes and was acquainted with Molière and Cyrano de Bergerac.

South of Boulevard Gassendi lie the upper town and St-Jerome's Cathedral approached by stepped and twisting streets.

**Municipal Museum** (B M). – *Open 10am to noon and 3 to 7pm; closed Mondays and certain holidays. 5F.*

The basement is devoted to archaeology: prehistoric, Gaulish and Gallo-Roman remains; the ground floor to conchology (shells), mineralogy, palaeontology (fish fossils).

Hanging in the first floor gallery is a **collection of paintings** from the French, Flemish, Dutch and Italian schools. One room contains stuffed animals. On the second floor, together with a Ziem, are several landscapes of Digne and Provence of late 19C.

**Great Fountain** (B B). – Two Doric porticos set at right angles in 1829 are now thick with a moss covered chalky deposit.

**Old Cathedral** (N.-D.-du-Bourg). – *Take D 900 north, ① on the plan. To visit the cathedral apply to the Keeper of the graveyard, white house behind the church on the right.*

The Romanesque church was built between 1200 and 1330. It has an elegant Lombard doorway, flanked by two lions couchant and surmounted by a huge rose window. The majestic rib-vaulted nave shows fragments of 15C and 16C murals and a very faint 14C fresco at the west end. A Merovingian altar stands in a niche on the north side.

## EXCURSIONS

**Courbons**★. – *Leave Digne by ③ on the plan, N 85 towards Marseilles, and turn right.*

The narrow road winds rapidly uphill through almond groves which offer wide **views**★ of Digne in its bare mountain site. The half ruined village of Courbons *(bear left at fork)* clings to a rocky ridge. The beautiful 14C Romanesque church, with a Gothic apse, looks out over a cypress-shaded graveyard to the Digne basin.

**Television Relay Mast.** – *8 km - 5 miles. Take the road to Courbons but bear right at the fork 4 km - 2 1/2 miles from Digne.*

From the road there are **views** of the Bléone valley. The cedar trees give way to scrub and flowers and then to bare ridges. From the top, 1 166 m - 3 825 ft, there is a **view**★ of the Pre-Alps (N), the heights of Grasse and Nice (E), Digne and the Bléone valley (S).

**DIGNE Pre-Alps** _____

Michelin map **BB** folds 7 and 17

The Provençal Pre-Alps of Digne, which lie between the Durance and Verdon rivers, are the least populated and most desolate in the French Alps. The slopes bear sparse, scattered vegetation. The summits are bare and whitish. Occasional small, cultivated basins open out in the valleys. The chalky ranges are cut at right-angles by torrents which have formed wild, narrow gorges *(clues)* in which the strata of soil reveal the geological complexity of the Southern Pre-Alps.

There is a Mediterranean clarity in the light and the sky. The district abounds in rare butterflies.

## ■ THE BÈS VALLEY★

**Round trip from Digne** – *85 km - 53 miles – about 2 1/2 hours*

*Leave Digne (p 56) by D 900A (Avenue Demontzey) which goes up the Bléone and Bès valleys.*

**Barles Rifts★.** – Road and river vie for space in the valley bottom. The second rift is the more remarkable; after a narrow passage compressing the turbulent waters of the Bès, a jagged arm of rock is silhouetted against the sky, blocking off the valley (beyond it the view is clear).

**Verdaches Rift.** – Lush green vegetation clothes the rift.

**Maure Pass★.** – Alt 1 347 m – 4 419 ft. The pass links the Blanche and the Bès valleys. In summer these torrential tributaries of the Durance shrink to a trickle of water. The long stretches of deserted valley are very striking.

Just off the road beyond the pass among the mountain pastures and larch trees is the winter sports station of **Le Grand Puy**, which has developed as an annex to Seyne.

**Seyne.** – Pop 1 242. *Facilities p 30*. It was Vauban who fortified the little town which commands the approaches to the Ubaye and Durance (N) and the Bès and Bléone (S) valleys from its sunny alpine site. Seyne is not only a summer and winter resort but also breeds horses and mules which are shown at the annual fair.
The **church** exemplifies the Provençal Romanesque mountain style. It is built in pink and blue stone with a stone spire, a large rose window and two elegant Gothic doorways. The interior contains 17C stalls and seats and a huge monolithic font.

*Leave Seyne by D 7 south.* The road runs through green pastureland and up a wooded hillside before reaching a pass.

**Le Fanget Pass★.** – Alt 1 459 m – 4 787 ft. There is a splendid **view★** to the north; in the foreground the Blanche valley with Seyne and Selonnet; to the east Mont Blanche (NE) and Dormillouse (NNE) 2 505 m – 8 219 ft; on the horizon the Grand Parpaillon (NE) and the mountains near Gap (NW).

The narrow road rejoins the outward route near the Verdaches Rift.

*The main car parks are indicated on the town plans.*

## DRAGUIGNAN

Michelin map **84** fold 7 – *Local map below* – Pop 22 406

Draguignan, whose name recalls legendary struggles against a dragon, developed from a Roman fort built on the isolated knoll where the clock tower now stands. In the Middle Ages a defensive wall with three gates, two of which remain, and a keep were built. In 19C Baron Haussmann laid out tree-lined walks and straight boulevards to the south of the town.

On market day the peaceful streets fill with people from the surrounding wine producing district. Draguignan boasts a huge and modern Youth and Sports Centre.

An Allied Military Cemetery, on the D 59 to the east of the town, recalls the fighting that took place in August 1944 in the region, notably round Muy, where 10 000 British and American soldiers were parachuted or landed from gliders on the morning of 15 August.

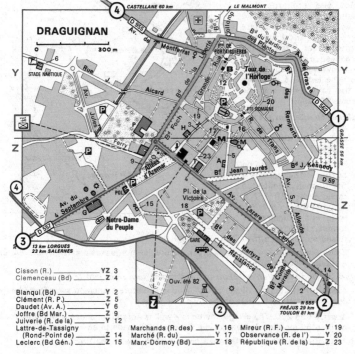

| | |
|---|---|
| Cisson (R.) _____ YZ 3 | |
| Clemenceau (Bd) _____ Z 4 | |
| | |
| Blanqui (Bd) _____ Y 2 | |
| Clément (R. P.) _____ Z 5 | |
| Daudet (Av. A.) _____ Y 6 | |
| Joffre (Bd Mar.) _____ Z 9 | |
| Juiverie (R. de la) _____ Y 12 | |
| Lattre-de-Tassigny | Marchands (R. des) _____ Y 16   Mireur (R. F.) _____ Y 19 |
| (Rond-Point de) _____ Z 14 | Marché (R. du) _____ Y 17   Observance (R. de l') _____ Y 20 |
| Leclerc (Bd Gén.) _____ Z 15 | Marx-Dormoy (Bd) _____ Z 18   République (R. de la) _____ Z 23 |

■ **SIGHTS** *time: 1 1/2 hours*

**Old town.** – *Key to Clock Tower available from Tourist Centre (Syndicat d'Initiative).*
To the east of Boulevard de la Liberté, between two of the original gateways – the Portaiguières (15C) and the Romaine (14C), a network of picturesque streets constitutes the old town. The market place is set with fountains and shaded by plane trees. The huge 13C façade (Y **B**) in Rue de la Juiverie was once part of a synagogue.

**Clock Tower** (Tour de l'Horloge) (Y). – It replaces the keep which was demolished in 1660. It has four flanking turrets and an ornate wrought-iron campanile. The **view** from the top takes in the town and the Nartuby valley; on the horizon are the Maures mountains.

**Museum-Library** (Z **M**). – Built as an Ursuline Convent in 17C the building was converted into a summer residence by the Bishop of Fréjus in 18C.

**Museum.** – *Open 10 to 11.45am and 3 to 6pm; closed Sundays, Mondays and holidays.*
The museum is well designed and has some interesting and rare items on display. Gallery 1 contains old furniture, Sèvres porcelain and biscuit ware and three paintings by Ziem. Gallery 2, devoted to French and Dutch 17C painting, contains a Rembrandt *(Child blowing bubbles),* a Franz Hals *(Kitchen interior)* and the *Siege of Maastricht* by Parrocel. Gallery 3 – archaeology – displays Etruscan vases and a handsome Roman lamp. Gallery 4 boasts the 14C illustrated **MS of the Romance of the Rose** and is hung with 17C and 18C canvasses: Teniers, the younger, Panini, the Boucher school, Greuze. Gallery 6 is devoted to china and porcelain.

**Library.** – *Open 9am to noon and 2 to 6pm; closed Sundays, Mondays and holidays.*
A 15C Book of Hours, sixteen icunabula, including a Latin Bible (1481), a Latin translation of Plutarch (1491), the works of Aristotle printed in Venice by Aldo Manuce in 1497 and many rare books are among the 20 000 volumes dating from 16C, 17C and 18C which are listed in the catalogue.

**Law Courts** (Palais de Justice) (Z **J**). – In the lobby is a fine statue of a woman seated, representing Justice, which came from the Valbelle tomb in Montrieux Charterhouse.

**Allées d'Azémar** (Z). – This magnificent avenue, shaded by six lines of hundred-year-old plane trees, is complemented by informal gardens and flanked by stately bourgeois houses. On the corner of Boulevard Clemenceau is a bronze by Rodin.

**Notre-Dame-du-Peuple** (Z). – The church was built in 16C in Flamboyant Gothic and enlarged later (west front in 19C). On the left is the central panel of a 16C altarpiece of the Nice School representing a Virgin saying her Rosary. Pilgrimage 8 September.

## EXCURSIONS

**Malmont Viewpoint★★.** – *6 km – 3 1/2 miles – about 3/4 hour. Leave Draguignan going due north by Boulevard Joseph-Collomp. After 6 km – 3 1/2 miles the road reaches a pass. Turn left into a narrow road which leads to a viewing table 300 m – 330 yds away.*
An extensive **view★★** covers Mount Vinaigre (E) in the Esterel range, Agay Roadstead (ESE), the Argens Valley (SE), the Maures Heights (S) and Toulon (SW).

**Flayosc.** – Pop 1 867. *7 km – 4 1/2 miles – about 3/4 hour. Leave Draguignan by D 557, ③ on the plan, going west.*
The typical local village, looking down on a smiling countryside of vineyards, fields and orchards, has retained its 14C fortified gates. Near the main square with its trees and fountain a narrow street leads to the Romanesque **church** which has a massive square bell-tower. From the terrace a long **view** of the countryside and the Maures Massif.

**Châteaudouble Gorges★.** – *41 km – 26 miles – about 1 hour. Leave Draguignan by ④, D 955.*

> **The Fairy's Stone** (Pierre de la Fée). – The stone is a fine dolmen of which the table, 6 m – 19 1/2 ft long, 4.50 m – 14 1/2 ft wide and weighing 40 tonnes, rests on three raised stones more than 2 m – 6 ft high.

> **Châteaudouble Gorge★.** – The deep, green, serpentine gorge was created by the Nartuby, a tributary of the Argens.

*Before reaching Montferrat, return to Le Plan and turn right into D 51.*

The road traverses the old village of Châteaudouble before branching away from the river through woodland; to the left of the road are caves.

> **Ampus.** – Pop 220. The village church is a well restored Romanesque building. A path marked by modern Stations of the Cross (1968) leads to an eminence.

Return to Draguignan by D 49 which gives a good **view** of the town.

**The Waterfalls.** – *45 km – 28 miles – about 2 hours. Leave Draguignan by N 555, ②
on the plan, and go to Trans-en-Provence.*

**Trans Waterfall** (Cascade de Trans). – Leave the car in the Place de la Mairie and follow
a path on the left, to a bridge above the falls. From the bridge, by which D 47 crosses
the Nartuby on leaving the village, there is a good view of the river deep in its narrow
valley below.

*Leave Trans by the N 555 and make for Les Arcs.*

**Les Arcs.** – Pop 3 431. The town, which is the home of the local wine authority, lies
at the heart of the vineyards which produce the well-known «Côtes de Provence»
wines. It is dominated by the ruins of Villeneuve castle where Ste-Roseline was born
*(below)*. The church attracts many visitors to the **mechanical crib** *(on the left on entering);*
the backdrop is the old village of Les Arcs. The side chapels is painted with frescoes:
on the left the miracle of Ste-Roseline's roses by Baboulaine; on the right a **polyptych★**
in 16 sections by Louis Bréa (1501) of the Virgin and Child surrounded by Provençal
saints. From the keep a watch was kept in the Middle Ages against Saracen invasion.
Around the medieval castle are the stepped streets and alleys of the old town winding
between and beneath the houses.

*Leave Les Arcs by D 91. About 4 km – 2 miles further on stands Ste-Roseline's Chapel,
once part of the old Abbey of La Celle-Roubaud.*

**Ste-Roseline's Chapel★.** – The 12C cloister *(not open to the public)* and the Romanesque
chapel are all that remains of the Abbey of Celle-Roubaud. Founded in 11C, it became
a Charterhouse in 13C and reached its apogee during the priorship of Roseline de
Villeneuve from 1300-1329.

**Chapel★.** – *Open 1 July to 30 September, Wednesdays, Saturdays and Sundays, 3.30
to 6.30pm; otherwise Wednesdays and Sundays, 2.30 to 4.30pm.* On the right of
the nave is the shrine of Ste-Roseline, whose corpse is amazingly well preserved.
Pilgrimages take place three times a year, the most popular being on 2 August
(collection of votive offerings). An elegant Renaissance rood screen separates the nave
from the choir, which contains a superb late 15C Baroque altarpiece (high altar),
delicately carved 17C choir stalls; a Renaissance altarpiece of the Nativity (on the
right) and a precious 13C predella hanging (on the left).

Contemporary works of art include a large mosaic by Chagall *(right aisle)*, a bronze
low-relief depicting Ste-Roseline's life, a lectern in the shape of a bush by Giacometti's
brother, a stained glass window by Bazaine, in irridescent colours, and others by Ubac.

*In the village turn left into D 47. After 200 m – 220 yds there is a signposted path on
the left to the Capelan Leap (Saut du Capelan).*

**Capelan Leap.** – The Nartuby drops 35 m – 115 ft.

*Return to D 47 and turn right; after 3 km – 2 miles bear left into D 25.*

**Pennafort Fall** (Cascade de Pennafort). –*1/2 hour on foot Rtn.* Near a swimming pool
a path leads to a magnificent waterfall where the St-Pons stream drops between walls
of porphyry rock.

*Continue along D 25.* **Pennafort Chapel** stands on a spur at the meeting of two streams.

*At Les Quatre Chemins turn left into D 562 and return to Draguignan.*

## The DURANCE ★

Michelin map 🔢 folds 5, 6, 15 and 16

The Durance, the most temperamental river of the southern Alps, opens a wide breach
in the mountains of Haute Provence. After defying all attempts by engineers over the years
to dominate it, the old Torment of Provence has been mastered and today plays a
considerable economic role. It is the last big tributary to enter the Rhône on its left bank,
rises on Montgenèvre near Briançon, and follows an uneven course for 324 km –
201 miles.

At Sisteron the Durance enters the Mediterranean region. The river bed is broader
and less steeply inclined and the stream flows between banks of shingle which are rarely
covered even when the river is in spate. The dams on the main stream and its tributaries
have regulated the flow of water.

### Sisteron to Manosque – *74 km - 46 miles – about 3 1/2 hours – Local map p 60*

*Leave Sisteron (p 140) by N 85, ② on plan.* The road follows the river which is chanelled
between embankments towards Salignac dam. After crossing the Jabron tributary, the
road is squeezed in between the river and the steep slopes of Mount Lure. At
Château-Arnoux, the river broadens into L'Escale Lake.

**Château-Arnoux.** – Pop 6 240. *Facilities p 30.* The town has a pleasant outlook
over the lake which provides fishing and pleasure boating while there is sailing
at the nearby St-Auban Centre. The castle in Renaissance style has mullioned
windows.

*2 km – 1 mile further on turn right following the signpost to Chapelle St-Jean.*

**St-Jean Chapel Viewpoint★.** – *1 hour on foot Rtn from town centre. Take the path to the
top of the rock where there is a viewing table near the telecommunications
mast. Parking and picnic area.*

The **panorama★** comprises Mount Lure (W), the Durance (N) and Sisteron (NNW) valleys,
L'Escale **lake** and dam (E) against the Digne Pre-Alps (E) and Les Mées Rocks (S) *(see
p 60)* in the foreground.

*Return to N 96 and continue southwards.*

At St-Auban the road is separated from the river by the Rhône-Progil chemical complex
and the Sailing Centre. Opposite **Montfort**, a picturesque village set in olive groves on the
right, is the confluence of the Durance and the Bléone.

# The DURANCE★

*4 km – 2 1/2 miles beyond Montfort, turn left at the crossroads into D 4'A.*

**Les Mées Rocks★** (Rochers des Mées). – The town is dominated by rocks formed of stones held together by natural cement. 100 m – 330 ft high, they are known as the Penitents of Les Mées owing to the way they have been shaped by erosion. There is a legend attached to them. During the Saracen invasions, the monks of Mount Lure were captivated by some Moorish women that a local nobleman had brought back from a campaign against the Infidels. To punish the monks for their covetousness, St-Donat petrified them as they were out walking in single file beside the Durance, in their pointed hooded cloaks.

*Return to N 96 and go straight across into D 101.*

**St-Donat's Chapel.** – Archaeologists have shown great interest in this large 11C pilgrimage chapel, one of the earliest examples of the Romanesque style in Provence. It has a high nave beneath a semicircular vault, buttressed by narrow aisles.

*Return to N 96; turn right towards Manosque.*

**Peyruis.** – Pop 1 621. The old village used to be cut off by a drawbridge. The 16C church has a hexagonal tower built of tufa-stone with lion-headed gargoyles.

*6 km – 3 1/2 miles beyond Peyruis, turn right into D 30 a narrow road which meanders steeply uphill above the Durance valley.*

**Ganagobie Plateau and Priory★.** – *Description p 73.*

*Take D 30 back down hill but just before N 96 turn right into a wooded road leading to Lurs, which follows the line of the Roman Via Domitia and crosses the Buès by a single-arched **Roman bridge** constructed in 2C.*

**Lurs.** – *Description p 92.*

*Leave the village by the road going south and rejoin N 96 via D 12.*

On the far bank of the Durance stands the Oraison power station, fed by a canal. After the confluence of the Durance and the Asse, opposite Villeneuve, the road diverges from the river and follows the foothills of Mount Lubéron to Manosque.

## Manosque to Sisteron via Mount Lure – *87 km – 54 miles – about 2 1/2 hours – Local map above*

*Leave Manosque by D 5 going north – Mort d'Imbert Pass road – with fine views of Manosque. Turn right into D 16 to Forcalquier.*

*From Forcalquier the route is described on p 92.*

## ▮ EMBIEZ Island ★

Michelin map **84** fold 14 – *Local map p 139*

*Ferries from Port du Brusc every hour; 12 mins; 10F Rtn. Enquiries "Domaine des Embiez": ☎ 25.02.42.*

The island is one of a group lying off Port du Brusc on rich fishing banks which are the delight of the amateur. The main island (95 ha – 235 acres) has an astonishing diversity of natural features; fine beaches, wild coastline full of coves, salt marshes, pine woods, vineyards (the rosé is popular).

There is a busy modern marina overlooked by the mediaeval ruins of Sabran castle; the local houses are built in the Provençal style. Sport facilities, agreeable walks and all the pleasures of the seaside are to hand.

**Ricard Oceanographic Foundation ★.** – *Open 9am to 12.30pm and 1.30 to 5.45pm; closed Wednesday morning in winter, 25 December and 1 January; 7F; time: ½ hour.*

The old naval gun site on St-Pierre promontory houses the Foundation which contains research laboratories *(not open)* for marine biology and pollution of the ocean.

A **museum** on the ground floor displays an extensive collection of molluscs, stuffed fish and fossils.

The sea water **aquariums** *(first floor)* provide a natural environment for a hundred species of Mediterranean aquatic animals some in gorgeous colours: gorgonias, hermit crabs, blue lobsters, spider crabs, octopi, sting rays, scorpion fish, little eels.

From the upper terrace there is a **view★★** over Le Brusc bay, Cap Sicié (SE), Sanary (N), the mountains behind Toulon (NE) and the approach to Marseilles (W).

Michelin map 195 fold 13 – Pop 688

Opposite the site of Roman Glandèves on the south bank of the Var, stands Entrevaux, for many years a frontier town between France and the Kingdom of Savoy. It was fortified by Vauban between 1692 and 1706 and lies grouped along the left bank of the Var at the foot of a curious rocky spine crowned by the town citadel. The **setting**★★ is characteristic of the Var countryside.

**Fortified town**★. – The drawbridge at the National Gate (Porte Nationale) leads into the old town untouched since 18C. It is pleasant to stroll through the cool and shady old streets, particularly those in the cathedral quarter. The approaches to the Italian Gate (Porte d'Italie) and the square on which the town hall stands form delightful esplanades.

**Old Cathedral.** – *To visit apply to the presbytery.*

The original see of Glandèves was transferred to Entrevaux where it remained until the Revolution. With its crenelated bell-tower and its incorporation in the ramparts, the 17C church accords with the town's military aspect. The huge Classical door is decorated with carved panels. The **interior** is richly decorated in a mixture of Classical and Baroque. A fine 17C painting of the Assumption, its frame decorated with gold leaf, forms an **altarpiece** at the high altar. The 50 choir stalls were carved by local craftsmen at the same date. Two "Descents from the Cross" by Jouvenet *(left)* and Ph. de Champaigne *(right)* face each other. To the left of the entrance a rich altarpiece of John-the-Baptist stands next to a silver reliquary. The organ (1628) has been restored *(concerts in summer)*. In the **sacristy**, formerly an armament store, are 15C and 17C furniture and 17C silk chasubles.

**Citadelle.** – *Open 1 March to 31 August, 9am to noon and 3 to 6pm; 1 September to 28 February, 10 am to noon and 3 to 5pm; closed Mondays; 4F.*

A fortified ramp with 20 bastioned gates leads up to the Citadel which overhangs the town from its rocky perch 135 m – 443 ft high. The walk *(3/4 hour on foot Rtn)* opens up **views**★ of the town and the Var valley.

Michelin map 195 folds 33 and 34

The Esterel between St-Raphaël and La Napoule has a breath-taking beauty. One of the loveliest areas of Provence, it was opened to large scale tourism by the Touring Club's creation in 1903 of the Golden Corniche (Corniche d'Or).

The contrast between the busy life along the coast and the loneliness of the inland roads is extraordinary – the latter will please tourists who prefer to leave the well beaten paths for the pleasure of exploring on their own.

## GEOGRAPHICAL NOTES

**The Massif.** – The Esterel, which is as old as its neighbour the Maures, from which it is separated by the Argens Valley, has been worn down by erosion so that its highest point, Mount Vinaigre, is a mere 618 m – 2 027 ft. However, in this mountain mass, the deep ravines and broken skyline dispel any impression of mere hills.

The Esterel is made up of volcanic rocks (porphyry), which were forced up at the period of the Hercynian foldings thus differentiating it from the Maures. These hard porphyry rocks, which give the range its characteristic profile, its harsh relief and vivid colouring, appear in full beauty in the red tints of the Cap Roux range. At Agay is found the blue porphyry from which the Romans made the shafts of the columns for their monuments in Provence ; elsewhere the colours are green, yellow, purple or grey.

The jagged relief extends even into the sea: the mountains thrust promontories into the sea; the sea cuts deep into the mountains. On the mainland rugged points alternate with minute bays, narrow strands and small shady beaches or creeks between vertical walls; offshore are thousands of rocks and islets coloured green with lichen, while underwater there are reefs which can be clearly seen.

The fiery red of the rocks makes a striking contrast with the deep blue of the sea.

**Vegetation.** – The Esterel, like the Maures, was entirely covered with pine and cork oak forests until ravaged on several occasions by fire. Following the widespread forest fire which decimated practically all the Esterel in 1964, the "forest" only exists today in a few places *(see p 13: forest fires)*. Reafforestation is especially difficult, since, in addition to being on a considerable scale, the problem is exacerbated by a disease affecting sea pines. Replanting has therefore to be undertaken with new strains. The National Forestry Office has planted large areas round Fréjus and St-Raphaël; work is also proceeding in cutting back the cork oaks.

A dense vegetation of shrubs and bushes covers the ground: heaths, arbutus, lentisks, cistus, gorse, lavenders, etc. These slow down erosion and in spring and autumn their flowers provide a glorious mass of colour.

## HISTORICAL NOTES

**The Aurelian Way.** – On its inland side the Esterel was bounded on the north by the Aurelian Way *(Via Aurelia)*. The great road, constructed during the reign of Aurelius, went from Rome to Arles, by way of Nice, Antibes, Fréjus and Aix and was one of the most important of the Roman Empire.

The roadway, paved and cambered and more than 2.5 m – 8 ft wide, was laid upon a cement base, as is the N 7, which follows much the same route. In the local dialect it is still called *lou camin aurélian*. Taking the shortest route, it made use of many bridges and other civil engineering works. At the end of each Roman mile (1 478 m – 1 617 yds) a tall milestone indicated the distances – one can be seen in the St-Raphaël museum. As the road approached the towns, it had raised pavements for pedestrians, which also served as mounting blocks. Stage posts, equipped with hostelries, horses and workshops, minimised delays to the imperial post.

## ESTEREL Massif ★★★

**The Esterel Gap.** – The road round the north side of the Esterel, which was for many years the only land route to Italy, was rife with highwaymen; "to survive the Esterel Gap" became a local saying. The most dangerous spot was to the west of Mount Vinaigre; in those days the coach road left N 7 at the Logis-de-Paris crossroads and ran nearer the foothills past the forest guard house at Le Malpey (Evil Mountain).

The exploits of **Gaspard de Besse**, in the 18C have remained legendary. After attacking and plundering the coaches and horsemen passing within reach, Gaspard and his band took refuge in a cave on the side of Mount Vinaigre. The brigand chief loved elegance: he wore a splendid red costume ornamented with brilliants and fine silver buttons and buckles. For many years the mounted constabulary were at his heels. He also frequented the inn at Les Adrets, on the N 7. Surprised in another inn near Toulon, the pillager of the Esterel was broken on the wheel in 1781 at the age of twenty-five. His head was nailed to a tree on the road which had been the scene of his many escapades.

Even in 1787 the naturalist Saussure showed real courage in exploring the region on foot. Until the end of the 19C the massif remained the fastness of convicts escaping from Toulon.

### ① ESTEREL CLIFF ROAD★★★
#### St-Raphaël to Cannes – 40 km – 25 miles – about 2 hours – Local map p 62-63

*Leave St-Raphaël (p 134) by N 98, ① on the plan.* The road skirts the marina. On the sea front is a memorial to the campaigns of the French Army in Africa.

**Boulouris.** – *Facilities p 28.* This small resort, where villas are scattered among pines in beautiful gardens, has several little beaches and a pleasure harbour.

**Dramont Beach** (Plage du Dramont). – An inscribed tablet, to the right of the road, commemorates the landing of the U.S. Army 36th Division on 15 August 1944. The beach is bordered by the Dramont Forest which covers the headland.

*Immediately after the Dramont camping site, turn right. 100 m – 110 yds further on, leave the car and take a lefthand path leading up to the signal station.*

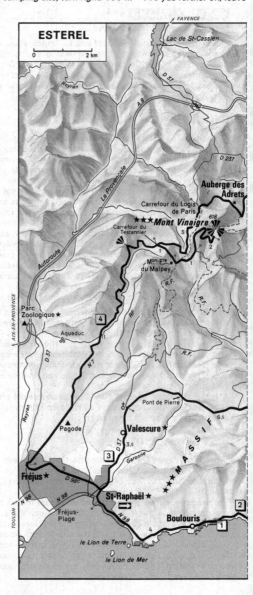

**Dramont Signal Station★★** (Sémaphore du Dramont). – *3/4 hour on foot Rtn.* From below the station there is a **panorama★★** : to the southwest of the Maures, of the two porphyry rocks guarding the entrance to the Gulf of Fréjus (the Lion of the Sea – *Lion de Mer* – and the Lion of the Land – *Lion de Terre),* Or Island *(Ile d'Or)* with its tower. On the horizon to the north is Mount Vinaigre; to the north east, behind the Rastel d'Agay peak in the foreground, can be seen the rocks of the Cap Roux range and lower down, on the right, the Agay roadstead and the lighthouse on the Baumette Point.

The road passes the beautiful Camp Long beach before reaching Agay.

**Agay★.** – *Facilities p 28.* The resort borders a deep anchorage, the best in the Esterel and used in earlier centuries by the Ligurians, the Greeks and the Romans. Beneath the waters have been found Roman *amphorae* which came, no doubt, from a ship which must have sunk some 2 000 years ago.

The bay is overlooked by the Rastel d'Agay, its slopes resplendent in red porphyry, and is lined by a large and sunny beach which extends eastwards as far as the small jetty and beyond by a more popular shady beach.

**Anthéor★.** – *Facilities p 28.* The resort of Anthéor is dominated by the three peaks of the Cap Roux range.

Just before Observatory Point there is a **view** inland of the red rocks of St-Barthélemy and Cap Roux. The Cap Roux peak road *(lefthand turning)* is described below.

**Observatory Point** (Pointe de l'Observatoire). – The ruins of a blockhouse look out over a beautiful **view★** with the blood-red porphyry rocks against the cobalt blue of the sea. From the point can be seen Anthéor (SW), Cap Roux Peak (inland) and Esquillon Point and La Napoule Bay further north east along the coast.

At this point the magnificent red rocks of the Esterel drop sheer into the sea.

**Le Trayas★.** – *Facilities p 28.* The resort is divided into two parts: one terraced on wooded slopes, the other by the sea shore. The creeks and inlets which mark the coast include many small beaches, the largest of which lies at the end of the Figueirette inlet. This bay was a centre for tunny fishing in the 17C when nets were cast offshore and left for four month. To watch the nets against marauders from the sea a tower, still standing, was built on the shore.

**Miramar★.** – An elegant resort with a private harbour in the curve of the Figueirette bay.

*On a bend near Tour de L'Esquillon Hotel, pull off the road into the car park. A path (signpost) leads up to L'Esquillon Point.*

**L'Esquillon Point★★.** – *1/4 hour on foot Rtn.* A beautiful **panorama★★** *(viewing table)* of the Esterel Heights, the coast, Cap Roux (S), the Lérins Islands and Cap d'Antibes (NE).

**La Galère★.** – The resort is built on wooded terraces on the slopes of the Esterel where it forms the western limit of La Napoule Bay. On the coast below is **Port-la-Galère marina** with unusual houses shaped like honeycombs.

The road rounds L'Aiguille Point, opening up a **view★** of La Napoule Bay, Cannes, the Lérins Islands and Cap d'Antibes.

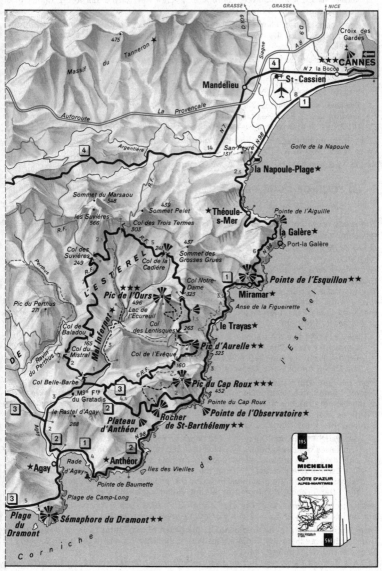

**Théoule-sur-Mer.** – Pop 798. *Facilities p 28.* This resort, which is protected by the Théoule promontory, has three small beaches. The crenelated building on the shore, now a château, was a soap factory in the 18C.

**La Napoule-Plage★.** – The seaside suburb of Mandelieu *(p 143)* lies at the foot of St Peter's Hill (San-Peyré); it has a marina and three sandy beaches. The view is magnificent.

**Castle Museum.** – *Guided tours at 3pm; closed in January, June, July and December and at other times. It is advisable to telephone 49.95.05. 8F.*
The three remaining towers of the massive 14C castle, were restored by the American sculptor, Henry Clews (1876-1937). The castle, a strange mixture of Romanesque, Gothic and oriental motifs, stands on a fine site★ surrounded by gardens which are included in the visit together with the chapel, cloister, rooms and studio. Henry Clews' sculptures belong to no particular school; they exhibit grim realism and fantastic romanticism. Art exhibitions and concerts are held in the castle in summer.

**San Peyré Viewpoint★.** – *Take Rue des Hautes-Roches from the Post Office; 3/4 hour on foot Rtn following the arrows.* From the top of the hill, the view extends over the Tanneron Massif (NW), La Napoule Bay and Cannes and Cap d'Antibes (ENE).

After crossing the river Siagne, N 98 skirts La Napoule Bay before reaching Cannes *(p 47)*.

## ② CAP ROUX PEAK ★★

*38 km – 24 miles – about 1 hour (excluding walks) – Local map p 62-63*

Leave St-Raphaël (p 134) by N 98, ① on the plan: the road as far as Agay is described on p 62.

Leaving Agay take the Valescure road and then at the fork bear right towards Ours Peak (Pic de l'Ours). Beyond the Gratadis Forest Hut bear right. After fording the river Agay, bear right again around the north side of the Rastel d'Agay in the direction of St Bartholomew's Rock (Rocher de St-Barthélemy).

**Anthéor Plateau.** – *Picnic area.* There is an overall view of the sea to the right and of neighbouring peaks to the left.

The road continues to climb; to the right there is a view★ of steep slopes plunging into the sea, to the left of the red rocks of St-Pilon and Cap Roux; in the background is the Ours Peak.

**St Bartholomew's Rock.** – *1/2 hour on foot Rtn from the car park.* A staircase carved into the stone leads to the top of the rock from where there is a magnificent view★★ of the Agay roadstead and the Bay of Fréjus (SW) and of the rocky inlets of Le Trayas and La Napoule Bay (NE).

**Cap Roux Peak★★★** (Pic du Cap Roux). – *2 hours on foot Rtn from the car park.* The path leading to Cap Roux Peak is indicated by arrows and orange marks. From the summit (452 m – 1 483 ft) there is a marvellous circular view★★★ *(viewing table)*.

From St Bartholomew's Rock, the road plunges down steep rocky hillsides and emerges on to N 98, 100 m – 110 yds from Observatory Point *(p 63)*.

Return to St-Raphaël by **Anthéor★**, **Agay★**, Dramont, and Boulouris *(p 62)*.

## ③ TOUR OF OURS PEAK ★★

*53 km – 33 miles – about 1 1/2 hours (excluding walks) – Local map pp 62-63*

The roads taken are hilly, narrow and not always surfaced and not regularly cleared of rock slides especially in the Trois Termes Pass and the Mistral Pass.

Leave St-Raphaël (p 134) by N 98, ① on the plan; the road as far as Agay is described on p 62.

From Agay take the Valescure road bearing right at the fork towards Ours Peak. After Gratadis Forest Hut, bear right and, having forded the Agay river, bear left to Ours Peak. The road climbs past evergreen oaks, barren land and red rocks, with the Mal Infernet ravine in the distance. Winding round the north side of St-Pilon and Cap Roux, the road reaches Evêque Pass, then slopes downhill to the Lentisques Pass with frequent glimpses of the sea to the right.

**Aurelle Peak★★** (Pic d'Aurelle). – *1 hour on foot Rtn by a marked path starting from the Lentisques Pass.* The Aurelle is one of the major peaks in the coastal chain of the Esterel. From the top (323 m – 1 060 ft) a fine panorama★★ takes in the area between the Cap d'Antibes and Observatory Point.

From the Lentisques Pass to Notre-Dame Pass is one of the most beautiful drives in the Esterel. Immediately overlooking the coast, the road offers breathtaking bird's-eye views★ of the Esterel Corniche and splendid perspectives of the shore looking towards the Cap d'Antibes. From Notre-Dame Pass (323 m – 1 060 ft) a remarkable panorama extends over Cannes, the Lérins Islands and La Napoule Bay.

**Ours Peak★★★** (Pic de l'Ours). – *1 1/2 hours on foot Rtn. Car park at Notre-Dame Pass.* The series of hairpin bends by which the road reaches the summit affords constantly changing views of the wooded ranges of the Esterel and the deeply indented coastline. The remarkable panorama★★★ from the summit (496 m – 1 627 ft) where there is a television transmitting station, includes the coast – from the Maures to the Alps – the Esterel range, dominated by Mount Vinaigre and the Var countryside.

*Return to Notre-Dame Pass. The road north via Cadière Pass is for the adventurous who are not daunted by 9 km – 6 miles of rough unsurfaced tracks.*

From Notre-Dame Pass the road clings to the peaks of the Petites Grues and the Grosses Grues before reaching the Cadière Pass where the view★ opens to the north towards La Napoule and the Tanneron range.

At Trois Termes Pass, bear left on to a track *(poor surface)* towards the Suvières Pass.

Along the heights of the porphyry rocks at the summit of the Suvières *(to the right),* the evergreen and cork oaks cling to the face of the mountains. At the Suvières Pass, bear left *(towards the Mistral Pass)* along the harsh Baladou road; to the right are the red porphyry rocks of the Perthus Peaks. At the Mistral Pass the track joins a metalled road; turn left to the Belle-Barbe Pass.

**Mal Infernet Ravine★.** – *1 1/2 hours on foot Rtn.* At the Belle-Barbe Pass, a track to the left leads to a car park.
Continue on foot into the ravine, an awe-inspiring landscape bristling with jagged rocks. The path ends at Ecureuil Lake.

*Return to Belle-Barbe Pass; turn left and then bear right. At the fork after the Gratadis Forest Hut, bear right into the road to St-Raphaël via Valescure.*

The landscape changes abruptly from the rocky wilderness of the Esterel to gentle hilly country where vineyards and orchards have been planted among the broom, eucalyptus and umbrella pines.

**Valescure★.** – The hotels and villas of this resort, the aristocratic extension of St-Raphaël, are scattered over the wooded hillsides, creating a huge landscaped park. It acquired its reputation from the English who used to come for the golf, the mild climate and the tranquillity.

## ④ AURELIAN WAY★
### Cannes to St-Raphaël – *46 km – 29 miles – about 3 hours – Local map p 62-63*

*Leave Cannes (p 47) by N 7, ③ on the plan.*

For most of the way this route runs through the Esterel Forest. After passing through the industrial zone of La Bocca, the road crosses the alluvial plain of the Siagne river. *Turn left into the road leading to Cannes-Mandelieu aerodrome.*

**St-Cassien Hermitage.** – The 17C chapel standing on a low rise in an oak plantation with a few cypress trees standing guard makes a charming picture. Tradition says it was once the site of a Roman temple; now it is a place of pilgrimage.

*Return to N 7.*

**Mandelieu.** – *Description p 143.*

On the left is the seaside development of Cannes-Marina. The road begins to climb the Argentière valley between the Esterel and Tanneron Heights. There are good views to the rear of Cannes and the Lerins Islands across La Napoule Bay.

**Les Adrets Inn.** – Favourite haunt of the highwayman Gaspard de Besse *(p 62)*.

At the Logis-de-Paris crossroads the road skirts the foot of Mount Vinaigre, the highest peak in the Esterel (618 m – 2 028 ft).

*At the Testannier crossroads, turn left into a road marked* "Forêt domaniale de l'Esterel". At the Malpey Forest Hut, follow the sign to Mount Vinaigre.

**Mount Vinaigre★★★.** – *1/2 hour on foot Rtn.* A path leads to the top. Bear left to the old watchtower and climb the steps inside to reach the platform which offers a splendid **panorama★★★** on all sides: on the coast Cap d'Antibes, Pointe de la Croisette, Cannes and La Napoule Bay (NE), Ours Peak with its tower and TV mast, Cap Roux Peak (SE) and Fréjus Bay (SW); inland the Maures Massif and the Argens valley (SW), and the limestone hills of Provence (NW). On a fine day one can see as far as the Alps (NE) and Ste-Baume (SW).

*Return to N 7.* At the second lefthand double bend, there is a **view** north-west towards Fayence; then the road follows the valley of the Maure. The original Aurelian Way however followed the line of the forest road on the opposite bank.

**Fréjus★.** – *Description p 69.*

*Return to St-Raphaël (p 134) by Bld. S.-Descuers.*

---

## ÈZE ★★
Michelin map ❶❾❺ fold 27 – *Local map pp 122-123* – Pop 1 860

Èze, a strange isolated village, is a prime example of a hill village *(see p 21 for information on hill villages)*: it clings, like an eagle's nest, to a rock spike towering 427 m – 1 550 ft over the sea. Each year numerous painters and tourists in search of the picturesque crowd its **site★★**.
Legend claims that it was founded by the Saracens but in origin it was a Ligurian settlement which subsequently came under the rule of the Phœnicians, Romans and Saracens and then of various families, even rising to the status of a county in 16C.

■ **SIGHTS** *time: 1 1/4 hours*

**Old streets★.** – A 14C double gateway with crenelations and a sentry walk leads into the steep narrow streets, sometimes stepped and sometimes running beneath the carefully restored houses which are now smart boutiques and artists' studios. At every turn there are flowers and shrubs and fountains and breathtaking views of the sea and mountains.

**White Penitents' Chapel** (B). – *Open 8am to 7pm all year.*
The simple 14C building is decorated with enamelled panels illustrating the life and death of Christ and his mother.
To the left on entering is a Crucifixion, an early example of the Nice school; on the high altar an unusual Catalan crucifix dating from 1258 in which Christ is smiling; on the right a 16C hexagonal ciborium in mahogany; on the left a 14C statue, the Madonna of the Forest, so called because the child she is holding has a pine cone in his hand.

## ÈZE ★★

**Tropical Gardens (Jardin exotique).** – *Open 8am (9am 1 October to 14 June) to sunset. 4F.*

Many varieties of succulents and cacti flourish in the gardens crowned by the remains of a castle built in the 14C and dismantled on the orders of Louis XIV in 1706.

There is a splendid **panorama**★★★ from the terrace of the Riviera (on a fine morning Corsica is visible).

**Church (D).** – The church was rebuilt in 18C with a Classical façade and a two-storey tower. The Baroque interior contains a fine statue of the Assumption (18C) attributed to Muerto and an emblazoned 15C font.

**Frederick-Nietzsche Path.** – *1 hour on foot Rtn.* Nietzsche first thought out his masterpiece *Thus Spake Zarathustra* on the picturesque mulepath which winds down towards the Lower Corniche (Corniche Inférieure). It leads through pinewoods and olive groves to the seaside resort of Èze-Bord-de-Mer *(p 124)* which has been built along the Lower Corniche road.

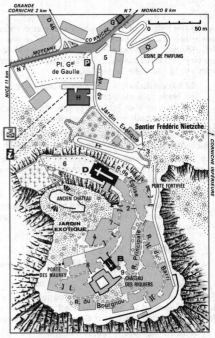

**ÈZE**

---

## FAYENCE

Michelin map 🗺 folds 7 and 8 – *Local map below* – Pop 2 146 – *Facilities p 30*

Fayence lies opposite its twin village, Tourrettes, on the Draguignan to Grasse road overlooking an important gliding field. It has an enviable position, between the mountains and the sea, ringed by picturesque villages and only 10 km – 6 miles from St-Cassien Lake. Potters, wood carvers (olive wood), weavers, painters and coppersmiths work there.

**Church.** – Built in 18C, the building is Classical with tall pillars supporting a gallery round the nave. There are two altarpieces of Christ and a predella of the Apocalypse.

From the terrace on the right of the church there is a **view**★ over the gliding field to the Maures and Esterel Heights.

**Old Castle Panorama.** – *Follow the signs from the church.* The view is to the north to the Pre-Alps of Castellane and Grasse.

**Old town.** – Below the church, steep streets, lined by handsome house doorways, lead to the town gates.

### *EXCURSIONS*

**Bel-Homme Pass**★. – *Round trip of 64 km – 40 miles – about 4 hours.* Key to N.-D.-des-Cyprès is available from the parish priest in Fayence (villa St-Pierre behind the church).

*Leave Fayence by D 563 going south. Almost immediately on the right is the turning (signpost) to N.-D.-des-Cyprès.*

**N.-D.-des-Cyprès.** – The Romanesque chapel, which contains a 16C altarpiece set in a Baroque frame, looks out over Fayence and Tourrettes.

*Return to D 563 which skirts Fayence aerodrome and turn right into D 562 which crosses several streams as it winds among trees.* To the north the villages of Fayence, Tourrettes and Montauroux are strung out along the ridge.

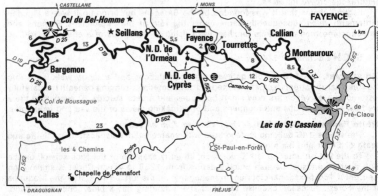

*At Quatre Chemins turn right into D 25.*

**Callas.** – Pop 708. Grouped round the castle ruins against a hillside of olive, oak and pine trees, Callas is still a typical village of the Haut-Var. A fire alarm disfigures the campanile but the Romanesque church, heavily restored in 19C, displays a 17C altarpiece above nine hooded penitents on their knees.

From the terrace the **view** south takes in the Maures and Esterel Heights.

Continue along D 25 which goes over the Boussague Pass and winds up a pleasant valley to Bargemon.

**Bargemon.** – *Description p 38.*

*Leave Bargemon by D 25 going north west.* The road climbs steeply offering fine views of Bargemon and its neighbourhood.

**Bel-Homme Pass★.** – Alt 951 m – 3 120 ft. A path on the left leads to the top. From the viewing table a **panorama★** extends south to the coast, north east to Grasse, north to the Canjuers Plateau and the mountains round Castellane.

*Return to Bargemon and take D 19 towards Fayence.* The road climbs above the town before turning eastwards through pine trees, evergreen oaks and broom. On the southern horizon rise the Maures and Esterel Heights.

**Seillans★.** – Pop 1 211. *Facilities p 30.* The pink and cream houses cascade down the steep slope of the Canjuers Plateau. Pleasant cobbled lanes lead up to the old castle with its ramparts and fountain and to the church (11C-15C) which contains two 15C triptychs and a marble stoup (1491). It is well known for its honey and herbs.

*Continue on D 19 towards Fayence for 1 km – 1/2 mile.*

**N.-D.-de-L'Ormeau.** – *Open Sundays 1 to 5pm in winter, 2 to 6pm in summer or apply to Mme Autheman, Rue de la Cappellette, ☎ (94) 76.05.02.*

The Romanesque chapel hidden in a clump of trees has a bell-tower of dressed stone but is marred by the later addition of an open porch. Inside is a remarkable 16C **altarpiece★★** carved and painted by an Italian monk: in the centre a crowd of people climbing the Tree of Jesse, on the left the Adoration of the Shepherds, on the right the Adoration of the Magi, very sensitively expressed. The predella, beneath a wooden peristyle, illustrates the life of Ste-Anne, the birth and marriage of the Virgin, the Annunciation *(damaged)*. On the right of the chancel is an early statue of Our Lady of the Elm and to the left of the main door a Roman tomb with an inscription.

Return to Fayence by D 19 with open views of the countryside.

**St-Cassien Lake.** – *Round trip of 29 km – 18 miles – about 2 hours. Local map p 66. Leave Fayence by the road to Tourrettes (SW).*

**Tourrettes.** – Pop 954. The unusual castle, modelled on the St Petersburg Cadet School, was built for a general under the Empire.

*Turn left into D 19, D 562 and D 56 to reach Callian.*

**Callian.** – Pop 1 230. Streets of old houses spiral round the castle on a delightful **site**. A fountain plays under the trees on the main square which looks south west over the local flower fields to St-Cassien Lake beneath the Tanneron Heights. The Esterel and Maures Heights dominate the horizon to the south.

Leave the village on the north side and turn right into D 37 which overlooks Callian and Montauroux.

**Montauroux.** – Pop 1 375. There are 17C and 18C houses in Rue de la Rouguière and a **view** from the square of St-Cassien Lake, the Tanneron Heights (SW), with a glimpse of the Maures and the Esterel. Standing apart is **St-Barthélemy's Chapel,** the former parish church *(key available at the Presbytery or Town Hall).* The building is Romanesque with a painted vaulted ceiling (17C) and a gilded wooden altarpiece (1748).

*Continue on D 37 crossing D 562.*

**St-Cassien Lake.** – From the Pré-Claou bridge there is a **view** of the whole lake which supplies water for irrigation. Its wooded slopes attract game hunters and fishermen. There are facilities for bathing and other water sports (except motor boating).

*Return to Fayence by D 37; turn left into D 562 and right into D 19.*

## FORCALQUIER

Michelin map **81** fold 15 – *Local map p 60* – Pop 3 436 – *Facilities p 30*

The town lies in a natural sandstone amphitheatre between the Lure and Lubéron mountains on a picturesque **site** overlooking the Durance. Its name derives from an old lime kiln *(furnus calcarius* in Latin, Fourcauquié in Provençal). In the Middle Ages it was the capital of the County of Haute-Provence.

**A powerful County.** – In 10C the Citadel of Forcalquier sheltered the relics of St Mary, St Donat's companion. Late in 11C a branch of the Count of Provence's family created the sovereign County of Forcalquier bordering the Durance from Apt and Manosque in the south via Forcalquier, Sisteron and Gap to Embrun in the north. By 12C the Counts of Forcalquier were a rival power to the Counts of Provence but in 1195 Gersende de Sabran, Countess of Forcalquier married Alphonse II, Count of Provence and their son, **Raymond Bérenger V,** inherited both counties early in 13C. This was the period when the Provençal language was made famous by the troubadours with their poems on chivalry and courtly love. Count Raymond Bérenger held a «court of love» at his castle in Forcalquier and Ugolin de Forcalquier was among the best known troubadours.

**Town with Four Queens.** – Raymond Bérenger's four daughters, who each married a king *(p 159),* were brought up in St-Maime to the south east of Forcalquier. The County passed to the House of Anjou and in 1481, together with the County of Provence, was willed to the French king who was henceforward styled Count of Provence and Forcalquier along with his other titles.

■ **MAIN SIGHTS** *time: 1 3/4 hours*

**Cemetery★**. – *Leave the town centre by D 16 going north and turn left after 200 m – 220 yds.*

A majestic central stairway leads down to the lower part of the cemetery where age-old yews and box hedges have been clipped into unusual shapes. The cemetery is enclosed by great walls of evergreen hollowed out into alcoves.

**Notre-Dame Church (E)**. – The former cathedral is Romanesque in origin (rib vaulting in the high nave) with many 13C Gothic additions. The massive square tower, built in 17C in Romanesque style, contrasts with the slender belfry supporting a lantern. An elegant Gothic door opens beneath a fine rose window. The transept and pentagonal choir are Gothic; the side aisles were added in 17C in the same style. The great **organ** (17C), has been twice restored and is among the finest in Provence *(concerts)*.

**Franciscan Monastery (Couvent des Cordeliers)**. – *Guided tours 1 July to 30 September, 10.30am to noon and 2.30 to 6.30pm; 1 April to 1 November, Sundays only 2 to 5pm; closed November to March; 8F; time: ¾ hour.*

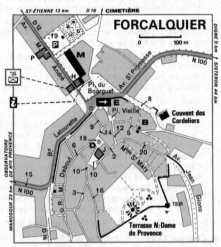

Originally a private house, the property was given to the Franciscans in 1236 by Raymond Béranger V; it was one of the earliest Franciscan foundations in Provence and remained in their possession until 18C. The buildings which date from 12C to 14C were damaged during the Wars of Religion and the Revolution and have been partially restored. The public may visit part of the cloisters which are lined with arcaded recesses – twin bays frame a Romanesque door into the Chapter House – and the restored conventual buildings: library (original ceiling), scriptorium, oratory (15C wooden statue of Virgin and Child), crypt and refectory, divided into three rooms.

Exhibitions and concerts take place in summer.

**Old town.** – The **Franciscan Gate** (Porte des Cordeliers) **(B)** is all that remains of the old fortifications. The house with balcony above is 14C. The gate leads into a network of narrow streets lined by tall houses designed to exclude the north wind *(Mistral)*. Many of the houses are dilapidated but here and there a handsome façade with twin bays survives or a fine doorway in the Gothic, Renaissance or Classical style. The **Gothic fountain (D)** in Place St-Michel is shaped like a pyramid and surmounted by St Michael fighting the dragon.

■ **ADDITIONAL SIGHTS**

**N.-D.-de-Provence Terrace.** – Starting from the Castellane-Adhémar mansion (arcaded door) Montée St-Mary leads up to the citadel past the castle ruins and traces of the first cathedral dedicated to St-Mary.

The octagonal chapel, built in 1875, is dedicated to Our Lady of Provence. There is a **panorama★** over the valley and the neighbouring mountain chains *(viewing table)* and a bird's eye view of town.

**Museum (M)**. – *Open 3 to 4pm; closed Saturdays, Sundays and holidays; 5F.*

The former convent of the Visitandines (17C), which later became a Jesuit College, has been converted into a museum which now houses a collection of local archaeology and artefacts (tools, furniture, china from Moustiers, Apt and Mane) and coins from Augustus to Louis-Philippe.

*EXCURSIONS*

**Lure Mountains★**. – *64 km – 40 miles – about 2 hours – Local map p 60 – description p 91.*

**Haute-Provence Observatory.** – *Round trip of 36 km – 22 miles – about 2 hours (excluding visit to the Observatory) – Local map p 60. Leave Forcalquier by N 100 going south.*

The rich countryside to the south of Forcalquier contrasts with the severity of the foothills of the Lure to the north.

**Mane.** – Pop 834. Large sections of the castle walls, some dating from 12C, are still standing; they circle the bluff above the town forming two ramps one above the other. The site has been occupied since Roman times and has been pillaged for stone to construct many of the local buildings. The 16C church has a Renaissance style west front.

500 m – 1 640 yds beyond Mane on the right is a small wall-belfry with two arches.

**N.-D.-de-Salagon.** – *Key available from the Town Hall (Mairie) at Mane.* The 12C church was part of a priory, a dependence of the Benedictine Abbey in Villeneuve-les-Avignon abandoned during the Revolution.

The **doorway** is framed by arch mouldings supported on slender columns crowned by Corinthian capitals which are repeated in the interior. Above and to each side of the doorway are strapwork and leaf mouldings; the tympanum shows traces of distemper.

Soon after the church, set back from the road on the righthand side, is a three-arched **Roman bridge.**

1 km – 1/2 mile further on Sauvan castle comes into view at the end of a carriage drive on the left.

**Sauvan Castle.** – *Guided tours Easter to 30 September, 2.30 to 7pm; closed Saturdays, Sundays, holidays and 1 October to Easter; 10F.*

One of the most beautiful Classical style houses in Provence, echoing the "Petit Trianon", it was begun in 1719 by Michel-François de Forbin-Janson. In 1793 the Mistress of Sauvan, Princess de Gallean, who strongly resembled Marie-Antoinette, is said to have tried to save the Queen by taking her place in the Conciergerie.

The main façade is ordered in the strictly Classical manner with a wrought–iron balcony and pediment. The porch is decorated with scroll work. The garden front is faced with tall columns in Mane stone.

*Return to N 100 and, 5 km – 3 miles further on, turn right into D 105.* On the right is **St-Paul's Chapel,** a simple oratory with thick columns terminating in Corinthian capitals, once part of a 12C priory.

**St-Michel-l'Observatoire.** – Pop 553. A few mediaeval houses and some of the defensive walls can be seen in the hillside village. The **lower church** has a curious silhouette: a pedimented Classical doorway beneath an ogival archivolt. The **upper church** at the top of the village *(key available from the bakery or on Wednesdays from the butcher)* is a well-proportioned white stone structure, flanked by a bell-tower in the Romanesque tradition. The barrel vaulted nave is 12C as is the cupola on squinches. At the entrance is a handsome stoup of marble carved with lions face to face. The arches in the chancel are supported by wreathed columns beneath Corinthian capitals. A 14C fresco shows Christ in Glory.

From the upper terrace there is a fine **view** of Forcalquier and the Lure (N) and Lubéron (SW) mountains.

*Take D 305 going north.*

**Haute-Provence Observatory★.** – *Open 3pm on Wednesday; 9.30am first Sunday in the month, April to September. 5F. 1 1/2 hours.*

The Observatory was established near Forcalquier because of the district's pure atmosphere. Fourteen domes contain astronomical instruments, laboratories, workshops and lodgings which are used by the staff of the National Centre for Scientific Research (CNRS) and foreign experts. There is an electronic **telescope**, 1.93 m in diameter. Some of the most powerful spectographs in the world are used to analyse starlight and to work out the chemical composition, the temperature and the radial speed of the stars.

From the Observatory a **view★** extends out over a sea of holm oaks to the Lubéron (SW), the Pre-Alps of Grasse (E) and Digne (NE), Forcalquier and the Lure (N).

*Return to St-Michel-l'Observatoire and take D 5 to Dauphin, then D 16 and finally D 13 to Forcalquier.*

## FRÉJUS ★

Michelin map ███ fold 33 – *Local maps pp 62-63 and 94-95 – Pop 30 607 – For additional plan of Fréjus see the current Michelin Guide France.*

Fréjus lies between the Maures and the Esterel, in the alluvial plain of the Lower Argens, where vineyards and fruit orchards flourish. The town itself is built on a rock plateau whose slopes descend gently towards the sea about a mile away.

Fréjus attracts lovers of the past; its Roman ruins, although unspectacular, are among the most varied in France and its episcopal city, is of architectural interest.

The construction at Fréjus-Plage on the coast of flats and houses for holiday letting has encouraged a local tourist industry.

## HISTORICAL NOTES

**Birth and Hey-day (1C BC).** – Fréjus takes its name "Forum Julii", a village founded by Julius Caesar in 49 BC , as a trading and staging post on the great coastal road which was to become known as the Aurelian Way *(p 61).*

Octavius, the future Emperor Augustus, turned the market town into an important naval base, where he built and trained the fast, manoeuvrable light galleys which were later to win the battle of Actium (31 BC) against the heavy ships of Cleopatra and Antony.

Augustus established in Fréjus a large colony of his veterans (soldiers who had finished their military duties and to whom were given, along with the full rights of a Roman citizen, a sum of money and some land). The city developed (construction of the Platform or military headquarters and St Antony's Mound) until it numbered 40 000 inhabitants. It was exceedingly prosperous.

**Fréjus 2 000 years ago.** – The plan shown on p 71 gives an idea of Forum Julii. Ramparts surrounded it, pierced by four gateways corresponding to the two large perpendicular streets, quartering the town, in the tradition of Roman cities. Soldiers, sailors and citizens enjoyed the arenas, theatre and baths free of charge.

An aqueduct 40 km – 25 miles long brought fresh water from the Siagnole near Mons *(p 78)* as far as the water tower *(castellum)* from which it was piped to the fountains and public installations.

Among the naval bases of the Roman world only Fréjus and Ostia, in Italy, offer sufficient remains to be reconstructed: from the eastern end of the Paul Vernet Square (Roman forum), one can look down on the plain where the port lay 2 000 years ago and, with the aid of the traces which are still visible, one can evoke fairly easily its shape, size and facilities.

The port, which was created in the first place by dredging and deepening a lagoon, was reconstructed during the reign of Augustus.

The harbour of some 22 ha – 54 acres, a considerable area for those times, included well over 2 km – 1 mile of quays of which traces still remain. It was linked with the sea by means of a canal, protected by a wall from the mistral and approximately 30 m – 98 ft wide and 500 m – 1 640 ft long – the shore line has receded since Roman times. The entrance was guarded by two large symmetrical towers, of which one, bearing the Lantern of Augustus, still rises high above the plain at the end of the south quay. An iron chain, which lay on the bottom all day, was stretched between the towers at night.

A strong outward current, obtained by a secondary canal from the Argens, prevented the harbour from silting up.

A large tower, boatyards, baths and buildings – the harbour-master's office, a health control office and fuller's earth laundry – completed the installations, together with the *palaestra* (sports ground) and hospital, of which traces are to be found at the Villeneuve farm, south-west of the town.

**Decline.** – During the long years of Roman peace, the military aspect declined and in late 2C AD the fleet was moved away but the port remained a lively commercial centre until 4C. Under Constantine an archbishopric was established. The harbour and canal, however, were neglected and began to silt up.

At the beginning of 10C the town was destroyed by the Saracens. In 990 under Bishop Riculphe the city rose again on a much smaller scale; the mediaeval town walls *(plan p 71)* followed the line of Rue Jean-Jaurès and Rue Grisolle.

Henri II turned Fréjus into a large naval base, but the sailors complained of the fevers they contracted in the now marshy country.

Finally, under the Revolution, the whole port was sold as a national estate and was filled in by its new owner.

■ **THE CATHEDRAL CLOSE**★★ *time: 3/4 hour*

This fortified unit comprised: the cathedral, the cloister and annexes, the baptistry and the bishop's palace. From the Place Formigé go down a few steps beneath the cathedral porch until you come to the stairway into the cloister; on the left is the baptistry, on the right the cathedral entrance.

*To visit apply at the bottom of the stairs (bell on the left) leading to the cloister. Guided tours 1 April to 30 September, 9.30am to noon and 2 to 6pm; the rest of the year 9.30am to noon and 2 to 4.30pm; closed Tuesdays and some holidays; 5F.*

**Portal.** – Under an ogee arch are two **panels**★ (1) *(the keeper will open the protective shutters)* carved in 16C to illustrate scenes in the life of the Virgin, St Peter and St Paul, portraits (resembling Francis 1 and Claude of France) and military motifs.

**Baptistry**★★. – This building, one of the most ancient in France, is thought to go back to the end of the 4C or beginning of the 5C. Separated from the cathedral by the porch, it has a square external appearance with sides about 11 m – 36 ft long; the inside is in the form of an octagon with, alternately spaced in the walls, round and flat-backed niches separated by black granite columns. These are topped by capitals of marble taken from Fréjus ancient forum and support the cupola which was reconstructed in 19C. Excavations have uncovered the original white marble pavement, the mosaics in the niches and the piscina.

A wrought iron grille (2), given by Cardinal de Fleury, tutor and minister to Louis XV, who was at one time Bishop of Fréjus, leads to the baptistry. Formerly the two doors on either side of the grille were used: by the lower door (3) the candidates for baptism entered and, after being baptised by the bishop, left by the upper, triumphal door (4) as new Christians. Dressed in a white tunic, they then went to the cathedral, attended full mass for the first time and received their first communion.

Baptism was often administered to adults. It is believed that originally the bishop washed the feet of

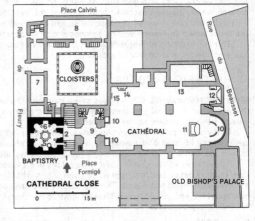

candidates in an earthenware basin *(dolium)* (5) found in the ground. Then immersion took place in the octagonal font (6) situated in the centre of the baptistry. A curtain, fixed to columns, surrounded the font. Unction was then administered on the head with holy oil.

**Cloisters★★**. – The 13C cloisters were intended for the chapter canons and comprised two storeys; only one upper gallery remains. The ground level clerestory is formed by a series of twin columns of white marble with varied capitals. The groined vaults which once covered the galleries were replaced in the 14C by a pinewood ceiling with visible beams, decorated in the 15C with curious little painted panels of animals, chimera, grotesques and characters from the Apocalypse. On the first floor the columns are finer and the arches round; on the ground floor the arches are pointed – such variations are often found in the architecture of Provence.

In the garth there is a well. The west gallery is flanked by a once fortified building (7), where the monks lodged. It has beautiful windows on the first floor.

**Archaeological Museum (8)**. – It contains a good collection of Gallo-Roman antiquities recovered from the Fréjus excavations. Particularly outstanding are a Roman mosaic with floral motifs and geometrical designs, a two headed Hermes in marble, a head of Jupiter (1C BC) and several statues in marble and bronze. One room is devoted to Old Fréjus.

**Cathedral★**. – Bishop Riculphe had built at the end of the 10C, on the remains of an old basilica, itself built over a former temple to Jupiter, a fortified church which exists in part to this day.

The porch (9) supporting the belfry was erected two hundred years later. Over the apse rises the battlemented tower which once defended the episcopal palace.

The nave, flanked by an aisle with a semi-circular vault, is roofed with heavy vaulting supported on enormous square pillars.

The lovely **choirstalls (10)** in the chancel date from the 15C and the high altar (11) of white marble from the 18C.

There are also two 14C tombs (12); a **triptych (13)** painted by the Nice artist, Jacques Durandi above the sacristy door and at the end of the aisle, near the tombs (15) of the bishops of Camelin, a wooden Renaissance Crucifix (14) especially venerated by the faithful.

The cathedral is dedicated to Our Lady and St Stephen and is an interesting example of early Gothic art in Provence.

**Old Bishop's Palace.** – The façade on the square is modern, the other overlooking Rue du Beausset formed part of the palace dating from the 14C which was built in pink sandstone from the Esterel.

**Chapter House.** – The uncut stone façade of the Chapter House, known locally as "Le Capitou" or the Provost's House (Maison du Prévot), looks down on Rue de Fleury. The doorway pierces a fortified tower at ground level; on the first floor twin windows beneath round arches.

■ **THE ROMAN CITY★** *time: 1 hour*

The Roman city covered about 40 ha – 99 acres.

**Arena★ (or amphitheatre).** – *Open 1 April to 30 September, 9.30am to noon and 2 to 7pm; the rest of the year, 9am to noon and 2 to 4.30pm; closed Tuesdays and from 25 October to 25 November; 3F. Four bullfights take place in July and August.*

The arena was the oldest in Gaul and is relatively badly damaged. It measures 113 m long by 82 m wide – 124 x 93 yds (Nîmes 143 yds by 109 yds; Arles 149 yds by 117 yds), and could accommodate approximately 10 000 spectators. Half the amphitheatre lies against the flank of the hill crowned by ramparts.

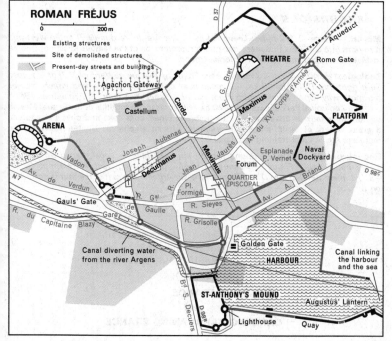

ROMAN FRÉJUS

0 ____ 200 m

Existing structures
Site of demolished structures
Present-day streets and buildings

THEATRE
Rome Gate
Aqueduct
Agachon Gateway
Castellum
PLATFORM
ARENA
Naval Dockyard
Esplanade P. Vernet
Forum
QUARTIER ÉPISCOPAL
Gauls' Gate
Golden Gate
Canal diverting water from the river Argens
HARBOUR
Canal linking the harbour and the sea
ST-ANTHONY'S MOUND
Augustus' Lantern
Lighthouse
Quay

Destined primarily for the pleasure of soldiers and veterans, the arena was clearly built with an eye to austerity and economy. It differs in this respect from the amphitheatres which were erected at Arles and Nîmes. These were destined for a much more sophisticated public.

Two columns discovered on a Roman wreck in the Gulf of St-Tropez in 1954 and brought in 1968 to the flat junction of the N 7 and D 37 can be seen to the southwest from the grass surrounding the arena.

**The Gauls' Gateway.** – The old gateway through the Roman ramparts is half-moon shaped. Of the two towers which once flanked it only one remains.

**Theatre.** – This theatre, contemporary with the arena, consists now of only the radial walls on which once rested the arching supporting the tiers of seats. It measures 84 m by 60 m – 92 x 66 yds.

Inside, the orchestra pit is clearly visible, together with the stage foundations and the groove into which the curtain was lowered.

**Aqueduct.** – Only pillars and ruined arcades now remain of the aqueduct which reached the city at the height of the ramparts. The water was then carried round beneath the northern parapet walk as far as the water tower *(castellum)* from which the distribution conduits started.

**The Platform.** – Still known as the eastern Citadel, this area shows traces of a Roman platform which served as the military headquarters: offices, storerooms, lodgings and baths. To the south lay the naval dockyard.

**Orée Gate.** – The gate consists of a fine arch and the remains of a chamber which formed part of the harbour baths.

**St Anthony's Mound (Butte St-Antoine).** – It formed a western citadel. Boulevard Descuers skirts the western wall ; the eastern wall would have overlooked the harbour; some towers remain on the southern front, one of which may have been a lighthouse. Nearby stood the military laundry where the soldiers' uniform was cleaned by a process using Fuller's earth and sulphur vapour.

**Augustus' Lantern.** – *Follow the signposted path skirting the south face of St Anthony's Mound.* Beside the base of a tower the path turns right on to the southern quay; part of the defence wall still exists.

At the far end of the quay a tower marks the entrance to the harbour and the beginning of the canal leading out to sea. Although the tower was a ruin by the Middle Ages a construction called Augustus' Lantern was erected on it to act as a landmark to sailors entering harbour. The wall marking the line of the sea canal stretches away to the south-east.

## ■ ADDITIONAL SIGHTS

**Fréjus-Plage.** – *2 km – 1 1/4 miles from town centre by Boulevard Descuers and Avenue de la Mer.* Fine sandy beach stretching several miles eastwards towards St-Raphaël.

**Buddhist Pagoda.** – *2 km – 1 1/4 miles north of town centre by Avenue du XVᵉ Corps (N 7). Open 1 June to 15 September, 3 to 7pm; 2F.*

The pagoda was built in a pleasant wooded setting in 1919 by Vietnamese in memory of their compatriots who died while serving in the French Army during the First World War. The building is decorated in vivid colours and surrounded by statues and ritual monuments.

## EXCURSIONS

**Missiri.** – *4 km – 2 1/2 miles. Leave Fréjus by Avenue de Verdun (N 7) going west and turn right into D 4.* This Sudanese mosque, a reproduction of the famous Missiri of Djenné in Mali, is another memorial of Colonial troops.

**Zoological Park★.** – *5 km – 3 miles. Leave Fréjus by Avenue de Verdun (N 7) going west. Turn right into D 4. After 3 km – 2 miles bear right into a narrow road which crosses the motorway. Open 9am to 6pm (5pm out of season); 1/2 hour; 30F, children 15F.*

The Zoological Park covers about 20 ha – 50 acres in the foothills of the Esterel Massif. Visitors may walk or drive beneath the umbrella pines, cork oaks and olive trees to see a great variety of birds, many wild animals, African elephants, Tibetan yaks, zebras, monkeys etc. Animal training sessions.

**Roquebrune Mountain★.** – *Round trip 29 km – 18 miles – Local map p 95 – about 1 1/2 hours. Leave Fréjus by Avenue de Verdun (N 7) going west. After about 10 km – 6 1/4 miles, turn left into D 7 to Roquebrune-sur-Argens. The rest of the tour is described on p 125.*

## GANAGOBIE Plateau ★

Michelin map **81** folds 15 and 16 – *Local map 60*

The Ganagobie Plateau, an outlier of a quaternary terrace above the west bank of the Durance, is covered with pine trees, holm oaks, broom and lavender and has been inhabited since prehistoric times. It constitutes an archaeological site with megalithic monuments, a simple Carolingian oratory, the ruins of the fortified village of Villevieille, which was built on the site of an oppidum and abandoned in 15C, and, surpassing all, a priory which offers a far-reaching view of the Durance valley. The caves in the plateau slopes have often provided shelter, particularly to Resistance workers during the Second World War.

### ■ SIGHTS *time: 1 hour*

**Priory★.** – *Guided tours 9.30am to noon and 2.30 to 6.30pm (5pm 1 November to 31 March); time : ½ hour; donation.*
The Ganagobie Priory, an old Benedictine monastery, founded in the 10C and rebuilt in the 12C for a dozen Cluniac monks, was partially destroyed in 1792.

**Church.** – The **portal** is highly original. The pointed archivolts are separated from one another by curious festoons of stone which also frame the door where they alternate with slim engaged columns set on edge. A conventional Christ in Majesty carved on the tympanum contrasts with the fluid lines of the Evangelists' symbols and adoring angels. On the lintel are the 12 Apostles.

A single nave, with pointed vaulting leads to a double transept. The interior is very plain. The stone carving would have been complemented by draperies and frescoes, of which a few traces remain, and particularly by 12C multicoloured **mosaics★** *(removed for restoration)* in the choir and transept. There is oriental influence, probably inspired by cloth brought back by the Crusaders, in the fabulous animals and the surrounding strapwork.

*Ganagobie – Church doorway*

**Cloister.** – Each gallery boasts eight arches divided by twin columns beneath double capitals which are decorated with human figures and foliage; at the centre of each gallery there is a group of four columns. Each group of four arches is crowned by a broad surbased arch giving an impression of spaciousness to the whole.

**Refectory.** – In the south wing of the conventual buildings, the refectory comprises two bays of rib-vaulting supported on engaged columns. There are traces of frescoes and a model of the church mosaics.

**Monks' Walk (Allée des Moines).** – Beyond the east end of the church at the edge of the plateau there is an almost aerial **view★★** of the Durance valley, the Valensole plateau (SW) and the Pre-Alps near Digne (E); on a clear day the Alps are visible from Pelvoux Massif to Mount Viso.

**Forcalquier Walk.** – This walk leads to the western edge of the plateau from where there is a fine **view★** over Forcalquier to the Lubéron (SW) with Mount Lure in the foreground (NW).
To the left of the path are some standing stones and to the right some round stones and hollows in the rock – traces of early habitation.

## La GARDE-FREINET

Michelin map **84** fold 17 – *Local map pp 94-95* – Pop 1 241

In the heart of the Maures Massif, between the Argens valley and St-Tropez Bay, lies La Garde-Freinet (formerly called Le Fraxinet). From the surrounding forests of cork oaks comes the raw material for the local manufacture of bottle corks. There is also a trade in sweet chestnuts sold under the name *Marrons de Luc.*

**The Saracens.** – Owing to its strategic position La Garde-Freinet has known over a century of occupation by Saracens; in local tradition this name is applied collectively to the Moors, Arabs, Turks and Berbers who harassed the country from 8C to 18C.
After being defeated at Poitiers in 732 by Charles Martel, the Arabs drifted down into Provence. Although driven back several times, they managed to hold on to the region around La Garde-Freinet. On the height which dominates the present village they built a fortress from which they used to descend to pillage inland Provence. It was only in 973 that Count William, the Liberator, managed to expel them.
In contrast to the damage they caused, the Saracens taught the Provençals about medicine, how to use the bark of the cork oak and how to extract resin from pine trees. They also introduced the flat house tile and the tambourine.

**The Saracen Fortress.** – *1 km – 1/2 mile – plus 3/4 hour on foot Rtn. Take GR 9 on the south side of the village. Leave the car in the parking place levelled out at a bend in the road.* There is a good view of the Le Luc plain and the first Alpine foothills. *A path leads first to a mission cross (the Maures' Cross) and then climbs quite steeply to the fortress ruins.*
The ruins of the feudal castle attributed to the Saracens merge with the rocky site. From the summit, the **panorama★** extends out to sea and a long way inland.

## GOURDON ★

Michelin map 195 fold 24 – *Local map p 90* – Pop 254

Gourdon the Saracen was built on a remarkable **site**★★ on a rock spur *(details on hill villages, p 21)* over 500 m – 1 640 ft above the Loup river.

The old houses have been restored and converted into boutiques and lively workshops producing carvings in olive wood, glassware, pottery, distilled lavender and local honey.

There is a magnificent **panorama**★★ from the square by the church with a 50 km – 30 mile radius covering the coast from the mouth of the Var (SE) to Cap Roux (S) and from the Esterel Massif (S) inland to the Courmettes Peak (NE) beneath which the Loup river emerges from the Upper Gorge and winds its way to the coast.

**Castle.** – *Open 1 June to 30 September, 11am to 1pm and 2 to 7pm; 1 October to 31 May, 2 to 6pm; closed Tuesdays out of Season; 20 minutes; 9F (one museum only 6F).*

The old fortress of Gourdon, built in the 13C on the foundations of an old Saracen fortress and restored in the 17C, contains architectural features of the Saracens of the 9C or 10C, of the Tuscans of the 14C and of the Renaissance.

**Historical Museum.** – *Guided tours only.* It occupies the ground floor of the castle. The entrance hall contains a fine collection of arms and armour. The monumental chimney in the dining room is 14C and the furniture 17C.

In the salon the furniture is 16C; there is also an Aubusson tapestry, a secretaire which belonged to Marie-Antoinette, a self-portrait by Rembrandt and a fine painting (1500) of the Cologne School: **St Ursula.**

The chapel contains a 16C triptych, a Descent from the Cross from Rubens' studio, a Golgotha of the Flemish School and a wood sculpture of St Sebastian by Greco.

The Guard Room contains a collection of 16C and 17C oriental arms.

In Henry IV's tower, the documents displayed bear the Royal Seal; an opening in the floor reveals the former dungeon.

**Museum of Naive Painting★.** – Seven rooms on the second floor are hung with an exceptional collection covering the period 1925-1970 and including a Douanier-Rousseau (portrait). Other artists represented are Seraphine, Bauchant, Vivin, Lefranc, Caillaud, Fous from France; the Yougoslavs Kovacic and Vercenaj (the Croatian School); O'Brady the American; Greffe a Belgian and Vivancos a Spaniard.

**Gardens.** – The terraced gardens were designed by Le Nôtre on three levels and have now been transformed into a botanical centre, preserving typical flora of the Pre-Alps (above 1 000 m – 3 280 ft).

*The Michelin Sectional Map Series covers (1:200 000)*
*the whole of France, showing:*
- *the road network*
- *the width, alignment, profile and surface*
  *of all roads from motorways to footpaths*
- *emergency telephones.*
*These maps are a must for your car*

## GRASSE ★★

Michelin map 195 fold 14 – *Local map p 77* – Pop 35 330 – *Facilities p 30*

Grasse has a seductive charm and much to please the visitor as it stretches out over the foothills of the high limestone plateaux and looks over the perfumed plains which have brought it fame and riches. There are wide views from the modern town with its terraced houses with split level gardens, while below in the old Provençal town narrow alleys are linked by steep ramps or steps which wind between houses four or even five storeys tall.

Grasse is not only a perfume town *(details p 75)*, it is also famous for its crystallised fruit and flowers and preserves. A high grade olive oil is also produced.

## HISTORICAL NOTES

**A Small Republic (12C).** – In the Middle Ages, Grasse was a tiny republic, administered by a council whose members called themselves "Consuls by the Grace of God". It based itself on the Italian republics and had diplomatic relations with Pisa. By way of Cannes, it exported soap, oil and tanned skins to Pisa; in exchange it received raw hides and arms. Raymond Bérenger, Count of Provence, put an end to this independent existence in 1227.

**A Great Provençal Poet.** – Bellaud de la Bellaudière (1532-1588), a soldier-poet, was born and died in Grasse although he lived mainly in Aix, Marseilles and Avignon. His work, inspired by Rabelais and Petrarch, is both tender and vigorous and briefly revived the Provençal language in literature between the troubadours (12C) and Mistral (19C).

**Fragonard, child of Grasse (1732-1806).** – Fragonard's father, a tanner and glovemaker, tried to make his son a lawyer's clerk rather than an artisan, but the demon of drawing possessed the young man, who soon left for Paris for the studio of Chardin and then of Boucher. Winner of the Prix de Rome at the age of twenty, he achieved great celebrity, but the Revolution deprived him of his fashionable clientele and dictated a more severe style of painting.

Despite the protection of the artist David, Fragonard preferred to leave Paris and seek refuge in Grasse in the house of his friend, Maubert. Fragonard had brought with him five of his finest canvasses, painted for Mme du Barry, who in a fit of caprice had refused them. He sold them to his host for a minute sum.

However, the painter became bored at Grasse and returned to Paris, where he lived economically, without, however, losing his happy-go-lucky airs.

One hot afternoon in August 1806 this now elderly artist entered a café to eat an ice and suddenly died of a stroke.

**How Grasse became a Climatic Resort.** – During the winter of 1807-1808 the gay and impetuous Princess Pauline Bonaparte, separated from her husband, Prince Borghese, and on bad terms with her brother, the Emperor, came to Grasse to seek relief from family worries and regain her strength in a warm climate. Every day she was carried in a sedan chair to a grove of holm oaks which she particularly liked and which is now known as "Princess Pauline's Garden" *(p 77)*.

Later, Queen Victoria spent several winters at Grasse in the Grand Hotel and at the Rothschild property.

**Napoleon's Passage** (2 March 1815). – After the cold welcome reserved for him at Cannes, the Emperor decided to take the Alpine Road (Route des Alpes) by way of Grenoble and advanced on Grasse, but perhaps because of fear of a hostile demonstration from the populace, the Emperor went round the town by what is now the Boulevard Victor-Hugo and the Boulevard du Jeu-de-Ballon. He camped on what is now known as "Napoleon's Plateau", but stayed scarcely an hour.

**Perfume Industry.** – Grasse had long specialised in leather work and glove making when in 16C perfumed gloves came into fashion. This was the beginning of the perfume industry. The great names were born in 18C and 19C and still enjoy international standing.

Distillation is the oldest process. Flowers and water are brought to boiling point in a still. The water and essence are condensed in a "Florentine" flask where they separate owing to the difference in density and to their insolubility.

In 18C enfleurage was invented using the ability of fats to absorb perfume. Fresh flowers are repeatedly laid on a layer of grease. Washing with alcohol separates the perfume from the grease; a pomade is obtained. Few firms use the process nowadays as it is labour-intensive.

The latest process is extraction by which the flowers yield their perfume in its most concentrated form. The flowers are brought into contact with a solvent which is then evaporated. A concrete is thus obtained which consists of perfume and wax. One tonne of jasmine blossoms yields 3 kg of concrete – which cost over 24 000F per kg in 1980. The wax is removed by alcohol and the 40 % which remains is called absolute.

The essences produced in Grasse, which are the base material of the perfume industry, are mixed with a fixative and sent to Paris where the great perfume houses blend them according to secret formulas to produce the fascinating creations for which France is famous throughout the world.

## ■ THE OLD TOWN★ (Vieille Ville) *time: 2 hours*

**Place du Cours★** (Y). – This fine terraced promenade offers a charming **view★** over the cultivated and wooded countryside, which rolls gently to the sea ; the huge **fountain** (Y V) dates from the Revolution; a monument to Fragonard stands in the small square where the promenade and Boulevard du Jeu-de-Ballon meet.

*Go down the steps and turn left into Rue Mirabeau below Boulevard Fragonard.*

**Provençal Art and History Museum★** (Y M¹). – *Open 1 June to 30 September, 10am to noon and 2 to 6pm (5pm 1 October to 31 May). Closed 2nd and 3rd Sundays in the month, Mondays holidays and in November. 4.50F; joint ticket for Fragonard Museum 7F.*

The museum is in an 18C mansion erected by Louise de Mirabeau, sister of the tribune, at the time of her marriage to the Marquis de Cabris. The name "Petit Trianon" was given to this mansion which the Marquise planned and decorated with a view to entertainments on a grand scale, but all she ever knew there were days troubled by court actions and family scenes.

This museum provides a remarkable compendium of the art and history of eastern Provence and is decorated with pictures by Granet and local artists.

**Basement.** – One room is devoted to the Gallo-Roman period, another to local prehistoric remains; a third contains Provençal cribs and santons and a fourth 18C costumes; in a fifth the kitchen of the Cabris Mansion has been reconstructed. Elsewhere agricultural implements, harness, oil presses and earthenware jars are on display.

**Ground Floor.** – Chinaware from Apt and Marseilles is displayed in the entrance hall. One room is devoted to fine pieces of Moustiers china. Others are decorated in the style of Louis XIII, Louis XIV and Louis XV. Across the hall is a fine collection of *"bergamots"*, painted papier mache boxes, lined with bergamot peel – the bergamot is a fruit which resembles an orange and has a sweet clinging perfume.

**First Floor.** – Furniture, Provençal china and coins, 18C Masonic ceremonial dress from the Grasse Lodge.

*Continue along Rue Mirabeau and turn left up the slope to Place du Barri; climb the Tout-Petits steps and another flight of steps on the right leads to Place du Petit-Puy.*

**Cathedral N.-D.-du-Puy** (Y B). – The cathedral dates back to the late 12C but was restored and remodelled in the 17C; the double staircase at the entrance with its wide stone handrail and the two crypts were added in the 18C. Note the panels of the main door (1721) in the façade. The high narrow nave, with heavy pointed rib-vaulting, marks the beginning of the Gothic style in Provence; together with the robust round pillars it gives a grandiose air to the whole building.

In the south aisle there are three **paintings★** by Rubens (The Crown of Thorns, the Crucifixion and St Helen in Exaltation of the Holy Cross) executed in Rome in 1601 and offered to the town in 1827 by a citizen; a fine **triptych** attributed to Louis Bréa representing St-Honorat between St-Clément and St-Lambert ; the Mystic Marriage of St Catherine by Sébastien Bourdon (17C); finally, **the Washing of the Feet**, one of the rare religious canvasses by Fragonard.

**Place du 24 Août** (Y). – From the far side of the square the east end and bell-tower of the cathedral can be seen to good effect. There is also a fine **view** eastwards over the Grasse countryside. Close at hand is the so-called Clock Tower.

*Retrace your steps to Place du Petit-Puy.*

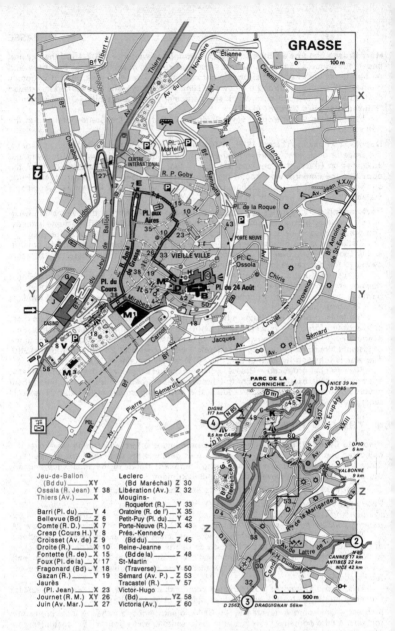

GRASSE

0        100m

**Watchtower (Tour de Guet)** (Y D). – The town hall, formerly the Bishop's Palace, boasts a massive square tower in red tufa stone, dating from 12C and bearing an inscription to the memory of the poet Bellaud de la Bellaudière (p 74).

**Marine Museum** (Y M²). – *Open 1 June to 15 September, 2.30 to 6pm; the rest of the year 2.30 to 5.30pm; closed Sundays, holidays, Mondays and in November; 3F.* Fine models of 18C naval ships; modern craft on the top floor.

*Return to the watchtower and turn left into Rue Mougins-Roquefort; turn right into Rue M. Journet which becomes Rue de Droite. Turn left up the steps of Rue Fontette which leads to Place aux Aires.*

**Place aux Aires** (X). – At the centre stands an elegant three-tiered **fountain**. The old houses which border the square are built over uneven arcades. **Isnard House** (E) on the north side, built in 1781, has a fine door and attractive wrought iron balcony at first floor level.
   Every morning there is a noisy **flower and vegetable market** in progress beneath the aged lotus trees.

**Rue Amiral-de-Grasse** (Y). – In this lively street at the town centre is 17C Fontmichel House (no 18).

## ■ ADDITIONAL SIGHTS

**Fragonard Villa-Museum** (Y M³). – *Same opening times as Provençal Art and History Museum; 4.50F; combined ticket for both museums: 7F. Ground floor rooms are closed to the public during municipal receptions.*
   In this elegant 17C country house Fragonard took refuge during the Revolution, when it belonged to Maubert, a local glove-maker and perfumier. It now belongs to the municipality and serves as a cultural centre and museum for a whole family of artists. A fine park surrounds it.

One of the ground floor rooms contains copies of the panels painted by Fragonard between 1771 and 1773 for the Countess du Barry. The stair well is decorated with republican and Masonic allegories executed in *trompe l'oeil* and monochrome by Fragonard's son, Alexandre-Évariste at the age of 14.

Upstairs the **Fragonard room★** displays a variety of the artist's work: original drawings and etchings, sketches, paintings. There are two self-portraits and a portrait of Mme Fragonard.

The work of Alexandre-Evariste (1780-1850), who was a pupil of his father and of David, is displayed in a room also devoted to a grandson, Théophile Fragonard (1806-1876).

A third room reveals the talent of Marguerite Gérard (1761-1837), Fragonard's pupil and sister-in-law.

**Perfumeries.** – *Open weekdays during working hours.* Fragonard *(20 Boulevard Fragonard),* Galimard *(les 4 chemins, Route de Cannes)* and Molinard *(60 Boulevard Victor-Hugo)* are open to the public and give a general idea of the manufacturing process. Other firms selling perfume are to be found in Cours Honoré-Cresp.

**Princess Pauline's Garden** (Z K). – *Access via Boulevard Albert-Ier and Boulevard de la Reine Jeanne.*

There is a good **panorama★** of Grasse, the Tanneron Massif, the Esterel and the coast from the viewing table in Princess Pauline's Garden.

**Corniche Public Park** (Z). – *Access as above; then turn sharp left into Boulevard Bellevue and then right into Boulevard du Président Kennedy; 1/2 hour on foot Rtn. At the bend a path to the right (signpost) leads to the edge of the steep Pre-Alps of Grasse.*

From the belvedere, the **viewpoint★★** extends from Baou de St-Jeannet and from the deforested Tanneron mountains to the peaks of the Esterel; on the horizon can also be seen La Napoule Bay, Juan Bay and the Lérins Islands.

## EXCURSIONS

**Round Tour into the Foothills of the Pre-Alps of Grasse★★.** – *Round trip of 104 km – 65 miles – about 5 hours – Local map below. Leave Grasse by Boulevard G.-Clemenceau and turn left into D11.*

After crossing the Napoleon Plateau *(p 75),* the road rises towards Cabris offering fine views of the Grasse countryside.

**Cabris★.** – This charming village occupies a magnificent **site★** on the edge of the Provence Plain, looking out over the Grasse countryside to the sea some 20 km – 12 miles away. Its name recalls the restless character of the Marquise de Cabris, Mirabeau's sister. The village and its neighbourhood has long been a favourite haunt of writers and artists.

The village is dominated by the 17C **church** which contains a painted wooden pulpit and a pleasant rustic altarpiece.

From the **castle ruins** there is a superb **view★★** : south-east to Mougins and the hills running down to Le Cannet, out to sea over La Napoule Bay to the Lérins Islands, south beyond Peymenade and over the brow of the Tanneron to the Esterel, swinging westwards to St-Cassien Lake with the Maures in the distance. On a clear day Corsica is visible.

By-pass Speracedes by turning right into D 513 at the beginning of the village. From Tignet there is a beautiful **view** of Cabris and Grasse. D 13 runs through magnificent sloping olive groves, passing the La Graou prehistoric tumulus.

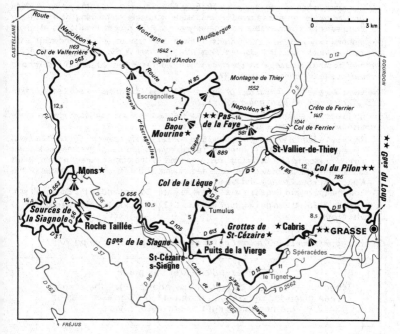

**Puits de la Vierge** (The Virgin's Well). – A righthand turning at the entrance to St-Cézaire-sur-Siagne makes a detour past a group of 9 wells, probably Roman in origin.

**St-Cézaire-sur-Siagne.** – Pop 1 046. From its **site**★ dominating the steep valley of the Siagne the walls and towers of this interesting village testify to its feudal past. Standing in its own graveyard is a pleasant Romanesque chapel which shelters the Gallo-Roman tomb of Julia Sempronia. From the church a marked path leads to a **point of view**★ *(viewing table)*.

*Leaving St-Cézaire by D 5, turn right into D 613 which leads to the caves.*

**St-Cézaire Caves**★. – *Open 1 June to 20 September, 10.30am to noon and 2 to 6pm (6.30pm in July and August); 21 September to 31 October and 1 March to 31 May, 2.30 to 5.30pm; closed November to February; ¾ hour; 9F.*

The caves, hollowed out of the limestone, have a constant temperature of 14°C – 57°F. Both the stalactites, which have great musical resonance and the stalagmites are remarkable for the variety of their shapes – toadstools, flowers, animals – and their red colour which is due to the presence of iron oxide in the rock. There are also beautiful rock crystallisations. The caves, which comprise several chambers known as the Hall of Draperies, the Organ Chamber, the Fairies' Alcove, the Great Hall, are connected by narrow passages one of which brings you suddenly, 40 m – 130 ft below ground, to the edge of an abyss.

*Return to the T-junction on D 5 and turn right.*

**Leque Pass.** – *5 km – 3 miles–about 1/4 hour.* To the right of the road leading up to the pass, near Puades, there is a group of tumuli. From the pass and on the return journey there are successive **views**★ of the Siagne gorge and the village of St-Cézaire piled up in its mountainous amphitheatre on the bluff.

*Continue towards to St-Cézaire and turn right into D 105.*

**Siagne Gorge.** – The road runs up the deep green valley which the waters of the Siagne have worn in the limestone.

*After crossing the Siagne,* (from the bridge, **view** up and down the gorge), *turn right into D 656, a very steep and narrow road.*

After serpentining steeply above the gorge, the road broadens out into a colourful rock circus before entering a wooded valley which brings it to the plateau.

*Turn left into D 56 following the hillside.* Fig and olive trees grow on the terraces which are retained by low drystone walls. *Cross the Siagnole.*

**Siagnole Springs.** – *1/2 hour on foot Rtn.* On the right beyond the bridge a path leads to a very pleasant spot where several Vauclusian springs rise to form the Siagnole river.

**Roche Taillée.** – There is a sign to indicate the remains of a Roman aqueduct *(on the left of the road)* which carried water from around Mons to Fréjus on the coast. **View**★ eastwards towards Grasse.

*Turn right into D 37 and then right again into D 563 to reach Mons.*

The road is cut into the hillside high above the Siagnole Gorge. Once over the Avaye Pass the road offers a magnificent **view**★★ reaching as far as the Esterel.

**Mons**★. – The wild and isolated **site**★ on a rock spur in the Provençal Plateau was chosen in the Middle Ages by a colony from Ventimiglia. The narrow streets and squares, well supplied with fountains, enjoy a sunny outlook. From **Place St-Sébastien**, which overlooks the Siagnole and Siagne valleys (SE), there is an exceptional **view**★★ which on a fine day can extend from Coudon (near Toulon) (SW) via the Lérins Islands to the Italian Alps *(viewing table)*.

The **church** *(when closed, key available from Mlle Sauvant, under the porch in Place du Centre)* is a much-altered Romanesque structure containing five Baroque altarpieces of a remarkable homogeneity and a 15C processional cross in silver.

The mountainous and wooded environs of Mons give way to an arid landscape with outcrops of white rock. *At Valferrière Pass turn right into N 85, the Napoleonic Road.*

*The road as far as Grasse offers spectacular views of the Riviera coast and is described in the opposite direction on page 127.*

**The Loup Gorges**★★. – *Round tour of 38 km – 24 miles – Local map p 90. Leave Grasse by D 2085, ① on the plan, going north east.*

The north-eastern suburb of Grasse comprises attractive villas scattered among olive, cypress and orange trees and fields of jasmine.

**Magagnosc.** – *Before entering the town, turn right at the sign saying : Église St-Laurent.* There are two churches. St-Laurent, in Tuscan style, is adorned with some fine stained glass and a copy of a Byzantine fresco painted by the contemporary painter, **Robert Savary**, who also decorated the walls and ceiling of the Romanesque chapel of the White Penitents *(lighting and taped commentary)*.

From the graveyard there is a **view**★ of the sea near Cannes and of the Esterel Massif.

*Return to D 2085.* At Pré-du-Lac, turn left into D 2210 facing the picturesque **site**★ of Le-Bar-sur-Loup.

**Le-Bar-sur-Loup.** – *Description p 39.*

*Continue to Pont-sur-Loup. The rest of the excursion is described on pp 90-91.*

---

The times indicated in this guide
when given with the distance allow one to enjoy the scenery
when given for sightseeing are intended to give an idea of
the possible length or brevity of a visit.

---

In the eastern sector of the Pre-Alps of Grasse, several deep and enclosed river valleys have been cut transversely through the mountain chains to form rifts *(clues)*, the characteristic features of this region.

This arid country, which is still quite cut off from the main lines of communication, has preserved several artistic treasures: it offers several fine vistas of the Esteron and Var valleys the slopes of which are dotted with natural viewpoints and hilltop villages.

## 1 SOUTHERN SLOPE OF MOUNT CHEIRON★

**Vence to Quatre-Chemins** – *62 km – 38 miles – about 1 1/2 hours – Local map pp 80-81*

*Leave Vence (p 159) by D 2 going north.* The road climbs the southern edge of the Pre-Alps of Grasse, bare limestone garrigue.

**Vence Pass★★**. – Alt 970 m – 3 182 ft. There is a wide **panorama★★** south from the pass: the heights along the left bank of the Var as far as Mount Agel; the coast including Cap Ferrat, the Baie des Anges, Cap d'Antibes, Ste-Marguerite Island and the Esterel. The white slopes of Mount Cheiron stand out dramatically against the sky.

The road, which crosses a desert-like countryside, overlooks the Cagne river which in rainy weather forms a splendid cascade; the view to the rear is of interest. *Turn off right to Coursegoules.*

**Coursegoules**. – Pop 155. Perched on a rocky spit at the foot of the Cheiron, the tall houses rise above the ravine of the nascent Cagne. In the church *(closed after 2pm)* is a **retable** by Louis Bréa of St John the Baptist between St Petronella and St Gothard; note the fine detail of the last figure *(light switches on the left of the entrance)*.

*Return to D 2.* At the lower end of a verdant valley the road suddenly comes out into the magnificent **upper valley of the Loup★**. Beautiful vistas before and after Gréolières.

**Gréolières**. – Pop 292. Hilltop village at the foot of the Cheiron; to the north the extensive ruins of Haut-Gréolières, to the south the remains of a major stronghold. The church with its Romanesque façade and squat tower has one side aisle. To the left of the entrance is a 15C silver-gilt processional cross and a fragment of a 16C altarpiece (St John the Baptist); opposite is a 14C Virgin and Child in wood; the finest work *(high on the right)* is the **St Stephen altarpiece★** by an unknown artist, the predella showing Christ and the Apostles (15C).

The road rises above the village and then turns westward snaking along the side of the gorge in and out of brief tunnels beneath huge rock spurs of fantastic shape and size; 400 m – 1 312 ft below flows the Loup.

**Gréolières Rift★**. – The rift *(clue)* was formed by a tributary of the Loup; its bare slopes are pitted with holes and spiked with curious dolomitic rocks.

The road emerges into the Plan-du-Peyron, a broad alluvial plateau.

*In Plan-du-Peyron turn right into D 802.* As the road climbs the side of Mount Cheiron, there are interesting **views** to the west and north.

**Gréolières-les-Neiges**. – Alt 1 450 m – 4 757 ft. The resort is the most southerly of the Alpine ski stations. It is well-equipped and easily accessible.

*Return to D 2 and continue to Quatre-Chemins crossroads.*

**Thorenc**. – *2.5 km – 1 1/2 miles west of the crossroads. Facilities p 30*. A pleasant quiet resort on a south facing slope, well shaded by pine trees, between the Aigle (E) and Bausson (W) peaks.

## 2 NORTHERN SLOPE OF MOUNT CHEIRON★

**Quatre-Chemins to Roquesteron** – *38 km – 23 miles – about 1 hour – Local map pp 80-81*

*The road is very steep and very narrow (passing often difficult). From Le Mas to D 17 drive carefully.*

The D 5 climbs the limestone face above Thorenc offering frequent **views** south of the Audibergue mountain and the Provence plateau.

**Bleine Pass★★**. – Alt 1 439 m – 4 721 ft. Magnificent **view★★**: below is La Faye ravine, ahead the superb Harpille rock (alt 1 686 m – 5 538 ft) with the ridge of Charamel Mountain eastwards to the snow peaks of the southern Alps on the sky line.

The descent from the Bleine Pass is over fir-clad slopes in sharp contrast to the preceding plateaux. *Bear right into D 10.* The road, winds down the hillsides affording an unusual view of the village of Le Mas which stands at the tip of a limestone spur, its rock sides strangely cut away so that they seem to resemble a bird's beak.

**Aiglun Rift★★**. – The Aiglun Rift, "the most mysterious of all the rifts", was formed by the Estéron. From the D 10, which crosses the stream as it emerges from the gorge, you get an astonishing view of the rift itself which looks like a blade thrust through the rock to divide Mount Charamel and Mount St-Martin.

**Vegay Waterfall**. – The stream cascades in a series of beautiful falls down the vertical cliff on the far side of the gorge.

From the Riolan bridge which crosses the southern end of the Riolan Rift *(p 80)*, there is a **view★** of the rift and its tumbling emerald green waters.

*Bear right into D 17.*

**Roquesteron**. – Pop 404. Before 1860 the river formed the frontier betwen Savoy to the north and France to the south. Today the two districts of Roquesteron-Puget (N) and Roquesteron-Grasse (S) are separately administered.

The fortified Romanesque church in Roquesteron-Grasse contains some fragmentary inscriptions.

## ③ TWO RIFT ROAD★★
### Quatre-Chemins to Roquesteron
*52 km – 32 miles – about 2 1/2 hours – Local map below*

The road from Quatre-Chemins over the Bleine Pass in described above. 5 km – 3 miles to the north of Bleine Pass, bear left at the fork. D 5 follows the Faye downstream before crossing over to join D 2211 on the west bank.

**St-Auban Rift★★.** – The Estéron, a tributary of the Var, has formed the grandiose St-Auban Rift, which is remarkable for its almost vertical sides, the deep potholes in its rocky bed and the huge caves in the steeply sloping cliffs.

From the entrance one can see to the far end of the gorge.

**Briançonnet.** – Pop 193. On a curious **site** at the foot of a huge rock stands a tiny village, which was originally a Roman settlement. The building stone of the ancients has been reused by later generations so that Latin inscriptions are incorporated in the house walls.

The church contains an altarpiece of the **Virgin of Mercy** by Louis Bréa: surrounded by angels playing musical instruments the Madonna protects a crowd of clerics and laity with her mantle; St Dominic and St Catherine, each reaching out to a rosary, have been added by a later less skillful hand.

From the east end of the church there is a **view★** of the Alps to the north.

Charamel Mountain on the south bank of the Estéron is separated from the road by the curious Gars mountains. After Collongues the Aiglun Rift *(p 79)* comes into view on the right; further on the Riolan Rift opens up.

**Riolan Rift★★.** – The breach was formed by a tributary of the Esteron cutting transversally through the mountain. High above, the road looks down on the gorge and the cascading river.

On an escarpment above the meeting of the Riolan and the Estéron stands the village of Sigale.

**Sigale.** – Pop 155. The former stronghold with its two main gates, Gothic houses and 16C fountain stands on a picturesque **site★** above terraced orchards.

A three-bayed Romanesque wall-belfry and later capitals adorn the **church.** In the right hand apse is a 17C gilded wood reliquary of St Lucy and a painting of the Virgin with scenes from the life of Christ.

*Climb the steps near the church.* On a rocky eminence stands a **clock-tower** crowned by an iron arcature. The **panorama★** extends over the village and the Estéron valley to the encircling mountains.

*The key to N.-D.-d'Entrevignes chapel is available from the town hall (mairie) in Sigale.*

There is an attractive **view** of Sigale to be seen from a lefthand hairpin bend.

**N.-D.-d'Entrevignes.** – Country chapel with porch and two-bayed wall-belfry. The 15C painting of the interior illustrates the Life of the Virgin : on the left, Presentation in the Temple, the Marriage of the Virgin ; below, the Virtues. Other subjects have been repainted and altered (Nativity of Mary, Annunciation, Assumption...).

## ④ RIDGE ROAD★★
### Roquesteron to Vence – *47 km – 29 miles – about 2 hours – Local map opposite*

The following itinerary links a series of high points in the Estéron and Var valleys, often occupied by a hilltop village.

*Leave Roquesteron by D 1 going south.* From the wooded slopes of the Estéron valley the road enters **La Bouisse Rift**, before passing in sight of **La Peguière Rift**, beyond Conségudes, and the hilltop village of Les Ferres.

D 1 continues as a *corniche* road above the deep ravine made by the Estéron; on the opposite side of the valley is the hilltop village of Gilette *(p 81)*; there are many magnificent **points of view★**.

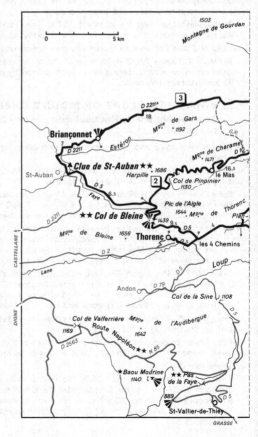

**Bouyon.** – Pop 202. Every part of the village offers a **view★** of Mount Cheiron, the Estéron and Var valleys and the Franco-Italian Alps. In the church *(key available from the house on the left)* there is a beautiful altarpiece of the Virgin and Child surrounded by saints (15C).

The road switches back into the Bouyon ravine before overlooking the Estéron flowing into the Var.

**Le Broc.** – Pop 360. The hilltop village has a fountain (1812) in the square which is surrounded by houses built out over arches. The 16C church has been decorated by the modern painter Guillonet.

On the road from Le Broc to Carros there are magnificent **views★** of the hilltop villages, of the confluence of the Estéron and the Var and of the Var itself flowing in multiple channels between dazzling white banks of pebbles on its broad flat bed.

**Carros.** – Pop 4 197. Huddled round its 13C-16C castle, the old village stands on a superb **site★**.
A little below the village a rock platform on which stands an old windmill has been laid out as a terrace and car park: **panorama★★** *(viewing table)*.

From the *corniche* road high above the Var there is an attractive glimpse of Gattières.

**Gattières.** – Pop 1 430. The hilltop village looks out over vineyards and olive groves to the Var valley and the neighbouring villages. The charming Romanesque-Gothic church contains a sculpture of St-Nicolas and the three children *(on the right in the choir)* and a beautiful modern Christ in the choir.

Bear left into D 2210 which looks down on the **site★** of St-Jeannet *(p 46)*.

## 5 DESCENT INTO THE VAR VALLEY★
### Roquesteron to Nice – *62 km – 39 miles – about 2 hours – Local map below*

*Leave Roquesteron by D 17 going east.* The road winds along half way up the north slope of the Esteron valley, doubling back into several ravines, some of which are true gorges. The opposite slope of the valley is cleft by **La Bouisse Rift** and then by **La Peguière Rift.**
Before the road loops north to Pont de Quinsoun, the curious **site** of Gilette comes into view.

**Gilette.** – Pop 504. From Place de la Mairie follow the signs to the castle ruins for a **view★** of the *corniche* roads, the Var and its confluence with the Estéron and the Pre-Alps of Nice. A pleasant walk, bordered by acacias and plane trees, skirts the castle looking out to Bonson on its hill *(p 82)* and the northern Alps.

*Return to the northern entrance to the village and bear right into D 227 and further on sharp right into D 27.*
The road looks down on the Var valley and Bonson perched on its hill.

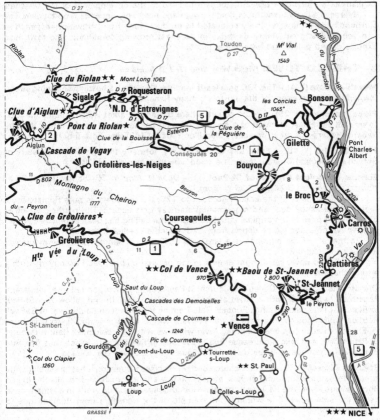

**Bonson.** – Pop 235. Built on a remarkable hiltop **site★** overlooking the Var valley, the village constitutes an exceptional **viewing point ★★**. From the church terrace there is a view of the Var and the Vésubie immediately below, of the Chaudan Defile (N), of the Vésubie Gorge (NE) and the Var flowing southwards beneath numerous hilltop villages.

The church *(key available from the Bar-Tabac if closed)* contains three fine examples of the early Nice school. On the west wall, **altarpiece of St Anthony** including Ste-Gertrude whit rats climbing on her shoulders (she was invoked against the plague); the work recalls the paintings of Durandi. In the right aisle, **altarpiece of St John-the-Baptist**, attribued to Antoine Bréa *(poor repainting on the central panel)*. At the high altar, in a Renaissance frame, **altarpiece of St Benedict ★** including St Agatha holding her wounded and bloody breasts.

*Leave Bonson by D 27 going south.* There are beautiful **views ★** of the Var valley as the road serpentines downhill to the river and crosses the bridge. *Turn right into N 202.*

*The stretch of N 202 from Charles-Albert Bridge to Nice (p 108) is described in the reverse direction on p 158.*

*You will find a selection of touring programmes on pp 24-25.*

*Plan your route with the help of the map of principal sights on pp 4-6*

---

**■ HYERES ★**

Michelin map 🅸🅸 fold 16 – *Local map p 94* – Pop 39 593 – *Facilities p 30*

Hyères lies in a well sheltered setting, the most southerly and the oldest of the Riviera climatic resorts. The old quarters cling to the southern slope of Castéou Hill (204 m – 670 ft) and overlook the modern town and the roadstead enclosed by Cape Bénat and the Giens Peninsula *(p 84)*. The new harbour is used by pleasure boats and the ferries which ply between the mainland and the Hyères Islands. The modern town is outstanding for its wide streets lined with magnificent palm trees.

**Early history.** – Excavations on the coast at Almannarre reveal that Greeks from Marseilles set up a trading station called **Olbia**, which was succeeded by a Roman town – Pomponiana. In the early Middle Ages the inhabitants removed up the hill where the Lords of Fos had built a castle. Agriculture and particularly the salt marshes brought Hyères success and the port of L'Ayguade (subsequently silted up) was a base for the Crusaders; St-Louis disembarked there in 1254 on returning from the Seventh Crusade. Soon afterwards the town passed to the Counts of Provence. In 1620 the Castle was demolished by Louis XIII and Hyères declined in favour of Toulon.

**Modern revival.** – The town became well-known in 18C and 19C, particularly to the English, as an inland resort; 20C tourism has led to the development of the beaches.

Hyères is a lively town throughout the year and not solely dependent on tourism. The surrounding plain is extensively cultivated to produce early fruit (strawberries, peaches) and vegetables; great vineyards thrive in excellent growing conditions. The town also exports potted palms and ornamental plants.

### ■ THE OLD TOWN (Vieille Ville) *time: 1 1/4 hours*

**Massillon Gate** (Y A). – The 13C gate leads into Rue Massillon, a bustling shopping street, formerly the main street of the old town; many Renaissance doorways.

**Place Massillon** (Y 29). – In the square where the daily market is held stands the 12C **Tower of St-Blaise**, last remnant of a Knights Templar commandery. To the left is the Rue Rabaton where the great preacher, Massillon (1663-1742) was born (no 7).

**Place St-Paul** (Y 48). – From this terrace square, formerly the site of the cloisters of St-Paul's Collegiate Church, there is a good **panorama★** *(viewing table)*.

**Former Collegiate Church of St-Paul** (Y). – *Open 1 June to 30 September, 2.30 to 6pm; 1 October to 30 May, 2.30 to 5pm.*

The oldest parts of the church go back to 12C; the bell-tower is pure Romanesque. A fine Renaissance door and monumental stairway give access. The narthex, which is probably the nave of the original structure to which a ceiling has been added, is covered with votive offerings (some dating from 17C) which embellish local history.

To the left of the entrance is a large **crib** of Provençal santons with the mediaeval town as a backdrop.

The Gothic nave, set at right angles to the original church, has Flamboyant Gothic lateral chapels.

**Old streets.** – Near the Collegiate Church St-Paul's Gate is incorporated in a handsome **Renaissance house** (Y E) with a turret at one corner. Pass beneath and follow Rue St-Paul to Rue Ste-Claire where stands Princes' Gate framing the chevet and bell-tower of St-Paul. Retrace your steps to Rue Paradis *(on the left)* where there is a fine **Romanesque house** (Y F), (no 6) which has been restored (twin windows with slim columns). Return through St-Paul's Gate and take picturesque Rue Barbacane to Rue St-Esprit which runs into Rue Bourgneuf. Continue to Place de la République with its shady plane trees.

**St-Louis Church** (Y K). – Former church of the Franciscan Convent, it has three elegantly simple doors beneath round arches, a rose window and a cornice and recalls the Italian Romanesque style. The nave, with its thick-ribbed pointed vaulting, ends in a square apse as do the side aisles. The whole is an example of the transition from Romanesque to Provençal Gothic.

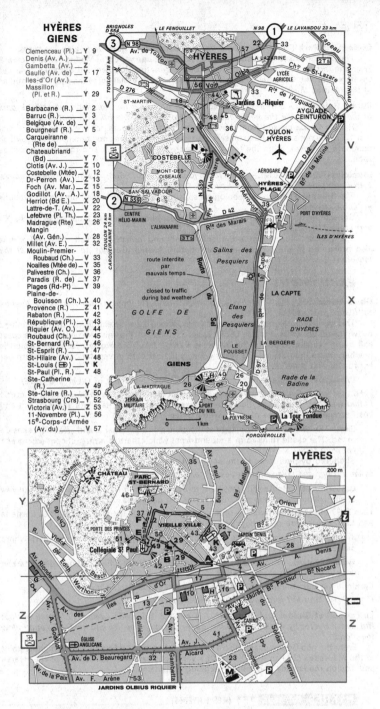

## HYÈRES
## GIENS

| | |
|---|---|
| Clemenceau (Pl.) | Y 9 |
| Denis (Av. A.) | Y |
| Gambetta (Av.) | Z |
| Gaulle (Av. de) | Y 17 |
| Iles-d'Or (Av.) | Z |
| Massillon (Pl. et R.) | Y 29 |
| | |
| Barbacane (R.) | Y 2 |
| Barruc (R.) | Y 3 |
| Belgique (Av. de) | Y 4 |
| Bourgneuf (R.) | Y 5 |
| Carqueiranne (Rte de) | X 6 |
| Chateaubriand (Bd) | Y 7 |
| Clotis (Av. J.) | Z 10 |
| Costebelle (Mtée) | V 12 |
| Dr-Perron (Av.) | Z 13 |
| Foch (Av. Mar.) | Z 15 |
| Godillot (Av. A.) | V 18 |
| Herriot (Bd E.) | X 20 |
| Lattre-de-T. (Av.) | Z 22 |
| Lefebvre (Pl. Th.) | Z 23 |
| Madrague (Rte) | X 26 |
| Mangin (Av. Gén.) | Z 28 |
| Millet (Av. E.) | Z 32 |
| Moulin-Premier-Roubaud (Ch.) | V 33 |
| Noailles (Mtée de) | Y 35 |
| Palivestre (Ch.) | V 36 |
| Paradis (R. de) | Y 37 |
| Plages (Rd-Pt) | Y 39 |
| Plaine-de-Bouisson (Ch.) | X 40 |
| Provence (R.) | Z 41 |
| Rabaton (R.) | Y 42 |
| République (Pl.) | Y 43 |
| Riquier (Av. O.) | V 44 |
| Roubaud (Ch.) | V 45 |
| St-Bernard (R.) | Y 46 |
| St-Esprit (R.) | Y 47 |
| St-Hilaire (Av.) | V 48 |
| St-Louis ( ) | K |
| St-Paul (Pl., R.) | Y 48 |
| Ste-Catherine (R.) | Y 49 |
| Ste-Claire (R.) | Y 50 |
| Strasbourg (Crs) | Y 52 |
| Victoria (Av.) | Z 53 |
| 11-Novembre (Pl.) | V 56 |
| 15e-Corps-d'Armée (Av. du) | V 57 |

# ■ ADDITIONAL SIGHTS

**Olbius Riquier Gardens★** (V). – The gardens are very extensive (6.5 hectares – 16 acres) and grow a rich variety of tropical plants, particularly varieties of palms and cacti, in the open.

In the **Show House** *(admission: 3.50F)* the more delicate varieties of tropical and equatorial plants can be seen together with a few rare animals.

The gardens include a small zoo in a special enclosure and a lake supports several species of water birds.

**Notre-Dame de Consolation Chapel★** (V N). – *Open 8.30am to 2.30pm.*

There has been a sanctuary on the top of Costebelle hill since 11C. The present chapel was built in 1955. The visitor is greeted by a huge coloured sculpture of Our Lady against the cross which forms the vertical axis of the tower. A series of sculpted groups depicting the main events in the Virgin's life are picked out in cement and stone on the principal front between the windows. The clean lines of the interior are complemented by the Apostle sculptures in the apse and the play of colours from the huge **stained glass windows★** designed by Gabriel Loir to illustrate the cult of Mary and the history of the sanctuary.

The neighbouring promenade gives a **view★** of the Hyères Roadstead *(left)* and of Toulon Roadstead *(right)*.

83

**St-Bernard Park** (Y). – *From Cours de Strasbourg drive north following the signs.*

The park encloses the castle ruins and boasts a huge variety of Mediterranean flowers. From the terraces there is a picturesque **view**★: from the old town and St-Paul's, over Les Oiseaux Peak and Costebelle Hill to the peninsula and the islands; to the east is the outline of the Maures Massif.

**Castle Ruins** (Y). – *Same route as above but go round the righthand side of the park to the car park. Take the well-trodden path up the hill (3/4 hour on foot Rtn).*

Hyères Castle passed from the Lords of Fos to the Counts of Provence who rebuilt it in 13C. The ruins are quite extensive, particularly the towers and crenellated keep which dominate the town. From the top a vast **panorama**★ of the coast and the interior can be seen.

**Municipal Museum** (Z M). – *Open 10am to noon and 3 to 6pm ; Saturdays and Sundays, 3 to 6pm; closed Tuesdays and holidays.*

The Greek and Roman archaeological specimens displayed come from the excavations at "Olbia" *(see p 82)*.

Collections of minerals, fossils, shells, fishes, birds. Gallery of local artists. Louis XV and Louis XVI furniture.

Background information on the local history and industries of salt, cane and cork is also presented in the former Anglican church, Avenue Godillot *(to visit, apply at the museum)*.

## EXCURSIONS

**Giens Peninsula**★ (X). – *31 km – 19 miles – about 1 hour. Leave Hyères by Avenue St-Hilaire, going south, N 559.*

This curious projection from the coast is formed by an island linked to the mainland by two sandbars which enclose Les Pesquiers salt marsh, the only one on the Riviera coast still being worked; south of the marsh is a huge lake. The western sandbar, which is nowhere more than 30 m – 33 yards wide, is almost bare of vegetation; the eastern bar is broader and greener.

**L'Almanarre.** – Long sandy beach near the Greek settlement of Olbia *(see p 82)*.

Take the "**salt road**" down the western side of the peninsula. *The road is closed to traffic in bad weather.* The picturesque drive passes the marsh with its white banks of salt and Les Pesquiers Pool, home of many water birds.

**Giens.** – *Facilities p 28*. The village at the centre of the former island, is a small seaside resort. The castle ruins form a mound from which there is a magnificent **panorama**★★ *(viewing table)*.

Sheltered by pine trees to the south is Le Niel Port.

*Drive through the village to the eastern end of the island.*

**La Tour Fondue.** – Boats sail from here to Porquerolles *(p 85)*. There is a beautiful **view** of the island out to sea and inland over the peninsula.

Take D 97 along the eastern side of the peninsula, through the pine groves of La Bergerie and La Capte before reaching Hyères-Plage.

**Hyères-Plage.** – *Facilities p 28*. A forest of umbrella pines shelters the port where passengers embark for the Islands.

**Ayguade-Ceinturon.** – *Facilities p 28*. The old port of Hyères where St-Louis disembarked is now a pleasant seaside resort.

Continue via Berriau-Plage to **Port-Pothuau**, a picturesque fishing port.

*From D 12, turn left into N 98 which returns to Hyères.*

**Le Fenouillet Chapel and Summit**★. – *4 km – 2 1/2 miles – plus 1/2 hours on foot Rtn. Leave Hyères by Avenue de Toulon. Bear right at La Bayorre into the D 554 and follow the signs.*

From the neo-Gothic chapel there is a marked path to Le Fenouillet, the highest point of the Maurettes (291 m – 955 ft) with a very good **panorama**★ particularly of the Hyères and Toulon roadsteads and the surrounding mountains.

## HYÈRES Islands ★★★ (ILES D'HYÈRES)

Michelin map 84 folds 16 and 17

*No cars or motorcycles are allowed on the islands.*

These well known islands which became detached from the Maures in a relatively recent geological age, close the south entrance to Hyères harbour. They are also known as the Golden Isles – Iles d'Or – a name given them during the Renaissance, no doubt because in certain lights their mica shale rocks have golden reflections. The short crossing and walks on the islands provide unforgettable memories.

## HISTORICAL NOTES

**Land of Asylum.** – In the 5C the monks of Lérins arrived in succession to the Ligurians, the Greeks and the Romans as the islands' overlords. In the following centuries they were constantly attacked by pirates until François 1 raised the three islands to the status of marquisate of the Iles d'Or on condition that the marquis kept them under cultivation and protected them from pirates.

Despite exemption from taxes, the islands lacked manpower until a right of asylum was established under which criminals were granted immunity provided they remained on the islands. This was a bad idea: jailbirds swarmed to the islands, where they turned to piracy, even being so bold as to attempt the capture of one of the King's ships from Toulon. Only in the reign of Louis XIV did the last of these doubtful characters leave.

**A British Coup.** – In 1793, after the capture of Toulon by the Revolutionaries *(see p 145)*, British and Spanish squadrons anchored off the Hyères Islands. The commander of Fort Ste-Agathe at Porquerolles, forgotten by the French authorities on his island, had but the vaguest idea of what was happening on the mainland. The British admiral invited him on board his flagship and the commander went unsuspectingly. While the whisky was circulating, British sailors landed, surprised the garrison and blew up the fort. The ships then raised anchor taking with them, as prisoner, the crestfallen commander of Ste-Agathe.

**Allied Landing** (August 1944). – During the night of 14 to 15 August American troops landed on the Islands of Port-Cros and Le Levant and silenced German batteries which could have had within their range Allied shipping lying at anchor.

## ACCESS TO THE ISLANDS

| Embarkation Point | PORQUEROLLES | PORT-CROS | LEVANT ISLAND |
| --- | --- | --- | --- |
| Toulon ................. | 1 hr 30 mins *(1)* | — | — |
| Giens (La Tour Fondue) ... | 15 mins *(2)* | — | — |
| Hyères-Plage ............ | 30 mins *(2)* | 1 hr 15 mins *(2)* | 1 hr 30 mins *(2)* |
| Le Lavandou ............ | 50 mins *(3)* | 35 mins *(3)* | 35 mins *(3)* |
| Cavalaire ............... | 2 hrs *(3)* | 1 hr *(3)* | 45 mins *(3)* |
| La Londe (Miramar) ...... | 30 mins *(3)* | 40 mins *(3)* | 1 hr *(3)* |

Shipping companies

*1) Transrade, Stalingrad quay, Toulon. ☏ (94) 92.96.82*

*(2) Société des Transports Maritimes et Terrestres du Littoral Varois, T. L. V., Av. F.-Roosevelt, Toulon. ☏ (94) 41.65.87.*

*(3) Cie Iles d'Or, 15 quai Gabriel-Péri, Le Lavandou. ☏ (94) 71.01.02.*

## ■ PORQUEROLLES ISLAND★★★

*Facilities p 28 – Local map below*

Porquerolles, the most westerly and largest of the Hyères Islands, measures 7.5 km long by 2 wide – 5 x 1 1/4 miles – and was called Prote (first) by the Greek colonists who came to live along its shores. The north coast is well supplied with sandy beaches bordered by pine trees, heather and scented myrtle; the south coast is steep and rugged with one or two inlets which are easily accessible. There are few inhabitants inland, only vineyards, pine and eucalyptus woods and thick Mediterranean vegetation.

The major part of the island has been acquired by the State to protect the natural heritage.

**The village.** – The small village of Porquerolles, which lies at the end of a minute roadstead now used as a harbour for pleasure boats, has given its name to the whole island. The village was built by the military about 100 years ago and consists of a main square, a modest church, containing an unusual Stations of the Cross carved by a soldier with his penknife, and a few fishermen's cottages. To this nucleus, which resembles a North African colonial settlement rather than a Provençal village, hotels and private houses have been added. 16C Ste-Agathe Fort has been converted into a police training college.

**Lighthouse** ★★ (Phare). – *1 1/2 hours on foot Rtn.* This walk is a "must" even for tourists with only a few hours on the island. The lighthouse, which stands on the most southerly point of the island some 96 m – 307 ft up, has a beam which carries 54 km – 34 miles. *(Closed to the public).*

There is a **panorama**★★ extending over most of the island: the hills of Le Grand Langoustier (W), Ste-Agathe Fort (S), the signal station (E) and the cliffs of the south coast, the Hyères Roadstead and the Maures Massif.

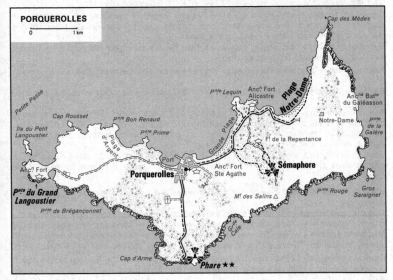

**Beach Walk★★.** – *2 hours on foot Rtn.* The walk by sandy paths continually in the shade of the pine trees, starts from Ste-Agathe's Fort *(bear left)* and skirts the Grande Plage. After Lequin Point the path dips towards the sea, revealing **Notre-Dame Beach,** a beautiful stretch of empty sand bordered by pine trees.

**Other Walks.** – The signal station (**sémaphore**), Argent Beach and **Le Grand Langoustier Point** all make good walks.

## ■ PORT-CROS ISLAND★★

*Facilities p 28 – Local map below*

Port-Cros, which was the Mesé – Middle Island – to the Greeks, owes its present name to the hollowed out *(creux)* shape of its small Harbour. A few fishermen's cottages, a small church, a castle, adorn the area around the bay which is commanded by the Eminence Fort.

Port-Cros Island is hillier and more rugged and rises higher above the sea than its neighbours; its covering greenery is unrivalled – it is a true Garden of Eden and a peaceful place in which to stay.

The island is 4.5 km – 3 miles long by 2 km – 1 mile wide and reaches 207 m – 679 ft at the highest point. Its rich vegetation is due to the springs which rise on the island. Port-Cros, together with its neighbouring islands, has been designated a **National Park** *(no camping, shooting, smoking or lighting fires)* and forms a nature reserve where Mediterranean flora and fauna (land and sea) are protected *(underwater hunting forbidden and fishing controlled)*.

*The principal walks are signposted at the quayside; possible variations are shown by a broken line on the plan.*

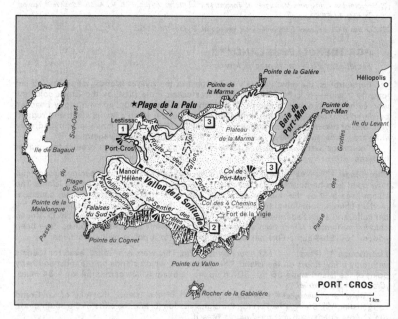

**La Palu Beach★** 1 – *1 1/4 hours on foot Rtn; path marked yellow.*
Climb up to the castle for a view of Bagaud Island. A **botanical path** planted with Mediterranean specimens winds round Lestissac Fort, built under Richelieu, and follows the curve of the bay before reaching the beach.
Between the shore and Rascas rock in La Palu bay an **underwater path** has been marked out with white buoys *(supervised dives)*.
Return to the village passing between Éminence Fort and Lestissac Fort.

**Solitude Valley★** 2 – *1 1/2 hours on foot Rtn; path marked first in yellow and then dark green.*
This is the classic walk for all visitors spending half a day on the island. At the beginning of Solitude Valley stands Helen's Manor (Manoir d'Hélène – now a hotel), so called after the heroine in Melchior de Vogüé's novel Jean d'Agrève which is set on Port-Cros. The path is in deep shade for almost all its length.
Once in sight of La Vigie Fort, start back along the cliff walk (Route des Crêtes), which affords **views** of the sea. At Mount Vinaigre bear right into La Fausse Monnaie (false currency) valley.

**Port-Man★** 3 – *Round tour of 10 km – 6 miles – 4 hours on foot Rtn; path marked dark green.*
This pleasant excursion is made along a shaded and nearly level path from which, at the end of the Port-Man Pass, there is a pretty **view** of the Levant Island, the coast and the Maures. It ends in a wonderful green amphitheatre which is well sheltered from the north winds, **Port-Man Bay**. Return via La Galère Point, La Marma plateau and the La Palu beach.

Other walks include La Palu beach by way of the Forts path and the Noir valley; the beach and the awesome cliffs along the south shore; Port-Man Point.

# ■ LEVANT ISLAND
*Local map p 86*

The island consists of a rock spine 8 km – 5 miles long but only 1 200 m – 1 300 yds wide rimmed by prodigious vertical cliffs inaccessible except at two points: the Avis and Estable inlets. The disembarkation point on the island is the Aiguade landing-stage from which a path leads up to Héliopolis.

When the Lérins monks inhabited the islands, Levant Island was the abbey's garden and granary. In the western part of the island the village of Héliopolis attracts a considerable number of nudists each summer.

Most of the rest of the island is occupied by the navy.

## JUAN-LES-PINS ★★

Michelin map **195** folds 39 and 40 – *Facilities p 28 – See town plan in the current Michelin Guide France*

This elegant winter and summer resort lies at the end of a magnificent bay, well protected by sumptuous Cap d'Antibes and La Croisette Point. A pinewood grows right down to a gently sloping beach of fine sand, some 2 km – 1 mile long, which is well protected from the wind. Port-Gallice is for pleasure boats.

In the evening activity centres on the restaurants, open-air cafés and night clubs round the casino. The summer season is marked by many events including the famous **World Jazz Festival** which takes place in the Palais des Congrès or under the pine trees.

## EXCURSIONS

**Cap d'Antibes★★.** – *Round tour of 10 km – 6 miles. Map and description pp 34-35.*

**Golfe-Juan★; Vallauris.** – *Round tour of 14 km – 8 miles. Go by the N 7 and Golfe-Juan (p 50) to Vallauris p 157). Return by way of Golfe-Juan and the coast (N 98).*

*The excursions described on p 50 starting from Cannes can also be undertaken from Juan-les-Pins.*

## Le LAVANDOU ★

Michelin map **84** folds 16 and 17 – *Local map pp 94-95 – Pop 3 800 – Facilities p 28 – See town plan in the current Michelin Guide France*

This charming resort in the shelter of Cap Bénat has so far preserved its Provençal character from modern building sprawl; its name recalls the lavender fields on the banks of the Bataillier. It is still active as a fishing **port** as well as offering mooring to pleasure craft. It is also a departure point for the Hyères Islands.

**Place Ernest-Reyer.** – The square, which has been laid out as a garden, offers a view of Levant and Port-Cros Islands; a broad beach curves south toward the port of Bormes-les-Mimosas with the wooded slopes of Cap Bénat in the background.

**Boulevard de-Lattre-de-Tassigny.** – Pleasant promenade beside the beach; view of the port and the coast eastwards to Cap Lardier.

## BOAT TRIPS

**Hyères Islands★★★.** – *One day. Sailing times, maps and description pp 84-87.*

**Cape Bénat★.** – *About 2 hours.* Make a private arrangement with the fishermen of Le Lavandou if you want to go on this tip. The trip of the cape, which is rocky and deeply cleft, is especially spectacular from the sea.

## Les LECQUES

Michelin map **84** fold 14 – *Facilities p 28*

This seaside resort to which families come in both winter and summer has a sheltered harbour at the far end of a tranquil bay. A lovely beach of fine sand bordering the fertile plain planted with vines and olives links Les Lecques with La Madrague, built at the foot of wooded hills where the coast abruptly changes to rocks and escarpments.

**Tauroëis.** – According to the Greek historian Apollodorus, a Phocean ship, a bull's head carved on its prow, foundered just off Les Lecques and the crew established a trading post called Tauroëis in memory of the ship (recent excavations have uncovered several bull figurines). The settlement was linked to Marseilles and passed to the Romans as Tauroentum. The town and harbour have now disappeared beneath the waves.

*Drive along the coast towards La Madrague.*

**Tauroentum Museum.** – *Open 1 June to 31 September, 3 to 7pm: 1 October to 31 May, Saturdays and Sundays, 2 to 5pm; closed Tuesdays; 5F.*

The museum is built on the foundations of a Roman villa ; on display are some wreathed columns with Corinthian capitals from the villa peristyle and a granite column from a pergola, 80 m – 262 ft long, which adorned the sea front. The museum also contains three 1C mosaics, fragments of frescoes and amphoras. In the showcases are many Greek and Roman objects: coins, pottery, glass, jewellery and figurines. In the grounds stands a double-decker tomb found in La Madrague: the burial chamber is lined with pink marble and the libation chamber above is covered wiht a 4C saddle-back roof.

Behind the museum a path leads to a pottery kiln and remains of houses (walls bearing traces of frescoes). The view is over Les Lecques Bay.

The interest and attraction of an excursion to the Lérins Islands lies in the enjoyment of the outing both at sea and on the islands themselves, in the fine panorama of the coast from the Cap Roux to the Cap d'Antibes, the visits to the Ste-Marguerite Fortress and the keep of the old fortified Monastery of St-Honorat.

**Access to the islands.** – *There is a boat service to the islands from Cannes, Antibes and Golfe-Juan. Crossing times from Cannes: 15 minutes to Ste-Marguerite; 30 minutes to St-Honorat. Information from the Campagnie Esterel-Chanteclair, Gare Maritime des Iles, Cannes. ☏ 39.11.82.*

*From 12 June to 15 September, Son et Lumière performances on Mondays, Wednesdays and Saturdays. Departure at 9.30pm from Service des Iles, Gare Maritime. Return 11.45pm. Prices including Rtn fare to Ste-Marguerite: 25F.*

## ■ SAINTE-MARGUERITE ISLAND★★

The higher and the larger of the two islands, Ste-Marguerite, is separated from the mainland by a shallow channel 1 100 m – just over half a mile wide. The island, which lies east-west, 3 km – 2 miles long and about 900 m – 1 000 yds wide, belongs to the State except for the Grand Jardin Domain in the south.

Pleasant walks have been laid out in the pine and eucalyptus woods.

**The Island in Antiquity.** – The Lérins Islands were mentioned by the ancient historians, the larger being called Lero. According to Strabo, this name commemorates a Ligurian hero to whom a temple was dedicated. Pliny, on the other hand, talks of a Roman port and town. Recent excavations near Fort Royal have uncovered houses, wall paintings, mosaics and ceramics dated between 3C BC to 1C AD. Various wrecks and port substructures found to the west of the island prove that Roman ships called in at Lero.

**The Riddle of the "Iron Mask".** – In 1687 the fortress of Ste-Marguerite, a state prison, received the famous "Man in the Iron Mask". Actually, the mask was made of velvet. His identity has never been established with any certainty. He is said to have been: an illegitimate brother of Louis XIV, a secretary of the Duke of Mantua who had tricked the "Sun King", a black sheep of the nobility and an accomplice of Madame La Brinvilliers the poisoner, etc. According to a recent version: Anne of Austria's doctor, having performed an autopsy on Louis XIII, expressed some misgivings about the king's ability to father a child. His son-in-law, who inherited the doctor's papers, is said to have let out this state secret and it may have been he, therefore, who was the prisoner on Ste-Marguerite. An even better theory maintains that a woman companion to the Man in the Iron Mask gave birth to a son who was immediately taken away to Corsica. Entrusted *(remis de bonne part* in French – *di buona parte* in Italian) to reliable foster parents, this nameless child is said to have been called "Buonaparte" and to have been the great-grandfather of Napoleon.

M. de Saint-Mars, charged with guarding the Man in the Iron Mask and bored to death on Ste-Marguerite, managed to obtain the post of Governor of the Bastille in 1698. His prisoner went with him and died in 1703.

### SIGHTS *time: 2 hours*

**The Forest★★.** – For the most part the island is covered with trees: tall eucalyptus and various species of pine protect a dense undergrowth of tree-heathers, arbutus, mastic trees, cistus, thyme and rosemary.

Many rides and broad paths cut through the forest to provide charming walks. Starting from the landward side of the Fort the Eucalyptus Walk – the trees are huge – leads to the Grand Jardin Domain; Ste-Marguerite Walk returns to the landing place. The cliffs are mostly fairly steep making it difficult to reach the shore. There is a path right round the edge of the island *(about 2 hours walk)*.

**Fort-Royal.** – *Open in accordance with the boat timetable; 0.25F.*

The fortress was built by Richelieu and reinforced by Vauban in 1712. Its main entrance on the west side is monumental. A small **aquarium** *(left)* contains Mediterranean specimens.

In the building beyond Marshal Bazaine was imprisoned from 1873 to 1874 when he escaped to Spain – official reports do not reveal how. From the terrace there is an extensive **view★** of the nearby coast.

**Prisons.** – Behind Bazaine's lodgings are the prisons. To the right of the corridor is the gloomy cell of the Man in the Iron Mask. The cells opposite were occupied by Protestant pastors imprisoned after the Revocation of the Edict of Nantes; the complete text of the Revocation and other relevant documents are on display.

**Marine Museum** (Musée de la Mer). – *Open 1 July to 30 September, 9.30am to noon and 2 to 6.30pm; 1 April to 30 June, 10.30am to noon and 2 to 5pm; the rest of the year, 10.30am to noon and 2 to 4.30pm; closed Mondays and in November and December; 3F.*

The ground floor of the old castle, near the prisons, was built above the original vaulted Roman rooms. The museum contains items of the Roman period excavated near the fort or from under the sea near the island shore (1C BC Roman wreck and 10C Arab wreck).

## ■ SAINT-HONORAT ISLAND★★

St-Honorat, nearly 400 x 1 500 m – a mile long by 400 yds wide has a less hospitable coastline than Ste-Marguerite, from which it is separated by a narrow strait known as the Central Plain (Plateau du Milieu). The island is the private property of the monastery but walking and bathing are permitted.

Some of the land is cultivated by the monks, who make a liqueur called "Lerina", but the rest is covered by a fine forest of umbrella and sea pines, of eucalyptus and a few cypress trees.

At the end of 4C, St Honorat settled on Lerina, the smaller of the two islands; his retreat soon became known and his disciples hastened to join him. Resigned to not living as a solitary, the saint founded a monastery which was to become one of the most famous and powerful in all Christendom. Pilgrims came in crowds to walk round the island barefoot – a pope on a visit followed this ancient tradition in all humility, Many of the faithful from France and Italy were buried in the monastery which became rich through endowments. In 660 St-Aigulf established the Benedictine Order in the monastery.

*(After photo : J. Delmas et Cie, Paris)*

St-Honorat – Trinity Chapel

Raids by Saracens and Genoese pirates, government by commendation, attacks by the Spaniards and the arrival of military garrisons were hardly favourable to monastic life so that by 1788 only four monks remained and the monastery was closed. During the Revolution, it was confiscated and finally sold.

In 1859 the monastery once more became a place of worship and in 1869 it was taken over by Cistercians from Sénanque Abbey.

## SIGHTS *time: 2 hours*

**Island Tour★★**. – Starting from the landing place, an attractive shady path makes a circuit of the island. Now close to the shore, now further inland, it offers many different views of the island, its crops, its trees and wooded walks; Ste-Marguerite Island and the coast on the mainland are also visible.

**Old Fortified Monastery★**. – *Open at times of boat arrivals, July to 15 September.*

The remarkable high "keep" or "castle" is set on a spit of land projecting into the sea from the southern coastline. It was built in 1073 by Aldebert, Abbot of Lérins, on Roman foundations, to protect the monks from Saracen pirates.

The gate is over 4 m – 12 ft above ground level and access to it was by a ladder which has now been replaced by a stone stairway. Facing the entrance, a staircase leads to a barrel-vaulted storeroom. On the left, a few steps go up to the first floor.

The **cloisters** with pointed arches and 14 and 17C vaulting (one of the columns is a Roman milestone) enclose a square courtyard covering a rainwater tank paved with marble. The upper gallery, with small columns of white marble, goes to the Chapel of the Holy Cross, a high room with Gothic arches still called The Holy of Holies owing to the many relics it contained.

From the platform, with its 15C battlements and crenelations, at the top of the old keep, the **view★★** extends over the Lérins Islands and the coast from the Esterel to Cap d'Antibes, with the often snow capped peaks of the Alps in the background.

**New Monastery.** – *Only museum and church are open.*

The old buildings occupied by the monks, parts of which date from 11C and 12C, have been swallowed in 19C construction.

The **museum**, on the left in the cloister, groups Roman and Christian lapidary fragments found on the island together with documents on the monastery's history and influence. There is also a panel from an altarpiece said to be by Louis Bréa.

The abbey **church** was built in 19C in the neo-Romanesque style. In the lefthand transept is an 11C Chapel of the Dead.

**Chapels.** – Seven chapels scattered about the island completed the monastery; they were intended for anchorites. Two have retained their former character.

**Trinité Chapel** situated at the eastern end of the island pre-dates 11C. It is built on a trefoil plan with an oval cupola on pendentives. The Byzantine influence leads some to propose 5C origin.

**St-Sauveur** which is near a restaurant under the trees in the north-west corner of the island is as old as Trinité Chapel but built to an octagonal plan. It was restored in 17C and more recently.

## LORGUES

Michelin map **84** fold 4 – Pop 4 453

Lorgues spreads up a slope towards wooded hilltops. The ground is well-suited to the cultivation of vines and olives. Oil, both from olives and grape seeds, is produced in large quantities.

It is a pleasant small town where the main square with its magnificent plane trees is one of the most beautiful in the whole region.

**Old town.** – The fortified gateways are 14C. From the square radiate streets of old houses with their attractive façades, lintels, wrought iron work, stairways and fountains.

**St-Martin Collegiate Church.** – The 18C church is unusually large with a dressed stone façade. The high altar in multicoloured marble is decorated with angels' heads. The Virgin and Child is attributed to Pierre Puget. The church has a fine organ and a carved pulpit.

**St-Ferréol.** – *1 km – 1/2 mile. Follow the signs to the north-east of the town.*

The chapel stands on a low wooded hill with a view of Lorgues and the Alpine foothills.

## *EXCURSIONS*

**Thoronet Abbey***. – *13 km – 8 miles. Description p 143. Leave Lorgues by D 562 going south east. Bear left into D 17 and turn right into D 79. The abbey is immediately on the right.*

**N.-D. de Benva Chapel.** – *3 km – 2 miles to north west (D 50) on the Entrecasteaux road. Key available from Lorgues Presbytery, 34 rue Bourgade.*
Our Lady of Benva (corruption of Provençal Ben Vai: good journey) stands on a hillside. Its porch is built astride the old Entrecasteaux road so that passers-by should notice it. Both the porch and the interior are decorated with 15C frescoes.

**Taradeau.** – Pop 535. *9 km – 6 miles – southeast by the D 10.*
A "Saracen" tower and a ruined Romanesque chapel crown the bluff dominating the village, which is a wine producing centre.

*Take D 73 north uphill.* On the right is a stony path marked "Table d'Orientation 800 m". Park the car and walk the last 100 m – 110 yards for a **panorama***. over Lorgues, les Arcs (NE), the Provençal Plateau (N) and the Pre-Alps of Grasse (NE), the Esterel (E) and the Maures (S).

## LOUP Valley ★★
Michelin map **195** folds 24 and 25

The region described is the lower basin of the Loup valley where the gorges rank among the most beautiful natural sights of Haute-Provence. The approach roads to the gorges pass through a picturesque region where there are many hill villages. The Loup rises at an altitude of 1 300 m – 4 250 ft in the Pre-Alps of Grasse (north face of L'Audibergue Mountain). For almost all of its short journey to the Mediterranean the river has cut a valley gorge through the mountains – and this is the most beautiful part of the drive.

### Round tour from Vence – *55 km – 21 miles – about 5 hours – Local map below*

*Leave Vence (p 159) by D 2210 going north west.*

The road is bordered by pleasant houses among the olive trees. There is a view back over the hills round Vence.

**Tourrette-sur-Loup***. – Pop 2 267. *Facilities p 30.* This is violet country; the flowers are grown under the olive trees. The unusual fortified village, its outer houses forming a surrounding rampart, stands on a rock plateau looking down over a sheer drop *(illustration p 9).* Weavers, potters, sculptors, engravers and painters living in Tourrette have made it an artistic and craft centre *(p 22).*
The 15C **church** contains a triptych by the Bréa School, carved wood altarpieces and 15-17C busts and reliquaries.
Seen from the southern corner of the square, under the bell-tower gate, the **old village*** has an almost entirely mediaeval aspect. The Grand-Rue describes a semi-circle through the village emerging at another gate. In 1959 **St-Jean Chapel** was decorated by Ralph Soupault with charming naive **frescoes.** On the far wall are the two St Johns (the Baptist and the Apostle) on either side of the cross symbolising the link between the Old and New Testaments.

The road loops round Tourrette revealing other views of this astonishing village, before negotiating the limestone fissures of the Loup valley. Soon the hilltop village of Le Bar-sur-Loup appears and Gourdon, perched on its promontory like an eagle's eyrie.

**Pont-du-Loup.** – Ruins of a railway viaduct destroyed by the Germans in 1944.

*Outside the village bear right into D 6.* The road runs through the very fine **Loup Gorges**★★, cut vertically through the Grasse mountains, with enormous potholes, smooth and round, hollowed out of their sides.

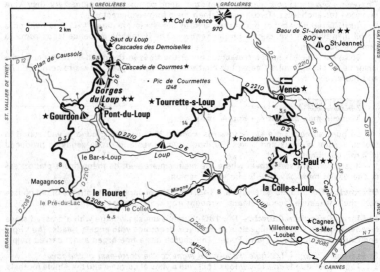

Just before the second tunnel, in a semicircular hollow, the **Courmes Waterfall★** (Cascade de Courmes) spills down on to a mossy bed (40 m – 130 ft).

*Leave the car beyond the third tunnel.* Retrace your steps to the **Saut du Loup** and the **Cascade des Demoiselles** embowered in lush vegetation.

*Just before Bramafan bridge, turn sharp left into D 3.* As the road rises to Caussols Plateau, the vegetation grows sparser but as far as Gourdon there are continual **views★** down into the depths of the gorges with a particularly breathtaking **view★★** where an overhang has been built out from a sharp righthand turn *(signpost)*. Beyond the end of the gorges the view widens out southwards towards the coast.

**Gourdon★**. – *Description p 74.*

Interesting drive downhill from Caussols Plateau by D 3. In Le-Pré-du-Lac turn right into D 2085.

**Le Rouret.** – Pop 1 807. The village lies on a slope where olives, vines and jasmine grow.

After Le Collet bear left into D 7 and drive down a wooded valley which becomes more and more enclosed until it joins the lower valley of the Loup, where there is a good **view** of the river and of the precipitous Pre-Alps of Grasse in the background.

After a *corniche* section, the road descends to the valley floor to cross the river.

**La Colle-sur-Loup.** – Pop 3 700. *Facilities p 30.* A picturesque village in the plain where fruit and flowers are cultivated. The church has a Renaissance door and a square bell-tower.

**St-Paul★★**. – *Description p 133.*

Beyond St-Paul the **view** broadens to include the rocky foothills of the Pre-Alps of Grasse.

## LUCÉRAM ★

Michelin map 🔟🟨🟨 fold 17 – *Local map p 154* – Pop 694

The village stands on a steep rock between two ravines in a wooded region beneath the Gros Braus peak; it was also defended by ramparts including the 13C tower which dominates the town. Lucéram not only boasts a remarkable **setting★** but is exceptionally rich in works of art.

**The Shepherds' Christmas Offering.** – The old ceremony always attracts a crowd. Each year shepherds from the neighbouring mountains make their offering of lambs and fruit to the church to the sound of fifes and tambourines.

### ■ SIGHTS *time: 3/4 hour*

*Place de la Mairie, follow the arrows pointing to the church (église).*

**Old village.** – A maze of stepped streets and vaulted alleyways make up the mediaeval town which was administered as a miniature republic by consuls. Note the Ionic columns framing a 14C doorway and the many Gothic houses. From the church terrace one can look down on Lucéram, its tower and crenelated walls, and over the hills behind Nice to the sea.

**Church.** – *To see the altarpieces illuminated and to visit the treasury apply to the Presbytery (☎ 91.51.87) on the right of the church. Keys to St-Grat and N.-D.-de-Bon-Coeur Chapels (see below) also available from the Presbytery.*

The interior of the simple 15C church was remodelled in 18C with elaborate plasterwork; it nevertheless contains some fine **works of art★★**, including five large altarpieces from the school of the Nice master, Louis Bréa *(p 19)*. They form the most complete group of the school and are the best presented in the country of Nice. Ourstanding are the 15C altarpiece to St Anthony in the south transept, and that to St Margaret, behind the high altar, which is divided into ten panels and attributed to Louis Bréa. In the nave stand two *pietàs:* one dating from the 13C in plaster on material, the other 16C of painted wood. In the chancel are some old wrought iron processional lanterns.

The **treasure★**, which is displayed in a chest, comprises some remarkable pieces: a chased silver statuette of St Margaret (1500), a finely engraved 14C reliquary, a statue-reliquary of St Rosalie from Sicily, two candlesticks and an alabaster Virgin (16C).

**St-Grat Chapel.** – *1 km – 1/2 mile to the south on D 2566.* The chapel is decorated with frescoes attributed to Jean Baleison : the four Evangelists writing; beneath a triple Gothic canopy the Virgin and Child who is holding a dove, St-Grat bearing the head of John the Baptist and St Sebastian in elegant attire, an arrow in his hand.

**N.-D.-de-Bon-Coeur Chapel.** – *2 km – 1 1/4 miles north west on D 2566, then 1/4 hour on foot Rtn.* Park the car on the open space and take the path on the left past a ruined house to the chapel.

The frescoes, attributed to Baleison, are interesting despite some unfortunate repainting. In the porch: Good and Bad Prayer and St Sebastian; in the chapel: the Adoration of the Shepherds, the Adoration of the Magi and scenes from the life of the Virgin.

## LURE Mountain ★

Michelin map 🔟🟨 folds 5, 6, 15 and 16

The Lure, which is an eastward extension of Mount Ventoux, dominates the middle reaches of the Durance with its impressive silhouette. It looks like an unbroken spine (30 km – 98 ft) sloping gently south to the Forcalquier basin while the north and east faces drop abruptly into the Jabron and Durance valleys. It is a bare rugged mountain; the cedars, holm oaks and lavender fields of the southern slopes give way to rough pasture and herbs at the summit, whereas the north face is densely forested with pine trees and spruces, beeches, oaks and maples.

LURE Mountain *

**Forcalquier to Sisteron** – *64 km – 40 miles – about 2 hours – Local map p 60. Between the Lure refuge and Valbelle the road is closed from 15 November to 31 May.*

*Leave Forcalquier (p 67) by D 12 going north west.*

The road winds through the scrub of the Lure foothills.

**Rochers des Mourres.** – The rock standing on the left of the road has been curiously shaped by erosion.

The Durance can be seen in the valley below *(right)*.

**Fontienne.** – Pop 24. The tiny village perched on a mountain shoulder has a Romanesque chapel with a two-bay wall belfry and a castle of which the lower part dates back to 13C.

The vegetation becomes less sparse as the road approaches St-Étienne.

**St-Étienne.** – Pop 561. *Facilities p 30.* The main road to the top of the Lure starts in St-Étienne, which owed its prosperity in earlier centuries to the many «drugs» which were prepared from the medicinal herbs growing on the mountain and hawked as far away as the Auvergne and Burgundy. Some of the houses with mullion windows and arched doorways date from 16C. The church choir is polygonal; next to it 18C towers have been added to the 13C castle.

D 113 climbs through lavender fields dotted with clumps of cedars and pines. The trees are scattered thinly at first but steadily develop into a dense woodland as the ground rises. Soon after St-Joseph's Oratory a narrow road leads off to the right to N.-D. de Lure.

**N.-D. de Lure.** – *Closed for restoration.* The rustic life of the Chalais Order is manifest in this simple monastery which was built in 1165 in this wild setting. The original buildings have mostly disappeared but the restored 17C chapel still stands beneath the lime trees. The semi-circular vaulting of the nave is continued into the choir which ends in three bays and – a rarity in Romanesque architecture – a cruciform oculus. The side aisles are barrel-vaulted and of later date.

*Return to D 113.* Beyond a holiday camp the woods recede and the view opens out.

**Lure Refuge.** – A modest winter sports station with six ski-lifts. From the car park the **view** attains its fullest extent.

1.5 km – 1 mile further on, a stele has been erected on the left hand side of the road to the 17C Belgian astronomer, Wendelin, who built the first observatory in France.

*Leave the car at a second platform 2.5 km – 1 1/2 miles further on.*

**Lure Beacon★★.** – *1/2 hour on foot Rtn (fairly steep climb).* From the top (1 826 m – 5 991 ft) there is a vast circular **panorama★★** of the coast, Mounts Viso, Pelvoux and Vercors, the Cévennes and Mount Ventoux.

A little further on the left a gap in the mountain ridge reveals the Jabron valley and the Baronnies in the distance. Beyond La Graille Pass the road enters the magnificent beech wood of La Fayée.

The road runs eastwards to circumvent Mount Sumiou before reaching the limestone bands of Valbelle circus. The forest continues steeply downhill into the Jabron valley. Bear left at the fork and after crossing the Jabron turn right into D 946 beside the river. After 3 km – 2 miles turn left into D 53 to Sisteron *(p 140)*.

---

**LURS**

Michelin map 🮲🮲 fold 15 – *Local map p 60* – Pop 275

Lurs is visible from far off, bathed in luminous light on its hilltop **site★** overlooking the Durance and the Forcalquier countryside.

**Episcopal Fortress.** – In the Middle Ages Lurs was a powerful stronghold with 3 000 inhabitants. It belonged to the Bishop of Sisteron who bore the title "Prince of Lurs"; it was the Bishops' favourite residence until 18C; they founded a seminary in the town (the building still stands beside the Forcalquier road).

**Capital of the Graphic Arts.** – Having neither running water nor electricity, the town was abandoned by its inhabitants early in this century and fell into ruin. It seemed destined to disappear after the second World War but was «discovered» and revived by a group of graphic artists, including Giono, led by Maximilian Vox, inventor of the universal classification of printing characters.

Since 1955 the **Lure International Meetings** – named after the neighbouring mountain – have provided an annual forum for experts in all forms of printing and made the village the capital of the Graphic Arts.

■ **SIGHTS** *time: 1/2 hour*

**The village.** – From Place des Feignants (Idler's Square) the Clock Gate with its campanile leads to the church with its three-bay wall belfry, narrow winding streets between overhanging houses with old doorways and the ruined mediaeval ramparts.

From the church a narrow street to the left leads to a renovated house, the **Chancellery of the Lure Companions**, and to a simple open-air theatre which has been built nearby; to the right a narrow street leads to the restored **Priory** which has been converted into a cultural centre, and to the Bishop's Palace *(closed to the public)* which has been partially rebuilt. On all sides there are views of the valley or the mountain.

**Bishop's Walk (Promenade des Évêques).** – Behind the castle on the north side is the Bishop's Walk, bordered by a rosary of 15 oratories, which was built in 1864 and leads to N.-D.-de-Vie Chapel. From the chapel there are many beautiful **views★** of the Durance valley, the Valensole Plateau and the Pre-Alps of Digne on the east and of Mount Lure and Forcalquier to the west.

Michelin map **84** fold 4 – *Local map p 60* – Pop 19 570 – *Facilities p 30*

For many years a quiet town in the lower foothills of the Lubéron above the Durance, Manosque has now begun to expand its local industry, to develop its agricultural land and to take advantage of its position on the Durance upstream from the power station at Cadarache. Modernisation has brought changes to the town so dear to **Jean Giono** (1895-1970) whose work was set in and around Manosque.

The old ramparts have for the most part been replaced by boulevards encircling the old town. The typical narrow streets are lined by tall houses which look down on patios and secret gardens at the rear.

**"Modest Manosque".** – Giono may claim that Francis I never visited Manosque but tradition maintains that the king was greeted at the Porte Saunerie by Péronne de Voland, the consul's daughter, who presented him with the keys of the city on a velvet cushion. The girl was very beautiful and the king very susceptible. To protect her virtue, the consul's daughter disfigured her face with sulphur and Manosque was known by the epithet "modest".

### MANOSQUE

| | |
|---|---|
| Grande (R.) | 10 |
| Hôtel-de-Ville (Pl. de l') | 14 |
| Marchands (R. des) | 15 |
| | |
| Arthur-Robert (R.) | 2 |
| Aubette (R. d') | 3 |
| Bret (Bd Martin) | 5 |
| Chacundier (R.) | 6 |
| Dauphine (R.) | 8 |
| Giono (Av. Jean) | 9 |
| Guilhempierre (R.) | 12 |
| Mirabeau (Bd) | 16 |
| Notre-Dame-de-Romigier (⊞) | D |
| Pelloutier (Bd C.) | 19 |
| Plaine (Bd de la) | 20 |
| Reine-Jeanne (R. de la) | 21 |
| République (R. de la) | 22 |
| Rousseau (R. J.-J.) | 24 |
| St-Lazare (R.) | 25 |
| St-Sauveur (⊞) | B |
| Saunerie (R. de la) | 27 |
| Soubeyran (R.) | 28 |
| Vraies-Richesses (Montée des) | 30 |

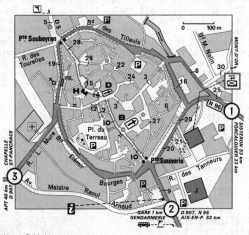

## ■ OLD MANOSQUE *time: 3/4 hour*

**Porte Saunerie★**. – The central section of the 14C Salt Gate is defended by two mantraps; the two side towers are crowned by fine machicolations. Its name comes from the salt which was stored nearby in former days.

**Rue Grande (10)**. – The main street of the old town has retained a picturesque and lively character; note the old doorways, stairways, courtyards and balconies (Nos 21, 23, 31, 39 and 42). No 14 was the shop where Giono spent some of his childhood; his father was a cobbler and his mother a laundress. Higher up the street the church looks down on an attractive fountain.

**St-Sauveur Church (B)**. – A Gothic doorway leads into a Romanesque nave with 17C rib vaulting. The transept is Romanesque with barrel vaulting and the crossing is surmounted by a cupola on squinches; there is oven vaulting in the apse. The organ casing was carved and gilded in 1620. The square bell-tower is crowned by a wrought iron **campanile**, the masterpiece of an 18C smith from Valensole.

**Place de l'Hôtel-de-Ville (14)**. – Three times a week there is a lively market. The town hall **(H)** on the left was built in 17C as an elegant private house.

**N.-D.-de-Romigier Church (D)**. – *Closed for restoration*. The elegant Renaissance doorway is surmounted by a marble Virgin by Pierre Puget. The Romanesque nave was refashioned in 17C when the side aisles were added.

The altar in the north chapel is made out of a 4C or 5C tombstone of Carrara marble, representing the Apostles facing a cross surmounted by a chrism. There is also a beautiful Black Virgin (12C), Our Lady of Romigier.

**Soubeyran Gate (Porte Soubeyran)**. – This 14C gateway, which has been restored, is decorated with a pretty stone balustrade and a campanile.

Go through the gate and turn left into Boulevard C.-Pelloutier continuing into Boulevard Elémir-Bourges which overlooks the foothills of Mount Lubéron before returning to Salt Gate.

## ■ ADDITIONAL SIGHTS

**St-Pancrace (or Toutes Aures) Chapel.** – *2 km – 1 1/4 miles south west. Leave Manosque by ③ on the plan and follow the signs.* From the top of the hill there is an almost circular view★ embracing Mount Lubéron (W), Manosque and to the east of the Durance the Valensole Plateau and the Pre-Alps of Digne.

**Mount Or (Mont d'Or).** – *1.5 km – 1 mile north east. From Rue Dauphine turn left into Montée des Vraies Richesses which climbs straight up a steep hill initially.* At the "Résidence Jean Giono" a dead-end turning to the right leads to **"La Paraïsse"** *(not open to the public)* a house hidden in the trees where Giono wrote his most important works. The **view★** which broadens as the road rises, reaches its full extent by a ruined tower on the summit: the roofs of old Manosque, the Durance valley, the Lubéron (W), Ste-Victoire Mountain and Ste-Baume Massif (S) in the distance.

Michelin map 🔢 folds 7, 16, 17 and 18

The wooded Maures Massif extends eastwards from Hyères to St-Raphaël, between the sea to the Gapeau and Argens river valleys. The coast is continuously indented, providing delightful viewpoints and beauty spots which can be seen from the magnificent tourist road, particularly the section from Le Lavandou to La Croix-Valmer known as the Maures' Corniche. The interior is broken up by shady valleys and wild ravines.

## GEOGRAPHICAL NOTES

The Maures, composed for the most part of crystalline schists (gneiss and mica-schists), are, with the Esterel, the oldest geological areas in Provence. The Hercynian folding pushed up a vast massif, Tyrrhenia, which included Corsica and Sardinia.

Successive thrusts originating from the Pyrenees and the Alps broke up this mass, forming the western basin of the Mediterranean and reshaping the Maures into four parallel lines of relief.

The Hyères Islands mark the southern chain which is partially submerged; the second chain along the coast reaches its highest point at Les Pradels (528 m – 1 725 ft); the two inland chains, La Verne and La Sauvette, are separated by the Grimaud (E) and Collobrières (W) rivers. La Sauvette, the most northerly chain, includes the highest peaks, Notre-Dame-des-Anges (771 m –1 523 ft) and La Sauvette (779 m – 2 556 ft), and ends in Roquebrune Mountain *(p 125)* (NE) overlooking the lower Argens valley

The coastline juts out in the blunt promontories of Cap Bénat and St-Tropez peninsula, the pointed headlands of Cap Nègre and Cap des Sardinaux and retreats into the Bormes roadstead, Cavalaire Bay and St-Tropez Bay.

The pines along the coast, and the cork oaks and chestnuts inland, which form the main vegetation of the Maures, are sometimes devastated by raging forest fires. The massif's principal industry, the manufacture of bottle corks, derives from the cork oaks which are carefully cultivated.

## HISTORICAL NOTES

"Maouro", a Provençal word applied to dark forests, has become "Maures" in French and is used to describe this densely wooded mountain range.

On the other hand, tradition sees in the name an allusion to the Moorish pirates from Spain, who ravaged the coast in the 8C and established themselves in the following century on the slopes around the Grimaud Plain; but these pirates were really Saracens *(see p 73)*. Driven out in 973, they continued to raid the coast up to the 18C and set up a reign of terror. To defend themselves, the inhabitants withdrew from the shore, going up into the hills from where they could watch the horizon *(details of hill villages p 21)*.

It was the 20C vogue for sea-bathing, limited at first to an aristocratic clientèle which brought this magnificent coast back to life and ended the economic isolation of the region.

On 15 August 1944, the Allied and French Armies landed on the Maures beaches to liberate the south of France *(p 17)*.

## ① MAURES CORNICHE★★

**Hyères to La Croix-Valmer** – *48 km – 30 miles – about 1 1/2 hours – Local map above*

*Leave Hyères (p 82) by N 98,* ① *on the plan.*

The *corniche* road along the foot of the Pradels coastal chain passes many enchanting beauty spots although the magnificence of the forest has been damaged by fire in some places. After crossing the Gapeau the road runs past the salt marshes across the Hyères Plain with **views** of Cap Bénat and Port-Cros Island.

MAURES

0        5 km

Le Lavandou★. –
*Description p 87.*

St-Clair. – *Facilities
p 28.* St-Clair, a short
distance from the main
road, has a beautiful beach.

Aiguebelle. – Pleasant, peaceful
seaside resort.

Cavalière★. – *Facilities p 28.* Cava-
lière has a fine beach, sheltered from
the mistral. The view extends over
Cap Nègre and the Bormes roadstead as
far as the Islands of Levant and Port-Cros.

Pramousquier. – *Facilities p 28.* A modest resort with
a sheltered beach of fine sand.

The road leaves the shore and winds among pine trees
and gardens.

Rayol-Canadel-sur-Mer. – *Facilities p 28.* Canadel, lying at the
base of the last foothills of the Pradels range and flanked by
two pinewoods, possesses one of the most sheltered beaches
on the Maures' coast.

Rayol's site★ terraced like an amphitheatre in the densely wooded hillside (cork oaks,
pines, eucalyptus and mimosa) is one of the most beautiful on the Maures' coast. A
monumental flower-decked flight of steps descends from Le Patek, a belvedere
decorated with a circular pergola, through the woods and well tended terraced
gardens, to the protected beach, which lies at the end of a narrow bay.

The road climbs disclosing a fine view from Cap Bénat to Cap Lardier.

Cavalaire-sur-Mer★. – Pop 2 710. *Facilities p 28.* At the foot of Les Pradels mountains
stretches 4 km – 2 1/2 miles of fine sandy beach facing east.
There is a boat service in summer from Cavalaire to the Hyères Islands *(p 84)*.

La Croix Valmer. – Pop 1 869. *Facilities p 28.* The village is a climatic resort and rest
centre. The local wine is well considered among Côtes de Provence. The site of La
Croix village is said to be where Constantine had his vision while on his way to Rome

to claim the Empire. According to tradition he saw a cross in the sky with the words "In hoc signo vinces : in this sign you will conquer", a prediction of his forthcoming victory which was shared by Christianity. A stone cross erected on the pass commemorates the legend and gives the village its name.

**Collebasse Pass.** – Alt 129 m – 423 ft. *8 km – 5 miles from La Croix-Valmer by the very winding D 93.* There is a superb **view★** of the Pampelonne Bight, Cavalaire Bay and the Hyères Islands.

## ② CIRCULAR TOUR OF THE MAURES MASSIF INTERIOR★★

*106 km – 66 miles – half-day – Local maps pp 94-95*

This beautiful circular tour, by very hilly but unfrequented roads, goes over at least seven passes and penetrates deep into the heart of the massif.

*Leave Le Lavandou (p 87) by N 559 going west and turn right into D 41.*

The road winds uphill among cypress, eucalyptus, mimosa and oleanders in white, pink and red. Fine **view** ahead of Bormes and its castle.

**Bormes-les-Mimosas★.** – *Description p 41.*

At Caguo-Ven Pass a righthand turning into a forest road marks the end of the circular tour. After winding downhill, D 41 reaches Gratteloup Pass (alt 200 m – 656 ft). Beyond the crossroads, D 41 runs over wooded slopes of cork oak and chestnut with glimpses of the sea and the mountains round Toulon to the left and deep valleys to the right.

**Babaou Pass★** (Col de Babaou). – Alt 415 m – 1 362 ft. There is an attractive **panorama★** from the pass of the Hyères roadstead, the Giens Peninsula and the Hyères Islands.

Beyond the pass rise the tallest of the Maures summits, their slopes wooded by magnificent chestnuts.

The road descends to the Réal Collobrier valley which widens to form the Collobrières basin. *Turn right into D 14.*

**Collobrières.** – Pop 1 135. The picturesque houses of the well-shaded town look down on the river flowing swiftly beneath an old hump-backed bridge. The local forests provide the raw material for bottle corks and the vineyards for rosé wine. The local speciality is marron glacé and other sweet chestnut products.

Six kilometres – 4 miles from Collobrières a narrow road *(uneven surface)* on the right leads to the ruins of the former Carthusian Monastery of La Verne, in its majestic forest setting.

**La Verne Charterhouse.** – *Open 10am to 7pm; closed Tuesdays from 1 October to 30 April; 1/2 hour; 10F.*
The ruins of the monastery (partially restored) stand on an isolated **site★** near a spring well off the beaten track deep in the Maures forest. The monastery was founded in 1770 and rebuilt several times until it was abandoned during the Revolution.
The buildings are of brown Maures schist but are distinguished by the use of ophite or serpentine, a stone with bluish green reflections, for the door jambs, arches, vaulting and other decoration.
Under the porch the main **doorway** is built of serpentine stone; two ringed columns flank the door under a triangular pediment. The guest house built round a court with its own fountain includes a bakehouse and 12C vaulted **kitchen;** a great stone staircase leads to the first floor which has been converted to a simple restaurant (17C wood statues).
Beyond the remains of the **small cloister** and the ruined Romanesque chapel, is the **great cloister,** partially preserved, with the monks' cells – each consisting of four rooms and a garden; one such cell has been reconstructed.
A postern in the great cloister leads to the remains of a windmill from where there is a fine **view** of the wooded Maures and the Verne valley.

*Return to D 14.*

After Taillude Pass the road looks across the valley of La Verne to the ruins of the Charterhouse crowning the opposite slope and then, after passing high above the hamlet of Capelude, makes its way into the upper valley of the Le Périer stream. From the centre of the valley there is a **vista** of the Grimaud Plain and the Bay of St-Tropez.

Abruptly the road turns into the Giscle valley (or the Grimaud stream valley) from where Grimaud can be seen in the distance overlooked by its beautiful castle ruins.

**Grimaud★.** – Pop 2 408. *Facilities p 30.* The village is named after the Grimaldi family who once owned it and offers fine **views** of the Maures and St-Tropez Bay. The ruins of the castle which was destroyed on the orders of Louis XIII dominate the mediaeval streets. **Rue des Templiers** with its basalt arcades and serpentine doorways leads to St-Michel's Church in pure Romanesque style.

*From Grimaud take D 558 which turns south.*

**Cogolin.** – *Description p 54.*

N 98 runs south west up the Môle valley for 8 km – 5 miles. Turn left into D 27 which winds up the north face of the coastal chain of hils.

**Canadel Pass★★.** – Alt 267 m – 876 ft. Suddenly the sea comes into view; there is a superb **panorama★★** of Canadel, the Pramousquier beach, Cap Nègre, the Bormes roadstead, Cap Bénat and beyond, on the horizon, the Island of Porquerolles.

*Turn right into the forest road to Caguo-Ven Pass.* It is a picturesque drive with magnificent **views★** of the Maures Massif, the coast and the Hyères Islands.

*15 km – 12 miles from Canadel Pass near a farm, park the car and take the path on the right; after 100 m – 110 yards follow the path to the left through the scrub and scramble up the rocks (easy climb).*

**Pierre d'Avenon★.** – Alt 442 m – 1 450 ft. From the top of this huge mound of giant boulders the **view★** extends on either hand over the whole Maures coastline from Cap Lardier (E) to Hyères (W) with the harbour installations of Le Lavandou and Bormes in the foreground.

**Caguo-Ven Pass.** – Alt 200 m – 656 ft. From the pass, there is a **panorama** of the Hyères and Bormes roadsteads and Porquerolles Island.

*Return to Le Lavandou, by Bormes-les-Mimosas and Le Pin.*

### ③ ST-TROPEZ PENINSULA★
**La Croix-Valmer to St-Tropez** *– 23 km – 14 miles – about 2 hours – Local map pp 94-95*

A tour of the country behind St-Tropez includes several charming villages and widespread views.

*Take N 559 going north.*

Shortly after La Croix-Valmer the village of Gassin comes into view while on the horizon to the left rise the twin peaks of La Sauvette (779 m – 2 556 ft) and N.-D.-des-Anges (771 m – 2 526 ft), the highest in the Maures Massif.

*Turn right into D 89.*

**Gassin★.** – Pop 1 519. The old village of Gassin, in complete contrast to the many seaside and holiday resorts which have developed in recent years, stands proudly apart at an altitude of 210 m – 605 ft. It is a typical example from the times when Saracen pirates used to plunder the region and villages were set up as look-out points. In the church there is a modern Way of the Cross with comments by the artist.
The **view★** from Gassin extends: northwards to the Bay of St-Tropez; southwards to Cavalaire Bay, the Hyères Islands and the Maures.

*From Gassin take D 98 south west and at Paillas Pass turn left into a narrow road.*

**Paillas Windmills★★.** – Near three ruined windmills stand a circular platform bearing a radio beacon.
Follow the perimeter fence round; through the gaps in the trees a fine **panorama★★** is visible: *(facing north east)* the broken outline of the Esterel Massif with Cap Roux, Ste-Maxime and St-Tropez Bay in the foreground; *(facing east)* the long beach at Pampelonne and the lighthouse on Cap Camarat; *(facing south west)* Cavalaire Bay, Hyères Islands out to sea, the Maures coast, les Pradels coastal chain; *(facing inland west)* Gassin opposite, Cogolin and Grimaud, La Sauvette chain; in the far distance are the Alps (NE).

*Make a U-turn and at Paillas Pass turn left into D 89.*

**Ramatuelle★.** – Pop 1 209. *Facilities p 30.* The village, built halfway up a slope, is a typical old Provençal market town with narrow winding alleys overhung with arches and arcades. A superb **tree** and one of the most remarkable survivors of the elms planted in Sully's time (16-17C) stands in the Place de l'Ormeau.

*Leave Ramatuelle by D 61 going south; turn left into D 93.*

**Cap Camarat★.** – 4 km – 2 1/2 miles *after joining D 93 turn right.* In a bleak landscape stands the lighthouse; its beam carries 60 km – 37 miles *(open during school*

*(After photo : Editions Mar, Nice)*

Ramatuelle

*holidays only, 2 to 6pm; closed Sundays and holidays).* The **view★** from the top extends from Cap Dramont (headland in the Esterel Massif) to the Hyères Islands.

*Return to D 93 and turn right.* The road runs through vineyards parallel to Pampelonne Beach. Bear right into a narrow road leading to **Ste-Anne Chapel** *(p 137).*

### ④ THE COAST ROAD★★
**St-Tropez to St-Raphaël** *– 39 km – 24 miles – 1/2 day – Local map p 95*

*Leave St-Tropez (p 136) by D 98ᴬ, ① on the plan.*

The road skirts the southern shore of St-Tropez Bay looking across to the opposite coast.
*After 4 km – 2 1/2 miles turn right.*

**Cogolin Marina.** – *See Cogolin p 54.*

*Return to D 98ᴬ; turn right into N 98 and right again to Port-Grimaud.*

**Port-Grimaud★.** – *Facilities p 28.* On St-Tropez Bay, this small port resembles a typical Mediterranean fishing village. In reality, it is an elegant residential ensemble with a well equipped marina offering a wide variety of leisure activities. Strolling in the village is pleasant *(parking obligatory at the entrance of the village)* with its colourful houses, canals, alleys and small bridges. Passenger ferries provide short cuts across the water. The ecumenical **church** was conceived as part of the overall plan and is resolutely modern although inspired by Provençal Romanesque. The interior is plain; no ceiling covers the wooden roof beams. The tower is open to the public *(donation);* the **view★** covers the modern village, St-Tropez Bay and the Maures Massif.

Return to N 98 which skirts the north shore of the bay, overlooking St-Tropez.

**Beauvallon.** – *Facilities p 28*. Beauvallon is a well situated resort on the north shore of St-Tropez Bay shaded by pine and cork oak woods.

At this spot the Maures slope very gently down to the sea where the shore, with scarcely any shade, forms a series of beaches from the end of the bay right round to Ste-Maxime.

**Ste-Maxime★.** – *Description p 138.*

The road, which skirts the coast closely as far as St-Aygulf, circles Cap Sardinaux.

**La Nartelle.** – The beach of what is now the resort of La Nartelle was one of the landing points for the Allied forces in August 1944.

The coastline between La Nartelle and St-Aygulf is broken up into several inlets *(calanques)* with small beaches and rocks emerging from the sea.

**Val d'Esquières, San Peïre, Les Calanques, Les Issambres.** – *Facilities p 28*. These four resorts combine to form a rapidly evolving tourist development. Houses of various sizes, some built in the Provençal style, have been discreetly sited in the hills. Les Issambres probably takes its name from "Sinus Sambracitanus", the Roman name for St-Tropez Bay.

**St-Aygulf.** – *Facilities p 28*. The resort of St-Aygulf is shaded by pines, cork and holm oaks; from the beach of fine sand, ringed with rocks, there is an attractive view of Fréjus Bay.

Beyond St-Aygulf there is a beautiful **panorama** of the plain of the Lower Argens which separates the Maures and the Esterel. The magnificent rocks of Mount Roquebrune stand out from the Maures Massif while in the Esterel chain, behind the Dramont semaphore, one can pick out the summit of Cap Roux.

**Fréjus★.** – *Description p 69.*

*Leave Fréjus by Boulevard S.-Descuers going south.*

**Fréjus-Plage.** – *Description p 72.*

*Take N 98 by the sea to reach St-Raphaël (p 134).*

## 5 THE CREST ROAD★★
### Round tour starting from St–Tropez – *103 miles – 64 miles – 1/2 day – Local map pp 94-95*

This excursion passes through wooded countryside *(Mediterranean vegetation, see p 12)* and affords some fine views. Quiet roads lead to the lower slopes of the twin peaks of N.-D.-des-Anges and La Sauvette.

*The itinerary is described as far as La Foux on p 97. At La Foux take the N 98 in the direction of Cogolin.*

**Cogolin.** – *Description p 54.*

The N 98 then follows the Môle valley. Shortly before the village of the same name, to the right of the road stands a château flanked by two round towers with pepper pot roofs. It was here that Saint-Exupéry (1900-1944) aviator and writer, spent some of his childhood years. Vineyards give way to forest covered slopes.

**Dom Forest★.** – This state forest composed mainly of pines, cork oaks and chestnuts, spreads over the Les Pradels and La Verne chains, which are separated by the steep sided Môle valley.

Jean Aicard (1848-1921), poet and novelist set his work *Maurin des Maures* in this area.

*At the Gratteloup Pass turn right into D 41 continuing until Collobrières (description of this section p 96). 3 km – 2 miles beyond Collobrières take the D 39 to the left.*

The road winds through wooded countryside overlooking a steep sided stream and affords to the right rare glimpses of La Sauvette peak. Shortly before La Fourche Pass the road forking off to the left leads to N.-D.-des-Anges, pinpointed by the television relay mast.

**Notre-Dame-des-Anges★★.** – The **hermitage** near the summit (771 m – 2 526 ft) stands in an attractive **setting★**, amidst schist rocks where only trees such as the chestnut thrive. The Merovingian foundation may well have superseded an earlier pagan place of worship. Remodelled in the 19C, the buildings included accommodation for pilgrims and a chapel *(open Sunday afternoons, April to November)*, the walls of which are covered with votive offerings.

The terrace affords an exceptional **panorama★★** of the Argens depression with the Alps behind (NE), over the Maures heights to the sea, the Hyères Islands (SE); Giens Peninsula and Toulon (SW); Ste-Baume (W) and even Corsica (SE) on a clear day. To the right of the chapel, behind the lotus tree stands a venerable **elm** over four hundred years old.

*Return to La Fourche Pass, turn left then right into the GR 9.*

Passing through Collobrières State Forest the road skirts the lower slopes of the Maures' highest peak, La Sauvette (779 m – 2 556 ft) and overlooks the Le Luc plain on the left. Shortly afterwards St-Tropez Bay comes into view.

**Les Roches Blanches Panorama★.** – This truly circular panorama includes La Garde-Freinet Forest stretching away to the Argens valley (NE), the St-Tropez Bay (E) and the maquis covered north facing slopes of the Maures (S).

The road climbs down to the village of La Garde-Freinet which is dominated by its castle ruins.

**La Garde-Freinet.** – *Description p 73.*

*Leave the village to the south by the D 558. Still descending the road passes cork oak and chestnut covered slopes and affords glimpses of the bay and peninsula of St-Tropez.*

**Grimaud★.** – *Description p 96.*

*Return to St-Tropez by the D 14 and the D 98 A.*

Michelin map **195** fold 28 – *Local map p 102* – Pop 25 314 – *Facilities p 28 – For additional plan of Menton see the current Michelin Guide France*

Menton claims to be the warmest resort on the Riviera and is a pleasant place to spend a winter holiday. Here, however, the sun is king and long sandy beaches, two marinas and numerous celebrations and cultural activities welcome the summer visitor.

The town is backed by terraced slopes planted with citrus fruits and olives. The climate is particularly favourable to flowers and tropical plants; lemon trees, which die if the temperature falls below – 3°C – 26°F, flourish throughout the year providing the famous Menton lemons much sought after by connoisseurs. The picturesque old town standing out against a mountainous backdrop constitutes a magnificent **site**★★.

**Early History.** – Evidence of human settlement in the paleolithic era from excavations near the Italian frontier is displayed in the Monaco Museum of Prehistoric Anthropology and in the Menton Municipal Museum but little is know about the town's origins. The name Menton first appears in 1261. In 1346 the town was bought by the Grimaldi of Monaco although it remained under the Bishop of Ventimiglia. Together with Monaco it oscillated between the protection of France and Sardinia until it was permanently attached to France in 1860.

**Modern town.** – In the late 19C Menton shared in the popularity of the Riviera with the European aristocracy. Rich and well-known foreigners came to live there including the New-Zealand writer Katherine Mansfield (1888-1929), the Spaniard Blasco Ibanez (1867-1928). 20C tourism brought new blood and light industry grew up in the Carei valley while the residential district spread west to Roquebrune-Cap Martin and east to the Italian frontier. The old town nonetheless is well supplied with parks.

**"Artium civitas".** – This inscription on the front of the Town Hall declared Menton's ambition to be a city of the arts. The aim is to offer a variety of cultural activity.

The Biennial International Art Exhibition (painting, sculpture, ceramics, tapestry) attracts the best among contemporary artists and offers a platform to the less well-known. The **Chamber Music Festival** has an international reputation and its guest artists are world-famous. A prize for the best short story is awarded each year by the Katherine Mansfield Foundation.

Shrove Tuesday brings the annual Lemon Festival and there are flower carnivals throughout the summer.

■ **SEA FRONT AND OLD TOWN**★★ *time: 3 hours*

*Start from the Municipal Casino going east.*

**Promenade du Soleil**★★ (Z). – The broad terraces of the promenade which follows the shore beneath the old town and the Alps in the background is a favourite with visitors.

**Quai Napoléon-III** (Z). – The jetty, which protects the harbour and ends in a lighthouse, is a good vantage point from which to look at the old town.

**Jean Cocteau Museum** (Z M). – *Open 15 June to 15 September, 10am to noon and 3 to 6pm; the rest of the year, 10am to noon and 2 to 6pm; closed Mondays, Tuesdays and holidays; 3F (combined ticket with Town Hall).*

The museum is housed in a 17C bastion built by Honoré II of Monaco. On the ground floor the Salamander, a mosaic of grey and white tesserae in the Menton tradition; on the left a tapestry: Judith and Holofernes. Upstairs, an unusual series of fantastic animals and an important collection of paintings, the *Innamorati* (variations on the theme of love), pastels, drawings and stage sets.

**Empress Eugénie Jetty** (Y). – From Volti's sculpture of Saint Michael (Y V) there is a fine **view**★ of the old town above the arcades with the mountains in the background and of the coast from Cap Martin to Bordighera in Italy; Ventimiglia is hidden by Cap Mortola.

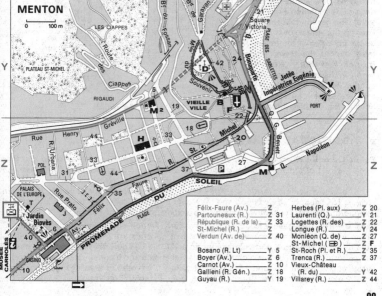

| | | | |
|---|---|---|---|
| Félix-Faure (Av.) | Z | Herbes (Pl. aux) | Z 20 |
| Partouneaux (R.) | Z 31 | Laurenti (Q.) | Y 21 |
| République (R. de la) | Z 33 | Logettes (R. des) | Z 22 |
| St-Michel (R.) | Z | Longue (R.) | Y 24 |
| Verdun (Av. de) | Z 40 | Monléon (Q. de) | Z 27 |
| | | St-Michel (⊞) | Z F |
| Bosano (R. Lt) | Y 5 | St-Roch (Pl. et R.) | Z 35 |
| Boyer (Av.) | Z 6 | Trenca (R.) | Z 37 |
| Carnot (Av.) | Z 10 | Vieux-Château | |
| Gallieni (R. Gén.) | Z 18 | (R. du) | Y 42 |
| Guyau (R.) | Y 19 | Villarey (R.) | Z 43 |

Return to **Quai Bonaparte** (Y) which skirts Les Sablettes Beach and the old town. A huge flight of steps leads up to St Michael's Church between tall narrow houses.

**St-Michel Parvis★★**. – At the top of the steps is a charming **square★★** in the Italian style, overlooking the sea and the coast, where the concerts of the Chamber Music Festival are held during August. The square is paved with a handsome mosaic of the Grimaldi arms in grey and white and framed by typical old houses and the façades of two churches.

**St-Michel Church★** (Y F). – It is the largest and finest Baroque church in the region. Its two-tier façade in yellow and rose exhibits a variety of architectural decoration. The Romanesque tower on the left, which belonged to an earlier edifice, was crowned with an octagonal campanile in 17C and the great Genoese style campanile (53 m – 174 ft) on the right was added in 18C. Above each of the three doors is a niche; the central one contains a statue of St Michael.

The interior was inspired by the Church of the Annunciation in Genoa, whence come the basilica plan with false transept and shallow chevet and barrel vaulting; it also resembles the church at Utelle *(p 155)*. Local artists such as Puppo and Vento contributed to the decoration of the side chapels which commemorate various local worthies.

*Go round the church anticlockwise.*

In the first side chapel is the fine Baroque **altarpiece of St-Nicolas** by Puppo, framed by gilt columns wreathed with vine leaves. Next door is a Crucifixion by Ferrari and an unusual 17C Virgin and Child. The third chapel contains an Assumption by Puppo garnished with angels, drapes and scrolls.

The choir contains the huge 17C **organ casing**; above the handsome 18C choir stalls is the **altarpiece of St Michael** (1569) by Manchello: the saint is flanked by Peter bearing papal insignia and John-the-Baptist; the upper sections show a fine *Pietà*. The exuberant Baroque high altar is crowned by St Michael slaying the Devil. Purple Genoese damask hangings. The next side chapel is devoted to the Princes of Monaco: an 18C painting shows Ste-Dévote, patron of the Principality, before the rock of Monaco. Another Ferrari: the Adoration of the Shepherds hangs in the first righthand aisle chapel and in the last chapel is an altarpiece by J. A. Vento: the Flight into Egypt.

**Façade★ of the Chapel of the Conception** (Y B). – On leaving the church climb a few steps on the left to admire the Chapel of the White Penitents (1762), with its garlands of flowers and basket-handled pediment surmounted by statues of the three theological virtues.

*Climb the steps into Rue du Vieux Château, very picturesque, which leads to the cemetery.*

**Old Cemetery** (Y D). – Laid out in the last century on the castle site, this cosmopolitan burial ground consists of four terraces devoted to different religious rites. From the southern corner of the English graveyard there is a beautiful **view★** of the old town, the sea and the coast from Cap Mortola to Cap Martin.

*Return to St-Michel Parvis by Montée du Souvenir, bordered by all shades of oleanders.*

St-Michel Steps are intersected by **Rue Longue** (Y 24) once the main street of the town and former Via Julia Augusta, which becomes Rue des Logettes and joins **Rue St-Michel** (Z). This pedestrian lane, lined by orange trees, links the old and new towns and is full of boutiques. Below on the left, **Place aux Herbes** (Y 20) with its coloured paving stones, plane trees, colonnade and fountain is a pleasant corner in view of the sea; nearby the covered market offers an animated daily spectacle.

*Avenue Félix-Faure, itself a lively street, leads to the Biovès Garden.*

**Biovès Garden** (Z). – This beautiful garden in the town centre is bordered by palms and lemon trees, planted with flowers and ornamented by fountains and statues (Goddess of the Golden Fruit by Volti). The garden follows the line of the Carei river and opens up a **view** of the mountains behind the town. The former Assembly Rooms *(right)*, in the style of the Belle Epoque, is now a conference and cultural centre and houses the Tourist Information Centre.

Biovès Gardens

## ■ ADDITIONAL SIGHTS

**Palais Carnolès Museum★**. – *Open 15 June to 15 September, 10am to noon and 3 to 6pm; the rest of the year, 10am to noon and 2 to 6pm; closed Mondays, Tuesdays and holidays; 3F.*

The former summer residence of the Prince of Monaco, which was built in the Italian style in 18C, decorated by Puppo and the Vento brothers – local artists – and surrounded by magnificent gardens, now contains a precious collection of paintings.

**Upstairs.** – The first gallery is devoted to the early French and Italian schools (fine 13C Virgin and Child from Tuscany). In the next two galleries are grouped religious themes from different countries, particularly a Virgin and Child by Louis Bréa. In the fourth gallery hangs Portrait of man by Bartolomeo Maineri. Galleries 5 and 6 contain the work of various European schools in 17C and 18C. The last gallery is devoted to drawings, gouaches and water colours by Manguin, Goerg , Kisling, Dufy, Picabia, Friesz etc.

**Ground floor.** – There are several rooms of modern and contemporary work by Camoin, Suzanne Valadon, Gleizes, Desnoyer, Paul Delvaux, Poliakoff, Sutherland, Gromaire etc. The other rooms are steadily filling up with works from the Biennial International Art Exhibition.

**Garavan★.** – Once a handful of elegant private houses, Garavan has now become – especially since the building of the marina – a luxurious residential suburb of Menton, between Quai Laurenti and Boulevard de Garavan, in a splendid setting.

**Tropical Garden★.** – *From Quai Laurenti take Chemin St-Jacques. Open 1 February to 30 September, 10am to noon and 2 to 5pm; 1 October to 31 January, 10am to noon and 2 to 4pm; closed Tuesdays and 1 May; 8F.*

Arranged around the Villa Val Rahmeh by the Natural History Museum of Paris, the garden includes Mediterranean and tropical flora, assembled according to theme: tropical garden, wilderness, aquatic plants and terraced olive groves. All these plants are acclimatized to the Menton climate and flourish abundantly. From the flower terrace near the house there is a magnificent view of the sea.

**Colombières Garden.** – *From Quai Laurenti take Chemin de Vallaya. Open 9am to noon and 3 to 8pm; closed 1 October to 31 December; 8F.*

A garden designed by Ferdinand Bac – writer, humorist and architect (1859-1952). An itinerary indicated by arrows conducts the visitor through 6 ha-15 acres of predominantly Mediterranean vegetation (clumps of yew trees, cypress hedges, boxwood borders), embellished with statues and follies.

At the east end, on the edge of the hill is a belvedere, with a beautiful **view★** of Menton, the port and Cap Martin.

In the villa several rooms are decorated in the ancient Roman Style: drawing room, dining room, bedroom.

**Town Hall** (Z H). – *Open 10am to noon and 3 (2 from 16 September to 14 June) to 6pm; closed Saturdays, Sundays and holidays; 3F, combined ticket with Jean Cocteau Museum.*

The building dates from 17C and was inspired by the Italian style. The **hall★** where marriage ceremonies are performed was decorated by Jean Cocteau. On the far wall the fisherman, whose eye is a fish, wears the characteristic headgear of the Menton fishermen; the girl opposite wears a Nice bonnet. On the side walls: the story of Orpheus and Eurydice, on one side, and a wedding, on the other. On the ceiling Poetry riding Pegasus.

**Municipal Museum** (Y M²). – *Closed for restoration.*

The elegant Italian façade is decorated with statues of the Four Seasons by contemporary sculptors (Summer by Volti).

Basement: popular art, local history and traditions.

Ground floor: pre-history and archaeology. Bones from local excavations, particularly the skull of "Menton man" (upper Palaeolithic); **female figurines★** from the same period. Neolithic and Roman ceramics; Gallo-Roman and Merovingian art.

## EXCURSIONS

**Roquebrune-Cap-Martin★★.** – Menton and Roquebrune-Cap-Martin form a ribbon of urban development. *Description p 125.*

**Mount Agel Tour★★.** – *Round tour of 47 km – 30 miles – about 3 1/2 hours – local map p 102.* The greater part of this tour is dominated by Mount Agel (1 110 m – 3 642 ft).

*Leave Menton by Avenue Carnot, N 7, going west. The road, La Grande Corniche, D 2584, as far as La Turbie is described on p 122. At La Turbie turn sharp right into D 53. This section of the tour is described on p 118. 2.5 km – 1 1/2 miles before Peille, turn sharp right into D 22 towards La Madone Pass; beautiful glimpses of the sea and the hilltop village of Gorbio (below).*

**St-Sébastien Pass.** – Alt 754 m – 2 474 ft. After winding round the south face of Biancon peak the road reaches St-Sébastien Pass which gives a particularly picturesque **view★** of Ste-Agnès village.

*At the crossroads go straight on to Ste-Agnès.*

**Ste-Agnès★.** – Pop 361. The **site★** is exceptional; at the foot of a pinkish grey limestone cliff the village blends harmoniously with the landscape. From the terrace at the end of the village there is a splendid **view★★** of the Provençal Motorway, of Menton between the Alps and the sea and of Mount Agel (SW).

There are many craft shops in the picturesque lanes of Ste-Agnès; in Rue Longue, which is cobbled, the houses meet overhead.

*Return to the crossroads and turn left into D 22 towards Menton.* The road is downhill all the way with views of the Gorbio valley and of the coast.

**Alternative route★ by Les Banquettes Pass.** – *Detour of 13 km – 8 miles.* Drive through **Peille★** *(p 119);* from there to St-Sébastien Pass the road is described on p 120.

**Gorbio★.** – Pop 635. *9 km – 5 1/2 miles – about 3/4 hour – Leave Menton by Avenue de la Madone, going south west; by the Palais Carnolès turn right into D 23, a narrow winding road where passing is often difficult.*

The Gorbio valley, with its flowers, its olives and pines and its luxurious houses, contrasts with the stark appearance of Gorbio village, perched on its wild and rocky **site★**. Near the entrance to the narrow cobbled lanes stands the old Malaussène fountain. The elm tree in the square was planted in 1713. Rue Garibaldi leads round the church to a fine viewpoint looking across to Bordighera Point.

**L'Annonciade Monastery★.** – *Round tour of 12 km – 7 miles – about 3/4 hour. Leave Menton by Avenue de Verdun running into Avenue de Sospel, D 2566 going north. Ignore a lefthand turning to L'Annonciade and continue on under the Provençal Motorway. After two hairpin bends D 2566 bears right to Sospel; bear left and go under the Motorway again and continue to Les Santons Inn where the path to the monastery begins.*

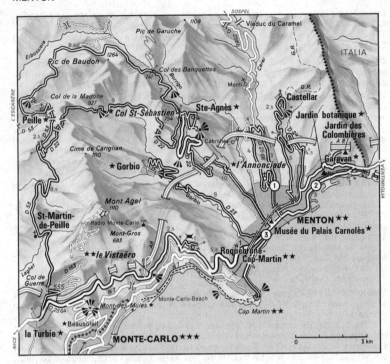

The **chapel** has been a centre for pilgrimages to the Virgin since 11C. The present building dates from the early 17C. From the terrace (225 m – 738 ft) there is a **panorama★** of the coast from Bordighera Point to Cap Martin and of the mountains ringing Menton. Return by a picturesque but winding road which rejoins Avenue de Sospel in Menton.

**Castellar.** – Pop 393. *Round tour of 13 km – 8 miles – about 3/4 hour. Leave Menton by Promenade du Val de Menton, D 24, going north.* Castellar is an attractive hilltop village. Its parallel streets are linked by covered alleys. It is a good centre for walking. From the terrace of the Café des Alpes, Place Clemenceau, there is a good **view** of the sea and the surrounding heights.

On the return drive, follow the same route for 2.5 km – 1 1/2 miles, then turn right into the winding "Chemin du Mont-Gros". Fine views of the coast and the Menton hinterland.

---

### MONACO Principality of ★★★

Michelin map **195** folds 27 and 28 – *Local map p 123* – Pop 24 600 – *For additional plan of Monaco see the current Michelin Guide France*

The Principality of Monaco, a sovereign state of only 192 ha – just under 1 sq mile, consists of: Monaco, the old town; Monte-Carlo, the new town; La Condamine which links them and Fontvieille the industrial section. Several million tourists flood into the Principality each year.

The native Monegasques pay no taxes and do no military service.

**The Grimaldi Family.** – It is with the Grimaldi dynasty that Monaco takes its real place in history. The exact origin of this family has never been definitely determined: some claim that their ancestry descends from Grimaldi, nephew of Charles-Martel, others say that the family came from Genoa. In any case, there are numerous branches of the family in France, at Cagnes and at Beuil, and in Italy at Genoa and Naples.

A Grimaldi bought the Domain of Monaco from the Genoese in 1308 and, since then, the name and the Grimaldi coat of arms have always been carried by the heirs to the title, whether these came from the House of Goyon-Matignon (1731-1949) or, as at present, from the House of Polignac.

**A Turbulent History.** – The history of Monaco has been turbulent and fraught with family dramas: in the 16C Jean II was killed by his brother Lucien, who in turn was assassinated by his nephew; political conflicts: in 1604 Honoré 1 was thrown into the sea by his subjects; foreign occupations: by the Spaniards from 1524 to 1641 (it was from the King of Spain that the Grimaldis received the title of Prince) and by the French from 1641 to 1814. In 1815 the Principality passed under the protection of the kingdom of Sardinia.

Menton and Roquebrune, which belonged to the Principality, were bought in 1861 by Napoleon III, at the time of the annexation of Nice.

**Birth of Monte-Carlo.** – The first casino was a mean establishment in Monaco itself, set up in 1856 by the Prince who was short of funds. Only in 1862 did the casino move to its own building in Monte Carlo where it remained in humble isolation for several years.

Within a few years the casino became fashionable and the surrounding land was covered with luxurious houses, most of them the property of the casino company, la Société des Bains de Mer. The gaming tables in Monte Carlo became the most famous and most popular in Europe.

**Unrestrained urbanization.** – To accomodate the influx of visitors attracted by the gambling tables and tax concessions, Monaco began to build at a furious pace until all the available space was occupied. Since the end of the last war sky-scrapers have arisen, road and rail tunnels have been bored and the shoreline has been extended into the sea.

Without neglecting the traditional visitor, Monaco has sought to capture the business traveller and the conference trade. The hotel complex at Les Spélugues, built on piles below the Casino, comprises a conference centre fitted with the latest equipment and capable of holding 1 400 people. Monaco now has facilities rivalling those of Cannes and Nice.

At Fontvieille light industry is being encouraged: clothing, printing, pharmaceutical products, plastics, precision engineering, perfumery, food processing. A man-made peninsula is slowly developing off the coast at Fontvieille.

**Non-Stop Entertainment.** – The Automobile Rally which has taken place in mid-January every year since 1911 is well known, as is the Grand Prix in May, when the cars race through the streets of the town on a narrow twisting circuit of 3 145 km – 1 954 miles. There is also the patronal Festival of Ste-Dévote, the International Arts Festival (December to April), the Circus (January), Television Festival (February), International Tennis (April), Flower Festival (May), Easter Ballet, International Boating Week,

*(After photo : Detaille)*

Monte-Carlo – Automaton

Concerts in the Palace Yard and Fire Works (July-August), National Festival (November). The reputation of the Opera and National Orchestra need no publicity.

## ■ MONACO★★★

Monaco, capital of the Principality, is picturesquely built on a rock which juts 800 m – some 875 yds out to sea and drops perpendicularly to the waves below on almost all sides. The upper part which stands 60 m – 200 ft above the mainland shore forms a terrace which is occupied by the old administrative offices of the town, the palace, the gardens and the oceanographic museum. Westwards, beyond the gully through which the road and railway run, are the steep cliffs and caves of the Tropical Gardens.

### Tropical Gardens Quarter★★ *time: 1 hour (excluding the Observatory Grottoes).*

**Tropical Gardens★★ (Jardin Exotique) (DZ).** – *Open 9am to 7pm in the season; 9am to sunset, out of season; closed 1 May and 19 November. Combined ticket for the gardens, the caves and the museum: 17F, children: 8.50F.*

The gardens cascade down a steep rock face which has its own microclimate favourable to cacti and other succulents particularly arborescents: huge candelabra-like euphorbia, giant aloes, "mother-in-law cushions", Barbary figs. There are 6 000 varieties of semi-desert flora; many of the unusual shapes and vivid colours are native to Mexico and southern Africa. The garden offers many magnificent **views★** of the rock of Monaco, the harbour, Monte-Carlo, Cap Martin and the Italian Riviera *(viewing table).*

**Observatory Caves★ (Grottes de l'Observatoire) (DZ E).** – *558 steps Rtn; time: 1/2 hour; guided tour.*

The grottoes, which open off the Tropical Gardens, have been well arranged. The tour passes through a number of chambers at different levels, adorned with stalactites, stalagmites and other delicate and varied concretions. The rock is dolomitic limestone.

Excavations in the cave mouth have revealed signs of human habitation some 200 000 years ago; tools and prehistoric animal bones on display in the museum.

**Prehistoric Anthropology Museum★ (DZ M¹).** – *Access via the Tropical Gardens. Open 9am to 7pm (5.30pm out of season); closed 1 May and 19 November.*

The presentation and rich diversity of the exhibits make this museum of interest even to the non-specialist. The righthand room contains animal bones and stone-age tools. Owing to changes in climate not only reindeer, mammoths and cave bears but also elephants and hippopotami roamed the Riviera. The skeletons of homo sapiens are impressive: Grimaldi negroids, Cro-Magnon man, collective burials etc. The other room shows skulls and bones belonging to man's ancestors. One showcase is devoted to prehistoric figurines – Grimaldi Venus, mammoth, horse; another to the bronze age. The famous "treasure" discovered in La Condamine at the end of the last century comprises Punic coins, late Roman coins and gold medals, vases, lamps and Roman jewellery.

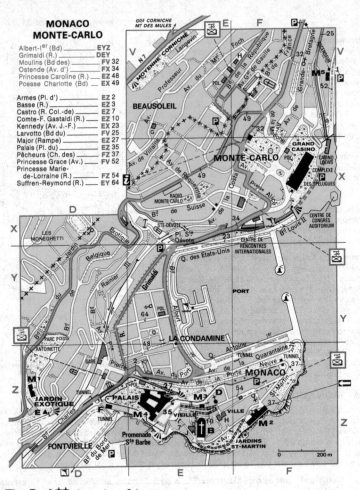

## MONACO
## MONTE-CARLO

■ **The Rock**★★ *time: about 3 hours*

*Leave the car in Fontvieille car park. From Easter to end October there is a bus service between Fontvieille and the Rock. Out of season walk up (1/2 hour) via Place d'Armes and Avenue de la Porte-Neuve.*

**Oceanographic Museum**★★ (FZ M²). – *Open 1 June to 30 September, 9am to 7pm (9pm in July and August); the rest of the year, 9.30am to 7pm. 27F, children 13.50F.*

The museum, which is also an institute of scientific research, was founded in 1910 by Prince Albert I, who was a passionate oceanographer. The **aquarium**★, in the basement, is one of the finest in Europe: Mediterranean and tropical species as well as crustaceans. On the ground floor, the main gallery is devoted to modern underwater exploratory devices. On the left the **oceanic zoology hall**★ contains the skeletons of large marine mammals: a whale, a narwhal, a sea-cow, a grampus; and specimens of marine fauna discovered by Prince Albert I and his successors on their scientific voyages.

On the first floor the large room in the centre contains the Prince's whaleboat, models of his yachts and the laboratory installed in his last boat; to the right is the room of applied oceanography; the showcases contain over 10 000 species of shells, pearls, mother-of-pearl, tortoiseshell and corals, many stuffed specimens, life-size reproduction of a giant squid 13 m – 43 ft long caught in the waters off Newfoundland.

From the terrace *(lift)* there is a magnificent **view**★★ of the coast from the Esterel to the Italian Riviera and of the Dog's Head (Tête de Chien) and Mount Agel inland.

**St-Martin Gardens**★ (EFZ). – Shady walks offer occasional glimpses of the sea. Statue of Prince Albert I by François Cogne (1951). The fragments of pillars and capitals come from St-Nicolas Church which preceded the Cathedral.

**Cathedral** (EZ B). – The neo-Romanesque cathedral was built on the ruins of St-Nicolas Church between 1875 and 1903 of white stone from La Turbie. The high altar, the organ loft and the Bishop's chair, its canopy supported by granite columns, are of white marble encrusted with mosaic and copper motifs. In the righthand transept chapel is a fine Spanish Renaissance style altar in red and gold. The Princes' tombs are in the ambulatory.

The cathedral contains several **early paintings of the Nice School**★★ (p 19). Three panels – St Roch, St Antony and the Rosary – decorate the Baptismal Chapel. The *Pietà* of the White Penitents in the ambulatory has a charming predella.

In the right transept above the Sacristy door is an **altarpiece** by Louis Bréa: Christ's body restored to his mother against a Monaco landscape. Here also surrounded by sumptuous Renaissance carving of leaves and dolphins is the **altarpiece of St-Nicolas** by Louis Bréa: 18 sections in glowing colours.

**Old town.** – Between the Cathedral and the Law Courts (Palais de Justice built in 1930 in imitation Italian Gothic) are the shady squares and narrow lanes of the old town. Rue Comte-Félix-Gastaldi (Renaissance doorways) leads to Rue Princesse-Marie-de-Lorraine.

**Misericord Chapel (EZ D).** – Opposite the town hall the classic pink and white façade was built in 1646 by the Black Penitents. Behind the high altar a **recumbent Christ★** by the Monegasque Bosio; on Good Friday this statue is carried through the streets of the old town.

*On leaving turn right into Rue Basse (picturesque restored houses).*

**Historial des Princes de Monaco (EZ M³).** – *Open 9.30am to 6.30pm; closed 1 December to 31 January; 10F.*

In a suite of handsome vaulted rooms the history of the Grimaldi family is set out in 24 scenes with life-size wax figures.

**Place du Palais★ (EZ 35).** – The square, ornamented with cannon given to the Prince of Monaco by Louis XIV, is bordered at its northeast end by a crenelated parapet from which there is a view of the harbour, Monte-Carlo and the coast as far as the Bordighera headland. At the southwest end is the **Promenade Ste-Barbe** with a view of the Cap d'Ail coastline.

The changing of the guard takes place just before midday.

**Prince's Palace★ (EZ).** – *Guided tours 9.30am to 12.30pm and 2 to 6.30pm; closed 1 October to 30 June; 10F; children 5F.*

The oldest parts of the palace are 13C; the buildings on the south side, in Italian Renaissance style, 15 and 16C. The perimeter is built into the vertical rock and presents a formidable front while a battlemented Moorish style tower commands the entrance.

An imposing doorway with the Grimaldi arms leads into the **Court of Honour** surrounded by arcaded galeries. A white marble staircase leads to the Hercules gallery decorated with 16C and 17C frescoes – particularly by Ferrari. The Throne Room and the state apartments where official receptions are held are decorated with carpets and precious furniture and hung with portraits signed by Rigaud, Ph. de Champaigne and Vanloo.

**Museum of Napoleon and Monaco History★ (EZ M⁴).** – *Open 1 July to 30 September, 9.30am to noon and 2 to 6pm; 1 October to 30 June, 10 to 11.30am and 2 to 5.30 pm; closed Mondays in winter and 1 January to 10 February; 8F.*

The ground floor of a wing of the Palace is devoted to Napoleon, to whom the Prince of Monaco is related. Numerous souvenirs and documents are collected here: lorgnette, watch, tabacco pouch, tricolour, hat belonging to the «little corporal», King of Rome's clothes; also coins, medals, arms, uniforms, military insignia, flags belonging to the grenadiers on Elba; busts of Napoleon by Canova and Houdon, bust of Josephine by Bosio; on the wall the family tree of the Bonapartes, originally from Florence, and of the Prince of Monaco.

Apart from a portrait of Napoleon by Gérard, the upper floor is devoted to the History of Monaco: charter granted by Louis XII recognising the Principality's independence, collection of stamps, coins and medals. A piece of rock brought back from the moon by the American cosmonauts is on display.

*In the season there is a bus service to the Zoo and Fontvieille car park. Otherwise walk down by the ramp (EZ 27) which starts from the north side of Place d'Armes, passing through 16, 17 and 18C gates as it descends the north face of the rock overlooking the harbour and La Condamine.*

**Zoo (Centre d'Acclimatation Zoologique) (DZ F).** – *Open 1 July to 30 September, 9am to 7pm; 1 October to 30 June, Sundays and holidays, 2 to 6pm except Tuesdays and Fridays. 17F.*

The zoo terraces on the south west face of the Rock present a large and varied collection of mammals, reptiles and birds and numerous monkeys. Fine view of the sea and Cap d'Ail.

■ **LA CONDAMINE** *time: 1/2 hour*

In the Middle Ages this term applied to cultivable land at the foot of a village or a castle. Nowadays La Condamine is the commercial district, between the Rock and Monte-Carlo. From Fontvieille car park Boulevard du Bord de Mer runs through a tunnel under the Rock to emerge on the harbour.

**Harbour (Port) (EFY).** – Prince Albert I was responsible for the harbour which is skirted by a broad terraced promenade and crowded with luxury yachts. The olympic swimming pool was added by Prince Rainier.

From the north west corner of the harbour a valley separating La Condamine from Monte Carlo runs up under a viaduct to Ste-Dévote Church.

**Ste-Dévote Church (EX).** – Restored in the 19C, it contains a fine 18C marble altar. Ste-Dévote was martyred in Corsica in the 3C when, according to tradition, the skiff carrying her body to Africa was caught in a terrific storm and was guided by a dove towards the French coast, finally landing at Monaco. In the Middle Age relics of the saint were stolen and taken away by ship. But the thieves were caught and their ship burned – a legend which has given rise to the ceremony which takes place every 26 January when a ship is burned on the square in front of the church. On the next day there is a procession.

■ **MONTE-CARLO★★★** *time: 1 1/4 hours – Facilities p 28*

Monte-Carlo is a name famous throughout the whole world. It brings to mind gambling and also the majestic setting of its palaces, casinos, rich villas, luxurious shops and its flowered terraces, trees and rare plants.

Monte-Carlo offers visitors attractions of all kinds: a theatrical and musical season, festivities at night, with floodlit terraces and gardens; floral processions and battles of flowers, etc.

To the east of the Principality are the artificial beaches, swimming pools and ultra-modern bathing facilities of Larvotto, a luxury development which has been partly built on land reclaimed from the sea and which complements the older facilities of Monte-Carlo Beach.

**The Casino** (FX). – *Open 10am to 4am; closed 1 May. In the hall, on the left, entry cards for the public or private gambling rooms are issued on presentation of a passport or identity papers to people over 21. 20F.*

The casino is surrounded by beautiful gardens and stands on a fine **terrace**★★ from which the view stretches from Monaco to the Bordighera headland.

The building comprises several different sections: the oldest (to the west), built in 1878 by Charles Garnier, architect of the Paris Opera House, faces the sea; the most recent dates from 1910. As one enters the huge central hall, the theatre is in front and the sumptuously decorated gambling rooms, on the left. First are the public rooms: the Renaissance Room, the European Grand Saloon, The America Room and the Room of the Graces. A small gallery separates the America Room from the rooms of the Cercle Privé (club), which you visit later, the two Touzet rooms and the vast and richly decorated François Médecin room. A monumental staircase goes down to the Ganne Room, where there is a tea room and a night club. Finally, there is the auditorium, designed by Charles Garnier.

**Museum of Dolls and Automata**★ **(National Museum)** (FV **M⁵**). – *Guided tours 10am to 12.30pm and 2.30 to 6.30pm; closed certain holidays; 12F.*

In a charming villa built by Charles Garnier and preceded by a rose garden ornamented with sculpture – note the Young Faun by Carpeaux – is displayed a collection of 19C automata *(illustration p 103)* and some 400 dolls dating from 18C to the present day. The very intricate internal workings are open to view. There is an 18C Neapolitan crib comprising 250 figures.

## EXCURSIONS

**Coastal Path to Cap Martin**★★. – *3 hours on foot Rtn (preferably in the afternoon). For a shorter walk, take the car to Roquebrune-Cap-Martin station and join the path below the station. Local map p 123.*

On the left of the Old Beach Hotel at Monte-Carlo Beach, take the steps down between two houses.

*The walk is described in the opposite direction on p 127.*

**Coastal Path to Cap d'Ail**★. – *1 hour on foot Rtn – Local map p 123. Park the car near the Marquet Beach (Plage Marquet) to the west of Fontvieille.*

From La Brise Marine Restaurant there is a path along the shore. Monaco Rock soon disappears from sight as the path rounds the headland where the sea throws up a fine spray as it crashes on the rocks. Slowly Cap Ferrat and Beaulieu come into view. On the left of La Pinède Restaurant steps lead up to the road and Cap-d'Ail station.

**Beausoleil**★; **Les Mules Mount**★. – *3 km – 2 miles then 1/4 hour on foot Rtn – Local map p 123 – description p 123.*

## █ MOUGINS █

Michelin map ▓▓▓ fold 24 – Pop 8 492 – *Facilities p 30*

On an extraordinary hilltop **site**★, clothed in flowers and bushes, the old village with its narrow lanes and restored houses is contained within the line of the earlier ramparts; the 15C fortified gateway is known as the Saracen Gate.

There is a festive atmosphere in Place de la Mairie where the solitary old elm and fountain are surrounded by bustle and craft shops. The town hall used to be a White Penitents' Chapel.

From the village there is a wide **view** of the Grasse countryside to the sea.

## EXCURSION

**N.-D.-de-Vie Hermitage**. – *Round tour of 6 km – 3 1/2 miles – about 3/4 hour. Take D 35 going east and turn right following the signs.*

The **site**★ is strikingly beautiful; the hermitage stands at the top of a long meadow bordered by two rows of giant cypresses (on the right beneath the trees a 15C cross). The **view**★ towards Mougins is reminiscent of a Tuscan landscape. Here Picasso chose to spend his last years; his house, well screened by trees and bushes, is just opposite.

The chapel is 17C; the bell-tower is roofed in coloured tiles. There are three Gallo-Roman funeral inscriptions inside the chapel. *(Open Sundays only for mass at 9am).* On the high altar is a fine altarpiece of the Assumption in blue and gold; on the lefthand wall a collection of votive offerings.

N.-D.-de-Vie was a "sanctuary of grace"; still-born babies were brought there, sometimes from great distances; during the mass the child was thought to revive for a few moments when it could be baptised.

*A track suitable for motor vehicles rejoins D 3.*

## █ MOUSTIERS-STE-MARIE █ ★

Michelin map ▓▓ fold 6 – *Local map p 162* – Pop 602 – *Facilities p 30*

Moustiers owes its name to a monastery founded in 5C by St-Maxime, Bishop of Riez, who came from Lérins Abbey. The **site**★★ is dramatic. A mountain torrent pours through a breach in the rock face above the village. Strung across the gorge is an iron chain (227 m – 230 yds long) from which hangs a gold star. The chain was secured to the rock in fulfilment of a vow made by a knight of Blacas on his return from the crusades after a long captivity.

Owing to its situation at the lower end of the Verdon Canyon on the main tourist roads, Moustiers is a good excursion centre. A leisure centre built some 3 km – 2 miles south east of the town adds to its attractions.

**Moustiers ware.** – According to tradition it was a monk from Faenza in Italy who gave Moustiers the secret of the beautiful glaze which was first used in 1679 by Pierre Clerissy to make the Moustiers ware which is decorated with a clear and luminous blue.

Originally the decoration was copied in the Italian style from prints – hunting scenes for example. Then came mythological subjects and geometric drapes and arabesques in the Bérain style.

In 1738 Joseph Olerys introduced the Spanish polychrome technique and decorations of birds, flowers and fabulous figures (grotesques) became popular. Moustiers began to rival Marseilles and every year great trains of mules loaded with china set out from Moustiers for the fair at Beaucaire.

About 1770 the Ferrat brothers and Féraud, the decorator, introduced Chinese and exotic themes, enigmatic and topical subjects.

By the end of the 18C there were twelve active potteries, but gradually the kilns cooled one by one until in 1874 the last one died.

In 1925 Marcel Provence undertook

Moustiers-Ste-Marie

the revival of pottery throwing at Moustiers. He built a kiln and with the cooperation of decorative artists and skilled craftsmen, evolved a new style of china with designs based on local flora and fauna as well as the traditional themes.

## ■ SIGHTS *time: 1 1/2 hours*

**Church (B).** – The church, an attractive building in golden brown tufa, boasts a three-tier **bell-tower★** decorated with blind arcading supported on slim columns and twin windows.

The Romanesque nave is decorated with a 15C canvas of the Communion of Saints (the background is contemporary Moustiers). The Gothic **choir**, set at an angle to the nave, comprises three aisles terminating in a flat chevet. The stalls are 16 and 18C. The chapel in the base of the bell-tower contains some votive offerings, one dating from 1702, items of religious art and a fine collection of Moustiers vases.

**Pottery Museum (Musée de la Faïence) (M).** – *Open 1 June to 31 August, 9am to noon and 2 to 7pm; 1 April to 31 May and 1 September to 31 October, 9am to noon and 2 to 6pm; closed Tuesdays and 1 November to 31 March; 3F.*

The museum is housed near the church beneath the Presbytery in a huge mediaeval crypt built by the Lérins monks. Each showcase is devoted to one of the master potters who made Moustiers famous in 17C and 18C: the Clerissys, Olerys, Fouque, Féraud and the Ferrat brothers. A fine collection of period moulds and tools is also on display.

**N.-D.-de-Beauvoir Chapel★.** – A picturesque path with many glimpses of the village and the Notre-Dame ravine winds up to the Chapel perched high above the village; along the way are oratories decorated by a contemporary master-potter, Simone Gar-

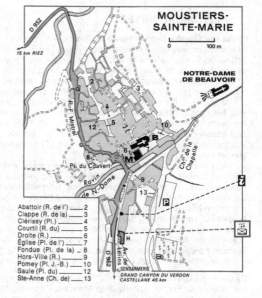

MOUSTIERS-SAINTE-MARIE

NOTRE-DAME DE BEAUVOIR

| | |
|---|---|
| Abattoir (R. de l') | 2 |
| Clappe (R. de la) | 3 |
| Clérissy (Pl.) | 4 |
| Courtil (R. du) | 5 |
| Droite (R.) | 6 |
| Église (Pl. de l') | 7 |
| Fondue (Pl. de la) | 8 |
| Hors-Ville (R.) | 9 |
| Pomey (Pl. J.-B.) | 10 |
| Saule (Pl. du) | 12 |
| Ste-Anne (Ch. de) | 13 |

GRAND CANYON DU VERDON
CASTELLANE 45 km

nier. From under the trees on the terrace in front of the chapel (the walls are part of the original fortifications), there is a good view of Moustiers, La Maire valley and the straight edge of the Valensole Plateau.

The first chapel was founded about 5C; a Gallo-Roman writer, Sidonius Apollinarius Bishop of Clermont, made a pilgrimage there in 470 and pilgrimages still continue today. Reconstruction in 12C was followed by alterations in 16C.

The chapel's Romanesque porch, protected by an overhanging roof, is dominated by a belfry of the same period. The carved wooden door is Renaissance. Inside, the first two bays of the nave are Romanesque, the remaining two Gothic, as is the pentagonal apse with engaged columns supporting the roof ribs. The statue of N.-D.-de-Beauvoir is enhanced by the Baroque altarpiece.

## NICE ★★★

Michelin map **195** fold 26 – *Local maps pp 117, 122* – Pop 346 620 – *Facilities p 28*
*– For additional plan of Nice see the current Michelin Guide France*

Capital and Queen of the Riviera, no title is too great for this magnificent winter and summer resort, which is also a famous centre for touring. Standing at the head of the Baie des Anges, Nice is sheltered by an amphitheatre of hills. Its popularity comes from the charm of its **setting★★**, the wonderful climate and innumerable attractions, including the proximity of the ski slopes, only one or two hours away by car, at Beuil, Auron, Valberg, Peira-Cava, Greolières, Isola 2000 etc.

Nice – Old street

The Paillon torrent, covered in part by esplanades and over which the Exhibition Hall has been constructed, divides the town in two: to the west, the modern town; to the east, the old town and the port, overlooked by the old castle hill from whose summit there is an extensive view.

Nice has several industries: olive oil, flowers and perfumery, crystallised fruit and macaroni.

Well served both by railways and roads, Nice now has one of the most modern airports of Europe and is third in passenger traffic in France after Paris.

Since 1966 Nice has also been a university town with faculties in law, science, arts and medicine.

**Festivals in Nice.** – The **Nice Carnival★★★** is famous. The entry of His Majesty King Carnival takes place on the Saturday, ten days before he is burnt in effigy on Shrove Tuesday; the two Saturdays and Sundays that fall between these are marked by processions, confetti battles, fireworks and masked balls, etc. The procession of floats, each one accompagnied by marchers or riders on horseback all wearing elaborate costumes, offer a picturesque spectacle and draw huge and excited crowds.

The summer season now prolongs the winter festivities with popular and fashionable fêtes, horse-racing (which takes place on the course at Cagnes), flower battles, open air theatrical performances and aquatic sports attracting crowds of visitors.

## HISTORICAL NOTES

**From the Greeks to the House of Savoy.** – Nice, as founded in 350 BC by the Greeks of Marseilles, was only a modest trading-post. The Romans concentrated their colonisation efforts on Cimiez, whose splendour obliterated the little market town on the east bank of the Paillon with a port at the eastern end of what is now the Quai des États-Unis.

Barbarian and Saracen invasions, however, reduced Cimiez to nothing, and it was Nice that began to develop under the Counts of Provence in the 10C.

In the 14C, the history of Nice was marked by an important event: Charles of Anjou and his cousin, Charles of Durazzo, Prince of Naples, both advanced their claims on Provence on the death of **Queen Jeanne**, Queen of Sicily and Countess of Provence, who had adopted them. Beautiful and beloved by the people of Provence, this princess was smothered to death on the orders of Durazzo (1382), after a romantic life which became almost legendary.

Amadeus VII, Count of Savoy, seizing a moment when troubles divided the country, installed himself in Provence. In 1388, working secretly with the Count of Savoy, who had been assured of the treachery of Jean Grimaldi, Governor of the town, Nice and its hinterland seceded from Provence and joined Savoy. Amadeus VII entered the city amidst popular rejoicing. Along the route of his procession the houses were decorated with tapestries, and flowers covered the ground; the people danced round bonfires; rich southern voices sang aloud; merchants set up their stalls on the streets; and everyone drank to the full in honour of the new sovereign. As Amadeus passed on horseback, cherubs hoisted on cords rose into the air waving palm leaves.

Except for a few short interruptions, Nice belonged to the House of Savoy until 1860.

**Catherine Ségurane.** – In the 16C Nice began to feel the effects of the rivalry between the Houses of France and Austria: François I and his Turkish allies launched military operations against the County of Nice, which belonged to the House of Savoy, allied to Charles V. In 1543 French and Turkish troops under the redoubtable leader, Barbarossa, besieged Nice; from the sea forty ships bombarded the town. It was then that, according to a local tradition, Catherine Ségurane, a woman of the people, earned her fame: as she was bringing food to a soldier on the ramparts, the order for the assault was given: some Turks appeared at the top of the wall. Catherine flung herself forward, knife in hand, hurled several attackers into the moat below, seized a standard and put fresh courage into the men of Nice: the attack was repulsed. From the ramparts, as a gesture of contempt, Catherine turned her back on the Turks and lifted up her skirts.

Other attacks met with greater success and the town fell after more than twenty days of siege; the defenders took refuge in the castle and their resistance was such as to force the besiegers to withdraw. A statue was erected to Catherine by her fellow citizens.

**Bonaparte at Nice.** – The County of Nice, which under the Convention became the Department of Alpes-Maritimes, had been occupied by French troops in 1792 and re-attached to France the following year. In 1794 Bonaparte, then General of Artillery in the army fighting against the Sardinians and the Austrians in the County of Nice, lived at no 6 in the street which today bears his name and proposed to the daughter of his landlord. It was in this house that he was arrested after the fall of Robespierre. Bonaparte, however, was on good terms with the Convention members and his brother was the people's representative with the army in Toulon. His detention was short as he put forward a skilful defence.

In 1796 he was in Nice again on his way to take over the post of commander-in-chief of the army in Italy. The house where he lived is in the Rue St-François-de-Paule, in front of the opera. He had married Josephine only a few days earlier and it was from Nice that he wrote the well-known letter: "My darling, anguish at our parting runs through my veins as swiftly as the waters flow down the Rhône... my emotion thunders in my ears like a volcano... I would like to tear out my heart with my teeth..."

At the fall of the Empire in 1814, Nice and its hinterland was handed back once more to the House of Savoy.

**The Plebiscite.** – As a result of the alliance of 1859 between France and Sardinia (House of Savoy), Napoleon III undertook to help the Sardinians drive the Austrians out of the provinces of northern Italy for which he would receive Nice and Savoy in return. But the Peace of Villafranca, signed prematurely by the Emperor, left Venice to the Austrians, thus not fully realising the aim of the alliance. The cession of Nice and Savoy was all the more compromised as it met with hostility from Britain.

In 1860 the Treaty of Turin between Napoleon III and the King of Sardinia, Victor Emmanuel II, stipulated the return of Nice to France "without any constraint on the will of the people". The plebiscite was a French victory: 25 743 in favour, 260 against.

The entry of French troops and the ceremony of annexation took place on 14 June 1860. On September 12 the Emperor and the Empress Eugénie received the silver-gilt keys to the city from the mayor of Nice in what is today the Place Garibaldi. These keys are kept in the Masséna Museum.

The region of Tende and Brigue were to remain Italian territory for eighty-seven years when the Treaty of 10 February 1947 *(p 129)* allowed France, once more, to extend its natural frontiers to the Alpine chain.

**Two men of Nice: Masséna and Garibaldi.** – Masséna (1758-1817), son of a wine merchant, went to sea until he was seventeen and then entered French service in the Royal Italian Regiment. Appointed sergeant-major, he waited fourteen years for the gold braid of a 2nd lieutenant and, disappointed, left the army. At the Revolution, he re-entered the service at Antibes where he was then living; by 1793 he was a divisional general. Napoleon called him "the cherished child of victory", and made him a Marshal of France, Duke of Rivoli and Prince of Essling. His military genius was accompanied by a ruthless ambition which sometimes caused scandal. During his career he is said to have shouted successively: "Long live the Nation! Long live the Emperor! Long live the King!" After Napoleon, he was the general most esteemed by Wellington.

Giuseppe Garibaldi (1807-1882), one of the principal authors of the Italian Revolution of 1860, had an extraordinarily turbulent political and military life in Europe and South America. A great friend of France, he served in the ranks of the French Army in 1870 with his two sons, and commanded a brigade in the Vosges.

In the 1914-1918 war Garibaldis fought in the Argonne at the head of Italian volunteers.

**Present day.** – Since 1860 the development of Nice, which then had 40 000 inhabitants, has been prodigious; it is today the second largest town of Mediterranean France after Marseilles and the fifth largest in France itself. Industry plays an important role in the local economy.

Nice is an administrative centre as well as a university town, with its Mediterranean University Centre, National School of Decorative Arts, Music Academy, important museums and International Book Fair, which is held each year in May, to add to the cultural life.

With its Exhibition Centre (20 000 places) and its many hotels, Nice remains the foremost tourist town in France and thereby gains its living.

## ■ MAIN SIGHTS

### The Sea Front ★★ *time: 3/4 hour*

**Place Masséna** (GZ). – Begun in 1815 in the Italian style the buildings form an architectural unit in red ochre with arcades at street level. A fountain stands in the southern section: four bronze horses rising from a basin.

The north side of the square opens into Avenue Jean-Médecin (formerly Avenue de la Victoire) which is the main shopping street, crowded with people and traffic. To the west extends what the 18C English called Newborough. Rue Masséna and Rue de France, its continuation, form the axis of a pedestrian precinct; here are smart shops, cinemas, cafés and restaurants between the tubs of flowers; it is a pleasant place to stroll at any hour of the day.

Avenue de Verdun skirts the **Albert I Garden** (GZ) a welcome oasis of greenery surrounding a fountain: the three Graces, sculpted by Volti.

**Promenade des Anglais★★** (EFZ). – This wide and magnificent promenade, facing due south and bordering on the sea for its entire length, provides wonderful views of the Baie des Anges which extends from Cape Nice to the Fort Carré at Antibes. Until 1820 access to the shore was difficult but the English colony, numerous since the 18C, undertook the construction of a coastal path which was the origin of the present promenade and gave it its name.

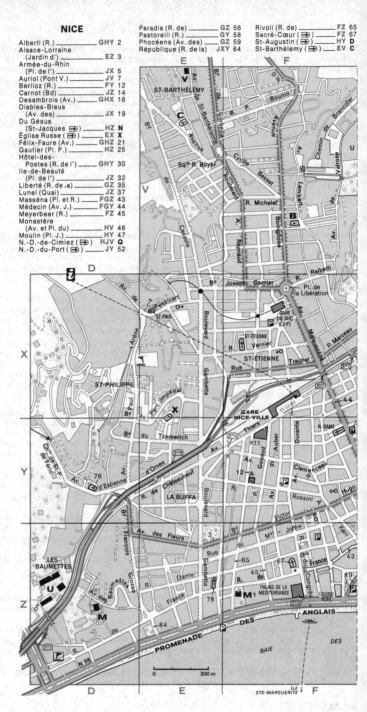

The famous Promenade has retained a sort of splendour despite being taken over by motor vehicles.

The white stone and glass façades of the north side overlooking the sea still attract the visitor: Ruhl Casino and Hotel Méridien (1973), Palais de la Méditerranée – fine example of 1930s architecture, the Negresco – a Baroque structure dating from the Belle Époque and the Masséna Museum.

**Quai des États-Unis (GHZ).** – The eastern extension of the Promenade des Anglais passes **Les Ponchettes Gallery (HZ Y)** and the **Contemporary Art Gallery (HZ X)** which put on interesting temporary exhibitions.

### Old Nice ★ *time: 3 hours*

The castle, Place Garibaldi and the hanging gardens where the Paillon river has been covered over define the limits of the old town which forms a network of twisting narrow lanes and steps on the lower slopes below the castle. The tall houses, bright with flowers or washing, exclude the glare of the sun and keep the streets cool. The many small shops, particularly near Boulevard Jean-Jaurès, the bars and the restaurants serving local dishes attract an endless flow of people to the district.

The western section, near the Préfecture and the Town Hall, was laid out in 17C on the grid pattern.

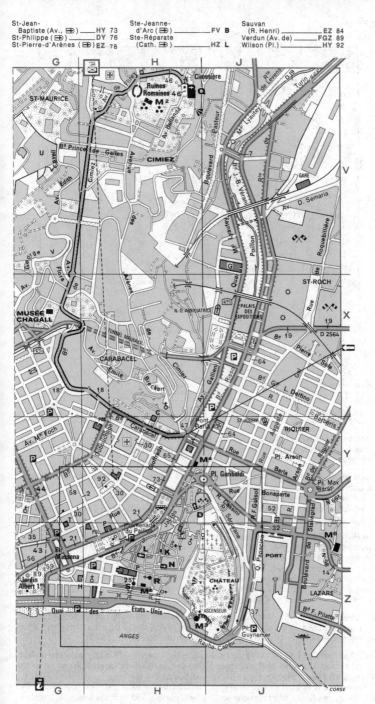

Park the car at the end of the Quai des États-Unis to walk up to the castle. Take the lift – the entrance is to the left of the 400 steps which also lead to the castle. Lift in operation: 9am to 8pm 1 June to 31 August; 9am to 7pm in April, May and September; 9.30am to noon and 1.30 to 5.30pm 1 October to 31 March. Rtn ticket: 2.60F.

Follow the arrows slightly downhill to visit the Naval Museum.

**Naval Museum** (HZ **M³**). – Open 10am to 12.30pm and 2.30 to 7pm (5pm 1 October to 31 March); closed Tuesdays, holidays and 15 November to 15 December.

    The museum is at the top of the Bellanda Tower, a huge 16C circular bastion where Berlioz once lived for a while. At the entrance are two 17C Portuguese bronze canons. Inside are models of ships, arms and navigation instruments. The walls are decorated with views of old Nice; a model shows the port at different periods in its history.

**Castle** (JZ). – "Castle" is the name given to the 92 m – 300 ft high hill, arranged as a shaded walk, on which Nice's guardian fortress once stood. Catinat blew up the powder magazine in 1691 and the fortress itself was destroyed in 1706 by Marshal de Berwick (1670-1734), the illegitimate son of James II who served in the French army.

    From the wide platform on the summit there is an almost circular **view**★★ (viewing table). Below the terrace is an artificial waterfall fed by water from the Vésubie. On the eastern side the **foundations of an 11C cathedral** (apse and apsidal chapels) have been uncovered. Below these ruins a Roman level and a Greek level have been excavated.

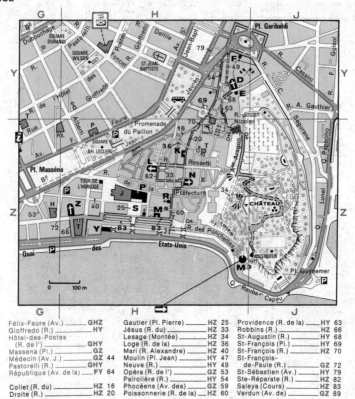

From the north west corner of Castle Hill *(follow the arrows to "Cimetière, Vieille Ville")* there is a path looking down on the roofs of old Nice. Steps lead down near a chapel on the left.

**Church of St-Martin and St-Augustin (HY D).** – In this, one of the oldest parishes in Nice, Luther celebrated mass in 1510 and Garibaldi was baptised. The church has a fine Baroque **interior★** with a *Pietà* by Louis Bréa on the left in the choir.

Outside opposite the entrance is a **monument** erected in 1933 to Catherine Ségurane (**HY E**) *(p 108)*.

**Place Garibaldi (HJY).** – The square was laid out at the end of 18C in the Piedmont style, the buildings coloured yellow ochre. It marks the northern limit of the old town and the beginning of the new. A statue of Garibaldi stands squarely among the fountains and greenery. **St-Sepulchre Chapel (HY F)** on the south side of the square belongs to the brotherhood of Blue Penitents; it was built in 18C with a blue Baroque interior.

Rue Pairolière, a shopping street, passes St-François bell-tower, part of a Franciscan convent which removed to Cimiez in 16C.

**Place St-François (HY 69).** – A fish market is held here in the mornings round the fountain.

Fixed to a house on the corner of Rue Droite and Rue de la Loge is a canon ball which dates from the siege of Nice by the Turks, allies of François I (1543).

**Palais Lascaris (HZ K).** – *1 July to 30 September, open 9.30am to noon and 2.30 to 6.30pm; closed Mondays and holidays. 1 October to 30 June, open 9.30 to noon and 2.30 to 6pm; closed Mondays, Tuesdays and holidays.*

The palace was built in Genoese style, influenced by local tradition, between 1643 and 1650 by the Count of Vintimiglia whose family was allied with the Lascaris, emperors of Nicaea in 13C. The façade is decorated with balcony supported on consoles and columns with flowered capitals; scrollwork ornaments the doorway.

On the ground floor a pharmacy from Besançon (1738) has been reconstructed to display a fine collection of flasks and tripods.

A **grandiose balustraded staircase★**, decorated with 17C paintings, Rococo niches and statues of Mars and Venus, leads to the second floor. The salon is hung with Flemish tapestries; the *trompe-l'oeil* ceiling is attributed to Carlone: the Fall of Phaeton, similar to the one in Cagnes *(p 44)*. In the next room hang two Flemish tapestries from sketches by Rubens. The state bedchamber is separated from the antichamber by a fretwork screen resembling a doorway with caryatids.

The private apartments display 18C ceilings, painted medallions framed in stuccowork and Louis XV woodwork inlaid with silver beneath landscaped piers.

**Ste-Réparate Cathedral (HZ L).** – Built in 1650 by a Nice architect, J.-A. Guibera and dedicated to the patron of Nice, who was martyred in Asia Minor at the age of 15.

Colours enhance the well-proportioned façade in which the Baroque style is very evident between the ground and the first cornice in the elegant arcading of the doorway and the decorative niches and medallions. The bell-tower is 18C and the church is roofed by a magnificent dome of glazed tiles. The **interior★** is a riot of Baroque plasterwork and marble. The high altar and choir balustrade are of marble adorned with heraldic bearings; the frieze and cornice are picturesque; 17C panelling in the sacristy.

**St-Jacques Church★** (HZ N). – Built as a chapel in 17C, it recalls the Gesu church in Rome.

Twin fluted columns support a barrel vault opening into side chapels containing loggias for the noble families. The general effect is highly ornate: there are 164 painted and 48 carved cherubs. The ceiling is painted with scenes from the life of St-James and there are several paintings presented by various brotherhoods; 16C *Pietà* on the right.

The **sacristy**, formerly the chapter house, contains 14 huge walnut cupboards (1696), some of which display the church treasure: pyxes, monstrances and reliquaries.

*Turn left into Rue Droite, right into Rue Vieille and left into Rue de la Poissonnerie.*

**St-Giaume Chapel** (HZ R). – Known locally as the Chapel of Ste-Rita, an Italian saint still venerated in Nice as the armfuls of flowers and pyramids of candles at her altar show *(left on entering)*.

The interior is a profusion of local Baroque **decoration★** : altars and rails inlaid with marble, sumptuous altarpieces (Lady Chapel), painted and coffered vaults, fine panelling.

The entrance door is handsomely carved outside.

**Cours Saleya** (HZ 83). – Once the elegant promenade of old Nice, it is now lined with shops and restaurants.

**Préfecture** (HZ P). – The elegant 18C façade of the Prefecture is decorated with alternate Corinthian and Doric columns and crowned by a balustrade.

The clock tower on the left is 18C.

**Flower Market.** – Long term repair work in Cours Saleya has forced the flower market to move to Rue St-François-de-Paule near the Opera. *(Daily 6am to 5pm except Sunday afternoons).*

## Cimiez★★ (HV) *time: 3 1/2 hours*

Cimiez hill is the sophisticated part of Nice with many large houses. At the top of Boulevard de Cimiez is a statue of Queen Victoria who used to stay in Cimiez.

*Starting from Barla Bridge, behind the Theatre, drive west along Boulevard Carabacel and follow the route marked on the plan.*

**Marc Chagall Museum★★** (GX). – *Open 10.30am to 3-4pm; closed Tuesdays; 8F, Sundays 4F, free on Wednesdays.*

The result of Chagall's donation to France, this museum built in 1972 by A. Hermant houses the most important permanent collection of the painter's works. Built in part in glass, hidden among the trees on a hill in Cimiez, the museum's cadre was realised especially for Chagall's "Biblical Message". The canvasses are shown to their best advantage owing to the set-back walls and the large windows opening on to the bright Mediterranean light. Greeting the visitor into a sacred world of lyrical fantasy, is a multicoloured tapestry, showing Chagall's personal feeling for the Holy Scriptures brought from his past – born (1887) of a poor Jewish family of Vitebsk in Russia.

This poetical lyricism is visible in all **17 canvasses** which make up the "Biblical Message" – an endeavour of thirteen uninterrupted years (1954-1967). In a large gallery are exposed twelve paintings evoking the Creation of Man, the Garden of Eden, the Story of Noah, Abraham, Jacob and Moses; among Chagall's world of rich translucent colours lies a magic spell of poetic enchantment which does not detract, however, from the seriousness of the subject matter. In a nearby gallery are five paintings illustrating the Song of Songs: dreamlike figures drift among glowing colours above the rooftops of sleepy villages.

There are also several sculptures by the artist; from the library door look outside and admire the large **mosaic**, which is reflected in the pool: it represents the Prophet Elijah, taken up to Heaven on a chariot of fire, surrounded by the signs of the Zodiac.

The circular gallery (used for concerts and conferences) is immersed in a bluish light emanating from the three large windows depicting the Creation of the World.

The other rooms are either taken up by temporary exhibitions or devoted to the development of the "Biblical Message". There is a series of thirty-nine gouaches painted by the artist in 1931 after his return from Palestine, some of the themes were taken up again and appear in his larger canvasses, 105 etchings and copperplate engravings for the Bible edited by Teriade in 1956; 200 sketches (oils, pastels, gouaches, drawings) showing the artist's preliminary study and a series of lithographs.

*Drive on to Place du Monastère and park.*

**Place du Monastère** (HV 46). – A twisted column of white marble, rising in the square in front of the church, bears a **Calvary** dating from 1477. On one side is the crucified seraph who appeared to St Francis and imprinted the stigmata of the Passion on his body; on the other St Clara and St Francis of Assisi stand together on either side of the Virgin.

**Monastery★** (HV Q). – The Franciscans, who in 16C took over the buildings of a former Benedictine monastery founded in 9C, restored and several times enlarged the abbey church.

**N.-D.-de-l'Assomption.** – The church possesses three **masterpieces★★** of the early Nice School *(p 19) (time switch).*

To the right of the entrance a **Pietà** (1475) by Louis Bréa, although a youthful work it is one of his most perfect. The arms of the cross and the stiff body of Christ emphasise the horizontal composition; the gold background reveals glimpses of a landscape. Weeping cherubs cluster round the cross while the lonely figure of Mary holds her son on her knees. One of the two side panels represents St Martin sharing his scarlet cloak; the slight inflection of the figures gives a rare elegance to the composition *(illustration p 19)*.

Quite different but as beautiful is the **Crucifixion** by the same artist which is on the left in the choir *(restoration in progress)*. It is a later work (1512); the gold background has been replaced by an elaborate landscape showing perspective. The predella is masterly, the lances reinforcing Jesus' arrest.

The **Deposition**, in the third chapel, is traditionally attributed to Antoine Bréa and shows less talent than the Crucifixion. A huge half Renaissance-half Baroque altarpiece carved in wood and decorated with gold leaf screens off the monks' choir which contains 40 stalls and a reading desk in walnut (17C).

**Conventual buildings.** – *Guided tours at 10 and 11am, 3, 4 and 5pm, except Saturday afternoons, Sundays and holidays; 6F.*

In the small cloister (16C) beneath groined vaulting some early engravings are on display. The great cloister, where concerts are given in summer, opens on to the Cimiez gardens. The sacristy leads to the oratory which contains some very curious 17C ceiling **paintings★** : symbolic characters are presented against a background of natural vegetation in combined biblical and alchemistic context which is unusual for a convent.

The oratory also contains a 14C Christ painted on wood, a 17C wood carving of St Francis and some magnificent books of antiphons from the same period. The sacristy is decorated with paintings on wood above handsome panelling.

**Franciscan Museum.** – *Open 10am to noon and 3 to 6pm, except Sundays and feast days.*

The museum recalls the work of the Franciscans in Nice from 13C to the present day. The social and spiritual message of the Franciscans is proclaimed through documents and audio-visual commentaries in a restored section of the old monastery.

**Gardens.** – On the south side of the monastery terraced gardens with flower beds and lemon trees look down on the Paillon valley from a **viewpoint** over Nice, the castle and the sea, Mount Boron (SSE) and the Observatory (E).

**Arena Villa** (HV M²). – *Open 1 May to 30 September, 10am to noon and 2.30 to 6.30pm; the rest of the year, 10am to noon and 2 to 5pm; closed Mondays, Sunday mornings, holidays and in November.*

17C Italian villa, on the site of ancient Cemenelum, housing two museums.

**Archaeological Museum.** – The exhibits come from excavations at Cimiez and the neighbourhood as well as from donations: objects of everyday life – ceramics, glass, jewellery, coins and tools; objects documenting local history from 7C BC to 6C AD – milestones, inscriptions, sculptures (statue of Antonia, Augustus' niece and a dancing Faun, Roman replica of the famous Greek faun from Pompei); reconstruction of cremation and burial practices (1 to 3C AD) with grave offerings – vases, lamps, glass phials.

There are collections from the Etruscan, Greek and Italic periods: ceramics, bronze statuettes (8 to 2C BC), particularly a very old Warrior from Mount Bégo, found in the Vallée des Merveilles (bronze age).

**Matisse Museum★.** – The various stages of Henri Matisse's (1869-1954) work are shown.

About thirty **canvasses** show the development of the painter from his early works, 1890 *(Still Life: Books)* to his blossoming, 1947 *(Rococo Armchair)*. He went from a dark realistic style to the discovery of the bright Mediterranean light passing through the influence of Cézanne *(Still Life: A Harmonium)* and Signac *(Young Woman with an Umbrella)* and culminating in 1916 *(Portrait of Laurette)* with an explosion of pure and brilliant colour *(Odalisque with Red Case* 1926; *Window in Tahiti* 1935); *Nude in An Armchair* 1937; *Reader at the Yellow Table* 1944; *Still Life: Pomegranates* 1947 as well as the "pure blue" of *Blue Nude* (1952).

**Drawings** of his many different periods are also on display. On a turnstile are thirty sketches for the mural The Dance (1933). Examples of book illustrations.

Two rooms contain sketches and models for the Chapel at Vence *(p 148)*. There are also preliminary designs for the tapestries: *The Sea, The Sky* (1947) and a huge Beauvais **tapestry**: *Polynesia.* The last work done by the artist is cut out gouaches: *flowers and fruit.*

There are about 50 **bronze sculptures,** the Serf (about 1900) and The Serpentine (1909). The development of more abstract form shows in the series of Jeannette, the Nudes, Henriette (1927) and culminates in the monumental Nudes from Behind (1913 and 1916).

Dispersed about the museum are his personal effects, his furniture and his private Art Collection.

**Roman Ruins★** (HV). – Cemenelum, the seat of the Roman Procurator, is estimated to have had a population of 20 000 at the end of 2C BC.

**Roman Baths.** – *Same opening times as Arena Villa; 1F.*

Steps lead down into the *decumanus maximus* (the main east-west street of a Roman town) with its central drain and shops. On the left are the **North Baths**, probably reserved for the Procurator and other worthies. The summer bath (1) consists of a marble basin surrounded by a peristyle with Corinthian capitals. On the eastern side are the latrines (2). The northern building contains the cold bath (**frigidarium**) (3) – it was vaulted and its dimensions (10 m – 33 ft high by 9 m – 30 ft wide) give an idea of the huge scale of the northern baths – the warm room (4) and the hot room (5), built above the **hypocaust,** and the public rooms partially excavated.

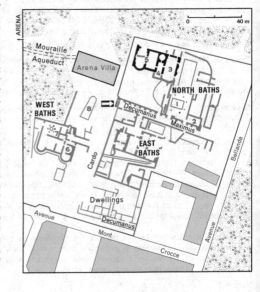

On the other side of the main street are the less elaborate East Baths for the general public. To the south of these baths is a parallel street lined with houses and shops; some of the paving stones have been uncovered.

The western end of this street opens into the *cardo* (main street running north south) which returns to Arena Villa. On the lefthand side are the **West Baths** for women only. The fabric is quite well preserved although it was used as a cathedral in 5C; the choir (6), in the *frigidarium*, contains traces of an altar and the neighbouring room to the north was used as the **baptistry** (7). On a terrace (8) near Arena Villa are some old sarcophagi.

**Arena.** – The elliptical arena which is only 67 m x 56 m – 220 ft x 184 ft, could hold 4 000 spectators. Traces remain of the gangways and of the brackets on the external façade which held the poles to which the sun awning was attached. The amphitheatre was designed for spear contests and gladiatorial bouts but not for animal fights. Modern spectacles are held here in summer.

## ■ ADDITIONAL SIGHTS

**Fine Arts Museum**★★ (Jules Chéret) (DZ M). – *Open 1 June to 30 September, 10am to noon and 2 to 6pm; the rest of the year, 10am to noon and 2 to 5pm; closed Mondays and holidays.*

The building, which was begun in 1878 in the Italian Renaissance style by the Russian Princess Kotschoubey, houses a rich collection of art.

**Ground floor.** – First comes the **Vanloo Gallery**; portraits of Louis XV and Marie Leczinska by Jean-Baptiste, a huge canvas by Carle. In the next room works by Fragonard, Hubert Robert, Ramsay, Zucarelli, Natoire, Joseph Vernet. The third room is devoted to 17C foreign schools, particularly Rubens and Caravaggio.

Two small galleries are devoted to Oriental art particularly from China and Japan: paintings, drawings and prints (especially Hokusai).

The great gallery contains a collection of sculptures by Carpeaux; paintings by masters of the Belle Époque, particularly portraits of women, hang on the walls and in neighbouring rooms (Bronze Age, sculpture by Rodin).

**Upstairs.** – The staircase and landing are devoted to the tapestries, pastels and oils of **Jules Chéret** and to sculptures by Rodin, Bourdelle, Pompon, Volti, also to glass by Marinot.

The **Impressionist Gallery** contains landscapes by Ziem, one by Bourdin. Renoir, Sisley, Guillaumin, Monet and Degas are represented as are the Post–Impressionists, Signac and Marquet.

In the **Dufy Gallery** portraits, nudes, landscapes, scenes and flowers give an insight into a career which extended over more than 50 years.

Two small galleries are devoted to the strange and fascinating world of the symbolist painter **Gustav-Adolf Mossa** and to works by Alexis Mossa, his father.

The room on the opposite side of the great gallery covers French painting from neo-Classicism to the first signs of Impressionism: touching self-portrait of the young Marie Bashkirtseff. Her major works are in the **Van Dongen Gallery**.

In addition to some fine works by Van Dongen and Dufy, the great gallery displays some huge cubist compositions by Survage (Dreamer – 1928) and a collection of **ceramics by Picasso** created at Vallauris in the 50s.

**Masséna Museum**★ (FZ M¹). – *Open 10am to noon and 2 to 5pm. Closed Mondays, holidays and in November.*

The building was constructed at the end of the 19C in the style of Italian villas of the First Empire, by Victor Masséna, Prince of Essling and great-grandson of the Marshal. In 1919 the Prince gave the Residence to the town.

**Ground floor.** – From the Empire style **interior** bay windows look out on the Promenade des Anglais. The gallery is decorated by statues, paintings and candelabra.

On the staircase are two remounted canvasses of the Masséna family by Flameng.

**First floor.** – The right wing contains a fine collection of **paintings** by the early Nice school *(p 19)*: altarpiece of St John-the-Baptist by Jacques Durandi – note the intense expression on the saint's face and the cat in his hand and the detailed painting of the predella; the predella of an altarpiece of Ste-Marguerite by Louis Bréa. All the paintings come from Lucéram church *(p 91)*. In the centre of the room is a reliquary known as "the Kiss of Peace", a magnificent piece of Italian Renaissance work in silver and enamel. 14C stone Virgin from the Roya valley. Early Italian paintings hang in the adjoining room.

The left wing contains a beautiful collection of regional religious objects. Several rooms trace the history of Nice, from its origins to the Revolution and the Empire (gold embroidered cloak worn by Josephine), and the history of the Masséna family.

On the staircase are reproductions in watercolour, by G. A. Mossa, of frescoes decorating the country chapels round Nice.

**Second floor.** – Local customs and local history are the principal theme on this floor (posters and models of the Carnaval). There is a fine collection of Provençal ceramics, arms and armour, antique jewellery and a 13C reliquary decorated with Limoges enamels.

**Russian Orthodox Cathedral** (EX X). – *Open 9am (9.30am in winter) to noon and 2.30 to 6pm (5.30pm in winter); Sundays and orthodox holidays, 2.30 to 6pm (5.30pm in winter); 5F.*

The pink brick, light grey marble and vivid coloured ceramics beneath six onion domes lend an exotic touch to the Nice scene. The cathedral was consecrated in 1912, largely as a result of the munificence of Csar Nicolas II and his mother.

The interior, which takes the form of a Greek cross, is richly decorated with frescoes, plasterwork and panelling. At the entrance to the choir is a sumptuous iconostasis, on the right an icon of **Our Lady of Kazan**, painted on wood and set off by chased silver and precious stones.

**Church of St Joan of Arc** (Ste-Jeanne-d'Arc) (FV B). – St Joan's is a modern church designed by Jacques Droz in concrete with three segmented cupolas and an ellipsoidal porch as main doorway. The stations of the Cross are frescoes by Klementief (1934).

**Vieux-Logis Museum** (EV V). – *Open Wednesdays, Thursdays, Saturdays and first Sundays in the month, 3 to 5pm. Apply to the curator, 59 Avenue St-Barthélemy.*

The museum consists of a priory reconstructed in a 16C farm and richly supplied with works of art, 14 to 17C furniture and items from everyday life (outstanding kitchen). There are numerous statues including a 15C *Pietà* from Franche-Comté.

**St Bartholomew's Church** (EV C). – The Renaissance façade, restored in 19C, is complemented by a modern bell-tower in the Italian Quattrocento style. At the far end of the righthand aisle *(switch on the right pillar)* is a triptych by François Bréa: Virgin in Majesty between St John-the-Baptist and St Sebastian.

**Law Faculty** (DZ U). – *Guided tours 9am to noon and 2 to 4.30pm; closed Saturdays and Sundays, holidays and 15 July to 15 September. Apply to the Dean.*

On the first floor landing a large-scale **mosaic**★ by Chagall covers the whole of one wall: Ulysses returns to Penelope in Ithaca.

**Natural History Museum** (Musée d'Histoire Naturelle) (HY M⁴). – *Open 9am (10am Sundays) to noon and 2 to 6pm; closed Tuesdays, certain holidays and in August.*

The museum, which is linked to a laboratory, houses a curious collection of 7 000 artificial fungi, fossilised marine creatures, stuffed fish, an exhibition of minerals, models of ships and various fishing tackle.

**Malacology Gallery** (HZ M⁵). – *Open 11am to 7pm; closed Sundays, Mondays and certain holidays.*

The Gallery, an annexe to the Natural History Museum, houses a collection of molluscs from all over the world: rare specimens of unusual shape and colour. Fish, molluscs and vegetation from the Mediterranean and the Red Sea are displayed in aquaria.

**Misericord Chapel**★ (HZ S). -*Open for guided tours only.*

The chapel, which belongs to the Black Penitents, is a masterpiece of Nice Baroque (1740) and was designed by the 17C Italian architect, Guarino Guarini. A bowed façade, garlands and oval windows accentuate the rounded motif of the exterior design.

In the sacristy are two early Nice **altarpieces**★ on the same subject: Our Lady of Pity. Jean Mirailhet's work is firmly in the Gothic tradition but the panel painted some 80 years later by Louis Bréa betrays the influence of the Italian Renaissance and shows the Virgin against a Nice landscape.

**St-François-de-Paule Church** (HZ Z). – The church is a fine example of Nice Baroque. The sanctuary (1750) is surmounted by a campanile roofed with coloured tiles; over the Dominican door on the left is a carving of the Virgin and Child.

The interior has the theatrical and wordly appearance so dear to Baroque art. The choir is surrounded by "stage boxes" behind grills reaching to the upper floor. The Communion of St-Benoit on the right of the entrance is attributed to Carle Van Loo. The statue of St-Dominique (1949) between the two chapels on the left is carved is olive wood.

**The Harbour** (Port) (JZ). – For 2 000 years ships putting in at Nice simply tied up in the lee of the castle rock. The excavation of a deep water port was ordered in 1750 by Charles-Emmanuel III, Duke of Savoy, in the marshy ground at Lympia. In 1870 and again in 1904 work was put in hand to deepen and extend the harbour; an outer harbour was created protected by two breakwaters. Merchant ships, yachts, pleasure boats and fishing boats, ferries and boats for hire make the harbour constantly busy and lively.

Behind the pleasing façades of Place Ile-de-Beauté on the waterfront the Riquier and St-Roch districts extend northwards, while elegant villas and comfortable houses are scattered on the slopes of Mount Boron to the east.

**Terra Amata Museum** (JZ M⁶). – *Open 10am to noon and 2 to 7pm (6pm 16 November to 14 April); closed holidays and Mondays.*

A model of a sand dune on a fossil beach, uncovered on the western slopes of Mount Boron, is reproduced on the ground floor of the museum built on the site of the excavation. An open hearth and a human footprint were found in the hardened limestone.

Bones, stone tools and traces of fire mark one of the earliest human settlements known in Europe. Articles, drawings, maps and a full scale reconstruction of a shelter made of branches illustrate the life of the Acheulean hunters some 400 thousand years ago (early paleolithic).

## BOAT TRIPS

In the season the *Gallus* boats run cruises right along the Riviera. *Apply to S. A. T. A. M., GALLUS 24 Quai Lunel, Nice:* ☎ *55.33.33.*

## EXCURSIONS

1 **The Eastern Heights**★★ – *Round trip of 11 km – 6 miles – about 3/4 hour – Local map p 117*

*Leave Nice from Place Max-Barel (JY) by N7, Moyenne Corniche, going east. After 2.5 km – 1 1/2 miles turn sharp right into a forest road. 1 km – 1/2 mile further on turn sharp left into a path leading to Mount Alban Fort.*

**Mount Alban**★★. – Alt 222 m – 728 ft. A footpath circles the height from which there is a splendid **view**★★ of the coastline: to the east are Cap Ferrat, Cap d'Ail, Bordighera and the limestone heights the Tête de Chien; to the west lie the Baie des Anges and the Garoupe Plateau. The fort, a massive 16C construction with bastions and watchtowers, can be explored on foot.

*Return to the fork and bear left to Mount Boron.*

**Mount Boron**★. – Alt 178 m – 584 ft. From the mountains there are **views**★ extending over the Villefranche roadstead and along the coast to the Cap d'Antibes. On the horizon can be seen the mountains around Grasse and, further to the left, the Esterel.

*Return to Nice by the Corniche Inférieure (N 98).*

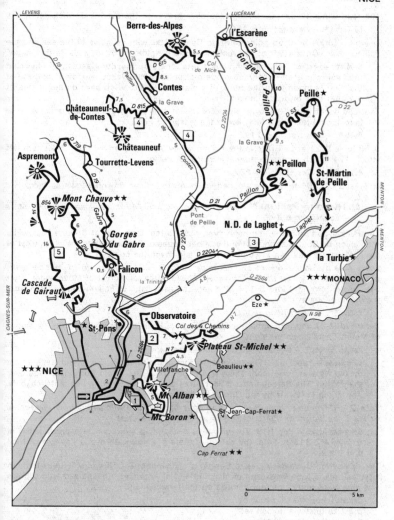

### ② St-Michel Plateau★★ – *Round tour of 19 km – 12 miles – about 1 hour –
*Local map above*

Leave Nice by ①, D 2564, Grande Corniche, which affords views of Nice and the Baie des Anges and later the Paillon basin. Ahead lie the forts of La Drète in the foreground and Mount Agel further back.

**Observatory.** – The private road on the right leads to the Observatory built on Mount Gros by Charles Garnier *(open 2nd and 4th Saturdays in the month at 3pm; commentary; 5F)*. It is an international centre for astronomical research.

Beyond the 4-Chemins Pass, Cap Ferrat peninsula and Villefranche roadstead come into view. *Drive along the D 34 for 500 m – 547 yds and leave the car in the car park.*

**St-Michel Plateau Viewpoint★★.** – A viewing table points out all the main features of the coast from Cap d'Ail to the Esterel.

*Continue along D 34 and then bear left into Moyenne Corniche (N 7).*

After a long tunnel there is a marvellous **view★** of Beaulieu, Cap Ferrat, Villefranche, Nice and Cap d'Antibes. The road winds round above Villefranche Roads. After the Villefranche Pass Nice with Castle Hill, the harbour and the Baie des Anges comes into view; on the horizon the outline of the Esterel and the limestone hills of Grasse.

*Return to Nice via Place Max-Barel.*

### ③ The Laghet to the Paillon★ – *Round tour of 59 km – 37  miles – about
*3 1/2 hours – Local map above*

The Laghet is a tributary of the Paillon. The suggested route goes up one valley and down the other with detours to La Turbie and Peille.

*Leave Nice by Boulevard J.-B.-Verani and Route de Turin (JV), D 2204 going north. In La Trinité bear right to Laghet, D 2204ᴬ.* The road goes up the verdant Laghet valley. The Roman road from La Turbie to Cimiez was on the opposite bank.

**N.-D. de Laghet.** – The sanctuary was founded in 1656 and is a pilgrimage centre; its influence is felt on both sides of the frontier. Innumerable votive offerings, touching and amusing in their naivety, cover the church and cloister. The best of them are displayed in the little **museum** in Place du Sanctuaire *(open 3 to 5pm)*. The interior decor is heavy Baroque. The statue of Our Lady of Laghet on the high altar is carved in wood.

**117**

The road winds steeply up through the olive groves to the Grande Corniche; turn left.

**La Turbie★**. – *Description p 152.*

Leave La Turbie by D 53 going north to Guerre Pass with its views of the sea and the Paillon basin. On the left of the road on a sharp righthand bend is St-Martin Chapel.

**St-Martin-de-Peille.** – The church stands in a lonely but beautiful setting of olive-clad mountains. It is an unadorned modern structure, with plastic windows; the base of the altar is made from the trunk of a giant olive tree. Wide bays on either side of the altar give on to the mountains.

The road winds round the lower slopes of Mount Agel before descending to Peille. Near the third tunnel there is a fine **view** of the village of Peille.

**Peille★**. – *Description p 119.*

D 53 joins D 21 at La Grave in the Paillon valley. After 2.5 km – 1 1/2 miles turn left into D 121 which climbs to the eagle's nest of Peillon.

**Peillon★★**. – *Description p 120.*

D 21 and D 2204 follow the wooded valley of the Paillon downhill towards Nice.

### ④ The two Paillons★ – *Round tour of 78 km – 49 miles – about 3 1/2 hours – Local map p 117*

The Paillon de l'Escarène, the main river, rises to the north east of St-Roch Pass while the Paillon de Contes springs from the upper slopes of Rocca-Seira to the north west of the same pass; they join at Point de Peille and reach the coast in Nice.

*Leave Nice by Bld J.-B.-Verani and Route de Turin, D 2204 going north. In Pont de Peille, turn right into D 21 up the Paillon valley.* Ahead is the long crest of Mount Agel. After Ste-Thècle, turn right into D 121. The eagle's nest village of Peillon can be seen from the steep bends in the road.

**Peillon★★**. – *Description p 120.*

*Return to D 21 and turn right.* Soon the village of Peille comes into view on the slopes of Mount Castellet on the right.

**Paillon Gorges★**. – Beautiful green wooded ravine.

**L'Escarène.** – Pop 1 553. The town at the foot of the Braus Pass is an old staging post on the Nice to Turin road. There is a good **view** of the whole from the bridge over the Paillon. The Baroque church is 17C as are the two flanking Penitents' chapels. The organ (1791) is by the Grinda brothers *(p 168)*.

*Take D 2204 south to Nice Pass and turn right into D 215, a wild and narrow serpentine. At the T junction turn right into D 615 up to Berre-des-Alpes.*

**Berre-des-Alpes.** – Pop 819. The village is a charming viewpoint in a pretty **setting** at 675 m – 2 215 ft. From the cemetery there is a **panorama★** of the Pre-Alps of Nice and the sea.

The drive from Berre-des-Alpes to Contes is enchanting. D 615 winds its way through a typical inland Nice landscape of chestnut and olive groves interspersed with cypress and pine trees and clumps of mimosa on the terraced land.

**Contes.** – Pop 4 215. *Facilities p 30.* Originally a Roman settlement the village is built on a rocky eminence which rears above the Paillon de Contes like a ship's prow; modern constructions extend into the valley. The church contains a remarkable altarpiece of the Nice school (1525). The central panel representing Ste-Madeleine has disappeared but the **predella★** illustrates her life in five scenes. The woodwork is 17C: doorway, gallery, pulpit.

An elegant Renaissance fountain plays before the church and the terrace has a fine view of the valley.

*Take D 15 downhill to La Grave.* Turn right crossing the Paillon into D 815 which winds uphill beneath the shade of pines and olives above the Paillon, until one can look down on Contes, on its rocky spit and on Berre-des-Alpes.

**Châteauneuf-de-Contes.** – Pop 260. The village nestles against the hillside among olive groves and vineyards on

*(After photo : J. Delmas et Cie, Paris)*

Contes

the site of a Roman camp. The 11C Romanesque church is decorated with festoons and Lombard bands; a Roman inscription is incorporated into the façade. The interior *(when closed enquire at the Town Hall (Mairie) or the café in the square)* was repaired in 17C and frescoes painted on the ceiling; behind the high altar a fine plaster altarpiece frames a 15C wooden statue of the Virgin and Child.

*2 km – 1 1/4 miles further on a lefthand turning leads to the ruins.*

**Old Châteauneuf.** – *1/2 hour on foot Rtn.* The deserted ruins of walls and towers make a strange spectacle against the rocky landscape. The people of Châteauneuf-de-Contes retreated up here in the Middle Ages to be safe from attack.
From the top of the bluff there is a huge **panorama★** taking in Mount Chauve (W), Mount Ferion (NW) and the Alps (NE).

*Return to D 15 which follows the Paillon-de-Contes valley back to Nice.*

5 **Mount Chauve★** – *Round tour of 53 km – 33 miles – about 2 1/2 hours – Local map p 117*

*Leave Nice by Avenue du Ray going north; turn sharp right into Avenue de Gairaut, D 14, towards Aspremont and after passing under the motorway (2 km – 1 1/4 miles) bear right following D 14 and then turn left following the signs.*

**Gairaut Waterfall** (Cascade de Gairaut). – In two great steps the waters of the Vésubie canal, which supplies Nice, tumble down into a basin. From the chapel terrace there is a beautiful view of the town.

*Return to D 14.* Soon there are fine views on the left of Nice and Mount Boron (S) and of Cap d'Antibes (SW). As the road climbs to Aspremont the view extends to include the Baous, the Var valley and the mountains.

**Aspremont.** – Pop 771. The village, built to a concentric plan, perches prettily on its hill site. The church *(if closed, key available from the priest)* has a Gothic nave, decorated with frescoes and supported on solid cubic capitals; on the left a painted wooden Virgin and Child. Above and behind the church stood the castle, now destroyed. From the terrace which overlooks the town is a **panorama★** comprising several hill villages, Vence (SW), Cap d'Antibes (SW), the hills behind Nice, Mount Chauve (SSE) and Mount Cima (N).

On leaving the village, take D 719 over Aspremont Pass between Mount Chauve and Mount Cima to the rich basin of Tourrette-Levens.

**Tourrette-Levens.** – Pop 2 644. The village clings to a knife-edged rock. The 18C church *(if closed enquire at Caravel the butcher's)* has a fine carved wooden altarpiece of the Virgin between St Sylvester and St Antony *(behind the high altar)*. A short walk through the village to the castle *(partially restored)* reveals views of the neighbouring mountains – Chauve (SW) and Ferion (N) – and the Gabre (S) and Tralatore (N) valleys.

*Return to D 19 turning left down into the Gabre valley.*

**Gabre Gorge.** – The ravine walls are limestone.

*Bear right into D 114 towards Falicon.*

**Falicon.** – Pop 877. Typical Nice village huddled on a rocky outcrop among the olive groves. The Bellevue Inn (panoramic view from the terrace) displays souvenirs of Jules Romains who wrote about Falicon in one of his novels.
In the church is a beautiful 17C Nativity framed in gold.
Climb up the stairway to the left of the church and turn right into a path leading to a terrace for a view★ of Nice, the sea, the hills and Mount Agel.

*Return to D 114 turning left.* At St-Sébastien Chapel turn right into D 214 a narrow and dangerous road to Mount Chauve. *Leave the car where the road ends.*

**Mount Chauve.** – *1/2 hour on foot Rtn.* Alt 854 m – 2 802 ft. "Chauve" means bald and the mountain lives up to its name. A disused fort stands on the naked summit offering a magnificent **panorama★★** : the snow-clad Alps (N) and the Nice hills and the coast from Menton to Cap Ferrat (S). On a very fine day Corsica is visible.

*Return to D 114 turning left; 2 km – 1 1/4 miles further on turn sharp right into D 19. Go under the motorway; 1 km – 1/2 mile later there is a righthand turning up to St-Pons.*

**St-Pons Church★.** – *To visit, ring at the door half way up the staircase.* The abbey of St Pontius was founded in Charlemagne's reign and played an important part in local affairs for 1 000 years. The church which was rebuilt early in 18C stands on a headland above the Paillon valley, its graceful silhouette and Genoese campanile visible on all sides. The elegant curves and counter-curves of the tall Baroque façade are echoed in the peristyle. The building forms an ellipse, preceded by a vestibule, prolonged by a semi-circular choir and ringed by side chapels opening out between powerful columns. Rich plasterwork decoration.

**PEILLE** ★
Michelin map ▦▦▦ north of fold 27 – *Local map p 117* – Pop 1 437

The village, which has maintained its mediaeval appearance, stands near the ruins of a castle once the property of the Count of Provence : three mountains tower over the wild site above the Faquin ravine : Pic de Baudon (NE), Mount Agel (SE) and Cime de Rastel (SW).

■ **SIGHTS** time: 3/4 hour

*Park the car on the north side of the village by the church which is approached by a steep slope behind the hospice.*

**Church.** – *Guided tour, ring at the door of the hospice next to the church.*
The church, dating from the 12 and 13C and with an elegant Romanesque belfry, is formed from two adjoining chapels; the one on the right having rounded vaulting, the one on the left crossed pointed arching. As you enter, an altar against the wall on the left is adorned with a fine altarpiece, divided into fifteen panels, by the 16C Honoré Bertone. A picture on the right shows Peille as it was in the Middle Ages. A 14C mural represents Ste-Anne, the Virgin and Child.

**The town**★. – *Car parking beside D 53, Place de la Tour.* Go down some steps which lead from the D 53 to the Rue de la Sauterie, a cobbled alley punctuated by steps and covered passageways and sloping down towards the Place A.-Laugier.

Rue Centrale on the right leads to a domed 13C building which was the old St-Sébastien Chapel. Now restored it houses the town hall. Turn left and left again into Rue St-Sébastien; on the left of the crossroads stands the former salt tax office (Hôtel de la Gabelle).

The street emerges into Place A.-Laugier. At the far end of the square, beyond the Gothic fountain, two arches beneath a house rest on a central Romanesque pillar: pass beneath the right arch and turn right into Rue Lascaris, then left into the Avenue Mary-Garden which goes up to the war memorial.

**Viewpoint**★. – From the memorial there is a view to the north of the terraced gardens of Peille, the Faquin ravine, the church and Pic de Baudon in the distance; to the south of Cime de Rastel and a glimpse of Nice and the Baie des Anges down the Paillon valley.

## EXCURSION

**Three Passes**★. – *Round tour of 23 km – 14 miles – about 1 1/4 hours – Local map p 102. Leave Peille by D 53 going west and bear right into a very narrow road.*

The road runs north and then east along the pine-clad slopes of the Erbossiera valley with fine views of the Paillon valley and of the sea.

**Les Banquettes Pass.** – Alt 741 m – 2 431 ft. From the south side of the pass, the sea at Menton and the hill village of Castillon are visible.

**St-Sébastien Pass**★. – Alt 754 m – 2 474 ft. **View**★ of Ste-Agnès village.

*At the crossroads, bear left to Ste-Agnès.*

**Ste-Agnès**★. – *Description p 101.*

*Return to the crossroads and take D 22 towards Madone Pass.*

The road winds round the south side of Cime de Biançon; above Gorbio rises Mount Agel with the Monte-Carlo Radio masts on its southern face. From the **Madone Pass** (alt 927 m – 3 041 ft) there are glimpses of the sea.

*Turn right into D 53 to return to Peille.* After the third tunnel the village comes into view.

## PEILLON ★★

Michelin map **195** fold 27 – *Local map p 117* – Pop 898

Set back on a narrow spur overlooking the Paillon valley, Peillon is one of the most spectacular villages on the Riviera. The strict architectural uniformity was imposed by the site and the need for defence.

**White Penitents' Chapel.** – *Key available at the Auberge de la Madone.*

Of most interest are the **frescoes**★ by Giovanni Canavesio: the Crucifixion with St Antony and Ste-Petronella; on the walls and ceiling scenes from the Passion. The similarity of style with N.-D.-des-Fontaines *(p 129)* is evident.

**Village**★. – Untouched since the Middle Ages, the village has few streets but many steep steps and covered alleys between the houses which crowd upon one another bedecked with flowers. The 18C church with its octagonal lantern crowns the village; inside are 17C and 18C canvasses and an 18C wooden statue of Christ.

## PUGET-THÉNIERS ★

Michelin map **195** folds 13 and 14 – Pop 1 520 – *Facilities p 30*

This amusing little Provençal town is huddled beneath the ruins of a Grimaldi castle where the Roudoule joins the Var surrounded by mountains.

**Old town**★. – The old houses with their elegant doorways and carved stone escutcheons are grouped on the west bank of the Roudoule around Place A.–Conil with its attractive fountain.

**Church** (B). – The Romanesque church built in 13C by the Templars was restyled in 17C. It contains many works of art. *Time switch at the left of the church entrance.*

Outstanding are the **sculptured groups**★ in walnut dating from the 15C on the first side altar on the left depicting from the top downwards: the Crucifixion, the Resurrection and the Placing in the Tomb. There is also a large primitive at the high altar dated 1525 and attributed to Antoine Ronzen; it is called **Our Lady of Succour**★.

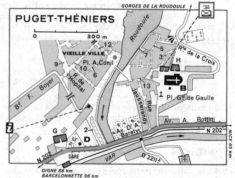

PUGET-THÉNIERS

| | |
|---|---|
| Adjudant-chef Rémond (Av.) | 2 |
| Conil (R. A.) | 3 |
| Docteur Gente (R.) | 5 |
| Judaïque (R.) | 6 |
| Maurin (Promenade R.) | 7 |
| Miss Pell (Av.) | 9 |
| Papon (R.) | 10 |
| Verdun (R. de) | 12 |
| 4 Septembre (R. du) | 13 |

Also at the high altar is a statue carved out of the trunk of an olive tree of the Virgin of the Assumption.

## EXCURSIONS

**Roudoule Gorges★**. – *15 km – 9 miles by a narrow and often impressive road – about 1 hour.*
Leave Puget-Théniers by the D 16 *(north on the map)*. There is a good general **view** of the old town before the road enters the Roudoule Gorge which shows some vertical strata.

**St-Léger Bridge.** – It has been built in a remarkable **setting★★**. Below can be seen the old Roman bridge with the paved Roman road still in good repair on either side.

Cross the suspension bridge (D 316) and 1 km – 3/4 mile further on where the road widens make a U turn for a fine **view★** of the Roman bridge and road, the village of La Croix and the Léouvé Circus on the horizon (N).

*Return to D 16 turning left and then turn right into D 416.*

**La Croix-sur-Roudoule.** – Pop 102. A small hill village, built up against the rock. Its **setting★** can be seen best from the downhill road. An old fortified gate guards the entrance. The Romanesque church with its wall belfry *(key available from the inn next door "Chez Jeanne")* contains three **altar panels** by François Bréa.

*Return to D 16 and continue to the right.*

**Léouvé.** – Those attracted by unusual coloured landscapes should go up the Roudoule valley as far as the **Léouvé Circus** (end of the D 16) which is entirely hollowed out of the red sandstone of the Dome de Barrot (alt 2 137 m – 7 011 ft).

## RIEZ

Michelin map **81** fold 16 – Pop 1 638

Riez stands at the confluence of the Auvestre and the Colostre and is dominated by Mount St-Maxime. It has played an important part in the life of the region over the centuries: it was a Gaulish city, then a Roman colony and finally a bishopric before settling to its present modest role.

## ■ SIGHTS *time: 1 1/2 hours*

**Baptistry★**. – *Guided tour: apply to Tourist Centre (Syndicat d'Initiative).*
The baptistry which is 5C, although its vaulting was reconstructed in the 12C, is one of only five or six edifices of the Merovingian period still to be found standing in France.

It consists of an octagonal room within a square building. Four apsidal chapels, of which one contains the altar, have been built into the corners, sunk into the thickness of the walls in such a way that they do not project externally. Eight antique granite columns surmounted by marble Corinthian capitals stand in a circle round the font of which only the ruins remain. A dome covers the chamber which now houses a lapidary museum. On the opposite side of the road facing the Baptistry the foundations of a Paleo-Christian cathedral have been excavated.

**Roman Columns (Colonnes Antiques).** – Four beautiful columns with monolithic grey granite shafts and white marble Corinthian capitals still supporting an architrave, are all that remains of a temple erected in late 1C and probably dedicated to Apollo.

**Old town.** – The old town is typically Provençal. Enter through the Aiguière Gate or the St-Sols Gate, the last remains, with the clocktower, of the old town ramparts.

**Provençal Natural History Museum (H).** – *Open 1 July to 30 September, 10am to noon and 3 to 7pm; the rest of the year, 10am to noon and 3 to 6pm; closed Tuesdays (and Wednesdays out of season) and 1 January to 15 February; 8F.*
Several rooms in the Town Hall, formerly the Bishop's Palace (15C), are devoted to the natural history of Provence from the Primary Era to the present day. There are fourteen display cases containing 3 000 samples of minerals, rocks and fossils, covering 600 million years. Particularly impressive is the **fossilised skeleton★** of a wading bird, 35 million years old, which had been perfectly preserved in the muddy marl of the period.
A beautiful vaulted room is used for a permanent display on the plants, insects and vertebrates of contemporary Provence and for temporary exhibitions.

**Mount St-Maxime.** – *2 km – 1 1/4 miles north east of the town – about 1/2 hour.*
*Leave Riez by Rue du Faubourg St-Sébastien going north on the plan.*
The mountain (alt 636 m – 2 087 ft) is a familiar landmark round Riez.

**St-Maxime Chapel.** – In the Romanesque apse the ambulatory is constructed with six beautiful Corinthian columns, a re-cycling of old materials.

**Panorama★.** – From the shade of the pine trees on the chapel terrace the view extends over Riez, the Valensole Plateau (NW), the Pre-Alps of Castellane (NE), the Canjuers Plateau (SE), the Lubéron (W) and Lure (NW) mountains.

The mountains plunge sharply down into the sea between Nice and Menton; the beaches are directly overlooked by the heights on which run the three famous highways known as the Great or Grande Corniche, the Middle or Moyenne Corniche and the Lower Corniche or Corniche Inférieure. The first affords the most beautiful views; the second, fine vistas along the shore and the third access to all the coastal resorts.

### ① GREAT CORNICHE★★★ (Grande Corniche)
**From Menton to Nice** – *31 km - 19 miles – about 3 hours – Local map below*

The Great Corniche, built by Napoleon along the route of the ancient Via Julia Augusta, is the highest of the three roads, passing through La Turbie from which it looks down from 450 m – 1 400 ft on to the Principality of Monaco. The views are breathtaking in extent. The road provides access to Roquebrune.

*Leave Menton (p 99) by Avenue Carnot and Avenue de la Madone (N 7) going west.*

**Roquebrune-Cap-Martin★★**. – *Description p 125.*

*Return to N 7. After 2 km – 1 1/4 miles bear right into D 2564.*

**The Vistaëro★★**. – From nearly 300 m – 1 000 ft above the sea where the Vistaëro Hotel stands, there is a marvellous **view★★** extending out over Bordighera Point, Cap Mortola, Menton, Cap Martin, Roquebrune and immediately below, Monte-Carlo Beach. To the right lie Monaco, Beausoleil, with the Tête de Chien rising above them. Further inland, in a pass, can be seen La Turbie and the Trophy of the Alps.

**La Turbie★**. – *Description p 152.*

The Great Corniche discloses distant **views** of Cap Ferrat and then of Èze village as the road reaches its highest point at 550 m – 1 804 ft. In Pical a stone cross on the left commemorates Pope Pius VII's return from exile in 1814.

**Èze Pass**. – Alt 512 m – 1 680 ft. Extended **view** to the north over the mountains and valleys of the upper Vésubie and Var. Owing to its strategic position, Mount Bastide on the left has been a Celtic-Ligurian oppidum and a Roman camp.

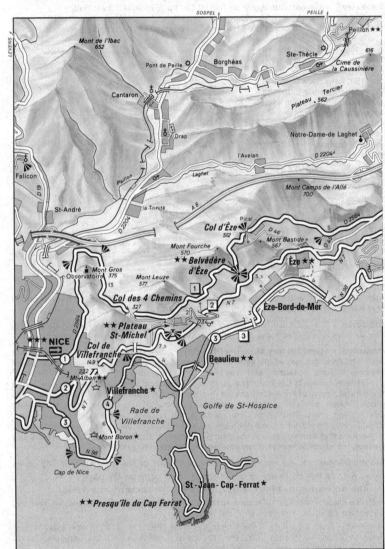

**Èze Belvedere.** – 1 200 m – 3/4 mile beyond the Pass opposite a small café named the "Belvedere" in a right bend, there is a wide panoramic **view★★** in which one can distinguish the Tête de Chien (E), Èze and the "Mer d'Èze", the Cap Ferrat Peninsula, Mount Boron (S), the Cap d'Antibes, the Lérins Islands, the Esterel chain with the Cap Roux Peak (SW), and the French and Italian Alps (NE).

**4-Chemins Pass.** – A short way beyond the pass (alt 327 m – 1 073 ft) one can see the Alps through an opening made by the Paillon valley.

Soon afterwards, the road, always descending affords a wide **view★** of the Pre-Alps, and then of Nice and Castle hill, the harbour, the Baie des Anges, Cap d'Antibes and the Esterel.

*Enter Nice from the east by Avenue des Diables-Bleus.*

### 2 MIDDLE CORNICHE★★ (Moyenne Corniche)

**From Nice to Menton** – *31 km – 19 miles – about 2 hours – Local map below*

The Middle Corniche is a broad modern road, well sited along the mountainside; it tunnels through the larger mountain chains and takes large sweeping curves into the smiling Mediterranean countryside; it offers good views of the coast and the coastal resorts and provides the only access by road to the amazing village of Èze.

*Unfortunately a parapet along a great part of the road obscures the view of the sea and the coast. Lay-bys, however, have been provided at all the best viewpoints.*

*Leave Nice (p 108) from Place Max-Barel by N 7 going east.* Initially the view comprises the town, Old Castle Hill, the harbour and the Baie des Anges; the Esterel chain and the limestone mountains of Grasse stand out on the horizon to the south west.

**Villefranche Pass.** – Alt 149 m – 489 ft. From a bend in the road soon after the Pass Villefranche Roadstead and Cap Ferrat come into view.

Just before entering a 180 m – 200 yd long tunnel, there is a very good **view★★** of Beaulieu, Cap Ferrat, Villefranche, Nice and Cap d'Antibes. After the tunnel the old village of Èze comes into view, perched high on its rock against the backdrop of the Tête de Chien (alt 556 m – 1 880 ft), the mountain promontory dominating Cap d'Ail and Monaco.

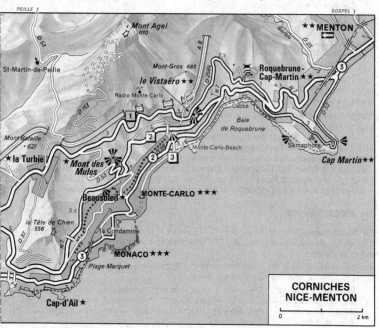

**CORNICHES NICE-MENTON**

**St-Michel Plateau★★.** – *2 km – 1 mile from N 7.* After the tunnel turn right into D 34 which climbs back over the tunnel for 2 km – 1 mile to a terrace carpark. Leave the car and walk up to the Mount Colomba viewing table on the edge of the plateau (375 m – 1 230 ft). The **panorama★** extends from Cap d'Ail to the Esterel.

**Èze★★.** – *Description p 65.*

Beyond Èze the Middle Corniche circles the rock escarpments of the Tête de Chien and brings into sight new panoramic views overlooking Cap Martin and the long Bordighera headland in Italy. Below, in the foreground, lies the Principality of Monaco. Before reaching Monaco bear left into N 7 which skirts the Principality and offers remarkable **views★** of the Principality, Cap Martin, the Italian coast and the coastal ranges.

**Beausoleil★.** – Pop 12 208. This resort forms part of the Monte-Carlo conurbation although it is on French territory. Its houses, reached by stepped streets, project from the slopes of Les Mules Mount like balconies over the sea.

**Les Mules Mount★.** – *Bear left into D 53 – 1 km – 1/2 mile plus 1/2 hour on foot Rtn along a marked path.* From the top there is a fine **panorama★** *(viewing table).*

Return to N 7 which passes below the Vistaëro before joining the Lower Corniche at Cabbé.

**Cap-Martin★.** – *Description p 126.*

*Enter Menton (p 99) by Avenue Carnot.*

**③ LOWER CORNICHE★★** (Corniche Inférieure)

**From Nice to Menton** – *33 km – 21 miles – about 6 hours – Local map p 123.*

The Lower Corniche was conceived and built as long ago as the 18C by a Prince of Monaco. The road, running at the foot of the mountain slopes and following the contours of the coast, serves all the Riviera resorts and gives access to the Cap Ferrat Peninsula and the Principality of Monaco.

*Leave Nice by Boulevard Carnot, N 98, going south east.* The road skirts the base of Mount Boron with **views★** of the Baie des Anges, Cap Ferrat, Villefranche Roads, Èze and the Tête de Chien in succession.

**Villefranche★.** – *Description p 167.*

Start from Pont St-Jean for a tour of the Cap Ferrat Peninsula.

**Cap Ferrat Peninsula★★.** – *Round tour of 11 km – 7 miles – about 2 1/2 hours. Description p 50.*

**Beaulieu★★.** – *Description p 39.*

**Èze-Bord-de-Mer.** – *Facilities p 28.* A long beach shelters beneath the cliffs below the eagle's nest of Èze.

**Cap d'Ail★.** – *Pop 4 282. Facilities p 28.* Sheltered by palm trees and pines, the elegant properties of Cap d'Ail extend over the lower slopes of the Tête de Chien escarpment to the sea.

**Cap d'Ail Coastal Path★.** – *1 hour on foot Rtn. To the east side of the station go down the steps into a subway which comes out on a road. Turn left and at La Pinède Restaurant take another flight of steps on the right down to the sea.*
A paved path running eastwards skirts the sea-drenched rocks at the foot of Cap d'Ail. To the west lie Beaulieu and Cap Ferrat; gradually Monaco Rock comes into view. The path ends on Marquet beach.

**Principality of Monaco★★★.** – *Description p 102.*

The road joins the Middle Corniche at Cabbé.

**Cap Martin★★.** – *Description p 126.*

*Enter Menton (p 99) by Avenue Carnot.*

---

## ROQUEBILLIÈRE

Michelin map ▦▦▦ fold 16 – *Local map p 166* – Pop 1 609

This important town has been rebuilt six times following rock falls or floods. The last landslide in 1926 left some of the austere old houses but rebuilding was forced to take place on the west bank of the Vésubie where the 15C church already stood.

**St-Michel-du-Gast Church.** – *In the new town. Apply to M. Gatti, carpenter (menuisier), quartier de la Bourgade.*
The church is one of the many examples in Provence of the Romanesque and Gothic styles combined. The Romanesque spire is unhappily disfigured by a clock. There are three Gothic naves supported on squat Romanesque columns. An **altarpiece** of the Nice school is dedicated to St Antony; the predella represents scenes from his legend. The Maltese cross carved on the volcanic stone of the font shows that the church was originally owned by the Knights of St John. A fine collection of 17C and 18C priestly vestments is kept in the sacristy.

## *EXCURSION*

**La Gordolasque Valley★★.** – *19 km – 12 miles – about 3/4 hour – Local map p 166. On leaving Roquebillière-Vieux, D 2565 going north, turn right into a narrow road leading up to Belvedere.*

A picturesque drive follows the course of the Gordolasque torrent upstream between the Cime du Diable and the Cime de Lavalette.

**Belvedere.** – Pop 430. Charming village in a **site★** overlooking both the Vésubie and the Gordolasque. The interior of the church is decorated with gilded wood and Baroque plasterwork; note the polychrome pulpit and naive paintings. *Open Sundays, 9am to 5pm.*
From the terrace behind the Town Hall *(Mairie)* there is a fine **view★** of the Vésubie downstream with Mount Férion and Turini Forest to the east and Mount Tourmairet to the west rising above Roquebillière.

Follow D 171 uphill through a landscape of magnificent rocks and sparkling waterfalls.

**Le Ray Waterfall★.** – The river gushes abundantly over twin falls.

The valley climbs northwards parallel to the Merveilles valley *(p 130)* from which it is divided by the Cime du Diable. Ahead rises the jagged outline of the Grand Capelet.

**L'Estrech Waterfall★.** – The road ends near the beautiful Estrech waterfall which drops from a **circus★★** of high snow-clad mountains above which rise Mount Clapier and the Cime du Gélas, both over 3 000 m - 9 840 ft.

*Join us in our never ending task of keeping up to date.*

*Send us your comments and suggestions, please.*

**Michelin Tyre Public Limited Company
Tourism Department
81 Fulham Road, LONDON SW3 6RD.**

Michelin map **84** fold 7 – *Local map p 95*

The proud silhouette of Roquebrune Mountain dominates the Argens valley to the south of the Provençal Motorway and N 7. It stands like an isolated outpost of the Maures Massif although its jagged red sandstone rocks link it to the Esterel. It is partially covered in cork oaks and conifers.

## MOUNTAIN TOUR★

### Round tour starting from Roquebrune-sur-Argens – *14 km - 8 miles – about 1 hour excluding climbing*

**Roquebrune-sur-Argens.** – Pop 5 053. The village clings to the rocky slope at the foot of Roquebrune Mountain. In 16C it was fortified and a few ramparts and arcaded houses remain from this period.

The 16C Gothic **church** includes two side chapels *(on the left)* with thick intersecting rib vaulting, part of the original 12C building.

One of the chapels contains a wooden altarpiece (1557) of John-the-Baptist in high relief, the other an altarpiece of the Last Judgement from the same period. In the nave, on the right of the entrance, is a 16C altarpiece composed of six carved panels depicting the Passion around a large Crucifix. There are two other 16C painted panels in the gallery.

*Take the narrow road on the south side of the village which leads up to N.-D.-de-Pitié.*

**N.-D.-de-Pitié.** – The chapel stands on rising ground amid pine and eucalyptus trees at the foot of a majestic red cliff. A 17C altarpiece incorporating a copy of Raphaël's *Pietà* is on the high altar.

From the chapel precincts there is a **view★** of the Argens plain, Fréjus, St-Raphaël and the Esterel Heights.

*Return to Roquebrune and turn left into D 7. After 500 m - 547 yds turn left. 1 km - 1/2 mile further on turn left again into a forest road. After 2 km - 3 1/4 miles leave the car where a path branches off to the right.*

**Roquebrune Summit★.** – *2 hours Rtn of hard walking; keep to the path.* From the summit (alt 372 m - 1 073 ft) there is an extended **view★** of the lower Argens plain, Fréjus Bay, the Esterel and the Alps on the horizon.

*Continue along the forest road; turn right into D 25 for 1 km - 1/2 mile (view of the Argens) then right again into a road which runs along the north face of the mountain, beside the Provençal Motorway, past La Roquette hamlet.*

**N.-D.-de-la-Roquette.** – *1/2 hour on foot Rtn.* Park in the car park beside the road and take the path on the right. The chapel is in an attractive **setting★** of trees and red sandstone, an ancient place of pilgrimage where walkers now meet.

From the terrace (alt 143 m - 470 ft) the **view** includes the lower Argens valley and the Provence Plateau.

*Return to the road turning right to reach D 7 and Roquebrune.*

*The layout diagram on page 3 shows the **Michelin Maps** covering the region. In the text, reference is made to the map which is the most suitable from a point of view of scale and practicality.*

## ROQUEBRUNE-CAP-MARTIN ★★

Michelin map **195** fold 28 – *Local map p 102* – Pop 11 246 – *Facilities p 28* – *For additional plan of Roquebrune-Cap-Martin see the current Michelin Guide France*

This pretty resort which covers the whole of Cap Martin and extends along the coast between Menton and Monte-Carlo, is watched over by the old hill village of Roquebrune and its castle keep.

The Roquebrune enclave is the only example in France today of a Carolingian castle, forerunners of the castles built 200 years later which marked the zenith of feudal times.

## HISTORICAL NOTES

The castle was built at the end of the 10C by Conrad I, Count of Ventimiglia, to stop the Saracens from establishing themselves once again in the area. After passing into the hands of the Counts of Provence and the Republic of Genoa, it belonged for several centuries to the Grimaldis *(p 102)*, who remodelled part of it and introduced artillery in its defences.

Originally, the castle was a fortress enclosing within its battlements, pierced by six fortified gateways, the keep and the village. In the 15C the keep became known as the castle and the rest of the fortress became the village, which up to the present time has preserved its mediaeval character.

For the past 500 years a procession representing in six tableaux the principal scenes of the Passion is held on the afternoon of 5 August. Unchanged since it was first performed by those who made a vow in 1467 during an epidemic of the plague, the ceremony goes on for about two hours between the church and the Chapel of La Pausa (Peace), about half a mile away.

At 9pm on Good Friday a Procession of the Entombment of Christ is held. This procession was instituted by the Confraternity of the White Penitents, which is now disbanded.

A train of some sixty people, dressed as Roman centurions and legionaries, disciples carrying the statue of Christ and holy women, walk through the streets of the village decorated with lighted motifs recalling the symbols of the Passion and illuminated with hundreds of little lights formed by snail shells filled with olive oil in which there is a small cotton wick.

# ■ THE OLD HILL VILLAGE★★ *time: 1 hour*

The town's remarkable situation and the mediaeval keep are not Roquebrune's sole attractions. To savour its charm, one should stroll through its covered streets, all apparently either steep slopes or stairways, which have preserved their ancient aspect despite the art galleries, craft and souvenir shops which have edged their way between the local tradesmen.

*Park in Place de la République.*

The square is the former barbican - the keep's advanced defence.

**Rue Moncollet★.** – Make for Place des Deux-Frères and then turn left into Rue Grimaldi. Bear left again into the unusual and picturesque Rue Moncollet with its long and narrow covered and stepped passageways. Mediaeval houses with barred windows where once lived those invited to join the seignorial court, give on to the road in front, while at the back they lie against or are cut into the living rock. Rue Moncollet, bending slightly to the right, leads into Rue du Château on the left.

**The Keep★.** – *Open 1 April to 30 September, 9am to noon and 2 to 7pm; the rest of the year 10am to 4pm; closed Fridays in winter, 1 May and 1 to 21 November. 5F.*

After crossing the "flowered enclosure" you enter the ancient keep of the oldest feudal castle in France. It overlooks by some 26 m – 80 ft the façades of the houses opposite in the Rue Moncollet. The walls, which are from 2 to 4 m – 6 to 12 ft thick, have every sort of defence: cannon embrasures, machicolations, battlements and loopholes, etc.

A flight of twenty steps leads up to the first floor and the Hall of Feudal Ceremonies. Note particularly: the placing of the baronial throne; the cell recessed into the wall; in the centre, a cube-shaped water tank; and the 15C mullioned window, replacing the oblique slots 20 cm – 8 in across which once provided light. Below this hall is the storeroom, carved out of the rock.

On the second floor is the small guardroom, on the right a comfortable prison and further on the archers' dormitory. On the third floor are the baronial apartments complete with furnishings: dining room, primitive kitchen with bread oven, and a bedroom containing old weapons.

The fourth floor includes the upper artillery platform affording a circular **panorama**★★ over the picturesque roofs of the village, the sea, Cap Martin, the Principality of Monaco, and Mount Agel (antenna of Radio-Monte-Carlo).

Go down by the parapet walk and the so-called English Tower which has been badly restored.

You can also visit the light artillery platform and the lookout post.

**Millenary Olive Tree.** – *Cross Place William-Ingram and turn right into Rue du Château.*

Opposite a souvenir shop, before an arched passage, take the Rue de la Fontaine on the left and the Menton road, which 200 m – 219 yds beyond the end of the village passes a 1 000-year-old olive tree, said to be one of the oldest trees in the world. Return to the Rue du Château which, on the left, leads to the church.

**Ste-Marguerite Church.** – The fairly plain Baroque façade masks the original 12C church which has undergone many alterations over the years. Against the polychrome plasterwork of the interior hang two paintings by a local painter, Marc-Antoine Otto (17C): a Crucifixion (2nd altar) and a *Pietà* (above the door).

*Turn right into Rue Grimaldi which leads, via Place des Deux-Frères, to Place de la République.*

# ■ CAP MARTIN★★

Cap Martin with its magnificent estates is the rich suburb of Menton. It is served by roads which cut through olive groves and clumps of cypresses, perfumed by pine woods and banks of mimosa.

A massive tower of feudal appearance rises at the centre; it was the old semaphore, now converted to a relay station for telecommunications. At its foot lie the ruins of St-Martin's Basilica, part of a priory built by the Lérins Island monks in 11C and destroyed by pirates about 1400.

Local legend gives the following account. One night the Prior, wishing to test the vigilance of the inhabitants who were obliged to protect the monks, sounded the alarm. The people came running, cursed to find it was a false alarm and returned to bed swearing not to be duped again. Some time later the pirates launched an attack; the monks sounded the alarm but nobody came to their rescue; they were massacred and the monastery burned down.

**East Coast.** – From the road along the eastern shore there is a marvellous **view**★★ of Menton in its mountain setting and of the Italian coast as far as Bordighera.

**Seaside resort.** – There are several beaches dominated by the old village: two at Cabbé facing south west and one at Carnolès on the east side next to Menton.

**Coastal Path★★**. – *From Cap Martin to Monte-Carlo Beach: 3 hours on foot Rtn (preferably in the afternoon). Park in the Avenue Winston-Churchill car park at the seaward end of Cap Martin. A sign "Promenade Le Corbusier" near a restaurant indicates the beginning of the path.*

The path leads westwards round the headland over the rocks. After several minutes a series of steps and inclines skirts the grounds of private properties through wild and abundant vegetation. Gradually the view takes in Monaco in its natural amphitheatre, Cap Ferrat, the Tête de Chien, La Turbie and Mount Agel behind Monaco, and the old village of Roquebrune with its castle.

*A flight of steps on the right crossing the railway line provides a short-cut back to Carnolès Beach via the Town Hall (Mairie).*

The coastal path continues beside the railway line to Roquebrune Station above a sheer drop into the sea. Skirting the Cabbé beaches and the Bon Voyage rocks the path goes on towards Monte-Carlo (rear view to Cap Martin), leaving La Vieille Point to seaward, and ending in a flight of steps near the Old Beach Hotel on Monte-Carlo Beach.

*There are frequent trains to Carnolès from Monte-Carlo or Roquebrune.*

## ROUTE NAPOLEON ★★

Michelin maps **195**, **84**, **81**, and **77**

The Route Napoléon – Napoleon's Road – follows the Emperor's route on his return from Elba from the point where he landed at Golfe-Juan to his arrival at Grenoble. The new road was opened in 1932. The commemorative plaques and monuments bear the flying eagle symbol inspired by Napoleon's remark "The eagle will fly from steeple to steeple until he reaches the towers of Notre-Dame".

## HISTORICAL NOTES

After landing at Golfe-Juan on 1 March 1815, Napoleon and his little troop, preceded by an advance guard, made a brief overnight stop at Cannes. Wishing to avoid the Rhône area, which he knew to be hostile, Napoleon made for Grasse to get to the Valley of the Durance by way of the Alps. Beyond Grasse the little column had a difficult time along mule tracks. It halted at St-Vallier, Escragnolles and Séranon, from which, after a night's rest, it reached Castellane on 3 March; by the afternoon it came to Barrême. The next day (4 March) the party lunched at Digne. Napoleon halted that evening at the Château de Malijai, impatiently awaiting news from Sisteron, whose fort commanded the narrow passage of the Durance.

Sisteron was not guarded. Napoleon lunched there (5 March) and left the town in an atmosphere of growing sympathy. Once more on a coach road he arrived that night at Gap and there received an enthusiastic welcome. Next day (6 March) he slept at Corps. The 7th, he reached La Mure, only to find troops from Grenoble

*(After photo : German National Museum, Nuremberg)*

Escape from Elba (popular print)

facing him at Laffrey. It was here that took place the famous episode which is commemorated today by a monument to Napoleon. That same evening he entered Grenoble to shouts of: "Long live the Emperor".

*The route followed by the Emperor as far as Sisteron is described below. The northern section of the route is described in the Michelin Green Guide – Alpes (French only).*

### From Golfe-Juan to Sisteron – *180 km - 112 miles – one day – Local map p 128*

*Leave Golfe-Juan (p 50) by N 7. The road winds round the west face of Super-Cannes hill, facing the Lérins Islands and the Esterel Massif. The view is best at sunset.*

**Cannes★★★**. – *Description p 47.*

*Leave Cannes by N 85, ④ on the plan. The road rises above the town and the sea past the hill village of Mougins (p 106). It passes through Mouans-Sartoux skirting the castle before coming in sight of Grasse spread out on the mountain slope.*

**Grasse★★**. – *Description p 74.*

*Leave Grasse by N 85, ④ on the plan, going north west, skirting Napoleon's Plateau where he halted on 2 March outside the town. The route through the Provence Plateau and then the Pre-Alps of Grasse, Provence's limestone mountains, crosses four passes in succession: the Pilon Pass (786 m - 2 578 ft), the La Faye Pass (Pas de la Faye, 981 m - 218 ft), the Valferrière Pass (1 169 m - 3 805 ft) and the Luens Pass (1 056 m - 3 467 ft).*

**Pilon Pass.** – From the southern slope up to the pass there is a magnificent **view★★** of La Napoule Bay with the Lérins Islands, Grasse, St-Cassien Lake (SW), the Esterel and Maures Massifs (SW).

**St-Vallier-de-Thiey.** – Pop 612. Former Roman stronghold grouped round a Romanesque church, St-Vallier is a traditional holiday resort for the people of Grasse, set in pine woods. A bust of Napoleon in the main square recalls his visit on 2 March.

# ROUTE NAPOLÉON ★★

As the road climbs to La Faye Pass there are very fine **views★**, particularly from the double bend.

> **La Faye Pass★★**. – Similar **view★★** to that seen from Pilon Pass. Those travelling south over the pass suddenly see the Mediterranean and the Riviera coastline spread out before them.

The road runs through arid country dominated by the Audibergue and Bleine mountains to the north and the Lachens mountain *(p 38)* to the east, with countless **views** to the south. 1 km - 1/2 mile before Escragnolles, by a filling station, a road to the Baou Mourine Belvedere branches off to the left.

> **Baou Mourine Belvedere★**. – *1 km - 1/2 mile plus 1/2 hour on foot Rtn. Path marked with red arrows.* Terrace **viewpoint★** over the Siagne valley, La Napoule Bay, the Esterel and Maures Massifs.

After Escragnolles, where Napoleon made a brief halt, there are further fine views to the south. Beyond Valferrière Pass the road enters the **Séranon Rift**: the Emperor spent the night of 2 March in Séranon village *(on the right)*.

After Luens Pass the road begins to descend the Pre-Alps of Castellane into the Verdon valley, where Castellane shelters beneath the Chapel of Our Lady of the Rock.

> **Castellane★**. – *Description p 52.*

From Castellane to Digne the road follows the Asse valley, scythed perpendicularly through the steep and rugged crests of the Haute-Provence ridges to form gorges and rifts, rock gateways displaying fine stratifications some of which have been tilted vertical.

The approach to Les Leques Pass (alt 1 146 m - 3 760 ft) offers **views** of Castellane, Castillon Lake and part of the Pre-Alps of Provence.

> **Taulanne Rift★**. – Through a spectacular opening cut into the rock, the road passes from the Verdon to the Asse valley.

*6 km - 3 3/4 miles further on, turn left over the Asse into Senez.*

> **Senez**. – Pop 126. In 4C the Gallo-Roman town of Sanitium was one of the oldest sees in France, hence the unusually large church in such a small village. By 17C its revenues were minimal.
> The **old cathedral** was built early in 13C of warm brown stone with Lombard arcading supported on slim engaged columns round the chevet.
> *Open Sundays 10.30am to noon; Thursdays, apply to the Town Hall (Mairie) 2.30 to 5pm; otherwise apply to Mme Ughetto, near the church or to M. Garnier at the presbytery.*
> A sober Gothic doorway opens into a plain Provençal Romanesque interior decorated with 16C Flemish and 18C Aubusson **tapestries★**, choir stalls, 17C altarpieces and pulpit, 18C antiphonaries.

*Return to N 85 turning left towards Digne.*

> **Barrême**. – Pop 435. Geologists have given the name «Barremian» to part of the lower cretaceous layer. A house bordering the N 85 near the square bears an inscription recording that Napoleon slept there on 3 March 1815.

Beyond Chaudon-Norante the road enters the Pre-Alps of Digne.

**Either** turn right into D 20 which follows the route taken by Napoleon, a narrow and picturesque road which passes the Digne Hydro.

**Or** continue along N 85 which abandons the historic route temporarily to pass through the **Chabrières Rift★**, enclosed between high limestone cliffs.

> **Digne**. – *Description p 56.*

*Leave Digne by N 85, ③ on the plan, going west.* The drive follows the Bléone valley between Valensole Plateau and the Pre-Alps of Digne. To the right rises the stark silhouette of Fontenelle castle, with its four candle-snuffer corner towers.

> **Malijai**. – Pop 1 471. Napoleon spent the night of 4 March in the 18C castle on the banks of the Bléone.

Beyond Malijai the view opens out over the Durance valley to the bluish bulk of the Lure mountain. The road turns north beside the Oraison Canal to the Escale hydro-electric dam on the Durance. Bear right into D 4 going north along the east bank of the Escale Lake.

> **Volonne**. – Pop 1 253. *Facilities p 30.* The twin towers of the picturesque village on its rocky spur stand out above the surrounding orchards.

Soon after the Salignac dam, as the road approaches Sisteron *(p 140)*, there is a superb view of the town in its **setting★★**.

*Respect the life of the countryside*
*Go carefully on country roads*
*Protect wild life, wild plants and trees.*

① Historical route.
② Historical halt.

ROUTE NAPOLÉON

① ∼ ②

0                    10 km

## ROYA Upper Valley ★★

Michelin map **195** folds 8, 9 and 18 – *Local map p 130*

When Savoy and the County of Nice were attached to France in 1860, the Italian minister, Cavour, obtained permission from Napoleon III to keep part of the French side of the Maritime Alps – the upper valley of the Roya – so that the sovereign of the new kingdom of Italy could retain his hunting grounds in the neighbourhood of Le Mercantour.

The peace treaty with Italy, confirmed by a plebiscite on 12 October 1947, put an end to this anomaly. The upper valley of the Roya, together with the Vésubie and the Tinée, were incorporated into France, thus bringing the frontier back to the watershed.

A tributary valley leads to a prehistoric site in the Merveilles valley.

### Breil-sur-Roya to Tende – *39 km - 24 miles – about 3 hours*

*Leave Breil-sur-Roya (p 42) by N 204 going north.* On the left the road to Brouis Pass *(p 44)* branches off.

**La Giandola.** – Attractive mountain hamlet with a Renaissance church tower.

Beyond La Giandola the road climbs the Roya Valley which becomes ever more enclosed.

**Saorge Gorges★★.** – The road follows the river's every curve in narrow *corniche* style and beneath overhanging rocks. The Nice-Cuneo railway also passes through these gorges by way of tunnels and other engineering undertakings.

As the road emerges from the gorges, you get a view through the gap between two rock cliffs of the extraordinary **setting★★** of Saorge, built in semicircular tiers, halfway up a hillside covered in olive trees.

**Saorge★★.** – *Description p 140.*

**Bergue Gorges★.** – Beyond Fontan, the road ascends gorges cut through red schists where the rock appears deeply coloured and foliated.

The valley widens out into the St-Dalmas basin.

**St-Dalmas-de-Tende.** – *Facilities p 30.* Attractive resort surrounded by chestnut forests. It is a good excursion centre, particularly for the Merveilles valley *(p 130)*.

*From St-Dalmas, bear right into D 43 up the green Levanza valley to the east to reach La Brigue.*

**La Brigue.** – *Description p 44.*

*Ask at the St-Martin Inn or at the Fleurs des Alpes Hotel for the key to the Chapel of Notre-Dame-des-Fontaines (see below).*

*Continue along the D 43, then turn right into the D 143 to Notre-Dame-des-Fontaines.*

**Notre-Dame-des-Fontaines★★.** – The Chapel of Our Lady of the Fountains stands in a lonely valley amidst intermittent springs, overlooking the main torrent. The sanctuary, which is the goal of pilgrimages faithfully observed by the local people, gives no idea from outside of the richness of its interior decoration where the walls are covered with well preserved **frescoes★★** forming a "catechism in pictures" with Latin titles.

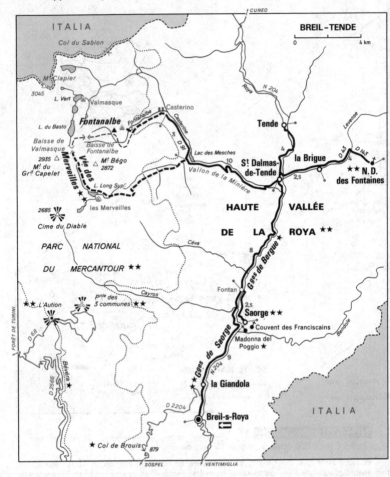

The choir is decorated by paintings attributed to Baleison depicting the life of the Virgin and the Evangelists and St-Thomas. All the other frescoes are by Canavesio. In composed scenes, rich in colour, an often poignant realism and a detail denoting keen observation, Giovanni Canavesio has depicted the principal events in Christ's life. In the chancel is the Childhood of Christ (note **the Flight into Egypt**), on the side walls the Passion (note **Jesus before Pilate**), on the back of the façade, the **Last Judgment**. This, together with the scenes of the **Crucifixion**, are among the most interesting compositions. The haunting portrayal of **Judas Iscariot** is particularly striking.

*Return to St-Dalmas and continue up the valley.* The meadows contrast with the olive growing regions round Sospel and Breil. At a bend Tende *(p 143)* comes into view.

## Merveilles Valley★★   *time: 1 or 2 days starting from St-Dalmas-de-Tende*

To the west of Tende, around Mount Bégo (alt 2 872 m – 9 423 ft), lies a region of glacial lakes and valleys, rock circuses and moraine, cut off by the lack of roads and the severe mountain climate. The Minière, Casterine and Fontanalbe valleys are clothed with larch woods but the Merveilles valley, which lies between the Grand Capelet and Mount Bégo has only a thin carpet of vegetation which flowers in the summer. The peaks and valleys and lakes make a gradiose spectacle but the region is famous for the thousands of rock engravings which have been discovered.

**Excursion by car.** – There are two possibilities.

**Merveilles Valley.** – *9 km – 5 1/2 miles starting from St-Dalmas-de-Tende by D 91 – allow 2 days.* Follow the Minière valley up to Les Mesches Lake and park the car. Walk on up the valley *(3 hours)* past the Lower Long Lake *(inférieur)* to the Merveilles Refuge and spend the night there *(meals available in theory).* In the morning explore the Merveilles valley as far as the Baisse de Valmasque and return to Les Mesches in the afternoon. Experienced walkers may go further as far as the Baisse de Fontanalbe and then strike due east *(no path for more than 2 km – 1 1/4 miles)* to the rock engravings near the Fontanalbe, returning to Les Mesches by the Fontanalbe and Casterine valleys.

**Fontanalbe.** – *12 km – 7 1/2 miles starting from St-Dalmas-de-Tende by D 91 – allow 1 day.* Drive up the Minière and Casterine valleys to Ste-Madeleine and park the car. Walk up Fontanalbe valley to the rock engravings near the Fontanalbe Refuge.

**Excursion by Jeep.** – *1 whole day.* Both Tende and St-Dalmas offer organised excursions in jeeps either to the Merveilles Refuge or to the Fontanalbe engravings: *terms to be agreed* as they do not all offer the same service; some include a guide who accompagnies the tourists to the engravings. Details from Tende Tourist Centre (Syndicat d'Initiative).

**N. B.** Whatever the route and mode of travel being used:
– the engravings may be covered with snow up to the end of June and from the end of September;
– without a guide it is very difficult to find the engravings which are spread over a wide area at various levels;
– detailed maps are essential: 1/25 000 scale maps of the National Geographic Institute or the 1/50 000 map «Haut Pays Niçois» by Didier et Richard-Grenoble;
– proper equipment is essential: compass, walking boots and warm waterproof clothing even in high summer;
– the Tourist Centre in Tende will supply whatever information is necessary.

**100 000 Rock Engravings.** – The Mount Bégo region is an open-air prehistoric museum; more than 100 000 engravings have been identified. The majority are to be found in the Merveilles valley but there are a few in the Fontanalbe and Vallaurette valleys and in Le Sabion Pass. The engravings are cut into the rock face worn smooth by glacial action 15 000 years ago.

While the linear engravings date from the Gallo-Roman period through the Middle Ages to the present day, the engravings which are of most interest to the archaeologists are earlier: the majority date from the early Bronze Age (about 1800 to 1500 BC). A stippling technique has been used; the contours and surfaces are obtained by the juxtaposition of tiny dots, between 1 and 5mm – up to 0.2ins across, punched in the rock face with flint or quartz tools.

**Magic Mountain.** – Although lacking in obvious artistic merit, the engravings reveal the preoccupations of the Ligurian people who lived in the lower valleys and made pilgrimages to Mount Bégo to which they ascribed divine power, both tutelary owing to the many streams which rise there and awesome owing to the sudden violent storms which rage there. Here, as elsewhere, the mountain cult was linked to that of the bull: drawings of horns and bovine creatures feature in half the engravings. Human figures however are quite numerous and the most well known have been given names: The Wizard, Christ, the Chieftain, the Dancer...

Ploughs and harrows harnessed to animals suggest that agriculture was practised; some criss-cross patterns may represent parcels of land. There are many representations of weapons which correspond quite well with those excavated on contemporary archaeological sites.

## St-ÉTIENNE-DE-TINÉE

Michelin map **195** fold 4 – Pop 1 938 – *Facilities p 30*

The smart little alpine town was rebuilt after a terrible fire in 1929 on its attractive **site★** beside the foaming river, surrounded by terraced cultivation and pasture at the heart of a beautiful circle of mountains. It is a popular centre for excursions and mountaineering as well as winter sports.

■ **SIGHTS** *time: 1 1/2 hours*

**Church.** – The fine four-storey Romanesque **bell-tower★** with Lombard bands, dated 1492, supports an octagonal stone spire with four gargoyle pinnacles. The high altar of gilded wood shows Spanish influence; to the left wood carvings in gold and silver depicting scenes from the life of Christ around a statue of the Virgin and Child.

**Chapels.** – *Guided tour from 1 July to 31 August: apply to Tourist Centre. Otherwise contact Mlle Fulconis: ☎ 02.42.59 after 8pm.*

**St-Sébastien Chapel.** – Some of the **frescoes** – on which Baleison and Canavesio collaborated – are in good condition. On the ceiling, the creation of Adam and Eve; on the far wall, Jesus between the robbers, with Sebastian and six other saints below; on the righthand wall, scenes from the life of St Sebastian.

**St-Michel Chapel.** – A small museum of religious art displaying items from the chapels in the neighbourhood.

**Trinitarian Chapel.** – Once part of the Convent of the Trinitarians, monks who devoted themselves to rescuing Christian captives from the Barbary pirates, the chapel is decorated with several 17C frescoes, one showing the Battle of Lepanto; below are two pictures depicting the life of the monks; some carved woodwork.

**St-Maur Chapel.** – *2 km – 1 1/4 miles down the Auron road, D 39.* Picuresque 15C frescoes by a local artist illustrating the legends of St–Maur and St Sebastian.

## ST-JULIEN

Michelin map **84** west of fold 5 – 14 km – 9 miles south of Gréoux-Les Bains – Pop 611

The small Provençal village of St-Julien is perched on an isolated mound from which it commands the Provence Plateau, a succession of rocky plateaux, covered with sparse scrub except where occasional small groups of houses have grown up, surrounded by well cultivated fields of cereals, vineyards and olive groves.

From the old threshing floor at the top of the village (579 m – 1 894 ft) there is a **view★** over Haute-Provence – the Valley of the Durance, the Valensole Plateau, the Provençal Alps as well as Ste-Baume and Ste-Victoire Mountains.

**Church.** – The church (IIC) is typical of Haute-Provence; there are also a 17C high altar of gilded wood and a well preserved rood-beam. The chancel is lit by a square belfry which forms a lantern.

**Ramparts.** – Continue right through the village to the north west where the road ends at a fortified gate which, together with traces of 13C ramparts, is all that remains of the former stronghold. There is a fine **view** of the country from here.

Michelin map **195** fold 6 – *Local map p 166* – Pop 1 188 – *Facilities p 30*

St-Martin-Vésubie, stretched out along a spiny rock between the Boréon and Madone-de-Fenestre streams, and encircled by tall summits, has become an important summer mountaineering centre and, because it is so cool, a highly popular resort.

*Climbing trips are organised by the Compagnie des Guides de la Haute-Vésubie; apply to the Tourist Centre, ☎ 03.21.28.*

■ **SIGHTS** time: *3/4 hour*

Start from the beautiful central square under the plane trees which line the Allées de Verdun.

**Rue du Docteur-Cagnoli.** – A narrow street, bordered by Gothic houses with handsome porches and lintels, runs north-south through the town with a small canal flowing down the centre.

**White Penitents' Chapel (B).** – A carved façade, a bulb-shaped bell-tower and, below the altar, a recumbent figure of Christ with cherubs at the four corners holding the instruments of the Passion.

**The Gubernatis' House (D).** – No 25 at the bottom of the street, the house built over an arcade, belonged to the Count of Gubernatis.

**Place de la Frairie.** – Turn left into Rue du Plan which ends in Place de la Frairie marked by a fountain. From the terrace overlooking the Madone de Fenestre torrent, there is a view of the rushing river and of the neighbouring mountains (Cime de la Palu (E) and Cime du Piagu (NE)).

**Church (E).** – The beautiful decoration dates from 17C. To the right of the choir is a richly dressed statue of Our

**ST-MARTIN-VÉSUBIE**

| | |
|---|---|
| Boréon (Ch. du) | 2 |
| Docteur Fulconis (Allées du) | 3 |
| Église (R. de l') | 4 |
| Kellerman (Av.) | 5 |
| Paulan (Av.) | 6 |
| Plan (R. du) | 7 |
| Saravalle (Av.) | 8 |

Lady of Fenestre, 12C seated figure of polychrome wood. On 2 July she is carried in procession to her mountain sanctuary *(below)* where she stays until mid-September.

In the second chapel in the lefthand aisle are two panels from an altarpiece attributed to Louis Bréa: St Peter and St Martin on the left, St John and St Petronella on the right. In the third chapel, a beautiful altar to the Rosary in carved and gilded wood (17C).

From the terrace a restricted view of the Boreon valley (N) and Venanson village below the round wooded Tête du Siruol (S).

## EXCURSIONS

**Le Boréon★★ and Le Mercantour National Park★★.** – *8 km – 5 miles to the north – Local map p 166. Leave St-Martin-Vésubie by D 2565 going north up the west bank of the Boréon.*

**Le Boréon★★.** – The resort stands on a superb site, 1 500 m – 4 021 ft up, by the Boréon **waterfall★** where the river drops 40 m – 130 ft in a narrow gorge; above the fall a small lake adds its calm beauty to the green landscape of pasture and woodland.

**Le Mercantour National Park★★.** – *No guns, dogs or transistors are allowed in the Park; camping and fires are forbidden.*
This region of natural beauty, some 70 000 ha – 270 sq miles, supports chamois, ibex, wild sheep, marmots, partridges and white hares; the rocks are covered by a varied flora rich in colour and rare species. The Park backs on to the Valdieri-Entracque Reserve in Italy.
Le Boréon is the starting place for walks in the forest, up to the high peaks and mountain lakes. One can drive by car to the Vacherie du Boréon *(2.5 km – 1 1/2 miles to the east)* beneath the distinctive silhouette of La Cougourde. There is also a road running west along the southern edge of the Park for 4 km – 2 1/2 miles up the Salèse valley.

**Valdeblore Route★★.** – *29 km – 18 miles – about 2 hours – Description p 156 – Local map p 166.*

**Madone de Fenestre Valley★.** – *12 km – 7 1/2 miles – about 1/2 hour – Local map p 166. Leave St-Martin by Avenue de Saravalle (north east on the plan). Turn right into D 94.* The road climbs rapidly up the Madone valley between the Cime du Piagu and the Cime de la Palu, crossing and re-crossing the river. A fine forest of pines and larches rises out of heavy undergrowth before giving way to high mountain pasture.

**Madone de Fenestre.** – The road ends in a rugged rock **circus★★** much appreciated by mountaineers. Cayre de la Madone, huge and pointed, rises nearby; the firm-covered slopes of the Cime du Gélas (3 143 m – 10 312 ft) dominates the northern horizon on the Italian border.
There are pilgrimages to the chapel on 2 and 26 July, 15 August and 8 September. During the summer it houses the statue of Our Lady of Fenestre which returns to St-Martin-Vésubie in solemn procession in the middle of September.

**Venanson★.** – Pop 84 – *4,5 km – 3 miles – Local map p 166. Leave St–Martin-Vésubie by the bridge over the Boréon and the D 31 going south.*

From Venanson, built on a rock spike 1 164 m – 3 819 ft high, there is a good **view★** of St-Martin, the Vésubie Valley and its mountain setting.

**St-Sébastien Chapel.** – *Key available at the presbytery or from the Town Hall (Mairie) at St-Martin-Vésubie.*
The interior is decorated with **frescoes★** by Baleison. At the far end beneath a Crucifixion St Sebastian pierced by arrows; on the side walls and the ceiling, scenes from the saint's life inspired by the Golden Legend. Another panel takes prayer as its theme.

**Parish church.** – On the left of the entrance is a triptych of the Virgin and Child, flanked by St John and St Petronella.
At the high altar is a Baroque altarpiece (1645) of the Coronation of the Vigin featuring the donor. On the right is an altarpiece of the Rosary.

## ST-PAUL ★★

Michelin map ⚏ fold 25 – *Local maps pp 81 and 90 – Pop 1 974 – Facilities p 30*

The tapering outline of St-Paul stands out from afar above the rolling hills and rich valleys of the Vence countryside which give it a very charming **setting★**. It is typical of the fortified towns which once guarded the Var frontier. Set on a spur, behind ramparts which are still more or less intact, it has retained much of its mediaeval appearance and attracts many visitors.

After a period of prosperity in the Middle Ages, the village declined in the last century to the benefit of Vence and Cagnes. It was "discovered" in the 1920s by painters such as Signac, Modigliani, Bonnard and Soutine who used to meet in a café which has since become the sumptuous Colombe d'Or Inn, its walls hung with pictures as in a gallery. Other artists followed: painters, sculptors, men of letters and entertainment, who have made St-Paul famous.

■ **SIGHTS** *time: 2 hours*

Leave your car before passing through the north gate where you will see the muzzle of a cannon captured at the battle of Cérisoles (1544). A square machicolated tower houses the Tourist Centre (Syndicat d'Initiative) together with a permanent exhibition of modern paintings.

**Rue Grande.** – The Rue Grande is the main street running the full length of the village but closed to traffic.
Many of the arcaded 16C and 17C houses bearing coats of arms are now artists' studios, antique shops and art and craft galleries.
The famous urn-shaped **fountain** with its vaulted washing place in the square is of particular interest.
*Climb up the stepped street above the fountain. Take the first right and then first left to the church.*

**Church.** – Gothic building constructed from 12C to 13C; the vaulting was rebuilt in 17C and the bell-tower in 18C. There are three naves supported on massive pillars.
It contains several works of art. In the north aisle near the font a 15C alabaster Virgin; at the far end of this aisle a painting attributed to Tintoretto of St Catherine of Alexandria in a magnificent red cloak, sword in hand.
The choir stalls are 17C carved walnut.
The south transept chapel is particularly noteworthy for the richness of its stucco decoration; before the altar a low-relief depicting the martyrdom of St Clement; above the altar a 17C Italian canvas of St Charles Borromeo; on the left, an Assumption of the Murillo school.
The next chapel is adorned with a Madonna of the Rosary (1588) with Catherine de Medici in the crowd. The Stations of the Cross are modern although painted in tempera, a 16C technique.
The **treasury** is rich in 12C to 15C pieces – statuettes, ciborium, processional cross, reliquaries and, in particular a 13C enamel Virgin and Child – demonstrate the talent of Provençal craftsmen.

**Keep.** – The keep opposite the church is now the Town Hall.
*Return to Rue Grande and continue down to the South Gate.*

**Ramparts★.** – From the South Gate bastion overlooking the cemetery there is a superb view of the Alps, the sea (Cap d'Antibes) and the Esterel.
The ramparts remain much as they were built between 1537 and 1547 in answer to the challenge of the Citadel of Nice. Follow the parapet walk where possible; it commands good views both of the orange trees and flower fields in the valley and of the hills and mountains inland.

**Maeght Foundation★.** – *Open 1 June to 31 October, 10am to 12.30pm and 3 to 7pm; 1 November to 31 May, 10am to 12.30pm and 2.30 to 6pm; 12F.*
This modern art museum is located northwest of St-Paul in a pinewood on La Gardette hill. The architect José Luis Sert, with the use of white concrete and rose-coloured bricks has created an architectural complex in the true Mediterranean style.
Incorporated in the pinewood park is a Calder stabile, as well as mobiles, sculpture, a bronze by Zadkine and Arp's "Giant Pip". In the garden is the Labyrinth with sculpture and ceramics by Miro and in the Chapel of St. Bernard are stained glass windows by Ubac and Braque; the Stations of the Cross are by Ubac.

## ST-PAUL ★★

A Braque mosaic forms the background to a pond while another by Chagall decorates the external wall of the sales room.

The **museum** is made up of two buildings divided by a court containing sculpture by Giacometti. Inside are housed works by Braque, Miro, Kandinsky, Chagall, Giacometti, Bonnard, Derain, Bazaine, Léger, Matisse and several young contemporary artists.

Other rooms are devoted to very good temporary exhibitions.

There are studios, a library, a cinema and an auditorium for the use of resident artists. Concerts are given as well as performances of ballet and poetry recitals.

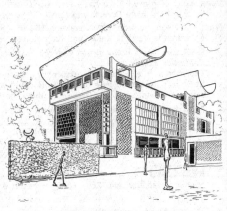

*St-Paul – Maeght Foundation*

## ST-RAPHAËL ★

Michelin map **195** fold 33 – *Local maps pp 62 and 95* – Pop 21 366 – *Facilities p 28 – For additional plan of St-Raphaël see the current Michelin Guide France*

St-Raphaël, a fashionable summer and winter resort situated on the Bay of Fréjus, has a well sheltered beach at the foot of the Esterel. The anchorage is deep enough for warships; the old harbour is used by fishing boats and trading vessels; a marina south east of the town can accommodate up to 1 800 pleasure craft.

**Origins.** – St-Raphaël, like Fréjus, is a daughter of Rome. A Gallo-Roman holiday resort stood on the site now occupied by the large Casino. It was built in terraces, decorated with mosaics, and included thermal baths and a vivarium (fish reserve). At that period rich Romans came there to take the sea air.

The villas were plundered by the Saracen pirates. After their expulsion (end of the 10C), the Count of Provence left these deserted lands to the Abbeys of Lérins and St-Victor of Marseilles. The monks built a village round the church. In the 12C its defence was entrusted to the Templars.

In the 18C the fishermen and peasants who lived in St-Raphaël occupied what are known today as the old quarters, but marsh fever so weakened the inhabitants that they became known in the region as «pale faces».

**Bonaparte at St-Raphaël.** – On 9 October 1799, the little village suddenly became well known. Bonaparte, returning from Egypt, landed there after a voyage of forty-eight days (a pyramid standing in Avenue Commandant-Guilbaud commemorates this event).

In 1814 St-Raphaël saw Napoleon once again, this time as a defeated man leaving for Elba, his new and minute kingdom.

**Alphonse Karr and the Origin of the Resort.** – The resort of St-Raphaël was discovered in 1864 by Alphonse Karr (1808-1890), journalist and pamphleteer (he was the author of the famous phrase "Let the murderers set to work!" when the abolition of capital punishment was being discussed) To his friends he sent enthusiastic descriptions of St-Raphaël. "Leave Paris," he wrote to one of them, "come and plant your walking stick in my garden; the next day, when you awake you will find that roses have grown from it." Writers, artists and musicians responded to his appeal. Dumas, Maupassant and Berlioz came to stay; Gounod composed Romeo et Juliette there in 1866.

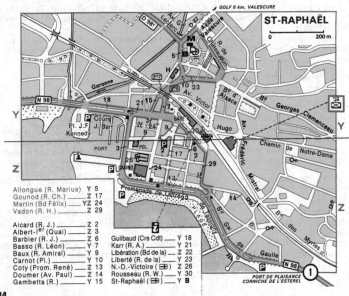

■ **SIGHTS** *time: 1 hour*

**Sea Front.** – There is great activity on the waterfront by the old harbour stimulated by the cafés and shops which line the broad pavements of Cours Jean-Bart and Quai Albert-I$^{er}$.

From beneath the palms and plane trees of Promenade René-Coty and Avenue du Général-de-Gaulle there is a fine **view** of the sea and the twin rocks known as the Land Lion and the Sea Lion. The road follows the coast eastwards to the marina with its terraces, shops and restaurants.

**Museum of Underwater Archaeology** (Y M). – *Open 15 June to 15 September, 10am to noon and 3 to 6pm (except Tuesday); 16 September to 14 June, 11am to noon and 2 to 5pm (except Sundays); closed holidays; 3F.*

This museum is used basically to receive the finds of the neighbouring scuba diving clubs. The 1st room contains an important **collection of amphorae**★ dating from 5C BC to AD 5. In the garden is a milestone set up on the Aurelian Way *(p 65)* under Augustus and found in the Esterel. The other rooms contain: a reconstructed scene of amphorae being loaded on a Roman ship, a collection of bottles, lamps and amphorae corks.

On the 1st floor there is skin diving equipment and in the display cabinet the treatment and conservation of ancient woods, once submerged underwater, is explained.

The history of St-Raphaël is evoked, in a room, with old photographs, drawings and a 13C bas-relief.

**St-Raphaël Church** (Y B). – *Same times as for the museum; combined ticket.*

This church, built in the 12C in the Romanesque-Provençal style, served as a fortress and a refuge for the population in case of attack by pirates. The watch tower, which tops one of the apsidal chapels, recalls the military constructions of the Templars.

In one of the side chapels a red sandstone monolith, formerly a pagan altar, now supports the altar table. The gilded wood bust of St Peter is carried by the fishermen in procession to the Sea Lion in August.

Near the church fragments of the aqueduct which brought water to St-Raphaël can also be seen.

---

## ST-ROCH Pass Road ★

Michelin map ██ folds 16, 17 and 27

This road also called the Sunshine Road (Route du Soleil), follows the Paillon de Contes valley into the back country of Nice.

### Nice to Lucéram – *51 km – 32 miles – about 2 hours*

*Leave Nice by Avenue de Turin, D 2204, going north; at Pointe de Contes bear left into D 15.*

For several miles beyond Pointe de Contes the countryside is marked by cement works.

**Châteauneuf-de-Contes and Old Châteauneuf.** – *7 km – 4 1/4 miles – from D 15 plus 1/2 hour on foot Rtn. Description pp 118-119.*

**Contes.** – *1 km – 1/2 mile along D 715. Description p 118.*

The beautiful road to Berre-des-Alpes (D 615) branches off to the right *(p 118)*. Continue on D 15 which winds north through terraced countryside dotted with chestnut, pine and cypress trees.

**Bendejun.** – Pop 396. A scattered village, most unusual in this region.

The road skirts the eastern edge of the Férion Chain until Coaraze comes into view on its hill.

*Turn right off D 15 up a steep narrow road to the village.*

**Coaraze**★. – Pop 327. *Park the car in Place Alexandre-Méni.*

Craftsmen have taken up residence in this nicely restored mediaeval village. The tourist will enjoy strolling through the terraced public garden, flanked by cypress trees, with its lovely view down into the valley and north to the Cime de Rocca Seira. The old cemetery, where cement boxes take the place of vaults because it is impossible to carve into the rock, leads to the 14C **church**. The interior is Baroque. At the far end an early painting of St Sebastian pierced by arrows.

From the top of the steps the church dominates the village square which is decorated with sundials designed by Cocteau, Goetz and Ponce de León. **Old streets**★, winding and narrow, crossed overhead by vaults and arches, cross little squares decorated with fountains and lead back to the starting point.

*To visit Our Lady-of-Mercy Chapel (Notre-Dame-de-la-Pitié) ask for the key at La Madone Hotel, near the car park. Return to D 15 going north and almost immediately turn left into a narrow road.*

**Notre-Dame-de-la-Pitié.** – The «blue chapel» was decorated in 1962 with blue monochrome scenes from the life of Christ. Behind the altar a glass panel enhances a metal structure representing a *Pietà*. From the terrace there is a **view** of the village.

*Return to D 15 continuing north.* The numerous hairpin bends look down on the Paillon de Contes and the ridge which separates it from the Pighière. 7 km – 4 1/2 miles beyond Coaraze a particularly sharp lefthand bend offers a superb **view**★ of the village surrounded by terraced olive groves opposite the eastern face of Mount Férion.

A wild and rugged landscape of arid slopes flanks the approach to St-Roch Pass.

**St-Roch Pass.** – Alt 990 m – 3 248 ft. At this point four roads meet. There is a view south east to Mount Agel (Monte-Carlo radio mast) and the Pic de Baudon further north.

*Turn right into D 2566* which winds downhill to the Paillon de l'Escarène; round a bend Lucéram *(p 91)* suddenly comes into view.

Michelin map **84** fold 17 – *Local map p 95* – Pop 5 434 – *Facilities p 28*

On the southern shore of one of the most beautiful bays of the Riviera, facing Ste-Maxime and separated on the east from the graceful Baie des Cannebiers by a promontory topped by a citadel, the little port of St-Tropez has become one of the best known resorts of Europe, a crossroads where journalists and photographers, writers, artists and celebrities all meet.

## HISTORICAL NOTES

**The Legend of St Tropez.** – Tropez, a Christian centurion beheaded in his native Pisa by order of the Emperor Nero, was placed in a boat with his head beside him and cast adrift with a cock and a dog who were meant to devour his remains but they left them intact; the boat is supposed to have come ashore where St-Tropez now stands.

**The Republic of St-Tropez (15-17C).** – In 1470 the Grand Seneschal of Provence accepted the offer of a Genoese gentleman, Raphaël de Garezzio, to install himself and sixty Genoese families at St-Tropez, which had been destroyed by the war at the end of the 14C. De Garezzio undertook to rebuild and defend the town on condition that it was freed of all taxes. The revival of the town was rapid.

St-Tropez became a sort of small republic administered by the heads of the families and, later, by two consuls and twelve councillors who were elected.

**Judge Suffren (18C).** – Pierre André de Suffren was born in 1726 in St-Tropez. He first served in the Order of Malta where he earned his title of *bailli,* judge, and then in the French Navy. Appointed in 1781 to command five ships being sent as a reinforcement to the Indies, Suffren sailed from Brest with his fellow Provençal, Count de Grasse, with whom he parted company at the Azores.

Then began an amazing campaign, which went on for two years from the Cape Verde islands to the Cape of Good Hope, from La Réunion to Ceylon, from Sumatra to Madras but the Treaty of Versailles was signed in 1783, and Suffren, now an Admiral, had to return. He died in 1788 at the age of sixty-two from an unfortunate blood-letting. A statue has been raised in his honour on the quay in St-Tropez.

**Defiance.** – Two "Acts of Defiance" *(bravades)* take place each year.

The first of these acts, a simple religious procession in honour of St-Tropez, has maintained its local importance since the end of the 15C. On 16 and 17 May the gilded wooden statue of St-Tropez is carried through the town escorted by the town captain, elected by the municipal council, and corps of *bravadeurs*. Strangers flock to see this picturesque spectacle.

The second act has a page of local history as its origin. On 15 June 1637, twenty-two Spanish galleys, attempting to take the town by surprise and to make off with four of the king's ships anchored in the port, were forced to flee, thanks to the energetic defence of the St-Tropez militia.

**Notoriety.** – At the turn of the century St-Tropez was a charming little village unknown to tourists and poorly served by a narrow-gauge branch line. In the harbour tartans laden with sand and wine were moored beside the fishing boats. It was then that Maupassant discovered it but it was above all the painters who came in Signac's train who made it more widely known *(see p 137)*. Between the wars, Colette, who used to spend the winter here, contributed to its notoriety.

From the 50s St-Tropez became the fashion with the literary set from St-Germain-des-Prés and then with the cinema people, together with their fans, and so became internationally famous.

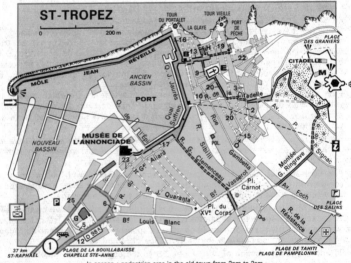

In season : pedestrian area in the old town from 2pm to 2am.

■ **SIGHTS** *time: 2 1/2 hours*

**Annonciade Museum★★.** – *Open 1 May to 30 September, 10am to noon and 3 to 7pm; otherwise, 10am to noon and 2 to 6pm; closed Tuesdays, certain holidays and in November; 8F.*

The former chapel of the Annunciation has been converted into a perfect setting for the bequest made to St-Tropez by Georges Grammont, patron of the arts. A dozen sculptures and a hundred paintings cover the years 1890 to 1940 and include among the best artists of the period those who lived or worked in St-Tropez.

When Paul Signac landed in St-Tropez in 1892, he fell in love with the place, stopped to paint and stayed permanently, attracting other painters such as Matisse, Bonnard, Marquet, Camoin, Dunoyer de Segonzac, who stayed for varying lengths of time.

**Ground Floor.** – There are six water-colours and 4 oils by Signac together with works by his disciples – H. E. Cross and T. van Rysselberghe; also a Marquet. Examples of Fauvism include Van Dongen, three fine oils by Derain and the famous *Gipsy* by Matisse. Sculptures by Maillol, Despiau and Wérick complete the distinguished collection.

**Mezzanine Floor.** – A study by Seurat, an oil by Gromaire, drawings by Dunoyer de Segonzac and a bust by Despiau are outstanding.

**First Floor.** – A splendid bronze by Maillol *(Nymph)* catches the eye at the end of the room. There are several works by Bonnard, some by Vuillard, a Braque, one by de la Fresnaye, others by Marquet, Rouault, Vlaminck... to which should be added oils by Utrillo, Matisse, Dufy, O. Friesz, Camoin and Manguin and water-colours by Dunoyer de Segonzac.

**Harbour★ (Port).** – The harbour teems with life. The fishing boats, commercial vessels and excursion craft share the mooring with a crowd of yachts – from the most humble to the most luxurious. On the waterfront and in the neighbouring streets the pink and yellow houses have been converted into cafés and pastrycooks', cabarets and restaurants, luxury boutiques, galleries and antique shops. In the season a picturesque and cosmopolitan crowd strolls beneath the bronze figure of de Suffren.

**Jean-Réveille Mole.** – The attractive **panorama★** from the top of the mole includes all of St-Tropez – Le Portalet Tower, the harbour, the town and its commanding citadel; the head of the bay and the plain at the foot of the Maures overlooked by Grimaud and its castle ruins; Beauvallon; Ste-Maxime; Cape Sardinaux; the Issambres Point; Le Dramont headland; Cap Roux summit and, in the distance, the Esterel.

**La Ponche Quarter.** – Turn right at the seaward end of Quai Jean-Jaurès into Place de l'Hôtel-de-Ville; on the left stands the massive **Suffren castle (B)**. Turn left beyond the Hôtel-de-Ville to reach La Glaye Bay; Rue de la Ponche leads through the old gateway to a beach overlooked by the Old Tower (Vieille Tour) where the fishing boats ride at anchor: two typical corners which have attracted painters.

*Retrace your steps turning left into Rue du Commandant-Guichard.*

**Church (E).** – The 19C edifice in Italian-Baroque style contains some finely carved woodwork and to the left of the high altar, a bust of St Tropez and, laid around it like a tribute of votive offerings, several old blunder-busses which exploded during a bravade. At Christmas a beautiful 19C Provençal crib with dressed figures, is brought into the church.

*On the south side of the church, turn right into Rue du Portail-Neuf and then left into Rue de la Citadelle.*

**Citadel★.** – The citadel stands on a hillock at the east end of the town. A fine hexagonal keep with three round towers was built in 16C. In 17C a fortified wall was added.

Each summer a festival of classical and modern music is held in the Citadel. From the ramparts there is a good **panorama★** of St-Tropez, the bay, Ste-Maxime and the Maures.

**Maritime Museum (M).** – *Open 15 June to 15 September, 10am to 6pm; the rest of the year 10am to 5pm; closed Thursdays, certain holidays and 15 November to 15 December; 7F.*

This museum in the citadel keep, is an annexe to the Chaillot Palace Museum in Paris. In the courtyard are two handsome 16C Spanish bronze cannons. Within the keep are displayed models of ships, engravings and seascapes illustrating the history and local activities of St-Tropez with an explanation of the 1944 Allied Landing. An amazing reconstruction of a Greek galley. Full-scale cross-section of a torpedo.

There is a magnificent **view★★** from the keep terrace of the town, St-Tropez Bay, the Maures and the Esterel; on a clear day the Alpes are visible.

## EXCURSIONS

**St-Tropez Beaches★.** – The nearest is the Bouillabaisse Beach *(1 km – 1/2 mile by D 98A, ① on the plan)*. To the east of the town is the **Graniers Beach** *(2 km – 1 1/4 miles by Rue de la Citadelle)* in the Cannebiers Bay. Further east round the headland is the **Salins Beach** *(4.5 km – 2 3/4 miles by Avenue Foch)*. Further south *(4 km – 2 1/2 miles by Route de la Belle-Isnarde)* lies the sheltered **Tahiti Beach** which extends south into the immense **Pampelonne Beach**, 5 km – 3 miles of fine sand.

**Ste-Anne Chapel.** – 4 km – 2 1/2 miles. Leave St-Tropez by ① on the plan; turn left into D 93; after 2 km – 1 1/4 miles turn left into a narrow signed road.

Standing on a volcanic rock spike in the shelter of huge trees, this attractive Provençal chapel is a place of pilgrimage for seafarers and «*bravadeurs*» (p 136) with a **view★** of the sea in all directions, particularly of St-Tropez and the Bay.

**St-Tropez Peninsula★.** – Round tour of 35 km – 22 miles – about 2 1/2 hours – Local map p 95. Leave St-Tropez by D 98A, ① on the plan, and turn left in La Foux into N 559. From La Croix-Valmer onwards the road is described on p 97.

**Circular Tour of the Maures Massif★★.** – Round tour of 103 km – 64 miles – 1/2 day – Local map and description on p 98.

### BOAT TRIPS

Motorboats run services across and also round St-Tropez Bay from Easter to 15 September. There are also daily services from St-Tropez to Port-Grimaud, Ste-Maxime and in summer to St-Raphaël and the Hyères Islands. *Apply to the Tourist Centre or to MMG Office ☎ (96.51.00).*

## STE-MAXIME ★ _____

Michelin map **84** folds 17 and 18 – *Local map p 95* – Pop 6 627 – *Facilities p 28* – *See town plan in the current Michelin Guide France*

The fashionable resort of Ste-Maxime, lies along the north shore of the Gulf of St-Tropez. It faces due south in a pretty setting protected from the mistral by wooded hills. As well as the fishing harbour there is a well-appointed marina and a beautiful beach of fine sand. In summer the town centre is a pedestrian precinct.

**Church.** – A modern ceramic tympanum decorates the doorway. Inside there is a fine 17C marble altar from La Verne Charterhouse; the choir stalls are 15C. From the terrace a view over St-Tropez Bay.

**Les Dames Tower.** – *Opposite the church on the waterfront.* Originally a defensive tower built by the Lérins monks, it later served as a law court.

**Place Victor-Hugo.** – Beneath magnificent plane trees, the square opens into tree-lined Avenue Charles-de-Gaulle which follows the shoreline westwards.

**Semaphore★.** – *1.5 km – 1 mile. Leave by the Boulevard Bellevue following the signs north.*

The road climbs steeply to the semaphore (128 m – 420 ft); there is a view★ out to sea from the Sardinaux Cape to Cape St-Pierre and inland to the Maures.

### EXCURSION

**St-Donat Park.** – *10 km – 6 1/4 miles north – about 1 hour. Leave Ste-Maxime by Boulevard G.–Clemenceau, D 25, going north.* A leisure park has been laid out in the woods between Gratteloup Pass and St-Donat's Chapel. The main attraction is the Museum of mechanical musical instruments.

**Museum of Mechanical Musical Instruments and Recording Machines.** – *Guided tours Easter holidays and 1 May to 30 September, 10am to noon and 2.30 to 6.30pm; closed Tuesdays and 1 October to 30 April; 7F.*

The huge Provençal country building houses an astonishing collection of 300 musical instruments and sound recording machines; among the rare and bizarre exhibits are a melophone (1780, forerunner of the accordeon), musical boxes from all periods, barrel organs and pianolas, phonographs from 1878 (Edison) to the present day, a 1903 dictaphone, a Pathegraphe for the study of foreign languages (first audio-visual machine) and even a talking doll (Edison, 1889).

## SANARY-SUR-MER ★ _____

Michelin map **84** fold 14 – *Local map p 139* – Pop 10 106 – *Facilities p 28* – *See town plan in the current Michelin Guide France*

The name Sanary derives from St-Nazaire who is venerated in the local church. The charming resort, all pink and white, is popular at every season and boasts a smart little harbour, bordered by palms, where fishing boats and pleasure craft put in. The bay is fairly well protected from the mistral by wooded hills dominated to the north by the Gros Cerveau and has several fine beaches.

**Notre-Dame-de-Pité.** – *Access by Bld. Courbet.* The chapel built in 1560 on a hillock, west of the town is decorated with votive offerings. From the stepped approach bordered by oratories there is an attractive view★ of Sanary Bay with the Toulon hills in the background, and the coast as far as the Embiez Archipelago behind which rise the heights of Cap Sicié.

### EXCURSIONS

**The Gros Cerveau★★.** – *13 km – 8 miles – about 1 1/4 hours – Local map p 139. Leave Sanary by Avenue de l'Europe-Unie going east, D 11.*

Flowers, vines and fruit trees are cultivated on the fertile land. At the entrance to Ollioules turn left into D 20.

At the start of the climb through terraced gardens and vineyards, the view extends both over the hillock on which the Six-Fours Fort stands and over the inner anchorage of Toulon at the foot of Mount Faron. Gradually the panorama extends south east over Toulon and the Cap Sicié peninsula from an impressive *corniche* road.

Further on the view★ is magnificent: to the right, the Grès de Ste-Anne – enormous rocks riddled with caves, the Beausset Plain, the Ste-Baume Massif, the Evenos hills and the Ollioules Gorge; on the left, a view of the coast. 8 km – 5 miles after Ollioules *(signpost)* make a U-turn to a platform for a marvellous view★★ of the coast from the Giens peninsula (SE) to Ile Verte off La Ciotat (W).

**Mount Caume★★.** – *23 km – 4 1/4 miles to north east – about 2 hours – Local map p 139. Leave Sanary by Avenue de l'Europe-Unie going east and follow D 11 to Ollioules.*

**Ollioules.** – Pop 8 810. Old arcaded houses and a Provençal Romanesque church stand at the foot of the 13C castle. A cut-flower market is held here.

*Beyond Ollioules turn left into N 8 which immediately enters the gorge.*

**Ollioules Gorge★**. – The arid and sinuous Gorge was created by the Reppe which empties into the sea in Sanary Bay. As the road emerges at the northern end there is a view on the left of the Grès de Ste-Anne, a curious mass of sandstone rocks, hollowed and pitted by erosion.

*In Ste-Anne d'Evenos, turn right into D 462. The road climbs an enclosed ravine dominated by the abrupt Barre des Aiguilles on the left. Turn right towards Evenos and park the car near a cross set in a rock.*

**Evenos★**. – *1/4 hour on foot Rtn.* Pop 700. The village is a jumble of half ruined and abandoned houses, built of basaltic stone, clinging to the steep rock slopes. The 13C church has a belltower with two bays. Over all brood the ruins of a 16C castle; the keep, also of basaltic stone, stands on the edge of a volcano from which the

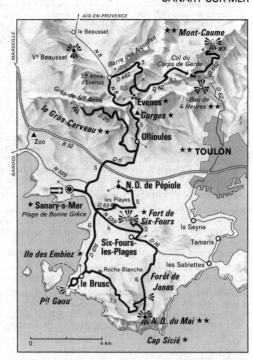

lava slag is still visible. From the platform there is a **view** of the Destel Gorge (N), the Croupatier Hill (SE), the Ollioules Gorge and the Gros Cerveau (W) in the foreground and of Cap Sicié (S) and the Ste-Baume Massif (N) on the horizon.

*Continue east along D 62 turning left at Corps de Garde Pass into D 662.*

**Mont Caume**. – Alt 801 m – 2 628 ft. The steep approach road offers fine viewpoints; from the top *(climb the mound to the right of the small fort)* there is a magnificent **panorama★★** of the coast, from Cap Bénat (E) to La Ciotat Bay (W) and inland to the Ste-Baume Massif.

## Cap Sicié Peninsula★. – *Round tour of 25 km – 15 1/2 miles – about 2 hours (excluding Les Embiez Island) – Local map above. Leave Sanary by Avenue d'Estienne d'Orves.*

The road skirts Bonnegrâce Beach and Pointe Nègre offering attractive views of Sanary Bay and Bandol.

**Le Brusc**. – Fishing village and resort; ferries to Les Embiez Island leave from the port.

**Les Embiez Island★**. – *Description p 60.*

**Petit Gaou**. – The rocky promontory, once an island, pounded by the sea, resembles a Breton seascape. There is an extensive **view** of the coast and the neighbouring islands.

*Return to Le Brusc and leave by D 16 towards Six-Fours; in Roche-Blanche bear right.*

The road follows the coast about 1 km – 1/2 mile inland but gives glimpses of La Ciotat, Bandol, Sanary. At the crossroads there is a **view★★** of Toulon Roads, Cap Céret, Giens peninsula and the Hyères Islands. *Turn right and park next to the radio station.*

**Notre-Dame-du-Mai★★** (Our Lady of the May Tree). – Walk round the radio station to the chapel *(open every day in May).* It is a place of pilgrimage, also known as Our Lady of Good Protection, and contains many votive offerings. From the top of Cap Sicié there is a dizzy drop to the sea and a splendid **panorama★★** of the coast from the Hyères Islands to the inlets *(calanques)* east of Marseilles.

Return to the crossroads continuing straight across into a narrow road which cuts through **Janas Forest**, planted with conifers, before rejoining D 16; turn left.

**Six-Fours-les-Plages**. – *Description p 142.*

*Return to Sanary by N 559.*

**N.-D.-de-Pépiole**. – *5 km – 3 miles – about 1 hour – Local map above. Leave Sanary by Avenue d'Estienne-d'Orves going east, skirting Bonnegrâce Beach, and turn left towards Toulon, D 63. After a short stretch turn left into a narrow road marked with a "Monuments Historiques" sign. Park the car on a terrace, 100 m – 110 yds from the chapel.*

The chapel *(open afternoons in principle)* of yellow, rose and grey stone, surmounted by two charming campaniles, stands in a most attractive **setting★** of pines and cypresses, olives, vines and broom, against the mountainous backdrop of Toulon.

For many years unrecognised under layers of wash, the chapel, which was built in 5C to 6C, is one of the oldest paleo-Christian buildings in France. Originally composed of three separate chapels, later linked together by huge lateral arcades of blue stone, it contains a 17C statue of Our Lady of Pépiole in the lefthand chapel.

*The maps, Red Guides and Green Guides are complementary publications. Use Them together.*

## SAORGE ★★

Michelin map **195** fold 18 – *Local map p 130* – Pop 330

In a wild **setting**★★ the stone covered houses and the proud belfries of the church and chapels grip the steep slopes of a natural amphitheatre where the Roya valley temporarily broadens out. In the Middle Ages the town was reputed to be impregnable but it yielded to the French under Masséna in 1794 and again in April 1945.

**Old town.** – *Park the car at the north entrance.* The stepped and twisting street, sometimes arched, make an interesting walk past 15C houses with decorative doorways and carved lintels. On the far side of the square, go straight, then right and right again to reach a terrace offering a beautiful **view**★ into the bottom of the Roya Gorge.

**St-Sauveur Church.** – Built in 16C and revaulted in 18C, it comprises three naves supported on columns with Corinthian capitals and is decorated with altarpieces painted red and gold. The **organ**, which was built in 1847 by the Lingiardi of Pavia, was transhipped by sea from Genoa to Nice and thence to Saorge on muleback. To the right is an 18C canvas, a fine Renaissance tabernacle, a 15C font beneath a painting by a local artist (1532); on the left, a 16C primitive over the altar of the Annunciation.

*Leave from the southern end of the village, bearing right at the road fork.*

**Madonna del Poggio★.** – *Open 3 to 4pm except Thursdays and Fridays (☎ 04.50.22).*
The early Romanesque building boasts a soaring belfry with six rows of Lombard bands and a fine chevet. The three naves are supported by columns crowned by capitals decorated with a stylised leaf design. The partially effaced frescoes in the apse are attributed to Baleison. In the chapel are several 15C altarpieces, one a fine *Pietà*.

*Return towards the village* – fine *view* of Saorge and the terraced olive groves – *bearing sharp right at the road fork towards the monastery.*

**Franciscan Convent.** – The 17C buildings, to which the monks returned in 1969 after a long absence, are prettily set among olive trees.
A small cloister *(open 10 to 11am and 3.30 to 5pm)* is decorated with crude but pious paintings. From the terrace, a **view**★ of Saorge, the Roya and the gorge.

---

## SISTERON ★★

Michelin map **81** fold 6 – Pop 7 443 – *Facilities p 30*

Sisteron stands in an impressive rift in the Durance valley – that "grandiose portal dividing Dauphiné and Provence". The town is set in tiers up the side of a steep hill crowned by a citadel proudly facing the great rock of La Baume, in which the strata run almost vertically, seeming to rise from the riverbed. In 1957 a tunnel was bored through the rock keeping the town itself free of traffic and preserving much of its original character.
It was at Sisteron in the Franciscan monastery that in the 13C Bérenger V, Count of Provence, signed the will under which he bequeathed the county of Provence to one of his daughters, Beatrix, the future wife of Charles of Anjou, brother of St. Louis *(see p 159: the Lords of Vence).* From this bequest came the rights of France over Provence.

**The setting★★.** – The town with its old houses densely crowded together, massed in tiers up the hillside below the last bare rock slope to the citadel, is seen best from the D 4.

■ **THE CITADEL★** *time: 1 hour*

*Open 8am to 7pm; closed All Saints' Day to Palm Sunday; 7F.*
Nothing remains of the 11C citadel; the oldest parts still standing – the keep and the parapet walk – date from late 12C. The massive 16C fortifications which surround the rock are chiefly the work of a precursor of Vauban, Jean Erard, Engineer to Henri IV.
The fortress was bombed on 15 August 1944 when the Allies landed in Provence *(restoration work in progress).*

### SISTERON

| Droite (R.) | |
| --- | --- |
| Provence (R. de) | 25 |
| Saunerie (R.) | |
| | |
| Arcades (R. des) | 2 |
| Arène (Av. Paul) | 3 |
| Bourg-Reynaud (Pl.) | 5 |
| Combes (R. des) | 6 |
| Cordeliers (R. des) | 8 |
| Coste (R. de la) | 9 |
| Dr-Robert (Pl. du) | 10 |
| Gaulle (Pl. Gén. de) | 13 |
| Glissoir (R. du) | 14 |
| Horloge (Pl. de l') | 15 |
| Libération (Av. de la) | 16 |
| Longue-Androne (R.) | 18 |
| Marres (Chemin des) | 19 |
| Melchior-Donnet (Cours) | 20 |
| Mercerie (R.) | 22 |
| Moulin (Av. Jean) | 23 |
| Porte-Sauve (R.) | 24 |
| République (Pl. de la) | 26 |
| Ste-Ursule (R.) | 27 |
| Tivoli (Pl. du) | 29 |
| Verdun (Allée de) | 30 |

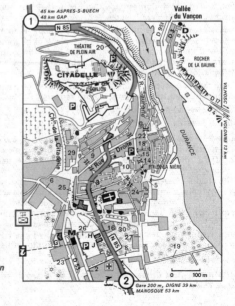

*For maximum information from town plans consult the key p 32.*

*Follow the marked path.* A series of stairways and stepped terraces, from which there are views of the town and the Durance valley, lead to the top of the wall which forms the parapet walk.

Go beneath the clock tower in which John-Casimir of Poland was imprisoned in 1639 to the terrace *(viewing table)* from which the **view★** plunges down on to the lower town and straight ahead northwards to the Laup and Aujour Mountains which enclose the Laragne basin. The old 15C citadel chapel, which was destroyed in 1944, has been rebuilt. Go next to the north side of the citadel to the "Devil's look-out" commanding the Durance rift and an impressive **view** of La Baume Rock, the petrified nightmare on the opposite bank. You can still go down the first few steps of the great underground stairway cut through the rock which formerly linked the fortress and the Dauphiné Gate which was also destroyed in 1944.

To leave, cross the open air theatre where a festival of music, dance and drama is held from mid-July to early August each year.

## ■ ADDITIONAL SIGHTS

**Notre-Dame Church★** (B). – This former cathedral is an example of the Provençal Romanesque school. The arch stones of the Lombard style doorway alternate in black and white and are prolonged on either side into a semi-circle resting on stout supports; the pediment flanked by two semi-pediments is similar; the short columns are decorated with carvings and capitals which form a frieze of fabulous beasts.

The chevet is unusual: a semi-circular apse is linked to two smaller flanking apses by strange small pendentives; it is surmounted by an octagonal lantern drum with short window piers, alongside a square tower surmounted by a pyramidal spire.

The dark interior is built to the basilica plan with broken barrel vaulting and narrow aisles, supported on square piers flanked by 2 half columns and crowned by carved capitals. The floor is paved with a lattice-work of stone bands with terracotta infill.

The painting on the high altar is by Mignard: the Holy Family listening to an angelic choir. The south chapels contain canvasses attributed to Vanloo, Parrocel and Coypel and an 18C statue of the Virgin and Child *(fourth chapel)*.

**Old Sisteron.** – *Start from the north side of the church and follow the arrows.* Between the Rue Droite and the banks of the Durance stands the old town, its narrow lanes lined with tall houses between which are steep alleys (**androns**), often covered in. Note the fine 13C Romanesque house in Rue du Glissoir (an icy slipway in winter), the 14C Niere doorway with its fountain, Rue Longue Androne and several charming little squares. On the way back in Rue Mercerie, note the façade with four pointed arches and twin bays. The Clock Tower marks the end of the tour.

**Town walls.** – The 14C walls contained five **towers** of which three are visible in Allée de Verdun, one abuts the Post Office and the last is at the foot of the Citadel.

**Museum** (M). – *Enquire at the Tourist Centre nextdoor or preferably to Maison Colomb, rue de Provence.*

The exhibits from the Gallo-Roman and mediaeval periods were found in the town: 2C tomb, stelae, inscriptions, capitals and statues.

**St-Dominique Church** (D). – The church of the former Convent of St Dominic founded by Beatrix of Savoy in 1248, still possesses an elegant Romanesque **belfry** in black and white stone. Musical and literary recitals are held in the church in summer.

## *EXCURSIONS*

**Upper Vançon Valley★.** – *92 km – 57 miles – about 2 hours. The morning light is best.* Leave Sisteron by the Durance bridge (north east on the plan), D 951 and then D 3. From the road which climbs by hairpin bends to the first pass there are good **views★** of Sisteron in its setting. The long rounded crests of the Lure Mountain stretch out to the southwest, while in the foreground lies the hollowed out basin of the Laragne where the Buech and the Durance meet.

Beyond the pass the view plunges to the Riou de Jabron river which, on emerging from the Pierre Écrite Defile, disappears downstream through a rift eventually to join the Durance below Sisteron.

**Pierre Écrite Defile.** – On the wall of this deep cleft on the left hand side of the road by a small bridge is a long Roman inscription to C. P. Dardenus, prefect of the Gauls and Christian convert, who opened this pass early in 5C. The inscription mentions a "City of God" of which traces have been found between Chardavon and St-Geniez further up the road.

Beyond St-Geniez there stands, to the right of the road, the curious humped Rocher du Dromon at the foot of which stands the 11C-12C chapel of **Our Lady of Dromon** which was visited by pilgrims until 18C.

Further on lies the wooded and deserted Vançon Upper Valley which the *corniche*-style road looks down upon from a great height. Look through a gap downstream to see, in the distance, Mount Lubéron and the Ste-Victoire. Beyond Authon, the D 3 goes through the Mélan National Forest to the Fontbelle Pass.

*D 17 passes through Le Planas and Barras to join N 85, Napoleon's Route (p 127). Turn right to return to Sisteron.*

**Vilhosc Priory.** – *10 km – 6 1/2 miles east – about 3/4 hour – Local map p 60. Leave Sisteron by D 4 (north east on the plan) going south towards Volonne. After 5 km – 3 miles turn left into D 217. 4 km – 2 1/2 miles further on, cross the Riou de Jabron and take a righthand turning and follow the sign.*

Underneath some farm buildings by the river is a curious crypt with three naves, the remains of an old priory *(the farmer acts as guide, ☏ (92) 61.26.70).* It represents some of the earliest Romanesque art in Provence.

## SIX-FOURS-LES-PLAGES

Michelin map 🔢 folds 14 and 15 – *Local map p 139* – Pop 21 525 – *Facilities p 28*

The community is scattered in 125 hamlets and residential districts; there are several beaches – the nearest and largest (2 km – 1 1/2 miles of sand) is Bonnegrâce near Sanary.

**Old Six-Fours.** – *Access by Avenue du Maréchal-Juin; turn left into a narrow road.*
The steep climb offers alternating views of Sanary Bay and Toulon Roadstead.

**Six-Fours Fort★.** – Alt 210 m – 689 ft. From the platform at the fort entrance a **panorama★** extends from east to west over Toulon Roadstead, St-Mandrier peninsula, Cap Sicié, Sanary Bay, Le Brusc and Les Embiez Island.

**St-Pierre Collegiate Church.** – *Open Wednesdays, Thursdays, Saturdays and Sundays, 2.30 to 6.30pm.*
At the foot of the fortress stands the church of the now abandoned village of Old Six-Fours. It has two naves at right angles; in 17C a Gothic style nave was built by the Marseilles architect Guillaume Borelli. The Romanesque nave which is well preserved contains a polyptych by Louis Bréa. In the Gothic chapels are a late 16C Flemish Descent from the Cross and a Virgin attributed to Pierre Puget.

## SOSPEL ★

Michelin map 🔢 fold 18 – Pop 1 931 – *Facilities p 30*

Sospel, a cool mountain resort, picturesquely extends its old houses along both banks of the Bévera. It lies in a cultivated basin (olive groves) surrounded by high mountains and is a good excursion centre owing to its position at the confluence of the Merlanson and the Bévera, where the road from Menton to the upper Vésubie meets the road from Nice to Turin via Tende Pass.

■ **SIGHTS** *time: 3/4 hour*

**Right bank.** – The church and arcaded houses in Cathedral square make a charming sight. The oldest house (palais Ricci) to the right of the church bears a plaque recording Pope Pius VII 's stay in 1809 when Napoleon had him brought to France away from the Papal States.

**St-Michel Church.** – At the time of the Great Schism it was the cathedral. The Romanesque bell-tower with Lombard bands flanks a Baroque façade. The interior decor is pure Baroque: altar with baldaquin, huge altarpieces, *trompe–l'oeil* frescoes, gilding; a denticulated cornice runs the length of the nave walls.

In the lefthand apse the Virgin of Mercy does not seem to belong to the Nice school but the **Immaculate Virgin★** is one of François Bréa's best works.

Sospel – The bridge

**Old bridge.** – The toll tower on the 11C bridge was destroyed during the 1939-45 war and rebuilt.

**Left bank.** – Cross the bridge to see the houses and paving in St-Nicolas Square and a 15C fountain beneath the arches of the old community centre.

## TANNERON Massif ★

Michelin map 🔢 folds 33 and 34

The Tanneron Massif is a northern extension of the Esterel from which it is separated by a shallow depression used by N 7 and the Provençal Motorway; however from its solid round contours and the nature of its rocks (gneiss) it is more closely related to the Maures.

**A bouquet of mimosa.** – The Tanneron is well known for its winter dress of brilliant yellow mimosa contrasting with the clear winter sky. Once the massif was covered with sea pines and chestnut trees but the forest has been much reduced under the triple assault of man (cultivation rights have existed since the Middle Ages), the cochineal (a parasitic insect which kills the pine trees) and fire. Mimosa was imported into the Mediterranean from Australia in 1839 and is first mentioned near Cannes in 1864. Since then it has invaded the bare slopes of the Tanneron and early this century brought financial success to the region.

Mimosa belongs to the acacia family of plants. There are many different types – some taking the form of shrubs and others growing into trees up to 12 m – 40 ft high – which flower at different times between November and March, although it can flower throughout the year. The commonest mimosa grows wild in huge swathes but the flowering can be brought forward or improved by forcing. Fronds are cut prematurely and shut up in a dark room 2 or 3 days at a temperature of 22-25 °C with very high humidity.

Mimosa can also be cut when the flowers are still in bud; a special powder mixed with hot water will cause the flowers to open. Tonnes of cut flowers from the Tanneron are sold in France and abroad each year.

## Round tour starting from Cannes – *56 km – 35 miles – about 1 1/2 hours*

*Leave Cannes (p 47) by N 7, ③ on the plan. As far as the Logis-de-Paris crossroads the route is described on p 65.* Then turn right into D 237 which offers glimpses of La Napoule Bay and Mount Vinaigre. Beyond les Adrets de l'Esterel the view extends to the Pre-Alps of Grasse. The road crosses over the Provençal Motorway on the edge of Montauroux woods before skirting St-Cassien Lake.

**St-Cassien Lake.** – *Description p 67.*

*Before the Pré-Claou bridge turn right into D 38.* The road rises through a pine wood with pleasant **glimpses** of the lake, the dam and the mountain peaks on the horizon.
Near Les Marjoris hamlet the road winds over mimosa-clad slopes down to the river Verrerie.

*Before reaching Tanneron village, turn right into a steep narrow road.*

**Notre-Dame de Peygros★.** – Alt 412 m – 1 352 ft. From the terrace of the Romanesque chapel, there is a fine **panorama★** of St-Cassien Lake, the Siagne valley and Grasse; Mount Agel on the coast and the Alps on the border with Italy stand out to the east; the Esterel and the Maures Massifs dominate the southern horizon.

*Pass through Tanneron to the Val-Cros crossroads;* each turn in the descent reveals fine **views** of Auribeau and its locality, of Grasse and the broad Siagne valley.

**Auribeau-sur-Siagne.** – *7 km – 4 1/4 miles – from Val-Cros.* Pop 950. A narrow twisting road sunk between banks of mimosa leads up to the charming village on a hill beside the Siagne. It was founded in 1490 by colonists from Genoa. Its stepped streets hide many surprises; the old houses now restored are grouped round the church which contains a 15C gilt-enamelled reliquary and a 16C chalice. From the church square there is a **view** of the wooded slopes of the Siagne valley and of Grasse in its ring of mountains.

*Return to the Val-Cros crossroads and go straight across towards Mandelieu, D 92.*

**Mandelieu Road★★.** – The slopes of the massif are covered by scrub. The rapid drive downhill to Mandelieu through the mimosa is marvellous with many **views★★** of the Esterel, Mandelieu with its airport, La Napoule Bay, Cannes and the Lérins Islands, the Siagne valley, Grasse and the Pre-Alps; on the horizon are the Alps (NE).

**Mandelieu.** – Pop 10 277 together with Napoule-Plage. – *Facilities p 28.* Chief town of the mimosa country beside the Siagne.

*Return to Cannes by D 92 and N 98 along the sea front.*

## TENDE

Michelin map 📕📗📘 fold 8 – *Local map p 130* – Pop 2 056 – *Facilities p 30*

The **site** of Tende in an alpine landscape on the banks of the Roya beneath the steep face of the Ripe de Bernou is unusual. The tall gaunt houses beneath their shingled roofs seem to be stacked one upon another. A jagged tooth of wall sticking 20 m – 65 ft into the air is all that is left of the Lascaris' castle which was pulled down in 1692. A curious terraced cemetery near the walls adds a bizarre touch.

Together with St-Dalmas, Tende is the starting point for organised excursions to Les Merveilles valley *(p 130).*

**Old town.** – Most of the houses, some date from 15C, are built of the local stone, green and purple schist. The maze of narrow streets boasts several carved lintels bearing escutcheons, huge overhanging eaves and balconies on all floors. Note the Renaissance bell-towers on the chapels of the Black and White Penitents.

**N.-D. de l'Assomption Church.** – Built of green schist the Church was constructed early in 16C except for the Lombard tower with its cupola. The Renaissance **doorway** comprises two Doric columns resting on two lions; the entablature is decorated with statuettes of Christ and his Apostles; a low-relief of the Assumption fills the semi-circular tympanum.

The use of green schist for the columns and paving of the interior gives a fine effect. The huge high nave is richly decorated. In the chapel on the right of the choir an 18C *Pietà* in olive wood; next, attractive predella (Christ and his Apostles) below the altarpiece. In the gallery the organ loft is dated 1673 but the mechanism is from Bergamo (1805).

## THORONET Abbey ★

Michelin map 📖📗 fold 6 – 9 km – 6 miles – southwest of Lorgues

Thoronet Abbey is hidden away in an isolated spot surrounded by wooded hills, in a setting well in keeping with the rigid rule of the Cistercian Order.

The church, the cloister and the conventual buildings all erected in the 12C form a remarkable group, comparable with Sénanque and Silvacane *(see Green Guide Provence).*

*Open 2 May to 30 September 10am to noon and 2 to 6pm, 5pm (March, April and October), 4pm (2 November to 28 February); closed 1 January, 1 May, 1 and 11 November and 25 December; 8F. Time: 1/2 hour.*

**Church★.** – The church belongs in style to the Provençal Romanesque school. The façade has no central doorway, the monks entering by a side door from the cloisters. Another door, in the south wall, led to the cemetery. Outside, on the side away from the cloisters, in a round arched niche is one of the few exterior funerary repositories of Provence.

The nave with broken cradle vaulting is flanked by half vaulted aisles and prolonged by a chancel and four apsidal chapels. These are rounded inside, but outside are incorporated in a massive square block of masonry which forms a straight wall as in most Cistercian churches.

The absence of any decoration – little remains of the 18C additions – is as the architect intended, allowing the majesty and purity of the church's lines to stand out.

**Cloisters★**. – The cloisters which open off the north side of the church are extremely austere. The massive arches, each divided into two with a central supporting column uphold, on three sides, an upper wooden gallery in the form of a trapezoid. At the centre was a garden.

The slope of the ground was compensated by seven steps between the gallery lining the church wall and the remaining galleries.

A small hexagonal building jutting out into the close served as the monks' lavabo; the tank above the basin was hollowed out into sixteen lobes, each pierced with a hole through which water flowed to sixteen taps.

**Chapterhouse★**. – The chapterhouse is early Gothic: its pointed arches with fan-vaulting are supported by two columns with crudely hewn capitals adorned with motifs inspired by the local flora. These are the abbey's only sculptures.

Thoronet Abbey – The Cloisters

**Annexes.** – After descending the steps from the south to the east gallery you will see an opening surmounted by a triangular lintel supported at its centre by a column – this is the library entrance. Beyond and abutting on the chapterhouse, is the parlour which forms a passage between the cloisters and the garden outside.

A covered staircase leads to the **dormitory** above the chapterhouse. The twenty windows have been glazed.

The doors which used to open off the north gallery gave on to the monks' common room, the boiler room, the refectory and the kitchen, all of which have now disappeared.

Millstones and a mortar can be seen in the tythe barn, later converted into an olive oil press, which stands to the south of the church.

## TINÉE Valley ★★

Michelin map **195** folds 4, 5, 15 and 16

The Tinée, which rises at La Bonette Pass, is a tributary of the Var which rises further west. The two rivers flow parallel southwards before the Var swings east to be joined by the Tinée at the northern end of the Chaudan Defile.

The Tinée valley now narrowing into gorges, now widening into basins, is covered with chestnut and pine woods.

### La Mescla Bridge to Auron – *87 km – 54 miles – 1/2 day*

*At Pont de la Mescla bear right into D 2205*

**La Mescla Gorge★**. – The road glides along the bottom of the gorge beneath overhanging rocks of grey limestone. La Mescla means the meeting of the waters.

On each side of the valley numerous villages cling to the slopes. In Pont de la Lune turn right into D 232 which makes a series of picturesque loops up above the Tinée.

**La Tour.** – Pop 176. This isolated village has a charming square bordered by arcades and served by a shady fountain.

The church with its Lombard bell-tower is Romanesque-Gothic in the interior; it has three fine altarpieces, Renaissance style, in the apse and apsidal chapels and two 15C stoups near the door.

At the northeast extremity of the village, beside the D 232, is the **White Penitents' Chapel** *(key available from M. Andisio; telephone in advance: 02.91.32 or 02.91.57)*. The side walls are decorated with frescoes, dated 1491 and signed by Bresevi and Nadale, depicting 20 scenes from the Passion as well as the Virtues and Vices. At the far end are some earlier unsigned frescoes with interesting scenes of the Last Judgement. In the chapel processional crosses and lanterns are displayed.

*Return to D 2205. Just beyond Pont-de-Clans turn right into D 55.*

**Clans.** – Pop 404. From 641 m – 2 100 ft the pleasant village looks down on the confluence of the Tinée and the Clans, surrounded by a fine forest of larch, spruce and pine. The place retains a mediaeval air with its fountains and richly decorated churches *(keys available from Marinette, the grocer's, near the church)*.

The former Romanesque collegiate **church**, now decorated in the Baroque style with a handsome carved doorway (1702), presents a **diptych** of the Nice school *(chancel)*, a Baroque altarpiece depicting the Mysteries of the Rosary in 17 sections *(side chapel)*, 11C hunting frescoes, the oldest in the County of Nice *(behind the high altar)*.

**St-Michel Chapel** *(at the end of the metalled road above the village)* has a square chevet decorated with 16C frescoes. From the terrace there is a **view** of Clans and of Bairols and the Pointe des Quatre Cantons across the valley.

**St-Antoine Chapel** *(500 m – 550 yds below the village on the left)* is decorated with realistic frescoes illustrating the life of St Antony, the Virtues *(partly obscured)* and Vices, with commentary in local dialect.

On either side of the valley deep gorges run back into the mountains through fine chestnut woods. On the right the Valdeblore Road *(p 156)* links the Tinée and Vésubie valleys. The limestone gives way to red schist.

**St-Sauveur-sur-Tinée.** – Pop 516. The village is tucked into a bend in the river opposite the Vionène tributary.

The mediaeval church is flanked by a Romanesque bell-tower with gargoyles, at the base of which stands a marble statue of St Peter (14C); inside note the altarpiece of Our Lady (1483) by Guillaume Planeta (choir), an anonymous painting (1648) of the mystic marriage of Ste-Catherine showing an early view of St-Sauveur (St Joseph's chapel), an unusual modern **mobile** (1977) which, when lit, casts moving silhouettes of Christ and the Virgin on the wall *(left of choir)*.

One of the typical old houses in the village near the church bears a carving of the hairdresser's sign – comb and scissors.

Beyond St-Sauveur the Vionène Road *(p 168)* branches off left linking the Tinée and Cians valleys by La Couillole Pass.

The road enters the **Valabres Gorge★**, a sombre ravine between bare rock walls at the foot of the Cime des Lauses and Mount St-Sauveur (E) and Mount Gravières (W).

**Isola.** – Pop 389. To the right of the approach to the village stands a fine Romanesque **tower** from an old church.

Bear left past the foot of the beautiful **Louch waterfall★** which drops from a hung valley 100 m – 330 ft above the Tinée.

**Chastillon Valley★.** – *17 km – 10 1/2 miles from Isola by D 97.* After a steep climb up the Guerche and then the Chastillon valley the road reaches a landscape of innumerable mountain streams tumbling over rocky falls among the larch woods and alpine pastures surrounding **Isola 2000★** *(Facilities p 30)*, a winter sports resort at the foot of an Alpine mountain circus on the Italian border.

North west of Isola D 2205 closely follows the border. The river is fed by frequent mountain streams rushing down from the snow-capped peaks to the north and from the slopes of Mount Mounier (S). The valley opens out as it approaches St-Étienne-de-Tinée.

**St-Étienne-de-Tinée.** – *Description p 131.*

Leave St-Étienne-de-Tinée by D 39, a **corniche road★** which climbs southwards to Auron *(p 36)* on the right bank of the Tinée facing the high peaks on the Italian border.

*The road from St-Étienne-de-Tinée to the Cime de la Bonette is described in the Michelin Green Guide Alpes (French text only).*

## TOULON ★★

Michelin map ▓▓ fold 15 – *Local map p 149* – Pop 185 050 – *For additional plan of Toulon see the current Michelin Guide France*

France's second naval port lies behind its **anchorage★★**, one of the safest and most beautiful harbours of the Mediterranean, surrounded as it is by tall hills crowned by forts. The suburbs lie along the shore and form terraces on the sunny slopes of the surrounding hills.

## HISTORICAL NOTES

**Toulon Purple.** – In Roman times Toulon was celebrated for the manufacture of the imperial purple. The dye was obtained by steeping in salt and boiling for ten days in leaden vats the colour glands of the pointed conches which abound along the coast. The purple obtained was used to dye silk and woollen materials.

This sumptuous colour was at first reserved for the emperors but later its use spread, though the imperial treasury maintained a monopoly over its manufacture. The foundations of the old Toulon dye-works were uncovered during reconstruction work in the arsenal.

**In the time of the Galleys (17 and 18C).** – One of the attractions for travellers of the 17 and 18C was to visit the galleys moored in the Old Port – Vieille Darse.

Each ship had only one bank of oars – twenty-five or twenty-six oars per side, each about fifty feet long and manned by four men. The sails were triangular; artillery had begun to be used. Thousands of galley slaves were needed. Criminals and poachers not being numerous enough, political and religious prisoners were added; Turks were bought and there were even some volunteers! All these men were bare-footed, wore a red cloak and a red or green bonnet; faces and heads were clean shaven but the Turks were allowed to retain a tuft of hair and the volunteers their moustaches. On board, the slaves rowed with one foot bound to the deck and one wrist chained to the oar, eating and sleeping without leaving their places. The slave-master stimulated their efforts with cuts from a rawhide whip.

The slaves were allowed to go ashore but were chained together in pairs. Players of musical instruments were much in demand at weddings when they played for dancing.

In 1748 the galleys were abolished and replaced by naval prisons. In 1854 these disappeared in their turn and the system of transportation overseas followed.

**Bonaparte's first feat of arms.** – On 27 April 1793, Toulon was handed over by the Royalists to an Anglo-Spanish fleet. A Republican army was sent to Toulon; the artillery was under the command of an obscure junior captain called Bonaparte. Between la Seyne and Tamaris where the Fort Carré or Fort Napoléon stands today the British had built a fortification so strong that it was called "little Gibraltar".

A battery was installed facing the British fort, which was subjected to a terrible fire and the gunners faltered. The young Corsican then wrote out a notice calling for volunteers to man a "battery of fearless men". He soon had enough volunteers. Bonaparte set the example; he laid the guns and manned the sponge-rod. It was in this engagement that Sergeant Junot distinguished himself. As he was writing down an order being dictated by Bonaparte, a shell burst nearby covering them both with flying earth: "Good!" said Junot, brushing himself down, "now I shall not need any sand to dry the ink".

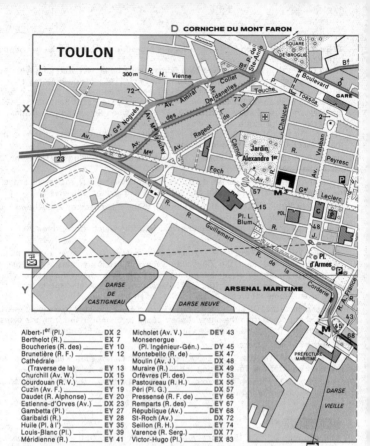

D **CORNICHE DU MONT FARON**

**TOULON**

| | | | |
|---|---|---|---|
| Albert-1er (Pl.) | DX 2 | Micholet (Av. V.) | DEY 43 |
| Berthelot (R.) | EX 7 | Monsenergue | |
| Boucheries (R. des) | EY 10 | (Pl. Ingénieur-Gén.) | DY 45 |
| Brunetière (R. F.) | EY 12 | Montebello (R. de) | EX 47 |
| Cathédrale | | Moulin (Av. J.) | DX 48 |
| (Traverse de la) | EY 13 | Muraire (R.) | EX 49 |
| Churchill (Av. W.) | DX 15 | Orfèvres (Pl. des) | EY 53 |
| Courdouan (R. V.) | EY 17 | Pastoureau (R. H.) | EX 55 |
| Cuzin (Av. F.) | EY 19 | Péri (Pl. G.) | DX 57 |
| Daudet (R. Alphonse) | EY 20 | Pressensé (R. F. de) | EY 67 |
| Estienne-d'Orves (Av.) | DX 23 | Remparts (R. des) | EY 67 |
| Gambetta (Pl.) | EY 27 | République (Av.) | DEY 68 |
| Garibaldi (R.) | EY 28 | St-Roch (Av.) | DX 72 |
| Huile (R. à l') | EY 35 | Seillon (R. H.) | EY 74 |
| Louis-Blanc (Pl.) | EY 39 | Varence (R. Serg.) | DX 77 |
| Méridienne (R.) | EY 41 | Victor-Hugo (Pl.) | EX 83 |

"Little Gibraltar" fell on 19 December. The foreign fleet withdrew after burning the French ships, the arsenal, and the provision depots as well as taking part of the population with them. While Napoleon was being made a brigadier-general, Toulon came near to being destroyed: 12 000 workers were requisitioned to raze "the infamous city", but at the last moment the Convention cancelled the order.

**1939-45 War.** – In November 1942, in answer to the allied landings in North Africa, Hitler decided to invade the French free zone. Owing to the element of surprise the French fleet was unable to get under way and, being unwilling to fall into the hands of the Germans, decided to scuttle its ships; on 27 November 60 ships went down in the Roads – only a few submarines escaped.

On 19 August 1944, four days after the Allied Landing on the beaches of the Maures, French troops attacked the Toulon defences, a plan of which had been smuggled out in 1942 by sailors in the Resistance. The city was liberated on 26 August. On 13 September the French fleet, which had taken part in the liberation, sailed into the anchorage, where the scuttled ships still lay on the bottom.

**Post-War.** – Up to 1939 Toulon had been too dependent on the naval dockyard and very isolated by its geographic position. After the war an effort was made to diversify: the Arsenal broadened the scope of its production, commercial trade in the port was developed and new industries were set up, the construction of holiday homes in the region sustained the building trade in the period after the post war reconstruction boom. Improvements in the road network made the town more easily accessible. Tourism, the creation of a university and of the Chateauvallon Cultural Centre point to a hopeful future.

■ **MOUNT FARON CORNICHE ROAD**★★ *time: 1/2 hour by car – For additional plan of Toulon see the current Michelin Guide France – Local map p 149*

For a first impression of Toulon drive up the Mount Faron *corniche* road, preferably late in the afternoon for the best light.

*Leave the town centre by Ste-Anne Bridge (DX), bear half right into Boulevard de la Victoire and left into Boulevard Ste-Anne.*

The drive along Boulevard Marius-Escartefigue, a magnificent *corniche* road over the slopes of Mount Faron, affords good views of Toulon and its outskirts. The old town is clearly visible huddled down by the harbour while the residential suburbs extend into the encircling hills.

The **view**★ of the anchorage is beautiful: the Inner Roadstead backed by Le Mourillon and La Seyne with the cliffs of Cap Sicié rising behind; the Outer Roadstead with to the south the St-Mandrier peninsula at the end of its low and narrow isthmus and to the east Cap de Carqueiranne; further east lies the Giens peninsula beyond Giens Bay.

*Before reaching La Valette turn sharp right into D 246 (Avenue Anatole–France) and take N 97 back into town (Avenue Colonel-Picot, Boulevard Maréchal-JOFFRE, Avenue F.-Cuzin).*

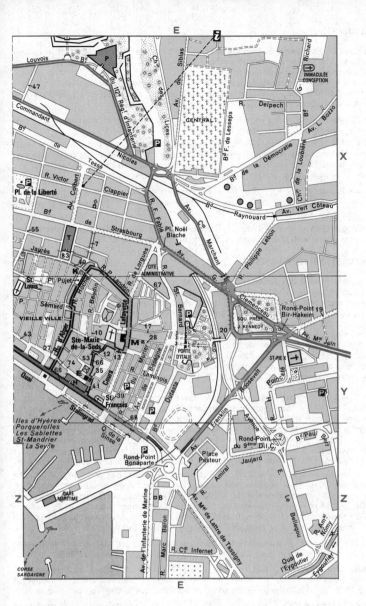

■ **THE OLD TOWN**★ *time: 1 3/4 hours*

*Start from Place Ingénieur-Général-Monsenergue and follow the route marked on the plan.*

**Naval Museum**★ (EY M). – *Open 10am to noon and 1.30 to 6pm; closed Tuesdays and holidays except Easter and Whitsun.*

At the entrance the visitor has the illusion of stepping on to the Quai de l'Artillerie of the old arsenal which is reproduced in gold leaf from a painting by Joseph Vernet.

On the ground floor there are many large scale models of a frigate and of an 18C vessel. The room is decorated with statues of great 17C admirals carved in wood by Puget's pupils and an impressive figurehead of Neptune. Fine paintings by Vernet's pupils, drawings and other exhibits recall Toulon's seafaring history and its prison.

Note in the stairwell another figurehead, Bellona in gilded and painted wood (1807). On the first floor, interesting collection of model ships and submarines from 19C to the present day.

**Quai Stalingrad** (EY). – Attracted by the shops and cafés an animated crowd throngs the waterfront. The tall modern buildings with their many coloured windows form a screen between the Old Port (Vieille Darse) and the Old Town. The only reminders of former times are the famous **atlantes**★ by Pierre Puget, which supported the main balcony of the old town hall.

**St-François Church** (EY). – A small building (1744) in the Nice Baroque style; it has three naves separated by coupled columns and railed galleries; the choir opens into a dome. In the righthand aisle a statue of Our Lady of Peace carved in wood by one of Puget's pupils.

*Go west along Avenue de la République, then right into Rue Méridienne.* Note the 18C **"House with carved heads"** in Place à l'Huile.

**Fish Market** (EY E). – The fish market is a Provençal style covered market bustling and picturesque in the morning when full of fishermen and fishwives.

**Cathedral of Ste-Marie-de-la-Seds** (EY). – The cathedral was constructed in the IIC, restored in the 12C and enlarged in the 17C. The belfry and façade are 18C and the great dark nave Transitional Gothic.

There are several interesting works of art: in the left aisle, an Annunciation by Pierre Puget; in the right aisle, two canvasses by J.-B. Vanloo and Puget and a Baroque altar in marble and plasterwork designed by a nephew of Puget.

**Cours Lafayette** (EY). – The vegetable and flower market held every morning in the Cours is a noisy, bustling, highly coloured occasion.

**Museum of Old Toulon** (EY M²). – *Closed for alteration.* Souvenirs of Bonaparte and de Lattre de Tassigny who liberated Toulon. Small sculptures by Pierre Puget. Pictures and drawings by local artists on subjects of local historical interest and religious works. Prints and drawings. Old weapons. Library on local and naval history.

**Dolphin Fountain** (EX K). – The three dolphins on the fountain in Place Puget were sculpted in 1782. The fountain is now so thickly encrusted with lime deposits that plants are growing on it forming a sort of rockery.

**Rue d'Alger** (EY). – The Rue d'Alger *(pedestrians only)* is the main commercial street and a favourite place with the Toulonnais for an evening stroll (5 to 7pm).

# ■ ADDITIONAL SIGHTS

**The Harbour★ and the Arsenal** (DY). – Construction of the Old Port (Vieille Darse or Darse Henri-IV) began in 1589 on the orders of the Duke of Épernon, Governor of Provence. Expenses were borne by the town of Toulon which imposed a 25 % tax on olive oil. The two breakwaters closing the harbour on the south side except for a 30 m – 100 ft wide passage across which a chain was slung, were completed in 1610.

The king, at that time possessed no royal fleet: when he required ships he leased them from lords and captains who had them built, armed and equipped. Richelieu changed all this by creating a military arsenal to build and repair warships. The port ceased to be big enough under Louis XIV, and Vauban had the New Port (Darse Neuve) dug out, further west, between 1680 and 1700. This became the naval port, the Old Port going over entirely to merchant shipping.

In the 19C the navy needed yet more space and in 1836 an annexe was built at Mourillon. In 1852 Prince Louis-Napoléon established the harbour at Castigneau but ten years later the port was again too small and Napoleon III created the Missiessy Harbour.

While retaining its position as a naval port, Toulon is increasing its commercial role. Merchant shipping is directed to the new facilities in Brégaillon Bay on the west side of the Inner Roads, while the east side is used by the passenger ferries plying to the Hyères Islands, Corsica and Sardinia and by pleasure boats and cruise liners throughout the year.

**Naval Arsenal** (Arsenal maritime) (DY). – *15 June to 15 September, a warship is on view to the public Saturdays, Sundays and holidays, 2 to 5pm; apply to the port authorities.*

The arsenal which covers some 1 500 ha – 3 707 acres overall and employs over 10 000 civilians, does repair work for both naval and merchant shipping. The wall of the old prison can be seen as well as the berths and dry docks (some date from 17C) where ships have put in or are being repaired: frigates, destroyers, oil tankers.

**Place d'Armes** (DX). – Alongside the Naval Arsenal the vast square with its elegant frontages and gardens in the middle was commissioned by Colbert in 1683.

**St-Louis Church** (EY). – A fine example of neo-Classical architecture, built in late 18C in the form of a Greek temple. It comprises three naves separated by architraves supported on a double Doric colonnade. Ten Corinthian columns in the choir support a cupola.

**Place de la Liberté** (EX). – The centre of the modern town is on the main axis – Boulevard de Strasbourg and Avenue du Général-Leclerc – where the cafés, shops and theatre are to be found.

**Museums** (DX M³). – A Renaissance style building houses two municipal museums.

**Natural History Museum.** – *Open 9.30 to 11.45am and 2 to 5.15pm; closed holidays.*

Two rooms on the ground floor are devoted to natural history: interesting collections of geology, zoology and botany.

**Museum of Art and Archaeology.** – *Open 10am to noon and 2 to 6pm; closed holidays.*

The archaeological gallery is devoted to Egyptian, Greek and Roman antiquities and local archaeological specimens from the prehistoric, Ligurian and Gallo-Roman periods.

A new Oriental gallery has several sections on the Near and Middle East, Central Asia (Gandharan art) and the Far East.

Old and modern paintings dating from the 13C to the 20C are displayed including works by the Byzantine and Italian schools in particular Vanloo, Fragonard, Joseph Vernet, David and Gustave Doré. Modern painting is represented by Vuillard, Maurice Denis, Vlaminck, Othon, Friesz and others. One room is devoted to photography.

**Alexandre Iᵉʳ Garden** (DX). – Attractive trees in the garden include magnolias, palms and cedars. There are a bust of Puget by Injalbert and a 1914-1918 War Memorial.

## MOTORBOAT TRIPS

All along the Stalingrad Quay are boats which go round the Inner Roads (Petite Rade. Fix the price with the boatman).

There are motorboat services leaving the Stalingrad Quay for:

**The Hyères Islands★★★.** – *Services July and August. Description pp 84–87.*

**Les Sablettes.** – *Services from May to October. 1/2 hour's crossing. Description p 150.*

**St-Mandrier-sur-Mer.** – *Services all the year round. 1/2 hour's crossing. Description p 150.*

## CAR TRIPS

The roads used in these excursions, although serving military installations, are classified as part of the civilian network. Traffic is permitted up to the entrance of these installations without formality. However, the military authorities categorically forbid anyone to enter certain places indicated by notices and signposts, particularly at the immediate approaches to the Forts of Croix-Faron, and Lieutenant-Girardon. It is also pointed out that the military authorities categorically forbid the taking of any photographs within a 10 km – 6 mile zone of military or naval posts.

**1 Mount Faron★★★** – *Round tour of 18 km – 11 miles – about 1 1/2 hours – Local map above*

*Leave Toulon by Avenue St–Roch (**DX 72**), Rue Dr–Fontan, Avenue Général-Gouraud and Avenue des Moulins and then turn right into the road to Fort Rouge.*

Mount Faron (alt 542 m – 1 778 ft) is the small limestone massif, bordered by deep valleys, which immediately overlooks Toulon. The drive, over pine-clad slopes, affords good **views★** of Toulon, the Inner and Outer Roadsteads, the St-Mandrier and Cap Sicié Peninsulas and Bandol.

**National Memorial to the Provençal Landing★**. – *Open 9 to 11.30am and 2.15 to 6.45pm (4 to 5.30pm out of season); 8F.*
Installed in the Beaumont tower, left of the road, is the memorial to commemorate the liberation of the southeast of France by the Allies in August 1944. One section is devoted to the memory of the English, American, Canadian, French and Resistants who helped make the Liberation possible. In the second part there is a diorama which presents the liberation of Toulon and Marseilles, and a movie theatre where films taken during the landing are shown.
From the terrace there is a magnificent **circular view★★★** *(three viewing tables)* of Toulon, the roadstead, the Mediterranean, and the islands and mountains all around Toulon.

**Zoo.** – *Open in season, 10am to noon and 2 to 7pm; the rest of the year, 2 to 5pm; closed Thursdays in winter; 16F, children 7F.*
There is a wide variety of wild animals – lions, tigers, jaguars – especially monkeys. It is also a breeding centre.

The road now running over the wooded plateau, ends abruptly in the north with a steep slope up to the Croix-Faron Fort from where there is a beautiful **view★** of the coast from the Giens Peninsula to Bandol. Walk 100 m – 110 yards north of the fort to enjoy a view of the Provence Alps.

*Return to Toulon on the Faron road turning right into Boulevard Faron.*

**2 Bau de 4 heures**★★ – *11 km – 6 3/4 miles – about 1 hour – Local map p 149*

*Leave Toulon by Avenue St-Roch (DX 72), Rue Dr-Fontan, Avenue Général–Gouraud and then turn left into Avenue des Routes and Place Macé, turning right into D 62 (Avenue Clovis).*

*After 4 km – 2 1/2 miles turn left into D 262. 3 km – 2 miles further on is a platform from which there is a magnificent view*★★ *of Toulon, the Roads and the coast.*

*The narrow road to the top (4 km – 2 1/2 miles) crosses a firing range (open to the traffic). At the top there is a fine panorama*★★ *of the coast from Cap Bénat to La Ciotat and inland from Ste-Baume to the Maures.*

**3 Tour of the Roadstead**★★ – *17 km – 10 1/2 miles – about 1 1/2 hours – Local map p 149*

*Leave Toulon by N 559, ③ on the plan.*

The road skirts the Brégaillon merchant shipping port. *Turn left towards La Seyne.*

**La Seyne.** – Pop 51 669. La Seyne, built beside the bay which bears its name, looks eastwards towards the Inner Roads. It has a harbour for fishing boats and pleasure craft but is basically an industrial town dependent for its livelihood upon the naval shipyards which were constructed in 1856 to build both naval and merchant ships and now are also employed in allied industries such as the construction of incinerators, condensers, turbines, etc.

The road skirts the small bay between the Eguillette and Balaguier forts, which were built in 17C opposite the Royal Tower *(below)* to seal off the harbour entrance. Close inshore are mussel beds and some old ships at anchor.

**Balaguier Naval Museum.** – *Open 15 June to 15 September, 10am to noon and 3 to 7pm, (2 to 6pm the rest of the year); closed Mondays and Tuesdays and certain holidays; 5F.* The fort was recaptured from the English in 1793 by the young Napoleon. In its round rooms with 4 m – 13 ft thick walls the museum displays two floors of model ships and other items made by the Toulon convicts; Napoleonic souvenirs.
From the terrace above a charming garden magnificent view★ of the coast from Toulon to Le Levant Island.

**Tamaris.** – In the shady resort on the hillside, George Sand wrote several of her novels. Fine view of St-Mandrier peninsula.

All along Le Lazaret Bay are small cabins perched on stilts above the mussel beds.

**Les Sablettes.** – *Facilities p 28.* Long wide beach of fine sand open to the sea. The houses were rebuilt after the last war in the neo-Provençal style, designed by F. Pouillon.

Take the road along the narrow sandy isthmus which links the peninsula to the land mass. Fine view of Toulon surrounded by mountains.

**St-Mandrier Peninsula★.** – The road offers a view★ of the whole anchorage and of Toulon and its setting before skirting St-Georges creek which harbours an aeronaval base as well as the fishing and leisure port of St-Mandrier-sur-Mer (Pop 6 767). A righthand turning at the entrance to the town climbs steeply to a small cemetery with a panoramic view★★ of Toulon, Cap Sicié and the Hyères Islands.

**4 Le Coudon★** – *Round tour of 38 km – 24 miles – about 1 1/2 hours – Local map p 149*

*Leave Toulon by Avenue F.-Cuzin (EY 19) followed by Boulevard Maréchal-Joffre and Avenue Colonel-Picot; bear left at the fork, cross Avenue Anatole-France and follow a narrow road north to D 46; turn left.*

*1 200 m – 1 312 yds further on turn right into Route du Coudon, D 446, a steep narrow road.*

**Le Coudon★.** – Alt 702 m – 2 303 ft. At the start of the climb you can see Mount Coudon entirely and also La Crau and the surrounding plain. The road, which narrows after going through pinewoods and then olive groves, finally comes out on to a wasteland scattered with evergreen oaks; the view★ widens continuously until at the entrance to the Lieutenant-Girardon Fort you can see the entire coast from the Giens Peninsula to the former Gaou Island near Le Brusc.

*Return to D 46 turning right and after 2.5 km – 2 miles – bear right again into D 846 which crosses a dam to Revest-les-Eaux.*

**Le Revest-les-Eaux.** – Pop 1 688. It is a delightful old village with 17C church on the side of a steep hill overlooked by a "Saracen" tower. Its 17C chateau is now an inn.

*Return to Toulon through the Le Las valley between Mounts Faron and Croupatier.*

**5 Var Corniche coast road to Cap Brun★** – *Round tour 11 km – 6 3/4 miles – about 3/4 hour – Local map p 149*

*Leave Toulon town centre by Avenue de l'Infanterie de Marine (south east on the plan) going straight on into Avenue des Tirailleurs-Sénégalais.*

**Royal Tower** (Tour Royale). – *Open 1 June to 15 September, 2 to 6pm; 16 September to 31 May, 3 to 6pm; closed Mondays and holidays and 1 November to 22 December and 4 January to 1 March; 6F.*
Known also as the Great or Mitre Tower, it was built by Louis XII in early 16C for defensive purposes (its walls are 7 m – 23 ft thick at the base) although it also served as a prison. It houses an annex to the Naval Museum: huge figureheads and armaments (bronze Chinese cannon).
From the parapet walk a fine panorama★ of Toulon below Mount Faron, the Roads and the coast from the Giens peninsula to Cap Sicié.

*Return to Boulevard Dr-Cunéo and turn right.*

**The Mourillon.** – Drive past the 17C St-Louis Fort; the Littoral Frédéric Mistral passes through a residential district with fine beaches and a view of the Outer Roadstead. The coast here has thrust forward two promontories: Cap Brun and Cap Carqueiranne. The Giens Peninsula stands outlined on the far horizon.

Continue along the D 642, the coast road known as the Var Corniche (Corniche Varoise).

*Near Cap Brun Fort turn sharp right into a narrow road which passes round the fort.*

**Cap Brun★.** – A pleasant setting with an attractive view: right over the Roadstead and left over Méjean Bay separated from Magaud Bay by a rocky promontory, over the point on which stands Ste-Marguerite Fort to Cap de Carqueiranne on the horizon.

*Return to Toulon by the D 42.*

### ⑥ Solliès-Ville – 15 km – 9 1/4 miles – 1 1/2 hours – Local map p 149

*Leave Toulon by N 97, ① on the plan. In La Farlède, turn left into D 67.*

The old town of Solliès-Ville clings to the side of a hill overlooking the rich Le Gapeau Plain; below lies Solliès-Pont, a town of the plain and a busy market in the centre of a region famous for its cherry orchards and other fruits.

**Church.** – *When closed, enquire at Maison Jean-Aicard.* This curious building with two naves combines Romanesque traits with Gothic arches. The monolith at the high altar is thought to be a 15C ciborium. The carved walnut organ (1499) is among the oldest in France. There is a fine 17C altarpiece and another from 16C near the pulpit. The wooden crucifix on the pillar is 13C. The lords of Solliès are buried in the crypt.

**Jean-Aicard House.** – *Open 10am to noon and 3 to 6pm; closed Wednesdays and in October.*

The house of the writer, Jean Aicard, has been converted into a small museum.

**La Montjoie Esplanade.** – From the ruined castle of the Forbins, lords of Solliès, there is a beautiful view★ of the Gapeau valley and the Maures Massif.

### TOURNEFORT Road ★

Michelin map ▮▮▮ fold 15 – *Local map p 166*

A picturesque road over the foothills of the Pointe des 4 Cantons between the Var and the Tinée makes an attractive short cut across the narrow spit of land between the river valleys and passes through Villars where the church contains several works of art.

#### The Var to the Tinée – 15 km – 9 1/4 miles – about 1 hour

*11 km – 6 3/4 miles west of Pont de la Mescla turn right off N 202 into D 26 which climbs up above the valley to the smiling site of Villars.*

**Villars-sur-Var.** – Pop 383. In the Middle Ages Villars belonged to the Grimaldi family of Beuil; its ruined fortifications, particularly St Antony's Gate, are evidence of former strategic importance. Its alluvial terrace sheltered by high mountains yields a good wine. The church square is adorned by a fountain and shaded by plane trees. The church contains several artistic treasures. A large **altarpiece★** *(high altar)* in 10 sections by an anonymous artist shows Franciscan influence; the central theme is a tragic **Entombment★★**; below against a gold lattice background are four saints, above three scenes from the life of Christ. The frame bears the Grimaldi arms. To the left of the choir is the **altarpiece of the Annunciation★** (Nice school, *c* 1520) opposite an alabaster statue of St Petronella. The lefthand chapels contain a statue of John-the-Baptist by Mathieu Danvers (1524) and a painting of the Martyrdom of St Bartholomew (Veronese school). On the right of the choir is a late 16C Madonna of the Rosary. To the right of the church a gate opens into the romantic **Allée des Grimaldi,** a verdant walk between standing columns which leads to a viewpoint above the Var valley.

D 26 winds through the woods on the southern slopes of Mount Falourde with fleeting glimpses of the Madone d'Utelle Chapel *(p 166)* beyond the Tinée.

**Massoins.** – Pop 42. This oasis in the mountains has a fine view of the Var valley.

From a bend in the road the hilltop village of Tournefort comes into view.

*After 2 km – 1 1/4 miles turn right.*

**Tournefort.** – Pop 46. The village clings to a rock escarpment. From near the chapel there is a very beautiful view★ of the Var and Tinée valleys cutting into the mountains and of the Madone d'Utelle and La Tour village *(p 144)* overlooking the Tinée.

*Return to D 26 turning right down into the Tinée valley.* The road runs through forest with magnificent walls of rock on the horizon and reaches the Tinée in Pont-de-Clans.

### TOUTES AURES Pass ★

Michelin map ▮▮ fold 18

It is by way of the Toutes Aures that a section of the Winter Alpine Road (Route d'Hiver des Alpes), N 202, is able to link the upper valleys of the Var and the Verdon, this last transformed into a lake above Castellane since the construction of the Castillon Dam.

#### St-André-les-Alpes to Entrevaux – 38 km – 23 1/2 miles – about 3/4 hour

South of St-André-les-Alpes *(p 165)* N 202 skirts the northern end of **Castillon Lake★** crossing over by St-Julien Bridge (attractive views on either side).

The torrents have cut wild and impressive gorges and rifts (*clues*) transversely to the crest lines through the steep and skeletal limestone ridges of Haute-Provence.

# TOUTES AURES Pass ★

**St-Julien-du-Verdon.** – Pop 66 – *Facilities p 30*. Pleasant lake-side village.

**Vergons Rift★.** – The road climbs through the rift; fine **views** back over the lake and the site of St-Julien-du-Verdon.

A lefthand turning soon after Vergons leads to the Romanesque chapel of Notre-Dame-de-Valvert.

**Toutes Aures Pass.** – Alt 1 124 m – 3 688 ft. The clean cut rock walls, revealing vertical or steeply inclined strata, contrast with the wooded slopes.

**Rouaine Rift★.** – Impressive narrow defile leading to the Coulomp valley.

Below Les Scaffarels the Coulomp valley is enclosed except where it joins the Var above Pont-de-Gueydan. The road continues along the Var valley, through an arid landscape which reflects the southern sun, to Entrevaux *(p 61)*.

## La TURBIE ★

Michelin map ▧▧▧ fold 27 – *Local maps pp 117 and 123* – Pop 1 826 – *Facilities p 30*

The village of La Turbie was built on the Great Corniche at an altitude of 480 m – 1 575 ft in a pass at the base of the massive Tête de Chien promontory which overlooks Monaco, and on either side of the Roman Via Julia which went from Genoa to Cimiez. In addition to the Alpine Trophy, a masterpiece of Roman art which has made the village famous, there are splendid panoramas of the coast and of Monaco. In the evening the lights of Monte-Carlo and Monaco are a magnificent spectacle.

## HISTORICAL NOTES

At the death of Caesar the region of the Alps was still occupied by several unconquered tribes threatening communications between Rome and her possessions in Gaul and Spain. After several campaigns, Augustus was victorious and established a new colony with Cimiez as its capital. In 6BC the Roman Senate and the people decided to commemorate their conquest with an imposing trophy, which was erected where the principal roads, built during the military campaigns, crossed the Alps.

There is one other Roman trophy still standing – Adam Klissi, 150 km – 93 miles from Bucharest in Rumania. Over the years the Latin name – Tropea Augusti – has been transformed into La Turbie.

## ■ SIGHTS *time: 1 hour*

*Start from Avenue Général-de-Gaulle and follow the route marked on the plan.*

**Fountain (E).** – Built in 18C at the end of the Roman aqueduct.

**Place Catherine-Davis.** – From the south-west corner of the square there is a fine **view★** of the coast as far as the Maures Massif.

**Rue Comte-de-Cessole (3).** – Part of the former Via Julia Augusta, built by the Romans, it now goes through the West Gate, climbing between mediaeval houses to the trophy. A house on the right bears a plaque with the verses Dante dedicated to La Turbie. Another plaque shows that the town appeared in the Antonine Itinerary (a reference list of the staging posts on the main roads of the Roman Empire with the distances between them).

**Church of St-Michel-Archange (B).** – Set back from the street stands a fine example of the Nice Baroque style. Built in 18C on an ellipsoidal plan, the church has a shallow concave façade – two storeys beneath a triangular pediment – and a bell-tower surmounted by a cupola covered with coloured tiles.

**Interior★.** – *Walk round clockwise.* The decoration of the nave and chapels is Baroque; the cradle vaulting, supported on tall pillars, is adorned with frescoes and mouldings.

There are two paintings by J.-B. Vanloo and a copy of Raphael's St Michael. The chapel on the left of the choir contains a *Pietà* from the Bréa school and a St Mark writing his Gospel attributed to Veronese. The 17C communion table is in onyx and agate. The high altar of multi-coloured marble

Banville (Pl. Th. de) _____ 2
Cessole (R. Comte-de)
  Via Julia vers la Gaule _____ 3
Guet (R. du) _____ 4
Incalat (R.)
  Via Julia vers l'Italie _____ 5
Philippe-Casimir (R.) _____ 6
Tête de chien (Rte de la) _____ 7

comes from St-Pons Abbey in Nice and was used for the cult of Reason during the Revolution; above it an 18C Christ in painted wood. Also 18C are the two triptychs in the choir: the one on the right shows Christ together with the Church, dressed like a queen in a white robe, and the Synagogue, turning away so as not to see the truth.

In the first chapel on the right is a canvas attributed to Ribera and a 15C Virgin and Child. In the second chapel a painting of Mary by the Murillo school and a Flagellation in Rembrandt's style; also St Catherine-of-Sienna by a pupil of Raphaël.

**Alpine Trophy★** (Trophée des Alpes). – *Open 1 April to 30 September, 9am to 12.30pm and 2 to 7pm; 1 October to 31 March, 9am to noon and 2 to 5.30pm; closed holidays; 7F, children 1F.*

The Alpine Trophy, 50 m high x 38 m wide (164 ft x 125 ft) comprised: a square podium bearing a lengthy inscription to Augustus and a list of the 44 conquered peoples; a large circular Doric colonnade with niches containing statues of the leaders who took part in the campaigns; a stepped cone serving as a base for the statue of Augustus, flanked by two captives. Stairways gave access to all levels.

The stone originally came from quarries in the Justicier Mountain on the far side of the Moneghetti Ravine beside the Great Corniche. In turn mutilated, fortified, blown up with explosives and exploited as a quarry, the monument has survived to our day in the form of a ruined tower emerging from a cone of rubble.

Skilful and patient restoration has been carried out through the generous help of Mr Edward Tuck, directed by M. Jules Fromigé. The trophy has been raised to a height of about 35 m – 115 ft and a large part of it has been left untouched. The inscription has been restored – Pliny had quoted it – and replaced in its original position; it is the longest left to us from Roman times.

**Museum (M).** – The museum contains a model of the monument as it looked at the time of Augustus and documents on its history.

**The Terraces.** – From these raised terraces there is a splendid **panorama★★★** over the Pincipality of Monaco, which one overlooks by more than 450 m – 1 350 ft and over the coast from Mount Agel to the Bordighera headland.

Return by Avenue Prince-Albert-I-de-Monaco turning left into Rue Droite, which passes through the east gate. It follows a part of the ancient Via Julia towards Italy: this later turns left and is called the Rue Incalat.

## TURINI Forest ★★
Michelin map ▓▓▓ folds 17 and 18

For people living on the coast between Nice and Menton the Turini forest means another world of cool green shade. The huge forest, only 25 km – 15 1/2 miles from the Mediterranean coast, is surprising for its trees are commonly found in more northerly latitudes. The lower slopes are covered with maritime sea pines and young oaks but higher up there are maple, beech, chestnut and spruce and superb pine trees, some of which on the northern slopes reach 35 m – 115 ft. Between 1 500 and 2 000 m – 5 000 and 6 500 ft the larch predominates. The forest covers a total of 3 500 ha – 1 350 sq miles between the Vésubie and Bévera valleys.

Several roads meet at the **Turini pass** *(Facilities p 30)* which is a good starting point for touring this beautiful district.

### ① L'AUTION ★★
**Round tour from Turini Pass** – *18 km – 11 miles – 3/4 hour – Local map p 154. The roads are usually blocked by snow in winter and sometimes late into spring.*

*Take D 68 north east from Turini Pass through the forest.* As the road climbs the mountain scenery becomes more magnificent. 4 km – 2 1/2 miles from the pass stands a War Memorial to those who died in 1793 and 1945.

**War Memorial.** – L'Aution has twice seen military action. In 1793 the Convention's troops fought here against the Austrian and Sardinians and in 1945 there was a bitter struggle before the Germans were driven out. Panoramic **view★** from the monument.

*At the fork bear left.* The larch and pine trees give way to pasture. After passing a military road on the left at 1 700 m – 2 077 yds, continue for 700 m – 765 yds to another monument; turn left into a track which after 500 m – 547 yds ends in a platform where it is possible to turn.

**3-Communes Point★★.** – Alt 2 082 m – 6 830 ft. Marvellous **panorama★★** of the peaks in Le Mercantour Park (N) and of the Pre-Alps of Nice (S).

*Return to D 68, turning right.* The road continues through Alpine pastures where cattle spend the summer months and past an old military camp which was damaged in the 1945 conflict. There is a magnificent and uninterrupted **view★** throughout the drive.

*The road comes full circle at the second monument and rejoins the outward route.*

### ② BEVERA VALLEY★
**Turini Pass to Sospel** – *25 km – 15 miles – 1/2 hour – Local map p 154*

Starting from Turini Pass the road, D 2566, runs south east downhill through the forest and along the Bévera valley.

**Moulinet.** – Pop 220. Charming village in a fresh green hollow.

The Bévera makes a succession of sharp bends between high wooded bluffs.

**Notre-Dame de La Menour Chapel.** – An oratory on the left marks the beginning of a path which leads to a huge flight of steps at the top of which stands the chapel, with a two-storey Renaissance façade.

**Piaon Gorge★★.** – In the most dramatic part of the ravine the *corniche* road runs beneath an overhang of rock high above the bed of the stream which is strewn with huge boulders. **Waterfall** on the left.

As the road approaches Sospel *(p 142)* the olive groves begin to reappear.

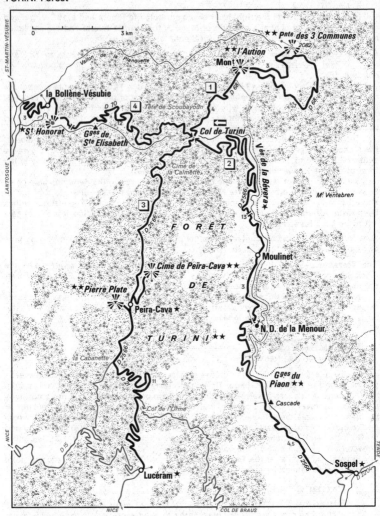

## ③ PEIRA-CAVA★
### Turini Pass to Lucéram – *21 km – 13 miles – 1/2 hour – Local map above*

*Take D 2566 south west.* The drive to Peira-Cava runs through the thickest part of the Turini Forest. There are fine views down into the Vésubie valley.

**Peira-Cava Peak★★.** – *1.5 km – 1 mile – plus 1/2 hour on foot Rtn. At the beginning of Peira-Cava village, near the Post Office, turn left into a steep hill; at the fork bear right. Park in the car park.* It is an easy climb to the top (follow the lift) for a **panoramic view★★**: west over the Vésubie valley and mountains, east over the Bévera valley, north to Le Mercantour Park and the high peaks on the Italian border and south to the Pre-Alps of Nice beyond which is the sea, with Corsica visible in fine weather.

**Peira-Cava★.** – Alt 1 450 m – 4 757 ft. The village stands on a narrow ridge between the Vésubie and Bévera valleys, with an almost aerial view of the district.

*Beyond the village a sharp right turn leads to a car park. A 50 m – 50 yds walk comes to some steps on the left.*

**Pierre Plate★★.** – The **panoramic view★★** is similar to the view from Peira-Cava Peak *(viewing table).*

*Return to D 2566 which continues through the forest. In La Cabanette turn left into D 21. A succession of steep downhill bends, with magnificent* **views★** *on all sides, reaches the edge of the forest. A lefthand turn takes a picturesque route over the Orme pass to the Braus pass, while D 21 continues to Lucéram (p 91).*

## ④ STE-ELISABETH VALLEY★
### Turini Pass to the Vésubie – *15 km – 10 miles – 1 hour – Local map above*

Take D 70 north west beneath the Tête du Scoubayoun overlooking the small Vésubie tributary which flows down Ste-Elisabeth valley.

**Ste-Elisabeth Gorge.** – A wild ravine between violently disturbed rock folds.

Soon after the tunnel at a bend in the road stands St-Honorat Chapel.

**St-Honorat Chapel Viewpoint★.** – The view extends from the terrace over the hill village of Bollène – good **view** from this angle; up the Vésubie from Lantosque to Roquebillière; north to Le Mercantour peaks.

**La Bollène-Vésubie.** – Pop 247. *Facilities p 30*. The village stands on a hill in a chestnut wood at the foot of Les Vallières Peak. The streets climb concentrically between 18C houses to the church. The interior is Baroque with *trompe l'oeil* painting on the ceiling. The sacristy *(key available from the Town Hall (Mairie))* contains: an early painting (1591) of the Virgin with Sts John, a precious ciborium and reliquaries from 17C.

The road follows a serpentine descent into the Vésubie valley *(p 165)* which it overlooks.

## UTELLE ★

Michelin map **195** fold 16 – *Local map p 166* – Pop 451

At 800 m – 2 625 ft the village projects like a balcony over the Vésubie valley facing the Turini Forest and the Gordolasque mountains to the north. It has retained its original character: fountain in the square, old houses with sun dials, ruined fortifications.

**St-Véran Church.** – *When closed, enquire at Auberge Utelloise in the square.*
Built in 14C on the basilica plan and altered in 17C, the church has an elegant Gothic porch with carved panels illustrating the legend of St Véran in 12 tableaux.

The architecture of the interior – groin and barrel vaulting supported on archaistic Romanesque columns and capitals – contrasts surprisingly with the generous Classical, even Baroque, decoration. At the high altar a **carved wooden altarpiece★** representing scenes from the Passion and dominated by a statue of St-Véran. Altarpiece of the Annunciation (Nice school) above the first altar in the left aisle and a 13C recumbent Christ below the altar in the right aisle. Fine 17C woodwork (choir, pulpit) and 16C carved font.

**White Penitents' Chapel.** – The chapel, which is near the church, contains a carved wooden altarpiece of the Descent from the Cross by Rubens and six large 18C paintings.

### EXCURSION

**Madone d'Utelle★★★**. – *6 km – 3 3/4 miles south west – Description p 166.*

## VALBERG ★

Michelin map **195** fold 4 – *Facilities p 30*

Valberg occupies a sunny site among larch woods and green pastures on a mountain shelf at an altitude of 1 669 m – 5 312 ft. It is a summer and winter resort facing the bare rock flanks of the Provençal Alps. Its slopes follow those of Beuil *(p 40)* and its ski runs lie between 1 500 m and 2 066 m – 4 900 ft and 6 800 ft below Le Raton peak (S).

**Chapel of Notre-Dame des Neiges.** – Our Lady of the Snows is a good example of a mountain church. The exterior is plain. **Inside★**, the vaulting, with exposed beams, is supported by arches springing directly from the floor. The decorated coffering presents as a theme the allegorical titles of the Litany of Our Lady painted over a blue background. The whole is a happy example of modern religious art.

**Valberg Cross.** – *3/4 hour on foot Rtn.* Start from the Le Sapet Pass road; the last part of the climb is a path. From the foot of the Cross (alt 1 829 m – 6 001 ft) an immense **panorama★★** unfolds from the Grand Coyer to Mount Pelat and from Mount Mounier to Le Mercantour (N).

### EXCURSION

**Guillaumes Road★ via Péone.** – *14.5 km – 9 miles – about 1/2 hour. Difficult road for several miles*. Leave Valberg by D 29 going north downhill through many hairpin bends to Péone, with views of the ridge linking the Grand Coyer to La Cayolle Pass.

**Péone.** – Pop 524. The village is surrounded by the dolomitic spikes which are one of the natural curiosities of the region.

Beyond Péone the road follows the river Tuebi which flows through a gorge before widening out towards Guillaumes *(p 159)* where it joins the Var. There are more strangely shaped rock formations on this part of the drive.

## VALBONNE Plateau

Michelin map **195** folds 24 and 25 – *Facilities p 30*

The Valbonne Plateau slopes gently from the Pre-Alps of Grasse to the coast with an average altitude of 200 m – 650 ft. It comprises some 2 000 ha – 4 940 acres of pines and holm-oaks and is drained by the Brague and its tributary the Valmasque.

**Valbonne.** – Pop 2 264. This hospitable spot has been occupied since antiquity. In 1199 the Chalais order founded an abbey, which came under the control of Lérins before becoming the parish church. The building, in the form of a Latin cross with a square chevet, has been badly restored on several occasions but has retained the austere character typical of Chalais building.

The village is a curious example of ribbon development, having been rebuilt in 16C by the Lérins monks. The main square with its 15C-17C arcades and old elm trees makes a noble sight.

**Sophia Antipolis.** – In the woods south east of Valbonne an industrial estate has been established for technological, scientific and cultural activities. In accordance with the scheme research groups, laboratories, light industry and residential developments are being installed with due regard for the natural features of the site; the buildings are of decidedly modern design. A sports ground and leisure park have been laid out.

## VALDEBLORE Road ★★
Michelin map **195** folds 5 and 6

The road linking the Tinée and upper Vésubie valleys passes through the Valdeblore district (Pop 475 – *Facilities p 30*), a region of green pastures and wooded slopes high in the mountains.

### St-Martin-Vésubie to the Tinée – *29 km – 18 miles – about 1 ½ hours – Local map p 166*

*Leave St-Martin-Vésubie (p 132) by D 2565 going north up the valley.* The road overlooks St-Martin and Venanson. Just before the tunnel there is a fine **view★** back down to the Vésubie and St-Martin, up the Madone valley and north to the peaks of Le Mercantour.

**La Colmiane.** – A ski resort in St-Martin's Pass (Alt 1 500 m – 5 000 ft) composed of chalets and hotels dispersed among the larches and pines.

*At St-Martin's Pass turn left into a narrow road which leads to the chair–lift.*

**Colmiane Peak★★.** – *Chair-lift to the top; Rtn 14F.* From the top there is an immense **panorama★★**; south over Mount Tournairet, the Vésubie valley and Turini Forest; east over Le Mercantour chain; north west over the Baus de la Frema to Mount Mounier with Valdeblore in the fore-ground.

Beyond the pass the road enters a green gulley, the highest part of the Valdeblore.

**St-Dalmas.** – The Romanesque **church** is striking with its pyramidal alpine style bell-tower, its stout buttresses and Lombard bands on the chevet. *To visit ask M Lewis Bertolini, ☎ 02.83.12.* Over an earlier groin-vaulted crypt, the church is built on the basilica plan. The interior

Valdeblore Landscape

was vaulted in 17C to hide the original roof. Above the high altar there is a polyptych by Guillaume Planeta. In the left aisle an altarpiece of St-Francis attributed to André de Cella. Behind an altarpiece of the Rosary (17C) in the right apsidal chapel are the partial remains of some very old frescoes.

The road looks down on the Bramafam valley and passes through La Roche at the foot of a grey rock spur.

**La Bolline.** – The town, which is the administrative centre of the Valdeblore district, makes a pleasant summer resort surrounded by chestnut woods which contrast with the Black Forest on the opposite slope. *The parish priest acts as guide to the church and chapel from Sunday to Wednesday in principle, ☎ 02.82.28.* The **church** – omanesque bell-tower – contains two 18C canvasses, one by Louis Vanloo and a triptych of the Virgin and Child (16C). In the **White Penitents' Chapel** is a Descent from the Cross by Rocca (1635) behind the high altar.

*Beyond La Bolline turn right into D 66.*

**Rimplas.** – Pop 55. The curious **site★** of the village on a rib of rock is very striking. From the chapel below the fort there is an extensive **view★** of the Tinée, Bramafam valley and the Valdeblore villages.

## VALENSOLE Plateau
Michelin map **81** fold 15

This region, which extends east from the Durance between the Bléone and the Verdon to the Pre-Alps of Castellane and Digne, resembles an ancient trench filled in at the end of the Primary Era with thick layers of pudding stone. It is now a large plateau, sloping downhill from east to west to finish some 200 m to 300 m – 656 ft to 984 ft above the Durance.

The plateau is divided in two by the river Asse. To the north lies a rough terrain of stunted woods where all signs of life are hidden in the valleys. The land to the south however is neatly parcelled out. The approach is the same from every direction: from a wooded ravine the road emerges on to the plateau where huge fields of wheat and lavandin *(p 15)* extend into the distance, with here and there an almond tree left over from an earlier economic system. It is a delightful drive in March when the almond blossom is out and in July when the lavender is in flower.

### SOUTHERN SECTION OF THE PLATEAU
**Round tour from Valensole** – *66 km – 41 miles – about 4 hours*

**Valensole.** – Pop 1 721. *Facilities p 30.* The town with its attractive fountains is spread out on a gently sloping hillside and dominated by the solid outline of the church, its massive tower flanked by a pinnacle turret. The interior is terminated by a square chevet, Gothic like the façade, and lit by six lancet windows; the choir stalls are 16C.

Leave Valensole by D 6 going east through wooded ravines to the Pre-Alps of Castellane.

**Riez.** – *Description p 121.*

*Leave Riez by D 952 going south west along the broad Colostre valley.*

**Allemagne-en-Provence.** – Pop 202. In the 13C the village was called Aramagna which became Alamania and then Allemagne.
On the edge of the village stands a surprising Renaissance château resembling those in the Loire valley.

Continue along D 952 through smiling country where vineyards alternate with lavender and tulip fields.

**St-Martin-de-Brômes.** – Pop 217. The streets are lined with old houses in Romanesque or Classical style; the porches bear curious inscriptions and the lintels are carved with the date of construction.
*To visit the church and tower apply to M. Royer, near the tower (Thursdays, 3 to 6pm, between Easter and end of September).*
The **church** is Romanesque with a fine rustic chevet and a belfry with three bays surmounted by a stone pyramid. Inside the transverse ribs rest on carved pendants; behind the altar is a curious tabernacle in painted plasterwork.
At the far end of the old castle site stands the 14C **Templar Tower,** which houses a Roman tomb containing a lead coffin and skeleton, excavated in the village in 1972 together with some coins which date the tomb somewhere in the first half of 4C.

*Take D 82 south of the village to Esparron.*

**Esparron-de-Verdon.** – Pop 104. *Facilities p 30.* The old village, built here and there in a ravine, is dominated by the Castellanes' castle *(not open);* its 18C façade is flanked by a high crenelated keep, the oldest parts of which date from 10C.
Since the building of the Gréoux dam to form a **lake** Esparron has become popular with sailing and fishing enthusiasts.

*Return along D 82 tuning left after 6 km – 3 3/4 miles towards Gréoux-les-Bains.*

From the road there are fine **views**★ of the lake.

**Gréoux Dam.** – The earth dam is 260 m – 853 ft thick at the base, 67 m – 220 ft high from the foundations and 220 m – 722 ft long at the top. It controls the flow of the Verdon to feed the hydro-electric station at Vinon and the Provence canal.

The road follows the green Verdon valley into Gréoux.

**Gréoux-les-Bains**★. – Pop 1 297 – *Facilities p 30.* This spa has been famous for its waters since antiquity; a dedication has been found which was made to the nymphs of Gréoux in 176AD. The water which comes from a single spring (200 million litres per day) is warm (36° C – 97° F) and sulphurous and used to treat rheumatism, arthritis and respiratory disorders. The very modern spa facilities occupy a well-shaded site to the east of the town on D 952. The town is smart and well endowed with greenery and sunshine. There has been considerable development in the hotel, commercial and leisure sectors.
Clustering at the foot of the castle, the buildings of the **old town** have been completely renovated. The church with its Romanesque nave and square Gothic apse has also been restored; the side aisles and chapels were added in 16C and 17C.
*Take D 82, towards Manosque, as far as the cemetery and turn sharp left.* Former Templar stronghold, the **castle** was still inhabited in 19C but is now in ruins. Its towers and walls are nonetheless impressive; from the platform there is a fine **view** of the valley.

*Take D 8 up the Laval Ravine to return to Valensole.*

## VALLAURIS

Michelin map **195** fold 39 – Pop 18 814 with Golfe-Juan – *For additional plan of Cannes see the current Michelin Guide France*

Vallauris lies 1 1/2 miles from the sea among rounded hills covered with orange trees and mimosa. The centre is laid out on the grid plan; the town was razed to the ground in 1390 and rebuilt and repopulated in 16C by immigrants from Genoa. The town's traditional craft of pottery was in decline when Picasso infused it with new life *(p 22)*. Today it is an important French centre for ceramics where a Biennial International festival of Ceramic Art is held. Glasswork and weaving have been added to the local commercial scene which also includes cut flowers and aromatic plants.

■ **SIGHTS** *time: 1 hour*

**Castle** (V D). – Built in 16C as a priory attached to Lérins, it is a rare example of Renaissance architecture in Provence. It is a rectangular two-storey building with a round pepper-pot tower at each corner. It houses two museums.

**National Museum of War and Peace**★. – *Open 10am to noon and 2 to 6pm (5pm 1 October to 30 April); closed holidays and in November; 5F.*
Only the chapel of the priory survived. Deconsecrated, it was decorated in 1952 by Picasso with a huge composition: War and Peace.

*(After photo : Galerie Madoura)*

Pottery by Picasso

157

**Municipal Museum.** – *Open 10am to noon and 2 to 6pm; closed Tuesdays and certain holidays; 3F.*

Temporary exhibitions of ceramics are displayed in the vaulted rooms.

A fine Renaissance staircase leads to the first floor where 6 rooms are devoted to the recent **Magnelli bequest** : works in oil, collage and gouache together with a large mural. Alberto Magnelli (1888-1971) was born in Florence but spent the greater part of his life in France. The rooms are arranged from left to right to trace the evolution of the artist's style.

**Place Paul-Isnard** (V 34). – At the centre of the town where the market is held in front of the church, stands a bronze statue presented by Picasso to the town of which he became an honorary citizen.

**Avenue Georges-Clemenceau** (V 17). – Here and in the neighbouring streets (Rue Sicard, Rue du Plan) are the pottery shops and studios, their displays of ceramics spilling out on to the pavement; high quality work vieing for attention beside second rate wares. The Madoura studio sells reproductions of Picasso's ceramics as well as its own work.

## VAR Lower Valley ★

Michelin map ▦▦▦ folds 26 and 16

Traditionally there have always been two main highways leading from eastern Provence and the County of Nice into the Alps of Haute-Provence: one is the Var and the other what is now known as Napoleon's Road *(p 127)*. The lower reaches of the Var are broad allowing the passage of heavy traffic in the valley. It is only above the confluence with the Vésubie that the river becomes narrower.

Despite growing industrialisation and urbanisation, the lower Var has many charms.

### Nice to Pont de la Mescla – *37 km – 23 miles – about 1 1/4 hours*

*Leave Nice by the Promenade des Anglais which becomes Promenade Corniglion Molinier, a pleasant drive along the Baie des Anges. Turn right into the access road to the airport.*

**Nice-Côte d'Azur Airport.** – It is the third largest in France in terms of traffic; 3.75 million passengers passed through in 1981. To meet the growing demand, the airport, which is on the east side of the Var estuary, is being extended out into the sea to provide an additional runway and a second terminal. From the terrace *(3F)* there is a view of the aircraft landing and taking off and of the Baie des Anges from Cap Ferrat to Cap d'Antibes and inland.

Shorts flights are organised by the Compagnie Avia-Sud.

*Return to N 98, then turn right towards Plan du Var.*

N 202 runs north past the Nice flower market and the vast facilities of the Sports Park, then underneath the Provençal Motorway which swings away east towards Italy negotiating the heights of Nice by a series of engineering feats.

The road hugs the east bank of the Var. In a landscape composed of flower beds and vegetable plots, of vineyards and olive groves, the hill villages of Vence and the Nice hinterland stand out one by one: on the west bank Gattières, Carros and Le Broc; on the east bank Aspremont and Castagniers at the foot of Mount Chauve, followed by St-Martin-du-Var and La Roquette-sur-Var.

The **view**★ includes the snow-capped Alps on the horizon.

**Charles-Albert Bridge.** – The **site**★ of Bonson village on an impressive rock spur high above the river on the opposite bank comes into view.

Beyond Plan-du-Var the road crosses the Vésubie where it emerges from the Gorge *(p 166)* to join the Var.

**Le Chaudan Defile**★★. – Downstream from La Mescla Bridge, the Var winds through a narrow gorge between sheer walls, scarcely leaving room for the road which often seems to be reaching a dead end. Four tunnels have been bored to carry the road through the gorge named after the village of Le Chaudan at the southern end.

## VAR Upper Valley ★★

Michelin map ▦▦▦ folds 2, 3, 13 and 14

The D 2202 borders the upper valley of the Var and offers views of several old villages set in the countryside. It is a main thoroughfare to the Nice region from the Alps.

*To reach Entraunes by the Cayolle Pass (Route des Grandes Alpes) see Michelin Green Guide Alpes – in French only.*

### Dowstream from Entraunes to Puget-Théniers – *51 km – 32 miles – about 3 hours*

**Entraunes.** – Pop 122. A pretty little village situated at the meeting of the Var and Bourdoux below La Cayolle Pass. The church has a rare asymmetrical bell-tower. On the north side of the town beside D 2202 stands **St-Sébastien Chapel** *(open every day 9am to 5pm; apply to M. Payan, carpenter near the chapel).* Frescoes (1516) by André de Cella cover the walls of the apse like a Renaissance style altarpiece.

Stark mountain scenery borders the road: bare rock relieved by patches of thin woodland. Below the tunnel the valley widens out into St-Martin's basin hollowed out of the black marl.

**St-Martin d'Entraunes.** – Pop 115. The village lies in a setting of greenery contrasting with the usual aridity of the upper Var valley. In the Romanesque **church** *(key available from M. Liautaud, house opposite the church door)* is an altarpiece of the Rosary by François Bréa.

*3.5 km – 2 1/4 miles beyond Villeneuve-d'Entraunes, turn left into D 74 which climbs above the Barlatte valley.*

**Châteauneuf d'Entraunes.** – Pop 36. The village stands on a desolate site above the Var valley. The church contains an early painting (1524) in the style of François Bréa *(key from the Café-bar in the village).*

*Return to D 2202 turning left.*

**Guillaumes.** – Pop 558. *Facilities p 30.* A defensive site above the confluence of the Var and the Tuebi, this summer resort is dominated by its ruined castle which has a fine view over the village.

Below Guillaumes the valley enters a gorge.

The wild and grandiose **Daluis Gorge★★**, created by the Var, is named after the village at the southern end. Between Guillaumes and Daluis the *corniche* road follows the contours of the west bank high above the limpid green waters of the river.
At the narrowest points tunnels have been made in the rock to carry the southbound traffic, while the other lane projects out over the gorge providing the best **views★★**. The Var has cut through the red schist, now spotted with greenery, to create a gorge which is outstanding for its depth, its starkness and its colouring.
Downstream stands the "Guardian of the Gorge", a curious shale rock, shaped like a bust of Marianne (symbol of the French Republic).

Below Daluis the road follows the river which makes a sharp turn to the east at Pont de Gueydan. After broadening out the valley closes in again at Entrevaux.

**Entrevaux.** – *Description p 61.*

There is a good view of the **site★★** of Entrevaux to the rear as N 202 approaches Puget-Théniers *(p 120).*

## VENCE ★

Michelin map **195** fold 25 – *Local maps p 90 – Pop 11 660 – Facilities p 30*

Vence is a delightful winter and summer resort, 10 km – 6 miles from the sea between Nice and Antibes, in a countryside where mimosa, roses, carnations and violets are cultivated and where olive and orange trees grow. It is a picturesque old market town, standing on a rock promontory bordered by two ravines and sheltered from the cold north winds by the last foothills of the Alps. The wines from the surrounding stony hillsides (La Gaude, St-Jeannet) are well esteemed.

## HISTORICAL NOTES

**An Episcopal Town.** – Vence, founded by the Ligurians, was an important Roman town. With the coming of Christianity, it took on a new influence: it acquired episcopal dignity. Among the bishops from 374 to 1789 were St Véran (5C) and St Lambert (12C), an Italian prince who became Pope Paul III (16C), and Antoine Godeau *(see below).*
During the wars of religion Vence was besieged in 1592 by the Huguenot Lesdiguières but held out; the victory is commemorated each year at Easter.

**The Lords of Vence (13C).** – The bishops of Vence were in continual conflict with the barons of Villeneuve, lords of the town. This family drew its fame from Romée de Villeneuve, an able Catalan who in the 13C re-organised the affairs of the Count of Provence, Berenger V. The count had four marriageable daughters and an empty treasury. Romée induced Blanche of Castille to ask for the eldest, Marguerite, for the future St Louis.
Eleanor married Henry III and became Queen of England and another became Empress of Austria. The last daughter, Beatrix, heiress of Provence, married Charles of Anjou, brother of St Louis in 1246, and became Queen of the Two Sicilies.

**Bishop Godeau (17C).** – The memory of Bishop Godeau has remained vivid throughout the region. His beginnings did not seem likely to lead him to a bishopric: he was the oracle of the House of Rambouillet. Small, skinny, swarthy and unusually ugly, he was nevertheless in great demand among some ladies of pretentious culture because of his wit, his fluency and his easy poetical vein: they called him Julie's dwarf (Julie d'Angennes was the daughter of the Marquise de Rambouillet) and also, ironically, the "Jewel of the Graces". His reputation was unprecedented; when later, anyone came across a text which was to defy the centuries, they said "It is by Godeau". Richelieu made him the first member of the French Academy.
At the age of thirty, Godeau, no doubt tired of verse-making, took holy orders and, the following year, was made Bishop of Grasse and Vence. The towns would not accept a joint bishop and so for several years he remained between the two dioceses, finally opting for Vence. The former wit and ladies' confidant took his new role seriously; he repaired his cathedral, which was falling in ruins, introduced various industries – perfumery, tanning and pottery – and brought some measure of prosperity to his poor and primitive diocese. He died in 1672 at the age of sixty-seven.

## ■ SIGHTS *time: 1 1/2 hours*

**Rosaire or Matisse Chapel★.** – *Open 10 to 11.30am and 2.30 to 5.30pm, Tuesdays and Thursdays except holidays; other days by appointment: Foyer Lacordaire, Avenue H. Matisse, Vence. ☎ 58.03.26; closed in November.*
"Despite its imperfections I think it is my masterpiece ... the result of a lifetime devoted to the search for truth". This was Henri Matisse's opinion of the chapel which he had designed and decorated between 1947 and 1951.
The fame of this artist and the daring of his design, which has revived in present times the genius of the mediaeval masters, has aroused an enormous interest in this building.

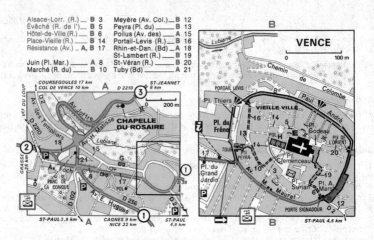

From the outside it looks like an ordinary Provençal house with a roof of coloured tiles surmounted by a huge wrought iron cross with gilt tips. Within the community nave and the parish nave meet at the altar which is set at an angle. Everything is white – floor, ceiling, tiled walls – except for the small high stained glass windows which make a floral pattern in lemon, bottle green and ultra-marine.

The decoration, the furnishings, the vestments are strikingly plain and simple. The mural compositions, notably the Way of the Cross and St Dominic, have been reduced to a play of black lines on a white background.

The gallery containing studies made by Matisse for his finished designs is worth a visit.

**Place du Frêne** (B). – Start from the Place du Grand-Jardin but before entering the old town look at the Place du Frêne and the enormous ash tree which gives the square its name and which, according to legend, was planted in memory of the visit to Vence of François I and Pope Paul III.

From the terrace in the Place Thiers, to the north, there is a good **view** of the Lubiane valley and the Rosaire Chapel.

**Old town** (Vieille Ville) (B). – The old town was enclosed in elliptical walls, parts of which can still be seen, and which were pierced by five gateways.

Go round the 15C square tower, adjoining the old castle, which was rebuilt in 17C, to reach and pass through the Peyra Gate (1441). This part of town is alive with artists, craftsmen and boutiques.

**Place du Peyra★** (B 13). – The square is picturesque with a dominating square tower and splashing fountain in the form of an urn (1822). It was the forum of the Roman town.

*From the south side of the square take Rue du Marché and turn left to reach Place Clemenceau.*

**Old cathedral** (B E). – The church, erected at the start of the Romanesque period on the site of a Roman temple which was replaced in 5C by a cathedral of which some carved stone still remains, has been modified many times. The building has a nave and four aisles but no transepts.

On either side of the door Roman inscriptions have been incorporated in the Baroque façade.

Inside there are St-Lambert's tomb *(second chapel on the right)*, 5C Roman sarcophagus said to be the tomb of St-Véran *(third chapel on the right)*; in the lefthand aisle a fine carved doorway and a 16C altarpiece of the Holy Angels; by the font a mosaic by Chagall of Moses in the bullrushes.

In the main gallery *(guided tour Tuesdays and Fridays, 11am to noon and 3 to 5pm)* are a lectern and some very beautiful 15C Gothic **choirstalls★** in which the misericords have been carved with delightful fantasy.

Vence – Place du Peyra

**The Ramparts.** – Leave the church by the east door which opens into Place Godeau, overlooked by the square tower with its parapet and surrounded by old houses. At the centre stands a Roman column erected to the god Mars. Take Rue St-Lambert and then Rue de l'Hôtel-de-Ville to reach the 13C Signadour Gate and turn left.

The next gate on the left is the Westgate (Orient), opened in 18C. Boulevard Paul-André follows the line of the ramparts; several narrow stepped streets open into it; there are fine **views** of the foothills of the Alps.

Re-enter the old town by the Gothic Levis Portal (13C) and walk up Rue du Portail Lévis between handsome old houses to Place du Peyra.

The Verdon, a tributary of the Durance, has created magnificent gorges in the limestone plateau of Haute-Provence, the most remarkable being the Grand Canyon, which is over 21 km – 13 miles long.

The magnificent gorge of the Grand Canyon extends from Rougon to Aiguines. The torrent has dug downwards using natural rifts in the soil. These have gradually become enlarged to form the great winding corridor that we see today.

The width of the gorges varies at the bottom from about 6 to 100 m – 20 to 320 ft, and at the top of the cliffs from about 200 to 1 500 m – 650 to 5 000 ft. The depth from the edge of the plateau varies from about 250 to 700 m – 800 to 2 500 ft.

**Exploration and Organisation.** – E.-A. Martel (1859-1938), the eminent founder of speleology, was the first to carry out a complete survey of these gorges in 1905. M. Janet and I. Blanc also took part in the venture.

In 1928 the Touring Club de France undertook to open up part of the Grand Canyon so that experienced walkers could explore it without danger. Protected belvederes were set up to lessen the effects of vertigo, and the main viewing points were marked.

In 1947 the Corniche Sublime (road D 71), cut in the solid rock, opened the south side to motoring and tourism on a considerable scale.

Since 1973, the Crest Road (Route des Crêtes, D 23) has opened the north bank to motorists.

**Access by road.** – There are two routes for visiting the gorges: D 71 (Corniche Sublime) on the south side and D 952 on the north side. *D 955 from Draguignan may very occasionally be closed to traffic when the Canjuers military firing range is in use.*

## THE CORNICHE SUBLIME★★★

*81 km – 50 miles – 1/2 day – Local map pp 162-163*

The route taken by the Sublime Corniche is perfect for tourists. It seeks out the most impressive ravines and viewpoints; the views down into the canyon are superb. Even the approach roads are interesting for the immense horizons they open up.

### From Castellane to the Balcons de la Mescla

*Leave Castellane (p 52) by D 952, ② on the plan.* The road follows the north bank of the Verdon, winding at the foot of impressive escarpments. Soon the rocky ridges of the Cadières de Brandis come into view on the right.

**Porte St-Jean★.** – St John's Gate is a magnificent defile cut vertically through a limestone chain.

The river begins to swing south in a wide bend.

**Chasteuil Rift★.** – A long rift *(clue)* between sheer rock walls.

At Pont-de-Soleils bear left into D 955 which turns away from the Verdon, crosses a small ravine on the edge of Les Défends wood and climbs the verdant Jabron valley.

**Combs-sur-Artuby.** – Pop 206. *Facilities p 30.* This market town is built against a hill of the Plans de Provence. Overlooking the village perched atop a rock is the interesting **St-André chapel,** *(ask for the key at the Town Hall 9am to noon and 2 to 5pm weekdays; access is by a path behind the parish church; 1/2 hour Rtn).*

A small Gothic façade of grey limestone, a covered nave with large diagonal ribs and an oven-vaulted apse recalls the church of St-Victor of Castellane *(p 52),* a church of Provençal Primitive Gothic Style. From the terrace is a beautiful view of the Plans de Provence and the Artuby Gorges.

*Leave Comps by D 71 going west.*

From a bend in the road there is a wide **view★** of bare mountain ranges (Pre-Alps of Castellane and Digne) sometimes strangely shaped; the hill village of Trigance is on the right.

**Balcons de la Mescla★★★** ① and ②. – *On the right of the road on either side of the Café-Relais des Balcons.* From these «balconies» or belvederes one looks down a dizzying 230 m – 755 ft to the Mescla below where the swirling waters of the Artuby meet the equally turbulent Verdon. In this wild and grandiose setting the Verdon bends sharply round a narrow knife-edge ridge. Upstream lies the north-south section of the gorges, steeply enclosed for between 400 and 500 m – 437 to 546 ft.

The upper belvedere ①, a short walk away, is the most impressive.

### From the Balcons de la Mescla to the Illoire Pass

*The road may be blocked by snow between December and March.*

**Artuby Bridge★.** – The Artuby Bridge, a magnificent feat of civil engineering in reinforced concrete, spans in a single 110 m – 361 ft arch the vertically walled Artuby canyon. *There is a carpark at the end of the bridge.*

The road, which makes an almost complete circle round the Pilon de Fayet, comes out above the canyon.

**Fayet Tunnels** ③. – Between and after two tunnels, there is an extraordinary **view★★★** of the bend in the canyon by the Cavaliers' Narrows.

**Cavaliers' Cliff★★** (Falaise des Cavaliers) ④. – The road leaves the gorges to follow the edge of the cliff where two viewpoints have been built. A fork to the right leads to the Cavaliers' Restaurant where, from the terrace *(free access April to October),* there is a striking view of the 300 m – 984 ft high Cavaliers' Cliff.

The next 3 km – 2 miles is one of the most spectacular sections of the drive, where the road overlooks a continuous precipice, which varies in height from 250 to 400 m – 800 to 1 300 ft.

**Falaise de Baucher★** ⑤. – Good view upstream of the Pré Baucher basin.

**L'Imbut Pass** ⑥. – The road offers a plunging view on a strait of the Verdon, dominated by awe-inspiring and perfectly smooth sided cliffs. The river disappears temporarily beneath a mass of fallen rocks.

The road draws away from the cliff edge to make two hairpin bends opposite the point where the Mainmorte Ravine enters the gorge, cutting through the far bank and opening up a vista of the Barbin Cliffs.

Continuing halfway up a moutain-side and some distance from the gorges, the road next enters a densely wooded area which hides the view.

**Vaumale Circus**★★. – A pronounced elbow-bend to the left marks the road's entry into a wooded circus where a magnificent view develops downstream to the Verdon's outlet.

The road, after reaching its highest point (1 204 m – 3 950 ft), offers wide views – ⑦ and ⑧ on either side of the Vaumale spring, some 700 m – 2 296 ft above the Verdon. The gorge itself and the heights along the right bank provide as impressive a spectacle as ever and the altitude is still sufficient to give the feeling that one is flying above the far bank.

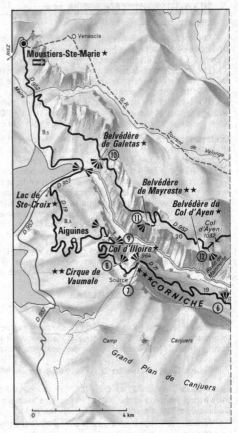

On coming out of the circus, the road leaves the hill slope overlooking the gorge for a short period to wind on in hairpin bends from which there are views★ downstream of the Verdon and Ste-Croix Lake, while in the far distance can be seen the Lubéron and the Lure and Ventoux Mountains on the right bank of the Durance.

**Illoire Pass**★ ⑨. – It marks the exit from the gorges. Stop to take a last look back at the Grand Canyon upstream, the bed invisible except for a short section.

## From the Illoire Pass to Moustiers-Ste-Marie

The **view**★ now extends over a world of distant bluish hills among which can be distinguished the spur of the Ste-Victoire Mountain. In the foreground the Valensole Plateau is so perfectly flat that it looks like mown grass.

**Aiguines.** – Pop 132. Prettily situated amidst cypress groves, Aiguines is proud of its 17C château, with its four pepperpot towers and glazed tiles.

After Aiguines the road descends in hairpin bends offering beautiful views of the lake of Ste-Croix. *Turn right into D 957.*

**Ste-Croix Lake**★. – With the recent construction of the dam, the already large Ste-Croix de Verdon was further enlarged and now takes up an area of 2 500 ha – 6 175 acres. It extends along the Plan de Provence to Valensole Plateau. The mean annual production of the power station is 162 million kWh.

The D 957 skirts the lake briefly and crosses the Verdon; from the bridge there is a **view**★ of the canyon and Ste-Croix Lake. Then the road follows the course of the Maïre Valley and passes a leisure centre before reaching Moustiers-Ste-Marie *(p 106).*

## THE NORTH BANK★★★

*73 km – 45 miles – 1/2 day – Local map above*

The direct road between Moustiers and Castellane, D 952, does not skirt the gorge in the middle section but D 23, the Crest Road, makes a great loop from La Palud-sur-Verdon along the edge of the gorge, filling in the middle section.

## From Moustiers-Ste-Marie to La Palud-sur-Verdon

Leave Moustiers *(p 106)* by D 952 descending the valley of the Maïre, at the foot of the Pre-Alps of Castellane. The straight edge of the Valensole plateau dropping into Ste-Croix lake, and Aiguines and its château appear on the right.

**Galetas Belvedere**★ ⑩. – There is a view of the impressive gap marking the end of the Grand Canyon, of the Rue d'Eau de St-Maurin upstream and of the Ste-Croix lake downstream.

The road enters the bare circus of Mayreste and climbs rapidly.

**Mayreste Belvedere**★★ ⑪. – *1/4 hour on foot Rtn by a marked path over a stony hill.* First view of the deep cleft upstream.

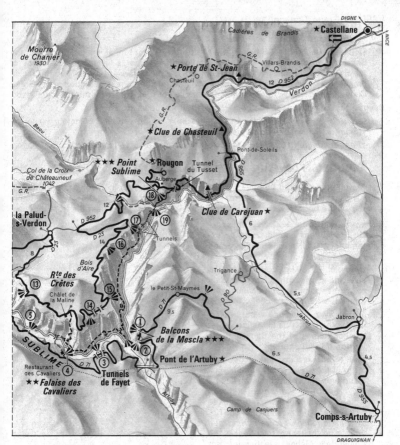

Ayen Pass Belvedere★ ⑫. – *1/4 hour on foot Rtn.* View upstream of its jagged course. The road leaves the Verdon to descend to the cultivated plateau of La Palud-sur-Verdon.

La Palud-sur-Verdon. – Summer excursion centre. Fine 12C Romanesque bell-tower.

*On entering La Palud, turn right into D 23, no signs.*

## Crest Road (Route des Crêtes)

*At Palud turn right into D 23, the Crest Road.*

The road returns to the Verdon by way of the Mainmorte ravine and emerges above the canyon. Belvederes with car parks follow one another, each offering plunging views upstream; only the main ones are mentioned below.

L'Imbut Belvedere★★ ⑬. – The Verdon disappears for 400 m – 440 yds beneath a mass of fallen boulders. View of the formidable polished cliffs of Baou-Béni. Upstream, beyond the Styx passage is the narrow Pré Baucher loop.

The road passes La Maline chalet, starting point for a walking tour *(p 164)* of the Grand Canyon, and then climbs rapidly to Aire Wood.

Les Glacières Belvedere★★ ⑭. – Impressive view of La Mescla and its huge knife edge rock, the Verdon and the Canjuers Plateau.

The ravine bends sharply to the left; the river is now running north-south.

Tilleul Belvedere★★ ⑮. – On the left are the impressive golden cliffs of the Dent d'Aire and the Barre de l'Escalès; opposite is the Baumes Frères defile, dominated by the Arme Vieille Ridge.

The road skirts the Aire wood.

L'Escalès Belvedere★★★ ⑯. – Unforgettable view of the Verdon gorge, from the top of the sheer cliffs to the footpath by the water's edge.

Trescaïre Belvedere★★ ⑰. – Plunging view of the incised meander of the river. To the left is the inn of the Point Sublime and above is the hill village of Rougon. Upstream the Verdon runs out among the rubble and retreats beneath the Baumes aux Pigeons.

The Crest Road turns west through Aire Wood to join D 952 east of La Palud-sur-Verdon.

## From La Palud-sur-Verdon to Castellane

From a bend in the road, D 952, ahead and to the left is a beautiful **view** of Rougon; from across the valley of the Baou, there is a full view of the gorges.

Point Sublime★★★ ⑱. – *1/4 hour on foot Rtn.* Leave the car *(car park)* at the inn and take the marked path: Point Sublime on the right. The belvedere looks down 180 m – 590 ft to where the Baou river joins Verdon. From this point, there is a splendid view of the opening of the Grand Canyon and of the Samson Corridor.

*Return to the car and take D 17 to Rougon.*

Rougon. – From the mediaeval ruins **view**★ of the opening of the Grand Canyon.

VERDON Grand Canyon ★★★

*Return to D 952 towards Castellane.*

**Samson Corridor**★★ ⑲. – On the right just after the Tusset tunnel is a marked route: the Belvedere of the Samson Corridor. It follows the slope as far as the confluence of the Baou and Verdon *(car park)* and meets the path marked by the Touring Club of France, coming from the Chalet de La Maline. From here the constriction of the Grand Canyon is grandiose and wild enormous piles of rock cluttering the torrential beds.

Beyond the Tusset tunnel, the *corniche* road drops down to the river.

**Carejuan Rift**★. – The limestone strata has an amazing variation of colour while the stream, as clear as ever, swirls roughly by.

*From Pont-de-Soleils to Castellane the drive is described on p 161 in the opposite direction.*

## EXCURSION ON FOOT IN THE GRAND CANYON ★★★

The Martel path, marked by the T.C.F, runs from the Chalet de la Maline to the Sublime Point and involves a whole day's hard walking but it provides a succession of unforgettable views from the bottom of the Canyon and a closer contact than is possible from the road.

**Recommendations and warnings. –** Certain precautions should be taken before embarking on a walk in the Grand Canyon.

**Equipment.** – Walking boots, food, torches and warm clothing are necessary as some sections, particularly the tunnels, are distinctly chilly.

**Drinking water.** – Drinking water is available at the Chalet de la Maline and at the confluence of the Baou and the Verdon (Merlet spring).

**Taxis.** – There is a taxi service between the Auberge du Point Sublime, La Palud and the Chalet de la Maline *(☎ (92) 74.68.20 Palud-sur-Verdon)* which enables walkers to return to the point where their car is parked. Out of season *(check before setting out)* there is no shelter nor telephone at the Chalet de la Maline. It is therefore not advisable to walk from Point-Sublime to La Maline out of season.

**Maps.** – In addition to the local map on p 162, the 1/50 000 (Moustiers – Ste-Marie) map produced by the Institut Géographique National and the map of the Grand Canyon du Verdon by A. Monier are useful *(on sale locally).*

Verdon Canyon

**Variations in the water level.** – The operation of the Chaudanne and Castillon power stations can cause rapid variations in the water level in the gorge; it is advisable to keep to the path marked by the Touring Club de France.

**Exploration of the bed of the gorge.** – This can be a dangerous excursion – it is made on foot (some swimming) or in canoes – and does not fall within the scope of this guide; information available from specialist sources.

### From Chalet de la Maline to the Point Sublime

*6 hours of hard walking (excluding halts) – Local map pp 162-163*

*The Touring Club de France path, G.R. 4, is signposted in white and red.*

The path descends by a winding stairway, providing fine views over the l'Estellié Pass.

*At the end of the descent pass a road on your right which leads to the Grand Canyon restaurant and the Corniche Sublime by way of the Estellié footbridge.*

At Le Pré d'Issane, you once again come to the torrent, which you follow in climbing the Étroit des Cavaliers where the steep cliffs are almost 300 m high – 1 000 ft. The gorge widens and you reach the Guègues, with high semicircular slopes around it.

Go down from the Guègues embankment to continue up the gorges. After the huge caves of the Baumes-aux-Boeufs, leave a path to the right which leads to the river and take the right fork to the **Mescla**★★★: the junction of the waters of the Verdon and the Artuby. In this grandiose setting there is a fine view upstream of the Baumes-Frères defile.

*Return to the fork and turn right.*

The path goes up in hairpin bends as far as La Brèche Imbert *(stairs)* from where there is a splendid view over the Baumes-Frères and Escalès. The gorges widen between cliffs 400 to 500 m high – 1 200 ft to 1 500 ft then narrow again.

To your right, the Trescaïre Chaos is a fantastic mass of fallen boulders.

You then pass through two more tunnels. In the last one an opening provides an overhanging view of the end of the Samson Corridor and the Baume aux Pigeons, an immense cavern hollowed out by whirlpools; a last opening affords another view of the Samson Corridor, a very narrow defile with smooth, vertical walls.

The path then passes over the Baou torrent by a footbridge and climbs up to the Samson Corridor car park *(above)* at the end of the road which joins D 952 by the Tusset tunnel. Walk to the Auberge du Point Sublime from where you can telephone for a taxi *(kiosk).*

*There are short cuts to D 952 coming out near the Auberge du Point Sublime.*
The excursion ends at the **Point Sublime★★★** *(p 163).*

*To reach La Palud without going by way of Point Sublime do not cross the Baou but take the left path which climbs up the right bank of the torrent and rejoins the D 952 about 4 km – 3 miles from La Palud. Short cut 3 km – 2 miles.*

## From the Samson Corridor to the Trescaïre Chaos

*2 hours walking – Local map pp 162-163 – torch essential*

This path provides a short walk into the bottom of the gorge and back.
*Leave the car in the Samson Corridor car park.*

Go down to the footbridge over the Baou, cross over and go straight on. The windows in the first tunnel show astonishing views of the Samson Corridor and the Baume aux Pigeons. After the second tunnel, the path reaches a promontory with a view of the Trescaïre Chaos and the high Barre de l'Escalès. On the way back there is a distant view of the hill village of Rougon beyond the Samson Corridor.

*Return by the same corridor.*

## VERDON Upper Valley

Michelin map **81** folds 8 and 18

Upstream from Castellane, the valley of the Verdon progressively loses its wild character. Mountain vegetation reappears with forests of beech, pine and larch, carpeting the lower slopes of the massive and majestic mountains. The relative coolness of the air and the bright clear sky make it a popular region with tourists.

### From Colmars to Castillon Lake – *30 km – 18 1/2 miles – 3/4 hour*

Leave Colmars *(p 55)* by D 908 going south which follows the right bank of the Verdon. The landscape is composed of woods and meadows.

**St-Pierre Gorge★.** – *3 km – 1 3/4 miles – plus 1 1/2 hours on foot Rtn.* Approaching Beauvezer from the north, turn left into the Villars-Heyssier road which becomes a track before ending in a car park. From there a marked path leads to the St-Pierre Gorge created by a tributary of the Verdon. From the *corniche* path there are impressive views of the wild ravine – the grey schist and white and ochre limestone.

**Beauvezer.** – Pop 233. *Facilities p 30.* Small summer resort in green countryside.

The road follows the valley bottom, beneath the imposing mass of the Grand Coyer (2 693 m – 8 835 ft).
Beyond Pont de Villaron bear right into D 995 to St-André-les-Alpes; it tacks between arid mountains covered with lavender and here and there a group of trees.

**St-André-les-Alpes.** – Pop 945. *Facilities p 30.* The town of St-André, which stands on the confluence of the Verdon and the Issole, is an important tourist junction, being well placed as a starting point for tours of Haute-Provence.

Below St-André the oak plantations which dominate the landscape have been drowned in some areas by the Castillon reservoir *(p 53).*

## VÉSUBIE Valley ★★

Michelin map **195** folds 6, 16 and 17

The Vésubie, a tributary of the Var, is formed by two torrents: the Madone de Fenestre and the Boréon. Rising amidst mountains of 2 500 m – 8 000 ft near the Italian frontier, the Vésubie is fed by the snows of the last high Alpine ranges. The valley, one of the most beautiful behind Nice, has many characteristics: the upper valley has Alpine green pastures, pine forests, cascades and peaks while the middle valley, between Lantosque and St-Jean-la-Rivière, shows signs of Mediterranean climate – the slopes are less steep and there are small patches of cultivation, set in terraces, with vines and olive trees. In its lower part, from St-Jean-la-Rivière, the torrent has created a gorge with vertical walls through which it passes to join the Var as it emerges from the Chaudan Defile.

### Access

Two roads lead to the Vésubie Valley from the coast:
– the road from Nice over the hills to Levens (D 19); and
– the main road from Nice (N 202) along the Var valley as far as Plan-sur-Var.

## ① VÉSUBIE GORGES★★★

### From Tourrette-Levens to St-Jean-la-Rivière (D 19) – *23 km – 14 1/4 miles – about 1 hour – Local map p 166*

From Tourrette-Levens *(p 119)* D 19 winds between the hillside villages, which look down on the lower Var valley, and the long Ferion Chain.

**Levens.** – Pop 1 422. *Facilities p 30.* Place de la Mairie opens into an attractive public garden, its shady terraces overlooking the valley; nearby stands the curved façade of the Baroque chapel of the White Penitents. In Rue Masséna is the house, dated 1722, of the Masséna family; some amusing frescoes on the life of Masséna, executed by the artist Dussour in 1958 in the style of strip cartoons, are to be found at the Town Hall *(apply to the Secretariat).*

Climb up towards the swimming pool; from near the 1914-1918 War Memorial, there is a pretty **view★** over the junction of the Var and the Vésubie in its setting of high mountains from the Cheiron (WSO) to Le Mercantour (NE).

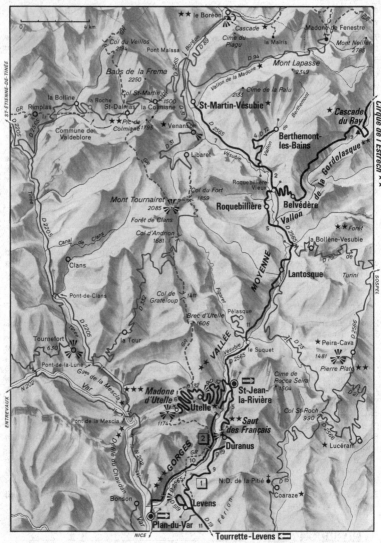

Shortly after Levens the road overlooks the gorges from a great height.

**Duranus.** – Pop 85. Pretty village set in the midst of vineyards and orchards.

**Frenchmen's Leap★★** (Saut des Français). – The leap, situated at the northern end of Duranus, is marked by a commanding belvedere. Two plaques recall the Republican soldiers who in 1793 were hurled over the edge by bands of Nice guerillas. The **view★★** is almost lost in the dizzy vertical drop to the bottom of the gorges.

D 19 runs downhill to meet the Vésubie in St-Jean-la-Rivière.

### ② From Plan-du-Var to the Madonna of Utelle Chapel – *25 km – 15 miles – about 1 hour – Local map above*

D 2565 follows the bed of the narrow, winding, steep sided Vésubie gorge: narrow, tortuous, steep and wild, the rock walls layered in many colours.

In St-Jean-la-Rivière turn left into D 32; there are numerous **views** of the Vésubie Gorge as the road climbs to Utelle.

**Utelle★.** – *Description p 155.*

*Key to the Madonna of Utelle Chapel available from one of the restaurants in Utelle.*

**The Madonna of Utelle Chapel★★★** (La Madone d'Utelle). – The sanctuary which was founded in 850 and reconstructed in 1806 is a popular place of pilgrimage (particularly 15 August and 8 September).
A short distance from the chapel there is a viewing table (1 174 m – 3 852 ft) covered by a dome. Splendid **panorama★★★** over a wide expanse of the Maritime Alps.

## MIDDLE VALLEY OF THE VÉSUBIE★★
### From St-Jean-la-Rivière to St-Martin-Vésubie – *59 km – 37 miles – about 2 hours – Local map above*

Beyond St-Jean-la-Rivière the valley squeezes between bluffs of rock, widening slightly at Le Suquet to skirt the eastern foothills of the Brec d'Utelle (1 606 m – 5 269 ft).

**Lantosque.** – Pop 884. It is sited on a limestone ridge which crosses the valley.

**Roquebillière; La Gordolasque Valley★★**. – *Description p 124.*

**Berthemont-les-Bains.** – *4 km – 2 1/2 miles – from the D 2565.* Berthemont-les-Bains is a holiday resort in a refreshing setting of shady trees and waterfalls. The sulphurous, radioactive waters were known even in Roman times; the St Julian Grotto stands over a well preserved Roman pool where 20 people could bathe at a time.

As the road climbs so the valley changes to a landscape of chestnuts, pines and green pastures which has earned the region round St-Martin-Vésubie *(p 132)* the title of "Little Switzerland". Venanson *(p 133)* overlooks the valley from the west bank.

## VILLECROZE

Michelin map **84** fold 6 – Pop 700 – *Facilities p 30*

The village has grown up round a group of caves, partially converted into dwellings. It lies in the foothills of the Provence Plateau surrounded by orchards, vineyards and olive groves.

**Old village.** – The flavour of the Middle Ages lingers in the clock tower, Rue des Arceaux and the Romanesque church with its wall belfry.

**Municipal Park.** – *Access by Route d'Aups, then a righthand turning leading to a car park at the park entrance.*

A beautiful waterfall cascades 40 m – 130 ft down the cliff face and forms a stream in an oasis of greenery. *Arrows indicate the path to the caves.*

**Caves.** – *Guided tours 15 June to 30 September, 9am to noon and 1.30 to 7.30pm; the rest o the year, Wednesdays, Saturdays and Sundays except holidays, 10am to noon and 2 to 5pm; 3F.*

In 16C the caves were partially converted into dwellings by the Lords of Villecroze; some mullioned windows let into the rock remain. The tour includes several little chambers with attractive concretions.

**Belvedere.** – 1 km – 1/2 mile from the village on the Tourtour road, there is a belvedere *(viewing table).* The **panorama**★ extends from the Provence Plateau (NE) over Tourtour, Villecroze and Salernes to the Bessillon peaks (SW) with the Maures (SE) and the Ste-Baume (SW) on the horizon.

## VILLEFRANCHE ★

Michelin map **195** fold 27 – *Local map pp 117 and 122* – Pop 7 258 – *Facilities p 28*

Villefranche, a fishing port and holiday resort, is built on the wooded slopes encircling one of the most beautiful **roadsteads**★★ in the Mediterranean. The deep bay of 25 to 60 m – 13 to 33 fathoms, where cruise liners and warships can lie at anchor, lies between the Cap Ferrat Peninsula and the Mount Boron heights.

Villefranche, with its port, its citadel, its old streets, has somehow preserved its 17C character.

Villefranche owes its name to the Count of Provence, Charles II of Anjou, nephew of St Louis, who having founded it at the start of the 14C gave it commercial freedom.

**The Congress of Nice.** – In 1538, at the time of the Congress of Nice convened by Pope Paul III, former Bishop of Vence, to bring peace between François I and Charles V, the latter stayed in Villefranche, François I in Villeneuve-Loubet and the Pope in Nice acting as intermediary.

### VILLEFRANCHE (ALPES-MAR.)

| | |
|---|---|
| Cauvin (Av.) | 2 |
| Corderie (Quai de la) | 3 |
| Corne-d'Or (Bd de la) | 5 |
| Courbet (Quai) | 6 |
| Église (R. de l') | 7 |
| Gallieni (Av. Général) | 9 |
| Gaulle (Av. Général de) | 10 |
| Grande-Bretagne (Av. de) | 12 |
| Joffre (Av. du Maréchal) | 14 |
| Leclerc (Av. Général) | 15 |
| Marinières (Promenade des) | 16 |
| May (R. de) | 18 |
| Obscure (R.) | 19 |
| Paix (Pl. de la) | 20 |
| Poilu (R. du) | 22 |
| Pollonais (Pl.) | 24 |
| Ponchardier (Quai Amiral) | 25 |
| Poullan (Pl.) | 26 |
| Sadi-Carnot (Av.) | 28 |
| St-Michel (🖂) | E |
| Senttimelli-Lazare (Bd) | 30 |
| Verdun (Av. de) | 32 |
| Victoire (R. de la) | 34 |
| Wilson (Pl.) | 35 |

*The town plans are orientated with north at the top.*

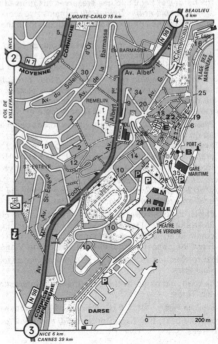

VILLEFRANCHE ★

The Queen of France, sister of Charles V, went to see her brother, whose ship was moored at Villefranche. Charles, giving his hand to the Queen and followed by the Duke of Savoy and lords and ladies of his suite, advanced majestically on the wooden gangway between the jetty and the ship. With a cracking noise the gangway collapsed and the Emperor, the Queen and the Duke splashed about in the water until, soaked and dishevelled, they were pulled ashore. The peace of Nice lasted only five years.

■ **SIGHTS** *time: 3/4 hour*

**Old town★.** – The old town is a picturesque jumble of narrow streets sometimes cut by steps, sometimes covered as in the **Rue Obscure. Rue du Poilu (22),** the main street runs parallel to the waterfront behind a face of brightly painted houses.

**St-Michel Church (E).** – This Italian Baroque church in style, contains 18C altarpieces; a Crucifix carved with impressive realism in the 17C from a single piece of boxwood by an unknown convict and a 16C polychrome wood statue of St Rock and his dog.
The organ, dated 1790, was built by the well-known Grinda brothers of Nice.

**St-Pierre Chapel★ (B).** – *Open in winter, 9.30am to noon and 2 to 4.30pm; in spring and autumn, 9am to noon and 2 to 6pm; in summer, 9am to noon and 2.30 to 7pm; closed Fridays, Christmas and 15 November to 15 December; 4F.*
This ancient chapel, which for many years served as a fishermen's sanctuary, was entirely decorated by Jean Cocteau in 1957. The theme of the frescoes is the life of St Peter together with scenes celebrating the women of Villefranche and the Gypsies, all linked by a geometric decor. The ceramics on either side of the door – staring eyes – represent the flames of the Apocalypse.

**The Harbour (Darse).** – Once a military port where galleys were built and manned, it is now an anchorage for yachts and pleasure boats. On 15 August a brilliant nautical fête is held, an illuminated procession of boats in the Roads.

**Citadel.** – The citadel was constructed in 1560 by the Duke of Savoy to guard the port.
It was much admired by Vauban and spared by Louis XIV together with Mount Alban Fort *(p 166)* when the defences of the County of Nice were destroyed.

## The VIONÈNE Road ★
Michelin map ▥▥▤ folds 4 and 5

The Vionène valley climbs east-west to the Couillole Pass between the Tinée and Cians valleys. The road linking the valleys is wild and beautiful. From Beuil there is a choice of route: south down the Cians valley *(p 54)* or west via Valberg *(p 155)* into the Var upper valley *(p 158).*

### From St-Sauveur-sur-Tinée to Beuil – *35 km – 22 miles – about 2 hours*

*Leave St-Sauveur by D 2205 going north. Bear left into D 30.*
The road crosses the Tinée and climbs the steep valley side above St-Sauveur through a series of tight bends. The red schistous rock is sparsely covered by thin woodland.
*After 4 km – 2 1/2 miles turn right into D 130.*
The narrow road climbs up to Roure. 1 km – 1/2 mile from the village, view on the left down into the Vionène and Tinée gorges.

**Roure★.** – Pop 1 089. An Alpine village overlooking the Vionène, it once belonged to the barons of Beuil and has preserved the ruins of the old château. The parish church *(key available at the Town Hall)* contains two works of art: 16C **altarpiece of St-Laurent★** *(high altar);* the altarpiece of the Assumption, in the style of François Bréa *(first chapel on the left).*
400 m – 440 yds north west of the village *(road signs)* is the **chapel of St-Bernard and St-Sébastien** *(keys at the Town Hall).* The frescoes illustrating the lives of the two saints are by André de Cella, with Renaissance friezes between the sections.

*Return to D 30 turning right.* The road glides through a verdant countryside above the Vionène then crosses the foaming torrent into a **landscape★** of red schist. Beautiful waterfall on the right before the first tunnel. Roubion comes into view. From a bend in the road there is a **view** of the Vionène valley and Roure on its hillside; beyond lies the Tinée valley.

**Roubion.** – Pop 62. The minute village stands on an impressive **site★** 1 200 m – 3 937 ft up on a ridge of red rock. It has original features: 12C ramparts, old houses, a belfry hewn from the rock and 18C fountain in the square. The parish church with its crenelated Romanesque bell-tower contains two 15C works of art *(lefthand chapel near the choir and second chapel on right);* note the decor of the first chapel on the right.

*Key to St-Sébastien chapel available from Mr. Louis Camas (☎ 02.00.76) or at the Town Hall (☎ 02.00.48). Return to D 30 turning left. At the first bend going east, park the car and take the path on the right down into the ravine. Over the bridge is the chapel.*

**Chapel of St-Sébastien de Roubion.** – The humble chapel is decorated with frescoes illustrating the life of St-Sébastien, painted in green, pink and ochre with a commentary in Provençal (about 1510).
From the chapel surroundings a **view** of the Vionène valley.

*Return to Roubion to hand over the key to the chapel and then continue west to the Couillole Pass.*

As the road climbs up to the pass there are interesting views of Roubion, the Vionène and the Tinée.

**Couillole Pass.** – Alt 1 678 m – 5 505 ft. Extensive **view** on either side of the pass.
Beyond the pass, the Cians Gorge *(p 54)* and Beuil *(p 40)* show through the spruce and larch trees.

# INDEX

**NOTES**

**MANUFACTURE FRANÇAISE DES PNEUMATIQUES MICHELIN**
Société en commandite par actions au capital de 1 300 000 000 de francs
Place des Carmes-Déchaux – 63 Clermont-Ferrand (France)
R.C.S. Clermont-Fd B 855 200 507
© Michelin et Cie, Propriétaires-Éditeurs 1983
Dépôt légal 1-83 – ISBN 206013301-7 – ISSN 0293-94-36

Printed in France 11-82-30
Photocomposition : MAURY-Imprimeur S.A. Malesherbes
Impression : MAURY-Imprimeur S.A. Malesherbes    n° C 82/11313

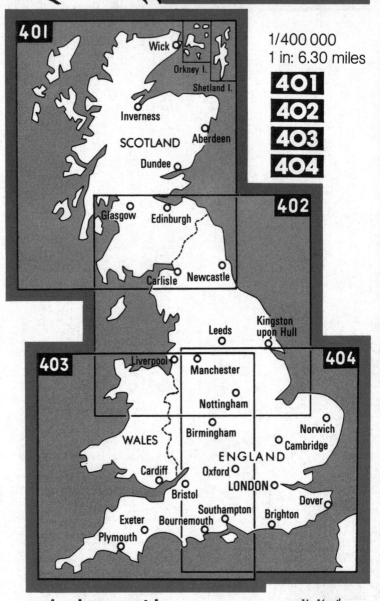

GREAT BRITAIN

# Use the new Michelin maps for the whole country

**401**

Wick
Orkney I.
Shetland I.

1/400 000
1 in: 6.30 miles

**401**
**402**
**403**
**404**

Inverness
SCOTLAND
Aberdeen
Dundee

**402**

Glasgow
Edinburgh
Carlisle
Newcastle

Leeds
Kingston upon Hull

**403**
Liverpool
Manchester
Nottingham

**404**

WALES
Birmingham
Norwich
Cambridge
Cardiff
ENGLAND
Oxford
Bristol
LONDON
Dover
Southampton
Brighton
Exeter
Bournemouth
Plymouth

**and enjoy your trip**

1 in: 16 miles

MICHELIN
GREATER LONDON

MICHELIN
GREAT BRITAIN
and IRELAND

**986** MICHELIN
Great Britain
Ireland
Großbritannien
Irland